Keep this book. You will need it and use it throughout your career.

MANAGING HOSPITALITY ENGINEERING SYSTEMS

Educational Institute Books

HOSPITALITY FOR SALE
C. DeWitt Coffman

UNIFORM SYSTEM OF ACCOUNTS AND EXPENSE DICTIONARY FOR SMALL HOTELS, MOTELS, AND MOTOR HOTELS
Fourth Edition

RESORT DEVELOPMENT AND MANAGEMENT
Second Edition
Chuck Y. Gee

PLANNING AND CONTROL FOR FOOD AND BEVERAGE OPERATIONS
Third Edition
Jack D. Ninemeier

STRATEGIC MARKETING PLANNING IN THE HOSPITALITY INDUSTRY: A BOOK OF READINGS
Edited by Robert L. Blomstrom

TRAINING FOR THE HOSPITALITY INDUSTRY
Second Edition
Lewis C. Forrest, Jr.

UNDERSTANDING HOSPITALITY LAW
Second Edition
Jack P. Jefferies

SUPERVISION IN THE HOSPITALITY INDUSTRY
Second Edition
Raphael R. Kavanaugh/Jack D. Ninemeier

SANITATION MANAGEMENT
Second Edition
Ronald F. Cichy

ENERGY AND WATER RESOURCE MANAGEMENT
Second Edition
Robert E. Aulbach

MANAGEMENT OF FOOD AND BEVERAGE OPERATIONS
Second Edition
Jack D. Ninemeier

MANAGING FRONT OFFICE OPERATIONS
Third Edition
Michael L. Kasavana/Richard M. Brooks

STRATEGIC HOTEL/MOTEL MARKETING
Revised Edition
Christopher W. L. Hart/David A. Troy

MANAGING SERVICE IN FOOD AND BEVERAGE OPERATIONS
Anthony M. Rey/Ferdinand Wieland

THE LODGING AND FOOD SERVICE INDUSTRY
Second Edition
Gerald W. Lattin

SECURITY AND LOSS PREVENTION MANAGEMENT
Raymond C. Ellis, Jr., & the Security Committee of AH&MA

HOSPITALITY INDUSTRY MANAGERIAL ACCOUNTING
Second Edition
Raymond S. Schmidgall

PURCHASING FOR HOSPITALITY OPERATIONS
William B. Virts

THE ART AND SCIENCE OF HOSPITALITY MANAGEMENT
Jerome J. Vallen/James R. Abbey

MANAGING COMPUTERS IN THE HOSPITALITY INDUSTRY
Second Edition
Michael L. Kasavana/John J. Cahill

MANAGING HOSPITALITY ENGINEERING SYSTEMS
Michael H. Redlin/David M. Stipanuk

UNDERSTANDING HOSPITALITY ACCOUNTING I
Second Edition
Raymond Cote

UNDERSTANDING HOSPITALITY ACCOUNTING II
Second Edition
Raymond Cote

MANAGING QUALITY SERVICES
Stephen J. Shriver

MANAGING CONVENTIONS AND GROUP BUSINESS
Leonard H. Hoyle/David C. Dorf/Thomas J. A. Jones

HOSPITALITY SALES AND ADVERTISING
James R. Abbey

MANAGING HUMAN RESOURCES IN THE HOSPITALITY INDUSTRY
David Wheelhouse

MANAGING HOUSEKEEPING OPERATIONS
Margaret M. Kappa/Aleta Nitschke/Patricia B. Schappert

CONVENTION SALES: A BOOK OF READINGS
Margaret Shaw

DIMENSIONS OF TOURISM
Joseph D. Fridgen

HOSPITALITY TODAY: AN INTRODUCTION
Rocco M. Angelo/Andrew N. Vladimir

MANAGING BAR AND BEVERAGE OPERATIONS
Lendal H. Kotschevar/Mary L. Tanke

POWERHOUSE CONFERENCES: ELIMINATING AUDIENCE BOREDOM
Coleman Lee Finkel

ETHICS IN HOSPITALITY MANAGEMENT: A BOOK OF READINGS
Edited by Stephen S.J. Hall

HOSPITALITY FACILITIES MANAGEMENT AND DESIGN
David M. Stipanuk/Harold Roffmann

MANAGING HOSPITALITY HUMAN RESOURCES
Robert H. Woods

MANAGING HOSPITALITY ENGINEERING SYSTEMS

Michael H. Redlin
David M. Stipanuk

Disclaimer

This publication is designed to provide accurate and authoritative information in regard to the subject matter covered. It is sold with the understanding that the publisher is not engaged in rendering legal, accounting, or other professional service. If legal advice or other expert assistance is required, the services of a competent professional person should be sought.

—From the Declaration of Principles jointly adopted by the American Bar Association and a Committee of Publishers and Associations

The authors, Michael H. Redlin and David M. Stipanuk, are solely responsible for the contents of this publication. All views expressed herein are solely those of the authors and do not necessarily reflect the views of the Educational Institute of the American Hotel & Motel Association (the Institute) or the American Hotel & Motel Association (AH&MA).

Nothing contained in this publication shall constitute a standard, an endorsement, or a recommendation of the Institute or AH&MA. The Institute and AH&MA disclaim any liability with respect to the use of any information, procedure, or product, or reliance thereon by any member of the hospitality industry.

1407 South Harrison Road
P.O. Box 1240
East Lansing, Michigan 48826

The Educational Institute of the American Hotel & Motel Association is a nonprofit educational foundation.

Printed in the United States of America
7 8 9 10 93

Library of Congress Cataloging-in-Publication Data
Redlin, Michael H.
Managing hospitality engineering systems.

Includes bibliographies and index.
1. Hotels, taverns, etc.—Maintenance and repair.
2. Motels—Maintenance and repair. 3. Restaurants, lunch rooms, etc.—Maintenance and repair. I. Stipanuk, David M. II. American Hotel & Motel Association. Educational Institute. III. Title.
TX928.R43 1987 647′.94′0682 87-15712
ISBN 0-86612-037-8

Editor: Timothy J. Eaton

Contents

Preface

This text has been prepared with the needs of three separate audiences in mind: students enrolled in hospitality management programs, hospitality facility managers interested in furthering their understanding of property operation and maintenance, and engineering/maintenance managers. The content and organization of the text have been carefully chosen to benefit each of these three groups significantly.

For the student enrolled in a hospitality management program and the instructor in such a program, the text affords flexibility in the amount and depth of exposure on any individual topic. This flexibility allows the text to be used for courses in both two- and four-year programs, where the amount of time available for the treatment of property operation and maintenance in lodging facilities varies considerably from program to program.

For the program which has less than a full semester to devote to the study of the engineering department and building systems, Chapters 1, 2, and 3 provide a concise treatment of these topics. Chapter 1 introduces the reader to some of the basic costs associated with the physical plant, starting with the building design and construction and including property operation and maintenance, energy, and renovation. Also included is a summary of the major duties and responsibilities of the engineering department in modern lodging establishments. In Chapter 2, the management function of the engineering department is discussed and developed in detail. Chapter 3 provides an overview of the major building engineering systems, their design, and their operational characteristics.

Chapters 4 through 9 discuss the major building systems traditionally covered in a course in building engineering systems: water and wastewater systems, electrical systems, heating systems, food service refrigeration systems, air conditioning systems, and integrated HVAC systems. Chapters 10 through 13 supplement these major systems with discussions of HVAC equipment, lighting systems, fire protection systems, and energy management. For full-semester programs, Chapters 1 through 13 should prove to be an ambitious yet realizable goal.

The hospitality manager reading this book with the goal of better understanding the engineering department will greatly benefit from Chapters 1 and 2, where the costs and responsibilities of the engineering department are developed and discussed in relation to the other departments in a facility and to a property's overall goals. The material should provide the manager with a number of suggestions for improving the operation of the department at his or her facility. Managers who wish to improve their understanding of building systems will benefit from the material in Chapter 3, which contains a great deal of basic information concerning building systems in non-technical terms. The hospitality manager with a further interest in a specific type of building system should find the appropriate chapter to be very readable, with a heavy emphasis on descriptive detail. When used with the Index, the book will be a very useful reference volume for any hospitality manager.

The building engineering manager reading this text may be in for a few surprises. The duties of the department, managerial responsibilities, and personnel characteristics discussed in Chapters 1 and 2 are more extensive and varied than some managers realize. Most engineers will want to skip Chapter 3 and use the detailed information on building systems contained in the remainder of the text. In these remaining chapters, the engineering manager will find the basic system description and variations on system design helpful in training new staff or in broadening the knowledge of existing personnel. With most chapters containing Applications sections which develop certain aspects of the chapter material in some depth, engineering managers should find each chapter helpful in improving their understanding and management of building systems. Engineering managers will also appreciate the text's two appendixes. Appendix A contains a refresher course in basic engineering principles, something which is often helpful as a reference. Appendix B discusses the relationship of temperature and humidity to human comfort, a topic of great importance in an industry dedicated to guest satisfaction. The Index provides a ready reference.

The text cites a number of references. Any reader desiring additional material on the topics contained in the text should refer to these books, magazines, and other publications. Regularly reviewing the various periodical publications is an excellent way of keeping abreast of the latest developments.

The authors represent the most recent standard-bearers in a long tradition of Cornell University School of Hotel Administration educators dealing with the physical plant. Beginning with Frank Randolph and continuing with our colleagues Richard H. Penner and Richard A. Compton, the School has long emphasized in its curriculum the importance of the physical plant. We have certainly been influenced by this tradition and acknowledge its contribution to the development of this text.

Dean John J. Clark of the School, formerly a member of the Properties Management faculty, will find woven into the fabric of the book several insights and approaches derived from his extensive course notes. His support in the allocation of time and resources to aid the development of this text has been a major contribution.

The Executive Engineers Committee of the American Hotel & Motel Association has provided a forum for discussing fertile ideas, many of which are incorporated here. Its encouragement and assistance is certainly appreciated. In addition, several of its members served as our review committee, contributing significantly to the style and order of the text and providing many worthwhile comments during its formative stages. Our thanks go to review committee members Robert E. Aulbach, Robach Inc.; Paul R. Broten, CEOE, Conrad Hilton College, University of Houston; Charles C. Cocotas, CEOE, Lehr Associates; and Raymond B. Hambel, CEOE, Hilton Hotels Corporation.

We have used numerous resources in the development of this text and are indebted to many authors. We have carefully attempted to credit all those whose work made a unique contribution to the text. Still, we know that we have been influenced by and owe much to the writings and comments of many unnamed others who have guided our thoughts through their articles in trade journals, books, and magazines.

Given the months which have been devoted to the preparation of this text, we must acknowledge the support we have received from our wives and children. They have endured hearing about "the book" for all too long. Their quiet understanding of the process of becoming an author is greatly appreciated.

Much of the art in the text has been prepared by Susan MacKay. Her professionalism has certainly contributed to the overall quality of the text and is much appreciated. Arianne Steinbeck was also involved in the production of some of the illustrations, providing excellent assistance in our efforts to meet the production deadlines for the text. In addition, our editor at the Educational Institute, Tim Eaton, significantly aided us in clarifying our wording and in developing a professional text. He has been very helpful and we hope we have not caused him to age too prematurely.

Finally, we must extend thanks to all the students who have attended our seminars and classes over the past years in maintenance, energy management, building systems, safety, and security. These students, both in the School and from the industry, have greatly contributed to our insights into the needs which exist in the hospitality field for an understanding of physical plant management.

Michael H. Redlin
David M. Stipanuk
School of Hotel Administration
Cornell University

1

Introduction to the Physical Plant and Building Operations

The Physical Plant

The term *physical plant* refers to the grounds, building structure, building systems, interior finishes (that is, paint, carpeting, wallpaper, and so forth), and furniture, fixtures, and equipment (FF&E) of a lodging facility. Many of these components of the physical plant are highly visible, such as the grounds, the exterior building structure, and the FF&E. Other portions of the physical plant, such as the structural steel in the building, the plumbing, and large amounts of the heating, ventilating, and air conditioning (HVAC) system, are seldom seen by the guests or most of the employees. The elements of the physical plant constitute a significant portion of the construction cost of a facility and consume a significant fraction of the maintenance and energy cost incurred over the building's lifetime.

The care and operation of the physical plant of modern lodging facilities is largely the responsibility of the engineering or maintenance department (the two terms are used interchangeably in this text). To understand the scope of this department's duties and responsibilities relative to the physical plant, a brief overview of the physical plant of modern lodging facilities and how these facilities have changed over time is helpful.

Yesterday and Today

The vast diversity of the modern lodging industry results in great variety in the complexity of the physical plant. As lodging facilities have grown in physical size, they have also grown in the complexity of their design, systems, and services. The physical plants of simple roadside motels in the 1930s and 1940s required little more skill to maintain and operate than that needed by a homeowner. In contrast, the "mega-hotels" of the late 1980s require several degreed engineers and individuals with specialized skills for their operation.

A list of some of the systems found in most modern lodging establishments would include:

- HVAC (heating, ventilation, and air conditioning)
- Water (hot and cold)
- Sewer (storm and sanitary)
- Lighting
- Telephone
- Refrigeration
- Cable television
- Fire protection

- Vertical transportation (elevators and escalators)

While not all establishments have every system, the list is impressive and growing. As recently as 20 years ago, it was rare for a property to have a cable television system and a health club and to *own* its telephone system. Today, such arrangements are almost standard. Systems and services which are relatively rare today but which are growing in popularity, such as personal computers in the guestroom, may become standard by the early 1990s. Each new system or service will bring with it new demands on facilities designers and on the engineering and maintenance function.

To operate the systems found in most properties, the properties need to purchase or produce certain basic services. At most United States properties, basic services such as water, sewer, fuel, electricity, communications, refuse removal, and so forth are purchased from a reliable local vendor. In many locations in the world, this is not the case. Properties in such locations may need to supply their own electricity, dispose of their own wastes, and operate other systems taken for granted in more developed countries. In many ways, lodging establishments in less developed countries find themselves in situations which are similar to those of United States hotels earlier in this century.

Many services and features of today's lodging properties were either non-existent in properties of the not-so-distant past or were provided by very different systems or equipment. During the early part of this century, hotels in urban areas burned coal to supply their heating needs, operated steam turbines and engines to produce electricity, provided space cooling only to a few dining areas, and used ammonia as the refrigerant in refrigeration systems.[1] The early 1900s saw Ellsworth Statler pioneer several then-new concepts in his Buffalo, New York, hotel, including installing individual bathrooms in hotel rooms, piping chilled drinking water to the guestrooms, carpeting the hallways to reduce noise, and more. In 1926, Statler stunned his board of directors by announcing he was going to put a radio in every room of his Boston hotel at a cost of $50,000.[2] The first complete guestroom air conditioning system was not installed until 1934 at the Detroit Statler.[3]

Engineering and Marketing

Technological innovations in the industry have often served as marketing elements for lodging facilities. When Statler installed individual bathrooms, he marketed his product with the slogan "A room and a bath for a buck and a half." In the early days of the motel business, properties clearly advertised that they offered television and were air conditioned. In communities where fire had taken a high toll, such as Chicago and San Francisco, properties prominently advertised their fire-proof construction and announced the presence of onsite water storage to combat fires. Lodging properties have been notable for their early adoption of new technologies in the constant quest for better guest service and an edge in the marketplace.

Spatial and Operating Characteristics: Some Managerial Aspects of Engineering

When the responsibilities of the engineering department are discussed, it is often easy to focus merely on the detail of the required activity, that is, to maintain and repair. But if we focus too narrowly on the detail, we may forget to see and appreciate the purpose of this department and its crucial role in the overall functioning of a lodging operation. A lodging property may benefit substantially if its management establishes broad goals for the engineering department. Identifying and clearly communicating such goals may help motivate personnel, define duties and responsibilities, and clarify interdepartmental relationships.

The following is a sample set of general operational goals for the engineering department which results in a functional way of viewing the department's responsibilities (and which is the basis for much of this text):

- Protect the investment in the physical plant.
- Control maintenance costs.
- Contribute as appropriate or necessary to overall guest satisfaction.
- Contribute to the efficient operation of other departments.

- Minimize the energy costs of the facility.
- Minimize potential safety problems.

The engineering department is organized to provide services to the guests and the remainder of the departments within a lodging facility. In order to provide the services, the staff of the department must accomplish functions that fall into two distinct categories: technical functions and managerial functions. The technical functions (for example, repairing the chiller) relate to the physical building and its landscaping, systems, interior finishes, furniture, and equipment, while the managerial functions (for example, planning the budget) relate to the operation of the department as a unit within the managerial structure of the property and, when applicable, the overall corporate structure of the operating company.

The success of the department in accomplishing the technical functions is totally dependent on the performance of the department in the managerial functions, which are similar to those functions necessary for the operation of any department. Engineering managers (whether the director of engineering in a very large first-class property or the head maintenance person in a small budget property) must have the ability to perform the typical management functions of planning, organizing, directing, controlling, staffing, setting goals, motivating their staff, communicating with their staff and with the rest of the property, and developing their staff. All of this is accomplished through a departmental structure that is appropriate to the size of the property.

For the department to be effective, engineering managers must also interact with the other managers in the property throughout the annual business cycle so that the technical functions completed by the department are compatible with the business objectives of the managers of the property. For example, the director of engineering must determine through the budgeting process that the level of maintenance and the cost associated with this level are sufficient to portray the appropriate image to the guests. Additionally, the head of the department in a chain property must interact with the central engineering group of the operating company in order to receive or provide information (for example, energy consumption reports, staffing reports) that is helpful for the coordinated operation of the specific property within the lodging chain.

Clearly, then, the managerial aspects of engineering are of vital importance. Managers must understand a variety of factors that influence engineering concerns. Just as important, they must understand that an approach to a problem that works at one property may not work at another property, even if the properties seem to be similar in many ways. In the next few pages, we will discuss a wide variety of general information and statistics concerning spatial and operating characteristics of lodging facilities that may provide important insights into the differences involved in managing different properties.

Types and Sizes of Facilities

Lodging facilities can be classified in numerous ways. Classification can be based, for example, on the market a property serves, the property's location, the rates it charges, and the facilities it provides. Thus, we could have a transient (market) facility at an airport (location) which is an economy (rate) property that provides lodging only (facilities). The variations in types of lodging facilities and the resulting variations in space and operating needs of these facilities could easily fill a book in itself (and has done so several times). One recent book, *Hotel Planning and Design* by Walter A. Rutes and Richard H. Penner, serves as the basis for the following discussion.[4] In their book, Rutes and Penner discuss various types of lodging facilities in detail, describing their characteristics, origins, and market growth. It is not possible in the limited space available here to summarize all the various types of lodging establishments. For a detailed discussion of the nature, variations, and requirements of lodging facilities, we suggest the reader refer to Rutes and Penner's book or a similar volume. We must assume that the reader is familiar with the industry.

Rutes and Penner discuss the facilities program as it relates to various classifications of lodging facilities. Exhibit 1.1 illustrates the space planning needs of various functional areas within the property for the major lodging property types considered in their book. Note how much the total area of a guestroom and total building area per guestroom varies from one facility type to another. Maintenance needs and

Exhibit 1.1 Space Requirements by Property Type: Area per Room

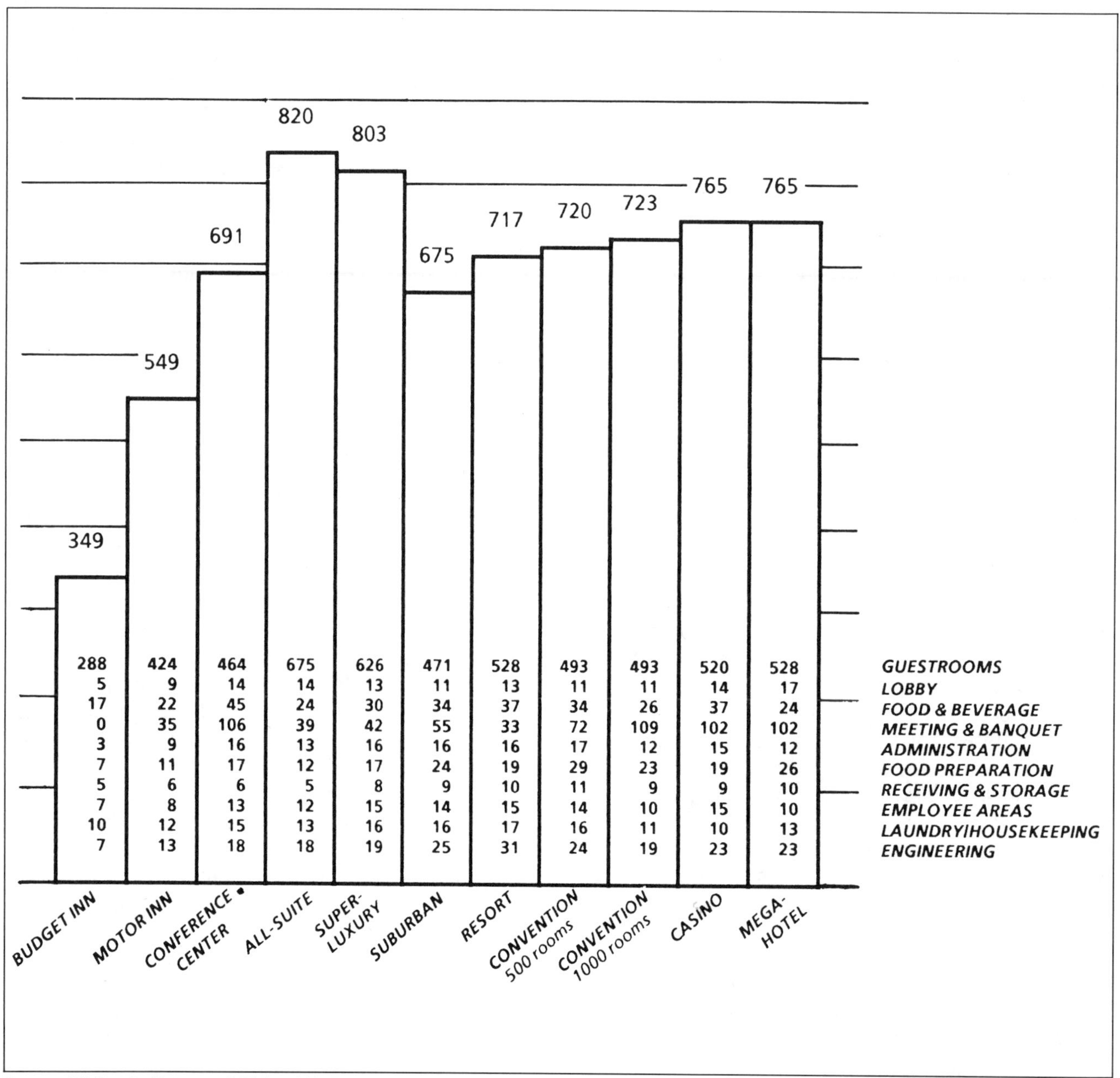

Source: Walter A. Rutes and Richard H. Penner, *Hotel Planning and Design* (New York: Whitney Library of Design, 1985), p. 158. Used by permission.

energy usage will be highly dependent on the size, facilities, and finishes of the property.

Exhibit 1.2 illustrates the distribution of lodging facilities by size of facility in terms of both the number of properties and the number of rooms. Exhibit 1.3 illustrates the distribution of these facilities in terms of location. Approximately 95% of the lodging establishments have under 300 rooms and approximately 71% of the total rooms are found in establishments under 300 rooms in total size. In 1985, the lodging industry (defined by Laventhol & Horwath—a national accounting firm—as all properties open all year and having more than 25 rooms) comprised approximately 54,000 establishments and 2.2 million rooms.

Exhibit 1.2 U.S. Lodging Industry: Distribution of Properties and Rooms by Size

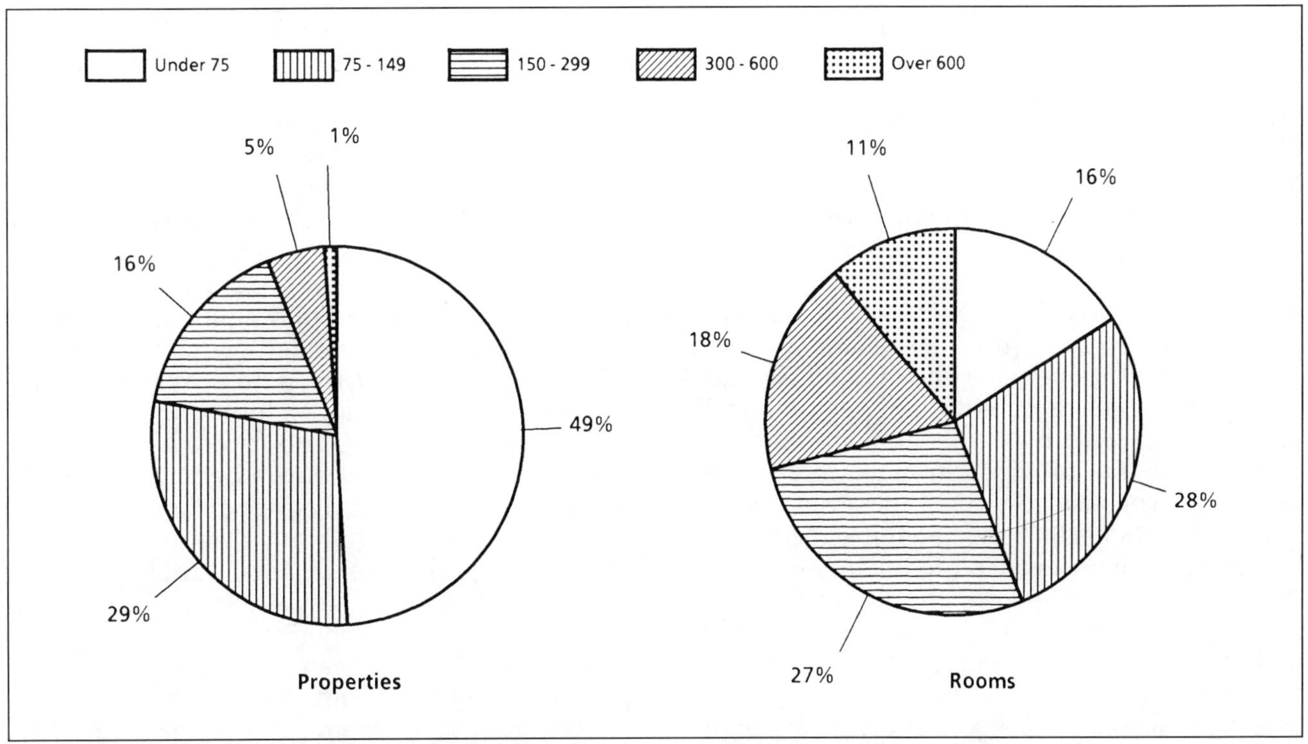

Source: *U.S. Lodging Industry—1985* (Philadelphia: Laventhol & Horwath, 1985), p. 91. Used by permission.

Exhibit 1.3 U.S. Lodging Industry: Distribution of Properties and Rooms by Location

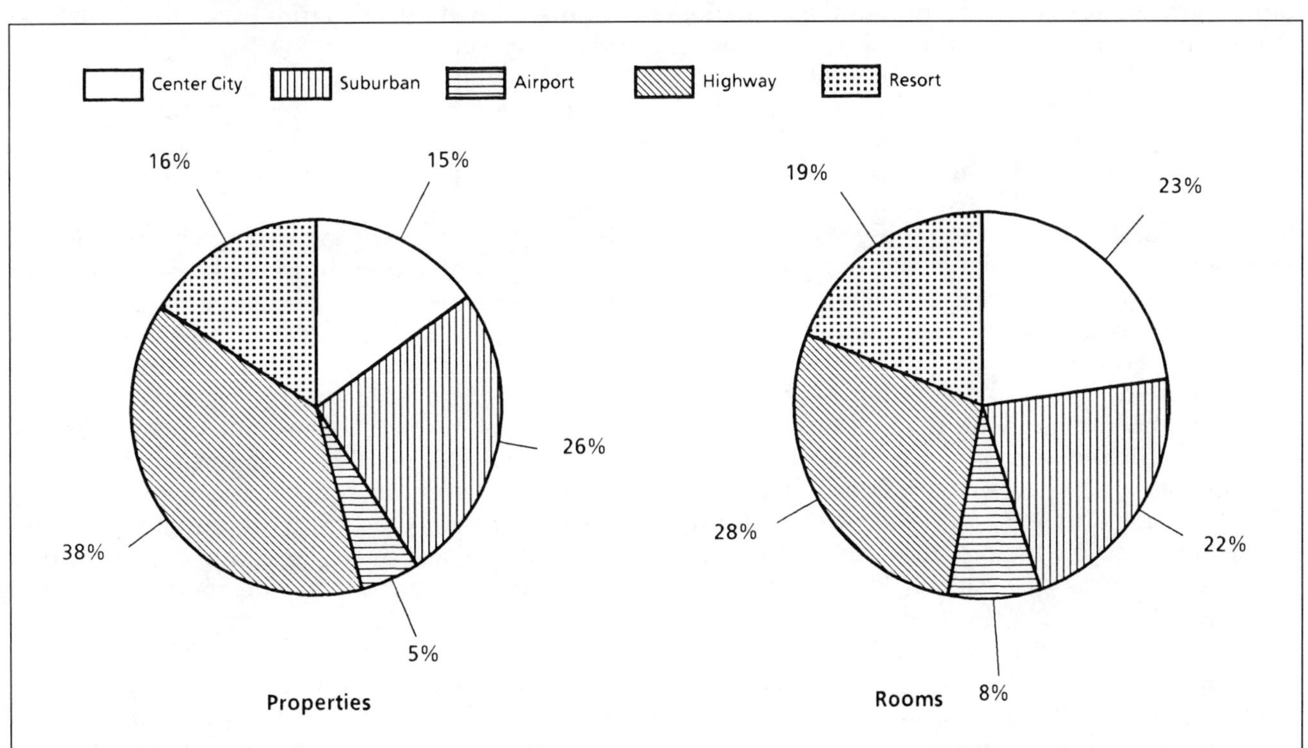

Source: *U.S. Lodging Industry—1985* (Philadelphia: Laventhol & Horwath, 1985), p. 91. Used by permission.

Costs of Construction

The costs of lodging facility construction vary significantly with the size and type of facility, its location, and the finishes used within the building. Of particular interest in this text is the cost of lodging properties' various components.

Rutes and Penner provide a discussion of the capital cost associated with a large (500-room) hotel. A copy of their data is shown in Exhibit 1.4. This data reveals a characteristic which is very common in the detailing of such costs: The components of the general construction cost—which represents over 50% of the total cost—are listed with little detail, while other cost components are provided in much more detail. It is this construction cost, the grounds, the parking facilities, and the FF&E installed within the building which constitute the major focus of the property maintenance effort over the building's life. We should also note, with regard to Exhibit 1.4, that the cost of many of a project's components are in some way directly related to the general construction costs; therefore, reductions in the general construction cost reduce other costs as well.

The distribution of the construction cost among its various components will vary from building to building depending on design, site, and facilities included. Exhibit 1.5 provides a component breakdown of the general construction cost for a small property and a convention property. Because of the greater complexity of systems and the greater difficulty in the design and construction of HVAC and electrical systems in larger buildings, these costs often represent a somewhat higher percentage of total construction costs in larger buildings.

As seen in Exhibit 1.5, the building HVAC, plumbing, and electrical equipment constitute approximately 30% of the building construction cost. When combined with the building conveying system and certain elements of fixed equipment, the percentage figure rises to 35–40%. It is this 35–40% of the building construction cost which is the primary focus of this text in terms of systems descriptions and operational concerns. In addition, these elements of the building are the primary consumers of energy at the facility. Basic elements of energy management at lodging facilities are also covered in this text.

Costs of Property Operation and Maintenance and Energy

The major operating costs associated with the engineering department are found in the *Property Operation and Maintenance* (or *POM*) and the *Energy* accounts of the uniform systems of accounts for lodging properties. The POM account is concerned with the expenses of the engineering/maintenance activity in the building. This account includes labor costs, materials and supplies used in building maintenance and repair, and building-related contract services. It does not include capital improvements. The Energy account includes not only fossil fuel purchases (such as oil and natural gas), but also electricity, purchased steam and chilled water, and potable water and sewer costs.

Laventhol & Horwath data for 1985 indicates the properties in their study expended about 10–12% of the total sales dollar on POM and Energy (each averaging about 5–7% of total sales). Exhibit 1.6 reveals variations in POM and Energy costs per room per year as they relate to the number of rooms at a property. In 1985, the resulting combined expenditures had a median value of about $2,000 per available room per year in properties in the size range of 150 to 299 rooms.[5] For properties with more than 600 rooms, the median figure rose to $3,400 per room per year.

While the absolute dollar expenditure on energy per room increases significantly as the size of the property increases, the percentage that these expenditures represent of total sales in properties with more than 300 rooms decreases as the property size increases. The reasons for the increase in expenditures relate to the generally greater overall building area per guestroom associated with the larger properties and the greater likelihood that energy-using facilities (such as in-house laundry, heated swimming pools, and multiple restaurant operations) will be associated with these properties. These features have a tendency to increase energy usage per guestroom. Offsetting these increases, however, is a greater overall revenue per guestroom which more than offsets the increased cost of energy.

The POM variations in Exhibit 1.6 do not fit as readily explainable a pattern as the energy cost variations do. POM costs per room increase with increasing property size, but the percent-

Exhibit 1.4 Capital Cost Outline for a Typical 500-Room Hotel

ITEM	PREDESIGN ESTIMATE BASIS		AMOUNT(S)
Land	Purchase		**2,000,000**
General construction			**23,000,000**
Sitework		$1,000,000	
Utilities	Allowance	200,000	
Surface parking roads	600 cars × 1,000	600,000	
Structured parking	None		
Landscaping	Allowance	200,000	
Basic building	500 bays × 600 sq.ft. (55.7 sq. m) = 300,000 sq.ft. (27,850 sq.m) 300,000 sq. ft. × 70	21,000,000	
Interior finishes	500 bays × 2,000	1,000,000	
Furniture, fixtures, and equipment	500 days × 14,000		**7,000,000**
Furniture and fixtures	55% × 7,000,000	3,850,000	
Kitchen, laundry, back-of-house equipment	25% × 7,000,000	1,750,000	
Inventories (linen, china, glassware, utensils, uniforms, supplies, printing)	15% × 7,000,000	1,050,000	
Purchasing fee	5% × 7,000,000	350,000	
Special systems			**550,000**
Telephone	500 bays × 900	450,000	
Computer (leased)	Allowance for conduit	50,000	
Special audiovisual equipment	Allowance	50,000	
Technical expenses			**2,450,000**
Architect-engineers (total)	3.5% × 22,000,000	770,000	
Architect (balance)	54% × 770,000	415,800	
Structural	12% × 770,000	92,400	
Mechanical, electrical, elevators, and civil engineering	28% × 770,000	215,600	
Audiovisual, acoustical, life safety, and landscape	6% × 770,000	46,200	
Interior designer (including lighting, signage graphics)	6.5% × 4,800,000*	312,000	
Menu graphics consultant	Allowance	20,000	
Food service equipment consultant	3.5% × 800,000	28,000	
Laundry equipment consultant	.2% × 400,000	8,000	
Site survey	Allowance	5,000	
Environmental consultant	Allowance	20,000	
Geotechnical consultant	Allowance	5,000	
Soils testing	Allowance	7,000	
Construction manager	2% × 25,000,000	500,000	
Hotel operators technical services	500 bays × 300	150,000	
Project field administration	1.5 years × 120,000	180,000	
Mock-up of typical guestroom	Allowance	25,000	
Lender's inspecting architect	Allowance	45,000	
Reimbursables	Allowance	150,000	
Construction testing	Allowance	150,000	
Permits	.2% × 25,000,000	50,000	
Feasibility study	Allowance	25,000	
Legal, financial, administrative			**750,000**
Financing fees	Debt: 70% × 40,000,000 = 28,000,000		
Loan commitment fees	1% × 28,000,000	280,000	
Brokerages	.5% × 28,000,000	140,000	
Owner's legal fees	Allowance	45,000	
Lender's legal fees	Allowance	55,000	
Developer's fee	None		
Appraisal	Allowance	10,000	
Investment tax credit study	Allowance	15,000	
Real estate taxes	Allowance	50,000	
Title insurance	Allowance	60,000	
Builders risk insurance	Allowance	45,000	
Liability insurance	Allowance	40,000	
Liquor license	Allowance	10,000	

* Cost of furniture, fixtures, accessories, and interior finishes designed and detailed by the interior designer.

(continued)

Exhibit 1.4 (continued)

Preopening expense	500 bays × 2,000	**1,000,000**
Working capital	500 bays × 500	**250,000**
Employee housing	None	
Interest during construction	Debt: 70% × 38,400,000 13% × 18 months × 55% (average cash flow balance)	**2,900,000**
Contingency	5% × 30,000,000	**1,500,000**
Total		**41,400,000**
Total cost per bay	**$41,400,000/480 keys**	**86,250**

Source: Rutes and Penner, *Hotel Planning and Design* (New York: Whitney Library of Design, 1985). Used by permission.

Exhibit 1.5 Average Lodging Property Construction Costs—Percentage Distribution

BUILDING SYSTEM	SMALL HOTEL/MOTEL	CONVENTION HOTEL
Foundations	5.5	4.0
Floors On Grade	0.5	1.0
Superstructure	21.9	28.0
Roofing	1.5	1.0
Exterior Walls	8.1	10.0
Partitions	9.1	13.0
Wall Finishes	5.4	3.0
Floor Finishes	4.5	1.0
Ceiling Finishes	3.7	1.0
Conveying Systems	6.0	6.0
Specialties	2.0	1.0
Fixed Equipment	1.8	0.0*
HVAC	9.4	16.0
Plumbing	11.2	5.0
Electrical	9.4	10.0

Note: The small hotel/motel category includes properties from 50,000 to 80,000 square feet. The convention hotel category includes properties from 700,000 to 900,000 square feet.

*Cost data for convention hotels was not reported.

Source: *Dodge Construction Costs—1985* (Princeton, N.J.: McGraw-Hill Information Systems, 1986). Used by permission.

Exhibit 1.6 1985 POM and Energy Cost Variations with Property Size (cost per available room)

	Under 150 Rooms	150-229	300-600	Over 600
ENERGY COSTS				
Per Room	$897	$1118	$1278	$1504
Ratio to Total Sales	5.9%	6.1%	4.9%	4.4%
POM COSTS				
Payroll Cost	$374	$417	$758	$966
Other	$425	$468	$740	$874
TOTAL	$789	$907	$1600	$1908
Ratio to Total Sales	5.0%	5.1%	5.7%	5.5%

Note: Since median values are reported for each item, the totals given above will generally not equal the sum of the median values for the component parts.

Source: *U.S. Lodging Industry—1986* (Philadelphia: Laventhol & Horwath, 1986). Used by permission.

age that these costs represent of total sales is relatively constant. As you view the POM data, keep in mind the variations in square footage per room (total property area divided by number of guestrooms) and the facilities and systems associated with these different size properties. As the number of rooms in the property grows, the amount of money necessary to maintain the property obviously increases. This increase in cost occurs in both the Payroll Cost and the Other categories, with the increase the greatest in the Payroll Cost category. While a portion of the payroll increase is due to an increased number of staff per room, a large percentage of the increase is due to an increased cost of labor for the larger properties. This increased cost may be due to the need to hire more skilled individuals for the more complex needs of the larger property and/or to the greater likelihood that the larger properties would be in urban areas with higher labor costs. Another factor which may contribute to increased labor requirements would be an increase in the amount of work which is done by in-house personnel instead of outside contractors.

Another Laventhol & Horwath study revealed the 1984 mean energy costs per occupied room per day for the study participants to be $1.10 for fuel, $3.63 for electricity, and 53 cents

Exhibit 1.7 Percentage Distribution of POM Expenditures (1984 mean for all establishments)

Payroll and related expenses	45.9%
Building	5.3
Electrical and mechanical equipment	11.7
Furniture	2.5
Grounds and landscaping	10.2
Operating supplies	5.0
Painting and decorating	2.5
Removal of waste matter	4.9
All other expenses	12.0
TOTAL	100.0%

Exhibit 1.8 Expenditures on Energy and POM—1985 for Various Types of Lodging Properties

	Resort Hotels	Motels with Restaurants	Motels without Restaurants
Energy Cost	$1616	$1102	$569
Energy as Percentage of Revenue	4.8	6.3	5.3
POM Cost	$1902	$787	$637
POM as Percentage of Revenue	5.6	5.1	6.0

All dollar figures are per available room per year.

Source: *Trends in the Hotel Industry*, USA Edition (Houston, Texas: Pannell Kerr Forster, 1986). Used by permission.

for water.[6] Clearly, electricity represents by far the greatest portion of the energy costs.

Exhibit 1.7 contains information concerning how the POM dollar is spent. Payroll represents slightly under 50% of the POM costs, with electrical and mechanical equipment and grounds and landscaping consuming significant percentages as well.

Comparisons of POM and Energy expenditures by type of property are possible using data compiled by Pannell Kerr Forster (PKF).[7] Exhibit 1.8 contains PKF data on resort hotels, motels with restaurants, and motels without restaurants. These types of properties exhibit very different total expenditures. The percentages these expenditures represent of total revenues

Exhibit 1.9 1984 POM and Energy Cost Variations with Property Age (dollars per available room)

	Built Pre-1960	1960-1969	1970-1979	Post 1980
Energy Costs				
Per Room	$1094	$990	$1032	$1074
% of Total Sales	5.1	6.5	5.4	7.0
POM Costs				
Payroll	$590	$328	$460	$492
Other	507	522	570	512
TOTAL	$1388	$877	$979	$876
% of Total Sales	6.2	5.4	4.8	4.2

Note: Since median values are reported for each item, the totals given above will generally not equal the sum of the median values for the component parts.

Source: *U.S. Lodging Industry* (Philadelphia: Laventhol & Horwath, 1985). Used by permission.

differ as well. Resorts have the highest dollar expenditure per available room of these three categories of properties, but with only one exception expend a smaller percentage of revenue in these areas. Motels with restaurants have greater costs per room than those without restaurants, but the POM costs are a smaller percentage of revenue.

Exhibit 1.9 shows the variation in POM and Energy costs as a function of property age. The variation with property age in energy expenditures (dollars per room) is rather slight. The age grouping with the lowest per room expenditure (1960–69) has the highest percentage of total sales expended on energy. This seeming anomaly is due to a reduced total sales per room for this age category of property relative to the others in the survey. The POM expenditure exhibits a significant variation with the age of the property. Those properties built before 1960 spend the most money and the highest percentage of sales on POM. Newer properties expend decreasing percentages of sales on POM, but not necessarily decreasing dollar amounts. The primary portion of the POM expenditures which vary depending on age is the Payroll component. The Other category of POM includes several contractual elements which are likely to vary little with the age of the property. Among these

Exhibit 1.10 How the POM Dollar Was Spent—By Age

POM CATEGORY	AGE Built Pre-1940	1940-1959	1960-1969	Post 1969
Payroll & Related Expenses	48.1	45.5	44.0	42.7
Building	5.6	10.1	6.7	5.8
Electrical & Mechanical Equipment	9.6	15.2	15.7	13.4
Furniture	2.1	2.2	2.4	2.3
Grounds & Landscaping	3.2	5.3	5.0	7.3
Operating Supplies	2.0	2.8	2.8	3.5
Painting & Decorating	5.5	4.8	5.0	3.1
Removal of Waste Matter	4.3	3.5	5.4	4.4
All Other Expenses	19.6	10.6	13.0	17.5
Total	100.0%	100.0%	100.0%	100.0%

Values are percent distributions based on arithmetic mean.

Source: *U.S. Lodging Industry—1984* (Philadelphia: Laventhol & Horwath, 1984). Used by permission.

are waste removal, elevators, and window cleaning.

Exhibit 1.10 illustrates some of the variations in the distribution of POM expenditures as the age of the property changes. The oldest properties (pre-1940) are somewhat more labor intensive than the younger and expend a considerably smaller portion of their POM expenditures on grounds and landscaping.

Responsibilities of the Engineering Department

Building and System Operation

Lodging buildings do not operate effectively without continuous attention. The buildings and the systems installed in these buildings require basic maintenance, repair or replacement of failed parts, calibration of controls and equipment, attention to factors which may pose safety problems, and, inevitably, a major renovation or rehabilitation. A failure to provide adequate attention to these needs can result in a poor operating performance of the building, which in turn may affect guest perceptions of quality, employee performance and morale, the safety of the guests and employees, and the profitability of the operation.

The building engineer is often placed in a position where he or she has little input into the design of the building. He or she arrives at a completed and operating building with the responsibility to continue the operation of the building at the level of appearance, comfort, and safety appropriate for the type of facility. If the building finishes, equipment, and systems are designed properly, the engineer's role may be largely that of a caretaker until a major renovation or change occurs. Unfortunately, many building engineers discover that:

- The building, equipment, or systems were not designed properly.
- The building, equipment, or systems were not designed with maintenance in mind.
- The individual previously caring for the building did not maintain it as it should have been maintained.

Under such circumstances, the caretaker role quickly becomes that of designer, problem solver, and fix-it expert—often in a chaotic environment of crisis after crisis coupled with little budgetary control and a poor rapport with and respect from fellow managers.

In a sense, the engineer tries to be as inconspicuous as possible. Many of the systems in the building should never be noticed if they are working properly. For example, an air conditioning system that is maintaining the types of indoor conditions which result in guest comfort should be almost invisible to the guest. It is the failure of systems to work properly which draws unwanted attention and creates managerial nightmares.

In the above discussion, the terms *building, equipment,* and *system* have been used. Each of these requires somewhat different types of attention from the building engineer and his or her staff. The discussion in the next few sections of this chapter provides further insight into the duties and responsibilities of the engineering department.

Building Maintenance

The actual physical structure of the building may initially seem like something which requires relatively little effort on the part of the engineering department. The stone, brick, asphalt, concrete, and steel of most lodging establishments would appear to last forever. However, there are a large number of basic maintenance activities which must be undertaken if the building is to preserve its initial appearance and function. Laventhol & Horwath data (see Exhibit 1.7) indicates that approximately 50% of the POM budget is spent on non-labor aspects of building maintenance.

The environment around many buildings sometimes results in rapid deterioration of building surfaces. In some urban areas, the exterior surfaces suffer pitting and erosion due to materials in the air. Cleaning of exterior surfaces may be required, but the engineer must be certain that the cure will not be worse than the disease since the use of some cleaning materials results in damage to surfaces. Other types of maintenance include the application of protective treatments to surfaces to retard corrosion and repel the attack of moisture-entrained pollutants.

One element of building maintenance which is an unavoidable and continual problem is roofing. Whether it is the repair of minor leaks (an expense item) or the reroofing of the entire building (a capital cost), roofing system maintenance is an important concern. This is especially true since a failure of any type usually generates problems elsewhere and is highly visible to guests and employees.

Maintenance of Guestrooms, Furnishings, and Fixtures

From the perspective of the lodging property guest, the guestrooms and the furnishings and fixtures of the property are very visible features which contribute to the overall experience of the establishment—either positively or negatively. The proper maintenance of these elements is usually a direct responsibility of the engineering department staff. Since these elements receive a lot of use, they are often replaced within the first ten years (a capital expenditure). The department may replace the items itself or supervise outside contractors.

The yearly expenditures on the maintenance of the guestrooms, furnishings, and fixtures of the establishment are charged against the POM account. Laventhol & Horwath indicates that 2–3% of the total POM budget is spent on furniture and 2.5–4.5% on painting and decorating. These are two obviously identifiable categories of expenditure which include guestroom, furnishing, and fixture maintenance. Although the labor component of the POM budget for these items is not broken out, it is probably somewhat larger than the portion of the budget consumed by the non-labor amount. Activities in the maintenance of these items are labor intensive, especially an activity such as painting. In many lodging establishments, a portion of the guestroom maintenance is included in the preventive maintenance schedule. These aspects of guestroom maintenance include various activities of inspection and checking which contribute to the estimated high labor cost component of guestroom, furnishing, and fixture maintenance.

Equipment Maintenance and Repair

The amount of equipment installed in a modern hotel or motel is astounding. In the guestroom, there are a television set, a room HVAC unit of some type, various electric lights, ventilation fans in the bath, and sundry other items. Public spaces have HVAC units with fans, chillers, pumps, and controls as well as lighting. Pools have pumps, filters, water treatment systems, and more. The kitchen and laundry are full of equipment requiring almost continual repair and adjustment. The repair and maintenance of all this equipment is the responsibility of the engineering department.

At this point, it may be helpful to define what is meant by the term maintenance. To maintain something is "to keep in an existing state" or "to preserve from failure or decline."[8] Unfortunately, with respect to equipment, a large fraction of the time spent in some engineering operations is directed at repair ("to restore by replacing a part or by putting together what is torn or broken") rather than at maintenance. As we will see later in this book, repair expenses (especially those resulting from a breakdown) have a significant effect on the cost of building maintenance.

The cost of equipment repair and maintenance includes the cost of parts and supplies for building equipment and the cost of labor used in the repair of the equipment. Laventhol & Horwath (see Exhibit 1.7) indicates that approximately 12% of the average property POM budget is directly expended for electrical and mechanical equipment maintenance (the labor percentage for this item is not stated).

Equipment maintenance and repair can be quite easily linked to the goals stated previously for the engineering department. With 12% of the POM budget expended in this area, cost control is potentially important. The equipment being repaired and maintained represents 30–40% of the initial investment in the property, certainly worth protecting through repair and maintenance. Failure of the equipment to operate properly is undoubtedly going to affect customer satisfaction or the ability of other departments to operate efficiently. If the deterioration reduces the efficiency of the equipment, it is very possible that increased energy expenditures will result. Finally, some modes of equipment deterioration or failure result in significant safety problems which could endanger guests, employees, or both.

Budgeting and Cost Control

With approximately 11% of the total property budget being the responsibility of the engineering department, the need for accurate budgeting and cost control should be apparent. Unfortunately, at many establishments, the development and control of this budget is not approached with the same level of care and analysis that is used in other areas.

While the engineering department expense budget is often distributed into two parts (POM and Energy) by the uniform system of accounts, the maintenance function consumes significantly more money than the POM account figure would indicate. Since activities by housekeeping and the kitchen steward are partially directed at maintenance, some of the cost of these functions is maintenance related. All capital investments in the building are directly or indirectly maintenance related. Many capital investments (such as equipment replacements) are directly linked to items which are commonly thought of as maintenance costs and others (such as renovation expenditures) reflect the replacement of worn out materials (either physically worn out or needing a new concept for marketing purposes).

Budgeting of the POM account is more difficult than budgeting of the Energy account. First of all, 40–50% of the POM account is labor related. This means an accurate labor forecast is necessary to adequately budget POM. Information about all costs of employee labor—base wages and fringe benefits—is necessary to complete the labor portion of the budget. For the Other portion of the budget, we can identify two major subcomponents. The first subcomponent would be all contractual elements of the budget. While it may be possible to solicit bids for all contractual services far enough in advance to develop a budget based on these bids, this is typically not the case. Budgeting is usually a mix of educated guesses coupled with input from contractors. The other subcomponent of the POM budget is primarily concerned with expendable supplies used to maintain the building. When budgeting these items, the standard practice is to adjust the previous year's expenditures, taking into account some estimated price changes and known fluctuations in expected usage.

The budgeting of energy usually relies upon an analysis of the previous year's expenditures and the development of a budget based on these values. This process requires information from the energy suppliers concerning estimated changes in the price of energy, an estimation of the effect of the previous year's weather and business on the historic energy consumption, some estimation of the effect on consumption of business plans for the next year, and the effect of energy cost control programs. If these factors are considered and properly incorporated, it should be quite easy to generate the energy budget.

For many properties, the budget for the engineering department has a ceiling based on a percentage of revenues. Under such an arrangement, the engineering manager generates the annual budget and then operates his or her department on a monthly basis subject to a percentage limitation of the actual property revenue. Operating under such circumstances results in quite a bit of month-end "creativity" for the manager as he or she tries to defer or make expenditures in a given month in order to stay within the revenue percentage target. This activity is somewhat difficult for the engineering manager since significant components of the budget are not deferrable or even controllable on a monthly basis—for example, contracts for various services and the property's utility bills.

Labor cost control in the department requires the same type of attention to personnel management that is required of any manager. Proper management of maintenance activities should contribute to a reduction in both the energy expenditures at the property and the need to perform breakdown maintenance using overtime labor.

Security/Safety Maintenance

Security concerns involve the physical assets of the property, the employees, and the guests. Safety concerns involve the potential for personal injury to both employees and guests. At smaller lodging establishments, it is not unusual for building safety and security to be largely the responsibility of the engineering manager. Since 95% of lodging establishments have under 300 rooms and approximately 71% of the total rooms in the United States are found in these establishments, the property engineer's contribution to security and safety within the industry is significant.

Some specific safety and security concerns which exist within the engineering area include key control, lock rotation and maintenance, control of tools and supplies, emergency response to fires and other potentially dangerous situations, safe operation of equipment and tools, and outside contractor interactions.[9]

Contractual and Regulatory Compliance

The terms *contractual compliance* and *regulatory compliance* refer to requirements imposed upon the property which are of a legal nature and are sometimes directly or indirectly the responsibility of engineering. National, state, and local governments are involved in establishing these requirements, as are unions within the property and contractors. Some of the requirements imposed by the governments which are entirely or partially the responsibility of engineering include elevator inspections and certification (contracted), fire code compliance, building code compliance, health/sanitary code compliance, Environmental Protection Agency compliance, and Occupational Safety and Health Act compliance.

The contractual responsibilities of engineering pertain to those contracts issued as part of the engineering department budget for work to be performed by outside vendors. Data from a sample of about 100 lodging properties indicates that among the costlier and more common contracts issued by engineering departments are elevator contracts (issued by 81% of the studied properties), window cleaning contracts (issued by 59% of the properties), and landscaping contracts (issued by 57% of the properties).[10] The engineering department may also contract for periodic calibration of controls, fire alarms, and communication systems. Outside contracts for water treatment, trash removal, fire extinguisher charging, cleaning and painting of kitchen ductwork, and maintenance of major pieces of HVAC equipment are also common.

Besides these basic maintenance contracts, major work to renovate or repair the building and grounds will also be contracted, but is likely to be considered as a capital improvement and handled separately from the POM budget.

Parts Inventory and Control

The nature of the work performed in engineering results in a need for parts and supplies which are unique in many instances. The uniqueness of these parts or supplies may mean they require long lead times when they are ordered. However, the ability to operate portions of the facility safely and comfortably often requires immediate access to parts or supplies in order to effect repairs. For this reason, an adequate parts and supplies inventory and control over the purchase and storage of these items are very important.

Development of an adequate parts and supplies inventory starts when the property is designed and constructed. If the property utilizes any unique FF&E, replacement parts for possible failure items should be supplied. An adequate number of duplicate and blank keys and locks should be stocked. A stock of appropriate replacement parts for equipment should be ordered—for example, replacement belts for all air handling units. The number of parts and supplies required is strongly influenced by the building design. If equipment is chosen with interchangeability in mind, then the needed supplies will be reduced. For highly sensitive pieces of equipment (for example, a circulating pump and motor for the building heating system), the building design may incorporate a

Exhibit 1.11 Renovation Cycle of an Existing Property

STAGE	COST/ROOM (approx.)	SCOPE
6-year refurbishment	$5000-10,000	Replacing fabrics, carpets, most furniture, vinyl wall covering, repainting
12-year major overhaul	$20,000-30,000	Repeating above plus upgrading systems and equipment (e.g. computers, life safety, kitchen, laundry)
50-year "gut-job" renovation and/or restoration	$50,000 +	Repeating all the above plus changes in partitions, areas, and circulation, and exterior restoration

Source: Walter A. Rutes and Richard H. Penner, *Hotel Planning and Design* (New York: Whitney Library of Design, 1985), p. 115. Used by permission.

backup unit or a replacement unit may be stocked.

If parts cost is considered during initial design, it may be possible to reduce the cost of maintenance at a later time. A hotel visited by one of the authors used an unusual size of disposable filter for guestroom HVAC units; this resulted in the need for special orders to restock filters and a significantly higher cost. Creating a set of washable filters for the units reduced the cost of filter changes by almost one dollar per change. This is a potentially significant dollar savings: when filters are changed 12 times per year and a property may average approximately one filter per room, a 100-room property could save $1,200 per year—money that falls directly to the bottom line. In other words, to cover the cost of not using the washable filters, a property would have to produce not *sales* of $1,200, but rather enough sales to produce *profits* of $1,200.

The control of parts and supplies inventory may often be relatively simple. Key elements in this control are ordering the proper items, knowing what items are in inventory, and being able to find them. When dealing with an offshore resort location, the lead times on such items and the sometimes unique needs of the location make inventory control more closely resemble that of a manufacturing plant where issues of par stocks, optimal order quantity, lead time, and so forth are rather important.

Renovations, Additions, and Restorations

The need to redecorate and renovate, whether because of wear and tear caused by use, because of changing needs for space, or in order to support a new concept, is a common feature of all lodging properties.[11] For many lodging chains, expenditures in these areas are greater each year than the expenditures on new properties. Depending on the magnitude of the project and the organization of the property and company, the work performed in some or all of these tasks may be the responsibility of the property's engineering department. This responsibility may include the actual performance of the work or the supervision of outside contractors as they perform the necessary tasks. Exhibit 1.11 lists the frequency, cost, and scope of common renovation tasks.

The construction of an addition is also a fairly common occurrence for a lodging property, especially if the property is successful. While this construction is almost always performed by an outside contractor, the involvement of the engineering department during the design, construction, and start-up of this addition is very helpful and usually necessary. The building engineer is often asked for information regarding the location of various building services, the necessity to shut down portions of the operation in order to effect interconnections, maintenance concerns in building design and equipment selection, safety during construction, and many other issues.

The need to perform a massive restoration will usually result in the removal of a lodging property from service for some time. The engineering department's responsibilities during this time will be similar to those for an addition as outlined above. An activity similar to restoration is *adaptive reuse*. When adaptive reuse is practiced, a building not originally built as a lodging property is modified for this purpose. Under this condition, there is no existing engineering department and the entire project is supervised by outside contractors and the staff of the building owner/operator. Involving the person who will become the building engineer in this process can give the engineer greater understanding of the building and enhance his or her ability to maintain it once it is finished.

Special Projects

With the introduction of new technologies and the needs of lodging customers for special services, the engineering department is called upon to perform many special projects. The introduction of property-owned telephone systems may result in the need to install the systems or supervise their installation by a contractor. Similar responsibilities may exist for energy conservation equipment. The introduction of computerized office equipment will sometimes create the need for dedicated electrical lines, additional electrical or HVAC services, special floor coverings, modifications to workspaces, and similar tasks often undertaken by the engineering department.

Special events may require the construction of display stands, protective barriers, and kiosks. Trade shows may need additional electrical service, phone connections, and special lighting. These projects require the input of the engineering department early in the negotiating stages of the contract for the event to ensure that costs are recovered and that the necessary services are ready for the customers upon their arrival.

Training of Staff

The training activities within the maintenance area may differ somewhat from those in other areas of the property. Many people hired in the maintenance department (electricians, painters, carpenters) already possess specific skills or abilities. While some responsibility exists to maintain their skill levels, the primary focus of training is to inform these employees of the standards and specific requirements of the property at which they are employed. This training may be grouped in the categories of general training, departmental training, and job-specific training.

General training involves informing employees about rules applying to all employees at the facility. Included is information concerning benefits, hours, building access, package passes, uniforms, time clocks, and other items common to all employees. Such training may be conducted by the personnel department for all newly hired employees or may be the responsibility of individual departments.

Departmental training is concerned with those activities which pertain to the general operation of the maintenance department. Such training includes work orders, inventory control, tool and supply requisitions, standards of conduct and dress, the employees' responsibilities and relationship with the guest, basic labor practices (especially as they relate to the union contract if one exists), and emergency procedures. The goal of this training is to address those unique items which pertain only to the maintenance department, but which affect all or almost all employees within this area.

Job-specific training deals with the development of specific skills or knowledge necessary to perform the assigned work function. This could mean training maintenance personnel to maintain new energy management equipment or it could mean offering a refresher course in basic electrical troubleshooting. This training should include standards of job performance at the property. Also included should be the safety standards at the property and an understanding of the responsibilities of other departments and their interactions with engineering. Many properties establish specific learning objectives for newly hired employees. Examples of these could be familiarity with building plans and layout and knowledge of specific procedures.

Since the work of employees will often be subject to inspection by someone representing the code authority, employees need to be instructed about applicable codes. Sometimes this instruction is part of the initial training the employee receives in order to earn a trade license. Continuing training in this area is important to avoid significant problems and costs which could arise if codes are not adhered to.

Because of the technical nature of some positions in the maintenance department and the desire of employees to advance, it may be desirable to establish a policy which provides employees with incentives for other more general maintenance or management training/education. Local trade, vocational, or technical schools will often provide training which is appropriate for the needs of maintenance employees. For certain types of equipment or systems, such as HVAC, equipment suppliers offer courses in the maintenance and operation of the equipment. These courses can be quite valuable and are often very reasonably priced.[12]

Corporate Reporting

In lodging chains, the engineering function at corporate headquarters, whether a subdivision of another department or completely separated, supports the operations of the engineering departments in the separate properties and strives to protect the company from the risks inherent in operating lodging facilities. This support can come in various forms:[13]

- Training in company policies and work-related skills
- Technical assistance on equipment and building
- Purchasing through national accounts or contracts
- Assistance in budgeting
- Analysis of operating results

Furthermore, the individual properties provide corporate headquarters with specific information which assists the central staff. This information generally includes:

- Proposals for operating budgets
- Proposals for capital expenditures
- Periodic reports on operating expenses
- Periodic reports on staffing and maintenance activities
- Reports on emergencies or disasters
- Reports on the failure of major equipment or systems
- Periodic reports on guest complaints

Organization and Staffing

Organization

Exhibit 1.12 shows fairly typical departmental organizational structures of a large property (over 350 rooms) and small property (under 150 rooms), both moderately priced. Although the property size varies, the relation of the engineering department to the other departments in the property remains quite similar. Regardless of the size of the property, the director of engineering is usually at a level equivalent to the other major department heads and often is a member of the executive committee with these other department heads. It is from this position of importance that the director performs the most important managerial functions. The goals, plans, functions, and activities of the engineering department should be coordinated with the other departments of the property. Usually, the ability of the director to operate well at this level affects the entire staff's perceived quality of the engineering function.

A sample organizational structure for the engineering department in a 650-room first-class chain property is shown in Exhibit 1.13. The top two individuals perform primarily managerial functions so that the remainder of the department's staff can effectively perform the technical functions expected of the department. Supporting the director and the assistant director are the administrative assistant who provides clerical services, the manager of the parts inventory, and several supervisors for each of the major trades. These supervisors perform both managerial and technical functions in that they schedule and monitor the performance of the workers for whom they are responsible as well as provide their technical expertise when repairing complex equipment.

In a chain property, the director of engineering may interact with the operating company through an engineering group headed usually by a vice president for engineering. This vice president and vice presidents for other functional areas may be part of a group that works with the individual responsible for lodging operations. Throughout this interaction, the technical expertise of the operating company is made available to the individual property, the company's goals are determined, and the operating standards are monitored by the staff of the company's engineering group.

Although we speak of fairly "typical" organizational structures, these structures may vary substantially from property to property due to several factors. The primary factors are the size of the property and the technical complexity of the building's systems. By necessity, large prop-

Exhibit 1.12 Organization Charts for a Large and a Small Property

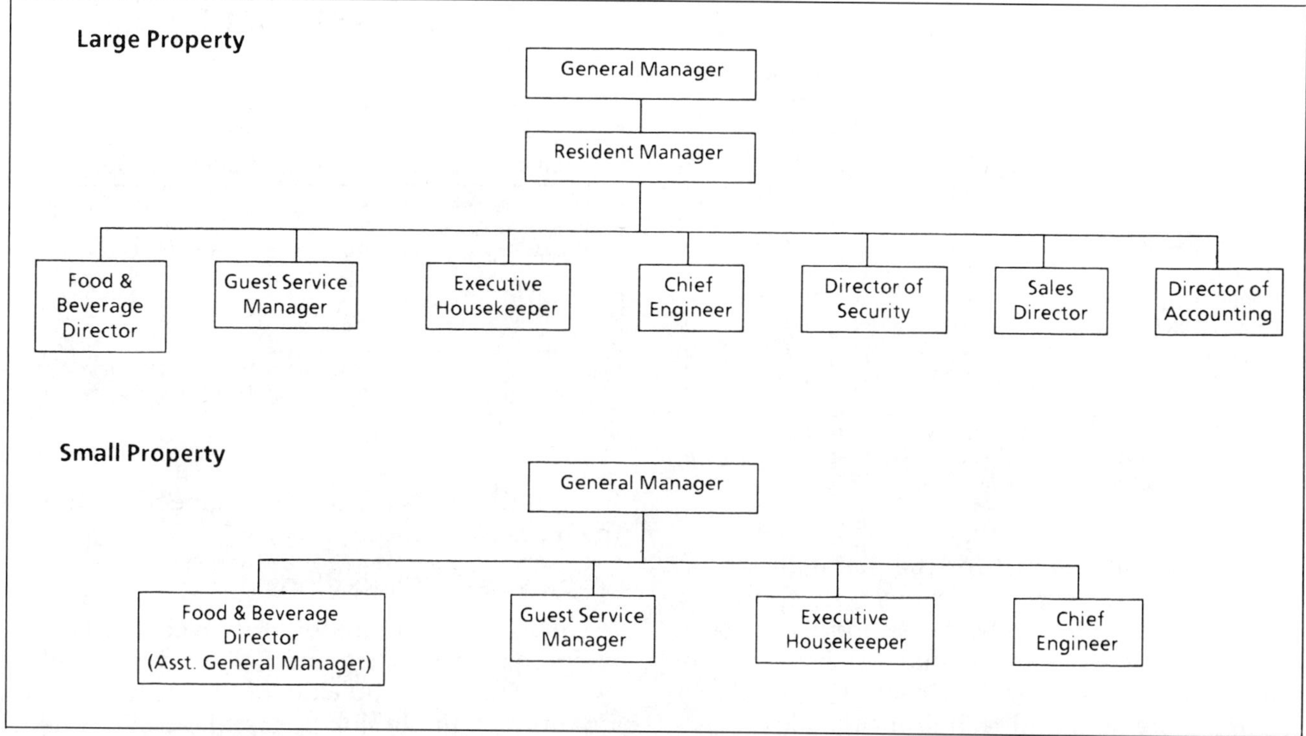

erties require several people to accomplish the volume of work. With the increase in the number of staff, the head of the engineering department must spend more time on the management functions and focus less time on the technical functions. On the other hand, the "department" in a small budget property may consist of a maintenance person working part-time who performs all of the work with no manager.

The second primary factor, the technical complexity of the building's systems, determines the level and range of the technical knowledge that the engineering department must possess. Buildings that have central heating and air conditioning systems with their sophisticated boilers, chillers, and controls require engineering staff who can maintain the systems. In contrast, the staff of a budget property would handle the breakdown of an individual air conditioning unit by replacing the unit and sending the broken unit out for repair.

Several other factors also influence the organizational structure of the department. The amount of services contracted out by the property, the amount (when applicable) of interaction with the operating company's central engineering group, and the types of services provided to the property's guests all have an effect. Less technical expertise is required in those

Exhibit 1.13 Typical Engineering Department Organization

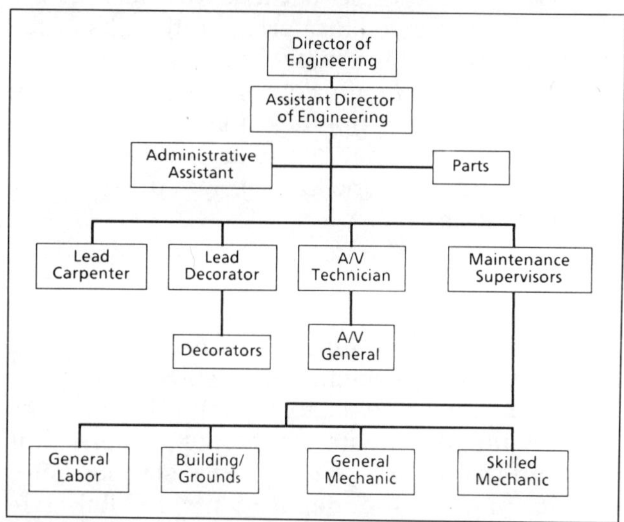

Source: Michael H. Redlin and David M. Stipanuk, *Survey of the Organization of the Operational Engineering Function in Lodging Companies* (an unpublished survey).

Exhibit 1.14 Staffing Levels for the Engineering Department

Type of Property	Number of Rooms	Total Number of Employees in Full-time Equivalents
Budget	110	1.0
Budget	220	1.5
Moderate-priced	150	3.0
Moderate-priced	350	7.0
Moderate-priced	600	10.0
First-class	280	6.0
First-class	400	16.0
First-class	2000	66.0

Source: Michael H. Redlin and David M. Stipanuk, *Survey of the Organization of the Operational Engineering Function in Lodging Companies* (an unpublished survey).

Exhibit 1.15 Engineering Staff for Moderate-priced Properties of Different Sizes

Title of Position	150 Rooms	350 Rooms	600 Rooms
Chief Engineer	1	1	1
Assistant Chief	0	1	1
Clerical Staff	0	0	1
All Others	2	5	7
TOTAL	3	7	10

Source: Michael H. Redlin and David M. Stipanuk, *Survey of the Organization of the Operational Engineering Function in Lodging Companies* (an unpublished survey).

properties that contract for the maintenance of major systems such as elevators, telephones, and computers. Less clerical support is necessary in those companies that do not require substantial interaction with a central engineering group. More staff and technical capability must be available in properties that have large convention spaces so that the setup of the rooms can be accomplished.

The direct impact of any one factor is very difficult to determine because the factors are usually interrelated. Properties with substantial convention services usually have a large number of rooms and contain complex systems. Conversely, budget properties that provide only sleeping accommodations usually have a small number of rooms and are designed with very simple systems.

Staffing

The number of employees required by the engineering department varies substantially because of the same factors that influence the organizational structure of the department. It is very difficult to determine precise standards for the staffing of the department. Exhibit 1.14 presents fairly typical staffing levels for different sizes and types of properties. Exhibit 1.15 breaks down the numbers for moderately priced properties into slightly more detail.

Another source of information is a study of luxury and first-class hotels that was performed in 1985. Exhibit 1.16 presents the distribution of the number of staff for the engineering department *per 100 rooms*.[14]

Employee Qualifications

The qualifications of employees within the maintenance department will vary depending on the size and complexity of the facility. Exhibit 1.17 is a sample job description for a chief engineer developed by the Executive Engineers Committee of AH&MA. The job description outlines various duties, but does not indicate their relative importance. Exhibit 1.18, in contrast, is taken from a survey of 74 chief engineers from properties averaging 609 guestrooms. The survey asked the engineers to rank the importance of and time spent on various engineering duties.

The degree to which the chief engineer performs rather than supervises the activities listed in the job description will depend on the property size. A 100-room property will probably have a three-person maintenance department and a POM budget of about $100,000. The maintenance manager is likely to be a skilled or semiskilled tradesperson with hands-on involvement in building maintenance who also performs supervisory activities. Much of the more complex work is contracted out. The maintenance and repair of the building conducted by the maintenance department resembles that which is undertaken by a moderately skilled homeowner in his or her home.

As the size and complexity of the property increases, the needs and qualifications of the employees also increase. The maintenance manager gradually shifts from a working manager to

Exhibit 1.16 Engineering Staff per 100 Rooms for First Class and Luxury Hotels

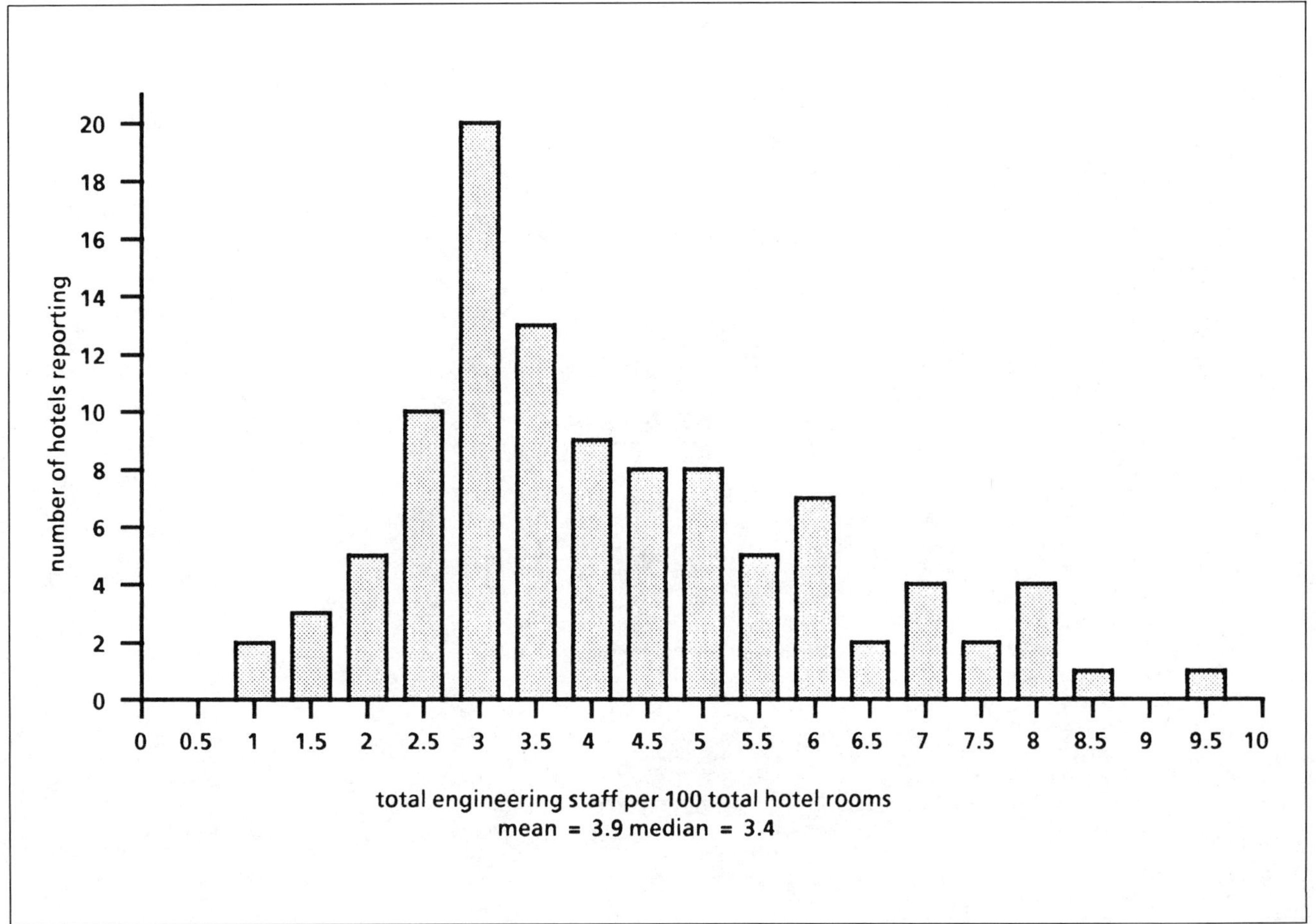

one who spends an increasing amount of time in the traditional management functions. In addition, if the property is unionized, there will be a greater subdivision of the labor force and fewer individuals who may function as "generalists" in terms of their duties. At somewhere around the 300-room level, the maintenance manager stops being involved in hands-on activity and is almost completely consumed with the managerial role. Since a property of 300 rooms will probably have a staff of 7 to 10, a POM budget of $350,000, and an energy budget of $375,000, the hiring of a full-time *manager* for such an operation certainly seems appropriate.

Some of the tradespeople who may be represented on the engineering department staff or retained by contract include painters, electricians, plumbers, carpenters, groundskeepers, mechanics for general maintenance, locksmiths, upholsterers, boiler operators, clerical staff, inventory control clerks, and paper hangers. Making hiring decisions for such a diverse group of trades may be difficult. One chain has developed a series of specific questions on individual trade areas and administers these to applicants. The questions cover basic elements of the trade which should be known by a qualified applicant. This process provides a quick screening of applicants (the really poor ones do not even take the test) and an objective way of assessing prospective employee knowledge of the trade.

Relationships Within the Property

The engineering department does not always benefit from a good working relationship

Exhibit 1.17 Job Description for a Chief Engineer

Job Title Chief Engineer Date

Basic Function:

Performs, manages, or supervises maintenance operations for exterior and interior facilities including electrical, refrigeration, plumbing, heating, cooling, structural, groundcare, parking areas, and other maintenance work necessary to maintain the property in an optimum and efficient condition. Also, ensures the safety and comfort of the guests and employees.

Responsibilities:

1. Maintain all distribution systems for electricity, water, steam, gas, etc.
2. Maintain and operate air conditioning, heating, ventilation, and refrigeration systems.
3. Maintain buildings and grounds.
4. Monitor and coordinate the services performed by outside contractors in accordance to all contracts, leases, service agreements, and warranties.
5. Keep all records pertaining to heat, light and power, and costs of the facility.
6. Ensure timely response to requests for services by guests, employees, and management to include repair or replacement of all interior fixtures and furnishings.
7. Schedule all work to be done on a daily basis at a minimum of inconvenience to guests and employees.
8. Plan, implement, and administer an effective preventive maintenance program in accordance with good engineering practices.
9. Plan, implement, and administer an energy management program.
   - Maintain appropriate equipment operating logs
   - Maintain utility consumption records
   - Educate other operating departments in energy management
   - Establish annual energy reduction objectives
   - Analyze and modify operation of the physical plant to conserve energy
10. Assist in the preparation of capital expenditures and maintenance budgets.
    - Select vendors and contractors that meet quality standards and pricing specifications
    - Initiate purchase orders
    - Approve invoices
    - Maintain adequate inventory of parts, tools, and supplies
    - Maintain purchasing records
11. Train and supervise subordinates and assist in safety and emergency training for other employees.
12. Conduct continuing inspection of buildings and grounds to ensure compliance with OSHA, fire and safety laws.
13. Recommend and/or take action to ensure compliance.
14. Maintain a clean and orderly work area free of hazards.
15. Perform other duties as assigned.

Supervision Exercised:

Assistant chief engineer, carpenters, electricians, grounds maintenance, lock and key, maintenance, painters, plumbers, refrigeration mechanics, and sound technicians.

Supervision Received:

- Supervisor:
  General Manager

Minimum Requirements:

- Education: high school or equivalent.
- Mechanical or equivalent training in the following: refrigeration, boilers, plumbing, air conditioning, power or building construction. Higher education or experience of such kind and amount as to provide a comparable background required.

Experience:

Five years in any combination of mechanical trades with hotels/motels, hospitals, high-rise apartments, or similar duties with the armed services. Must have license where required or qualifications to become licensed. Knowledge of carpentry and painting required.

Other:

1. Applicant should possess the following traits:
   - Effective communication skills
   - Administrative abilities
   - Good personal relations skills
   - Self-motivation
   - Mechanical aptitude
2. Applicant must be willing to relocate when and where directed.

Source: Executive Engineers Committee, American Hotel & Motel Association, 1981.

Exhibit 1.18 Importance of and Time Devoted to Various Engineering Duties

Time Devoted Ratings			Importance Ratings		
Rank	Duty	Mean rating	Rank	Duty	Mean rating
1.	Knowledge of maintenance of equipment	4.22	1.	Knowledge of maintenance of equipment	4.76
2.	Responsibility for leadership	4.08	2.	Energy conservation	4.66
3.	Responsibility for communicating with employees	4.04	3.	Energy management	4.59
4.	Responsibility for effective organizational ability	3.91	4.	Responsibility for communicating with employees	4.59
5.	Relations with housekeeping department	3.85	5.	Relations with top management	4.52
6.	Responsibility for safety	3.78	6.	Responsibility for leadership	4.51
7.	Relations with top management	3.76	7.	Responsibility for safety	4.49
8.	Energy conservation	3.65	8.	Responsibility for effective organizational ability	4.45
9.	Knowledge of types of equipment	3.64	9.	Energy costs	4.44
10.	Responsibility for motivation	3.60	10.	Knowledge of types of equipment	4.37
11.	Energy management	3.60	11.	Use of computers for control in monitoring energy costs	4.36
12.	Use of computers for control in monitoring energy costs	3.46	12.	Responsibility for budgeting	4.31
13.	Knowledge of the energy requirements of equipment	3.40	13.	Knowledge of the use of and training on equipment	4.31
14.	Energy costs	3.38	14.	Relations with housekeeping department	4.27
15.	Knowledge of the use of and training on equipment	3.36	15.	Responsibility for effective recordkeeping	4.27
16.	Computer use in the department	3.35	16.	Knowledge of the energy requirements of equipment	4.23
17.	Relations with food and beverage department	3.29	17.	Responsibility for motivation	4.22
18.	Responsibility for budgeting	3.25	18.	Computer use in the department	4.19
19.	Responsibility for effective recordkeeping	3.25	19.	Personnel function of training and continuing education	4.12
20.	Personnel function of training and continuing education	3.23	20.	Use of computers for control in preventive maintenance	4.09

Seventy-four chief engineers were asked to rate the importance of and time devoted to 58 job duties or factors on a scale of 1 to 5. The above were rated most important or time-consuming on average.

Source: Denney G. Rutherford, "The Evolution of the Hotel Engineer's Job," *The Cornell Hotel and Restaurant Administration Quarterly*, February 1987, p. 77. Used by permission.

with other departments. Since this department is a service agency, failure on its part to provide proper service to its customers—the guests, employees, and other departments—will result in a negative image. Certain departments in the property have significant levels of interaction with engineering.

The housekeeping department provides an important initial step in the property upkeep. Because its employees enter almost every guestroom every day, it is in a position to identify maintenance needs and initiate work orders for engineering. Unfortunately, it is a department with which the engineering department often seems to have an almost adversarial relationship. Engineering personnel may be upset if the misuse of chemicals and equipment by housekeeping results in work for the maintenance department. Housekeeping personnel sometimes resent having to clean up after various types of maintenance. In addition, Exhibit 1.18 indicates a potential source of problems. The chief engineers surveyed rated relations with housekeeping fifth in time spent, but only fourteenth in importance. This, combined with the fact that relations with food and beverage rated seventeenth in time spent, but did not make the top 20 in importance, may indicate a lack of appreciation by the engineering management of the importance of interdepartmental relations. In particular, engineering and housekeeping managers need to devote attention to improving the relationship between their departments at many properties.

The engineering department can make life at the front desk relatively easy or a virtual nightmare. If the overall maintenance program results in guestroom equipment and facilities which meet the guests' expectations, the number of complaints or problems which result are slight and the front desk does not have to deal with these and their implications. Failure of engineering to coordinate its activities with housekeeping and the front desk can result in the removal of rooms from service at awkward times or without the knowledge of those who need to know. The results can affect the bottom line at the property and the morale and performance of other departments.

At larger properties, engineering has a significant involvement with the convention and meetings staff. As special groups are booked into the facilities, they bring with them unique needs and concerns. These can range from facilities (protective enclosures around unsightly construction areas) and services (electrical supply for a computer show) to special security considerations (closed-circuit television for a diamond merchants' display). Close coordination between convention/sales staff and engineering is necessary to ensure that the needs of the client are met effectively and at a reasonable cost.

Notes

1. J. F. Musselman, "Power Plant and Refrigeration Equipment," *The Architectural Forum*, November 1923, pp. 254-258.
2. Floyd Miller, *Statler: America's Extraordinary Hotelman* (New York: The Statler Foundation, 1968).
3. *U.S. Lodging Industry, 1984 Edition* (Philadelphia: Laventhol & Horwath, 1984).
4. Walter A. Rutes and Richard H. Penner, *Hotel Planning and Design* (New York: Whitney Library of Design, 1985).
5. A median value is that number in a sample where one half the numbers in the sample fall on each side of this value.
6. *U.S. Lodging Industry—1985* (Philadelphia: Laventhol & Horwath, 1985).
7. *Trends in the Hotel Industry* (Houston, Texas: Pannell Kerr Forster, 1985).
8. *Webster's Ninth New Collegiate Dictionary* (Springfield, Mass.: Merriam-Webster Inc., 1983).
9. For a detailed treatment of lodging security and safety issues, see *Security and Loss Prevention Management* by Raymond C. Ellis, Jr., and the Security Committee of AH&MA (East Lansing, Mich.: Educational Institute of the American Hotel & Motel Association, 1986). The Institute also offers a complete security course, Hotel/Motel Security Management, based on this text, and a videotape, *Hotel Security on Trial*, which discusses the general issues surrounding lodging industry security.
10. Reed Alan Fisher, *A Documentation of the Factors Which Determine Staffing Levels for the Engineering Department of a Hotel Property*, MPS Monograph, School of Hotel Administration, Cornell University, Ithaca, N.Y., 1986.
11. The discussion which follows is derived from Rutes and Penner. The reader is referred to their text for a fuller treatment of this topic.
12. The Educational Institute of the American Hotel & Motel Association provides a correspondence training program which includes technical aspects of lodging property engineering, plus human relations, supervisory training, and elective opportunities. The engi-

neering or maintenance manager can participate in the Certified Engineering Operations Executive (CEOE) program offered by the Institute. There are several paths available to achieve this certification which combine varying amounts of experience and education. A comprehensive examination is required. Such certification could be a worthwhile component of the personal development for a junior level (aspiring manager) person at a hotel or motel.

13. This information comes from the authors' unpublished *Survey of the Organization of the Operational Engineering Function in Lodging Companies,* Cornell University, Ithaca, N.Y., 1986.
14. Fisher.

2
Management Methods and Systems

The engineering department manager is faced with the same set of general managerial responsibilities facing most management staff. Although this text is not a text on management principles, this chapter will focus on those managerial aspects which are either unique or particularly relevant to the engineering department. We will discuss budgeting, capital projects, maintenance methods and management systems, energy management methods, the uniform system of accounts, and personnel management.

Budgeting

Some managers see the preparation of a budget as a necessary evil, one which they perform in some manner but with little link to the actual performance of their "real" responsibilities. For others, preparation and adherance to the budget is the primary focus of their "management style." This text advocates neither approach. A clear understanding of the role of budget development and monitoring as a managerial tool can greatly assist any manager, whether building engineer or general manager.

The Budget as a Managerial Tool

A budget should be viewed as a tool which helps a manager perform his or her duties. The budgeting process specifically relates to the managerial functions of planning, organizing, controlling, and setting goals. The budget is also a means of communicating within the property.

The budgeting process is, by definition, one of projection. The manager is being asked to forecast needs for property funds for the next month, year, or longer. He or she must use information about both the expected business activity for the next year (a sales forecast) and the projected cost of the components of the budget. In addition, the engineering manager must take into account anticipated special needs for the budget year. While some of these special needs are components of the capital budget (discussed later in this chapter), there may be others which belong in the expense category (the primary focus of this section).

The usefulness of the budget at the property level and beyond is sometimes not understood by line managers. For example, the overall property budget is an important tool in estimating cash needs at the property. By accumulating departmental budgets, revenue projections, and other relevant cost information, the property controller can forecast the need to borrow funds or the appropriate time to invest excess funds.

The budget also functions as a means of communicating departmental needs and plans to management and other departments. In developing and presenting the budget, the manager must clarify his or her plans and not only develop these in monetary terms, but also clearly define the needs and their relation to the property's goals and plans. Using this information, management decides whether to initiate plans to address these needs.

Following the preparation of the budget, the building engineer should use the budget to monitor and control the department's expenditures. Exhibit 2.1 is a sample of the monthly reports of the Repairs and Maintenance (POM) and Heat, Light, and Power (Energy) components of the property costs as prepared within one large lodging corporation. Various information is provided to aid the manager. The forecasted expenditures (and percentages of revenue) for the month and year to date are provided, along with the actual expenditures in the month and year to date for both the current year and the previous year. The monthly and annual comparisons help the manager to identify problem areas in departmental costs, an activity which should lead to attempts to understand and/or remedy the problem.

In the following pages, the components of the engineering department budget are discussed in relation to some methods which should be applied in the budget development process. Factors which may result in deviations from this budget will be mentioned and linked to the monitoring and control process for engineering department expenditures. In addition, certain practices in the department and at the property which can result in budgetary problems will be mentioned. This discussion assumes the property's goal in budget development is to allocate funds to support the accomplishment of the engineering department's major goals stated in Chapter 1. While the budget total will certainly be subject to limits and constraints, we do not advocate the development of a budget based solely on adding a flat percent to the previous year's budget nor on a rigid "percentage of revenue" approach. If either of these approaches is used, the budget and budget development process lose a great deal of their utility as managerial tools.

Developing the Departmental Budget

In Chapter 1, the basic components of the engineering department budget were defined as the Energy and POM accounts. The Energy account (previously known as Heat, Light, and Power or HLP) includes all purchases of energy (oil, natural gas, liquified petroleum gas, steam, chilled water, and electricity), plus water and sewer costs. The POM account has two primary subcomponents—labor costs and all other departmental expenditures. The Energy and POM accounts each consume, on the average, 5–7% of property revenues.

Departmental expenditures are charged to various subaccounts of the Energy and POM accounts as they are incurred. The budget development process eventually produces a budget which follows the subaccounts of the uniform systems of accounts. (A complete listing of the components of the POM and Energy accounts appears later in this chapter.)

The process of budgeting energy costs should consist of two parts. Part one should be a forecast of projected energy use at the facility by month and should rely rather heavily on information about past energy use. Part two should convert the energy use forecast to a forecast of costs.

Energy use at the property is affected by business and climatic factors and by the efficiency of systems operation. If the engineer can develop some understanding of how occupancy affects the building's overall energy use, it may be possible to build into the energy budget a change in energy usage based on the property sales plan. If significant energy-conserving actions are taken to improve the efficiency of energy use at the property, the engineer should be able to incorporate the effect of these actions in the energy budget. Finally, the budget should be developed and monitored based on appropriate considerations of weather conditions. Developing a budget by assuming that the same abnormal weather which existed last year will exist this year, such as the hottest summer in 50 years, will usually not result in accurate budgets. Basing the forecasted energy consumption on average conditions is typically more appropriate and desirable. Of course, management should not attempt to hold the engineering department to an energy budget based on average weather when the coldest winter in 50 years hits.

The POM budget development process is probably better approached on a task basis than on an account basis. Task budgeting of POM budgets uses information the engineering manager has of the needs within and methods of the department (for example, contracts, types of maintenance, special projects). By assessing specific tasks, evaluating the costs associated with these tasks, and linking them to the appropriate accounts, the POM budget can be developed.

Exhibit 2.1 Monthly POM and Energy Report for a Large Property

MONTH OF: FEBRUARY FORECAST		THIS YR: 1987		LAST YR: 1986		REPAIRS AND MAINTENANCE	Y-T-D: JANUARY TO FEBRUARY THIS YR: 1987		LAST YR: 1986		FORECAST	
$	%	$	%	$	%		$	%	$	%	$	%
						PAYROLL & RELATED EXPENSES:						
20,100	1.4	20,449	1.6	19,009	1.3	SALARIES & WAGES	41,545	1.7	42,476	1.6	41,200	1.5
9,200	.6	9,807	.8	8,826	.6	PAYROLL TAXES & EMP. BENEFITS	21,148	.9	18,348	.7	18,800	.7
29,300	2.0	30,257	2.3	27,834	2.0	TOTAL P/R & RELATED EXPENSES	62,694	2.5	60,824	2.3	60,000	2.1
						OTHER EXPENSES:						
1,000	.1	2,418	.2	1,994	.1	BUILDING	2,681	.1	2,285	.1	2,000	.1
200						CURTAINS AND DRAPES					400	
700		690	.1	1,264	.1	ELECTRIC BULBS	1,563	.1	1,264		1,400	
						ELECTRICAL & MECH. EQUIPMENT						
2,100	.1	1,406	.1	1,936	.1	-AIR COND, HEAT, PLUMB & REFRIG	3,042	.1	3,418	.1	4,200	.1
400		59		228		-AUTOMOTIVE	122		419		800	
5,400	.4	5,343	.4	4,873	.3	-ELEVATORS & ESCALATORS	10,274	.4	9,833	.4	10,800	.4
1,300	.1	950	.1	1,693	.1	-GENERAL ELECTRICAL & MECH.	1,885	.1	3,793	.1	2,600	.1
600		1,044	.1	220		-KITCHEN	2,307	.1	896		1,200	
300		183				-LAUNDRY	1,556	.1	52		600	
400		149		168		-TELEVISION	302		253		800	
1,800	.1	1,746	.1	1,758	.1	-MAINTENANCE CONTRACTS (OTH)	3,654	.1	3,616	.1	3,600	.1
400		364		368		EXTERMINATION	728		368		800	
500		101				FLOOR COVERING	521				1,000	
400				67		FURNITURE & FIXTURES	16		927		800	
800	.1	1,537	.1	732	.1	GENERAL SUPPLIES	2,054	.1	1,510	.1	1,600	.1
800	.1	440		504		LANDSCAPING - EXTERIOR	1,108		1,008		1,600	.1
1,100	.1	1,348	.1	1,179	.1	LANDSCAPING - INTERIOR	2,518	.1	2,358	.1	2,200	.1
300		371		26		PAINTING & DECORATING	935		303		600	
100						POOL					200	
2,900	.2	3,887	.3	3,136	.2	REFUSE AND TRASH REMOVAL	6,574	.3	6,272	.2	5,800	.2
100		310		48		SIGNS - ON PROPERTY	482		48		200	
300		403		199		UNIFORMS	649		377		600	
300		56		265		MISCELLANEOUS	234		674		600	
22,200	1.5	22,805	1.7	20,657	1.5	TOTAL OTHER EXPENSES	43,203	1.7	39,673	1.5	44,400	1.6
51,500	3.5	53,061	4.1	48,491	3.4	TOTAL REPAIRS AND MAINTENANCE	105,897	4.3	100,497	3.8	104,400	3.7
						HEAT, LIGHT AND POWER						
29,600	2.0	21,752	1.7	26,446	1.9	ELECTRICITY	46,034	1.9	51,260	1.9	60,200	2.1
2,900	.2	2,083	.2	2,962	.2	FUEL (GAS & OIL)	4,167	.2	5,467	.2	5,400	.2
6,000	.4	5,540	.4	5,956	.4	WATER	11,137	.4	11,358	.4	11,400	.4
32,300	2.2	26,783	2.1	32,335	2.3	CENTRAL PLANTS UTIL CHARGES	53,567	2.2	65,622	2.5	65,500	2.3
70,800	4.9	56,159	4.3	67,699	4.8	TOTAL HEAT, LIGHT AND POWER	114,901	4.6	133,707	5.0	142,500	5.0

Budgeting of the POM account certainly requires a much different approach from that used for the energy account. The two major components of this account should be handled differently, and certain subcomponents of this account require special handling as well. The budgeting of the labor account requires an accurate forecast of labor needs (number of employees, normal work hours, and overtime hours) and an accurate input of all wage rates, including such items as fringe benefits and other indirect costs. The labor needs forecast should use data from previous years adjusted for relevant factors such as staff shortages or overages, shifts in work from outside contracts to in-house personnel, and projected special needs. Wage rate projections require input from the personnel department concerning expected average wage rate changes, contractual wage adjustments, and other relevant information.

Budgeting of the non-labor portion of the POM budget requires subdivision into two major categories, contractual services and purchased supplies. All contractual services included in the POM budget should be reviewed to determine whether they will be renewed for the following year. If so, then the cost can usually be estimated by applying some adjustment factor to the previous year's cost. If a contract will not be renewed, then the cost should either be removed from the departmental budget or entered in another section of the budget. For example, a decision to discontinue a window washing contract and conduct this work with in-house employees might shift the expense from the contract (non-labor) component of the budget to the labor line of the POM budget (if it was thought there was not enough "slack" available in the current labor budget).

The purchased supplies portion of the budget can generally be estimated by adjusting the previous year's expenditures to take anticipated market factors into account. If significant special activities are to be undertaken, such as a major repainting of the facility by the building engineering department, then adjustments to the budget should be made to account for these.

Special Considerations

Special concerns or considerations can sometimes aid in preparing engineering department budgets, adjusting to budget cuts, responding to unexpected revenue availability, and responding to other problems and opportunities. The following discussion focuses on some of the special considerations facing the engineering manager in the budgeting and controlling process.

Since no property can afford to make all of the expenditures each department head would like to make, the preparation of the budget, whether for expenses or capital items, is partially a sales job. The budgeting process is one of assigning priorities, lobbying, compromising, and creative planning in the attempt to have the overall budget satisfy the goals of management and needs of the property. The engineering manager's probability of success in "selling" his or her requested budget to upper management may possibly be increased by the use of supplemental materials. For special needs such as roofing, parking lot repairs, new major equipment, and so forth, submitting a photo showing the deteriorated items may significantly enhance the proposal. Documentation of maintenance expenses during the past few years illustrating the cost of repairs and potential savings can be very helpful. Also helpful can be consultants' reports or copies of quotations for repair or replacement.

Some managers may find that their budgets are compared with those from other facilities and that, on this basis, the amounts requested are questioned. This is often unfortunate because the maintenance needs of one facility can differ significantly from those of another facility. The types of systems or equipment installed, historic level of maintenance, site climatic or environmental factors, allocation of space in the building, design of the building, and expectations of the staff and guests will all affect the maintenance needs and the budget.

No matter how carefully the budget is prepared, there will often be unanticipated savings or expense. If savings occur, the opportunity exists to apply the excess funds to another project or activity. With some properties exerting particularly tight control on a monthly basis, money which is not spent in a given month is sometimes essentially lost to the department. If the accuracy of estimating monthly expenditures is poor, the result may be problems in subsequent months. One possible solution to this circumstance is the purchase of certain supplies when extra cash is available, thereby meeting departmental needs, though at an earlier time than originally planned. While both making and deferring purchases are not uncommon activities at the end of a budget year, similar activities can happen on a monthly basis. Care must be used when doing this to avoid ending up with excess supplies that eventually become obsolete. Another possibility in this instance is setting aside unspent funds for later use—assuming the property controller agrees to such efforts.

The department's budget can be affected by elements out of its control, such as the actions of other departments. For example, the engineering department does not actually pay the bills for the goods and services it purchases. One of these bills, the electric bill, is among the largest single bills received by the property. It is not unusual for the utility company to assign a surcharge to the bill for late payment. If the accounting department does not issue a check on time for this bill, the engineering department budget is charged with the surcharge (which can be substantial), even though it is not to blame for the late payment. A few late payments during the year can contribute significantly to engineering department expenditures. Even more problematic can be erroneous bills from the utility company which, when corrected, result in potentially huge unexpected charges.

Failure of a property to meet its sales forecast will result in pressures to cut costs in all areas, including engineering. While certain elements of the engineering budget may well respond to cost-cutting activities, others will not. Contracted services generally cannot be adjusted and may have little direct relevance to overall business levels. In the short run (approximately one year or less), these expenses may be thought of as fixed expenses. Examples are elevator service, refuse hauling, and snow plowing contracts. Failure to perform basic building maintenance activities to an adequate level can contribute negatively to property image and accelerate a poor sales trend. A lack of attention to basic safety needs due to budget cuts is also not desirable.

It is the responsibility of the engineering manager to communicate critical elements of his or her operation to upper management, documenting the department's needs and their relation to concerns and goals of the property. The manager may not win every battle, but he or she must adequately represent the interests and responsibilities of the department.

Capital Projects

Capital projects can have several definitions. Items may be considered capital projects because of their lifetime, their cost, their treatment in the accounting records, their treatment for tax purposes, or provisions in the management contract. Capital items are not expenses (that is, they are not charged to an account of the uniform system of accounts). Special approval is normally required for these items. Depending on the magnitude and/or type of expenditure, the initiation and/or approval of the request may follow the normal chain of approval or a completely different chain of approval.

Any capital investment affects the engineering department because it is this department which will be required to maintain whatever is purchased. In many instances, the engineering department is required to invest additional resources in the interconnection of the purchased item to the building systems and to budget energy funds for its operation. For these reasons, *all* purchase orders for equipment should be routed through the engineering department for their information and input.

Reasons for and Types of Projects

Capital projects may be performed for several reasons:

- To maintain the market position of the property
- To improve the market position of the property
- To expand the size or facilities of the property
- To improve the efficiency of the facility operation
- To sustain or improve the safety of the facility
- To replace necessary elements of the building physical plant
- To obtain tax advantages

Capital expenditures such as these are made for financial or physical reasons or both. The financial reasons may be directly related to income or profits at the property or may be linked to overall financial goals of the operating or owning company. The physical reasons for investment may concern appearance, may be the result of internal (not directly visible) deterioration in the physical plant, or may be related to life safety.

The methods used to evaluate a capital investment's desirability will depend on the type of and the reason for the investment. Investments made to maintain the market position of the property would include basic guestroom refurbishments and efforts to maintain the property's appearance. These investments are often performed on some sort of a timetable and are usually not formally subject to financial analysis. Investments made to improve the market position of the property, such as a change in the design concept of a restaurant or a major change in the quality of the FF&E, may be subject to a more careful payback analysis. Even more analysis of cost and benefit may occur when assessing expanding the size or facilities at the property; such an analysis would resemble the initial feasibility study performed to determine whether the property should be developed.

Expenditures to improve the efficiency of facility operations usually require extensive justification. For the engineering department, these types of expenditures typically involve energy conservation and the resulting decrease in energy costs. Such expenditures are often subject to rather rigid criteria for their acceptance, often much more stringent than those applied to market-related investments.

Expenditures directed at safety issues or the replacement of necessary elements of the building physical plant fall into the category of necessary expenditures. A property may be able to delay the investment in a code-required sprinkler system (a safety issue) or in replacing a deteriorating building chiller (a physical plant issue), but these investments eventually must be made if the property is to continue to operate. Investments such as these are sometimes made on the basis of the lowest bid, a method which may not be as useful as a life cycle cost approach (discussed in the following section).

Methods of Project Analysis

Any facility may be faced with demands for capital improvements which exceed the available resources for these purposes. There are several ways to analyze the economics of capital projects when assessing which projects should be undertaken. Among the more common methods of analysis are payback, internal rate of return, and discounted cash flow. Rather than focusing on the details of the financial analysis techniques for each method (which are better suited to an accounting text[1]), this portion of the text deals with some of the unique concerns which should be incorporated in capital project analyses at lodging facilities.

Capital investment decisions are usually "front loaded" decisions. That is, the decision deals with the expenditure or commitment of relatively large sums of money at the start of a project with some expectation of benefit over the life of the project. The need to consider all economic aspects of a capital investment has resulted in the project analysis technique called life cycle costing. Even projects with seemingly overwhelming initial costs may be justifiable when examined using life cycle costing.

Life cycle costing considers and quantifies all the costs and benefits associated with a given investment. In this process, the focus on the initial cost or benefit of the project is balanced with the other aspects of the project to develop a full financial picture. Some of the elements of a life cycle cost analysis for building equipment are:

- Initial costs—for example, costs of the item itself including costs of installation, interconnection, and modification of supporting systems or equipment.
- Operating costs—for example, costs of energy or water to operate the equipment and supporting systems or those systems affected by the equipment; maintenance labor and supplies or contract maintenance services.
- Fixed costs—for example, insurance and property tax changes resulting from the equipment or system.
- Tax implications—for example, income taxes and tax credits such as investment tax credits and depreciation deductions.

The desirability of evaluating projects on some sort of a life cycle cost basis is illustrated in Exhibit 2.2. In this exhibit, the life cycle cost of a building is shown in chart form illustrating the different ways the building cost can be viewed. At the far left of Exhibit 2.2, the building construction cost is broken down into basic components similar to those discussed in Chapter 1. In terms of the total project cost (the amount of money actually committed by the time the building opens), these construction costs amount to a little more than half of the total project cost. When the entire project cost is considered over its life cycle, however, the construction and other costs represent less than 25% of the total life cycle costs. For some individual pieces of equipment, this process is even more dramatic, with the cost to operate the equipment being greater in its first year than the cost of the equipment itself!

The development of all the relevant cost data necessary to conduct a life cycle cost analysis is not an easy task. While property records, engineering calculations, and property experience can be used for the initial data development, there are several factors which are highly variable. For example, while equipment life (a central issue in this type of analysis) can be stated as a statistical probability, this value is highly dependent on the care given the equipment at the property. The amount of maintenance the equipment or system requires is also dependent on several factors, among which is the competence of the engineering department. The forecasted cost of utilities, labor, and supplies is obviously questionable under the best of circumstances, as evidenced by the roller coaster performance of energy prices and inflation over the past 10 years. For such analysis methods as internal rate of return and discounted cash flow, the discount rate chosen for the analysis may also be subject to significant variation if the past is any indication.

Not all capital investments are undertaken based on an analysis of economic benefit to the company. Some projects are undertaken almost solely for non-economic reasons—for example, upgrading a building fire protection system. While there may be some direct, measurable economic benefits of the project (such as reduced insurance premiums), the project is essentially "pure cost" and, as such, will often be approached by attempting to secure the lowest price for the project. While this approach has certain favorable aspects, failure to integrate issues of initial cost with issues of operating cost, maintenance, reliability, durability and, most important, the suitability of the proposed system for the property and its staff can result in decisions which do not best serve the long-term interests of the property. (See Chapter 3 for a discussion of other important criteria in engineering system design and selection.)

Exhibit 2.2 Life Cycle Cost of a Building

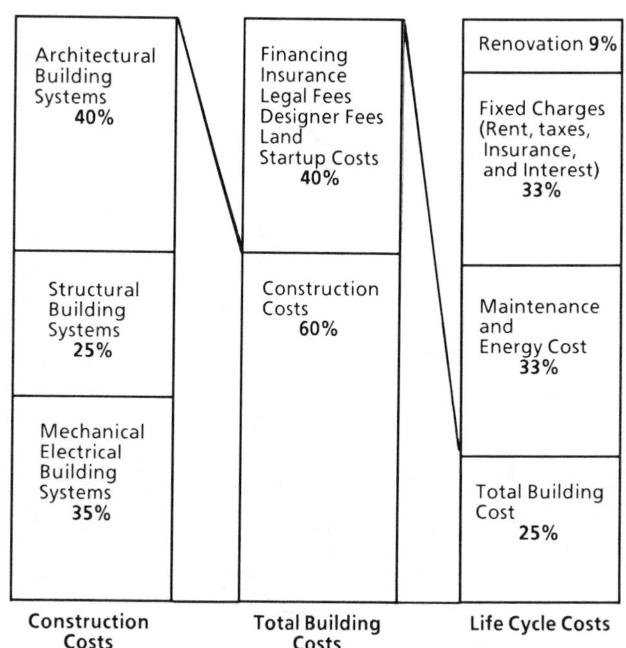

Types of Maintenance

A discussion of maintenance categories or types invariably results in difficulties with terminology. Different industries use the same terms to mean different things and each has special terminology as well. Even within the lodging industry itself, definitions of maintenance types frequently vary.

In this text, we have chosen to use the classifications *routine*, *preventive*, *scheduled*, and *emergency/breakdown*, terminology which agrees in general with that found in texts and articles on maintenance management. We have also included a discussion of guestroom maintenance. We encourage you to focus on the descriptive aspects of the maintenance activities and of the management methods related to these activities. The label assigned to the activity is ultimately much less important than understanding the activity and its importance to a well-run engineering operation and a well-maintained property.

Routine Maintenance

Routine maintenance activities are those which pertain to the general upkeep of the property, recur on a regular (daily or weekly) basis, and require relatively minimal training or skills. These are maintenance activities which occur outside of a formal work order system and for which no specific maintenance records (time or materials) are kept. Examples include sweeping carpets, washing floors, cleaning readily accessible windows, cutting grass, cleaning guestrooms, shoveling snow, and replacing burned out light bulbs.

Within the property, many routine maintenance activities are carried out by the housekeeping department. The contribution of this department to building maintenance is sometimes overlooked. Proper care of many of the surfaces and materials in the building by the housekeeping department is the first step in the overall maintenance program for many of these items. In most non-lodging commercial buildings, the engineering function and the housekeeping function do not report to separate managers as they do in most lodging functions. For these commercial buildings, this is a recognition of the need for a close working relationship between these departments and of the similarity in their goals and methods.

Preventive Maintenance

Our definition of preventive maintenance is a deliberately narrow one. In contrast to routine maintenance, preventive maintenance is much more directed and specific, has elements of inspection and decision which go beyond those generally engaged in by an individual in a janitorial position, is scheduled and recurs within a much longer time frame than most routine maintenance, and requires individuals with more advanced skills and training. Activities in preventive maintenance are usually performed based on guidelines from equipment suppliers and the building engineer. Preventive maintenance includes actions to prolong the life of a piece of equipment and to minimize the breakdown of equipment. It is directed at keeping the equipment operating at or near its rated level.

Preventive maintenance consists of three parts: inspection, minor corrections, and work order initiation. For the inspection, a checklist is usually used. The inspection can include taking readings from indicating or recording devices, looking for leaks, listening for unusual sounds, checking for unusual vibrations, inspecting the appearance of FF&E, checking the functioning of devices and equipment and, in general, being observant of the area or equipment receiving preventive maintenance.

The minor corrections portion of the preventive maintenance program consists of repairs, adjustments, replacements, and so forth which are made at the time of the inspection. The inspecting employee carries the tools and supplies needed to perform these tasks. The preventive maintenance form itself gives the employee information on what to replace.

The work order initiation phase is a logical outgrowth of parts one and two. Preventive maintenance, by its nature, sometimes identifies problems and needs beyond its scope. These should be brought to the attention of management via the work order system. The necessary work is then scheduled by the building engineer.

Scheduled Maintenance

Scheduled maintenance refers to those activities which are initiated at the property based on a formal work order or a similar document which identifies a known problem or need. While preventive maintenance is initiated to delay the occurrence of a problem or to make a minor correction, scheduled maintenance attempts to meet known needs in an orderly and timely manner consistent with overall needs and demands at the property.

Some people would classify certain scheduled maintenance activities as preventive maintenance—for example, annual maintenance of room HVAC units, acid cleaning of water heaters, and elevator service contracts. However, since the scope of these activities is relatively large, since they may remove the item from service for a time, and since the cost involved is more than that of a brief inspection and repair, we believe it is appropriate to label these as scheduled maintenance. Scheduled maintenance activities require additional planning and preparation not only by the engineering manager but by other departments as well. The timing of scheduled maintenance, planning of the work, and coordination of this work with other departments is discussed later in this chapter.

Emergency and Breakdown Maintenance

These two classifications of maintenance represent the primary mode of operation of the poorly managed engineering department. They are crisis-oriented, costly, and unpredictable. Operation of the maintenance department largely in these modes makes it almost impossible to fulfill the broad departmental goals stated in Chapter 1.

Emergency maintenance is without a doubt an expensive maintenance service, since it generally requires a disruption of scheduled activity and may result (or have already resulted) in a problem which could remove a room from service or cause guest discomfort, a deterioration in the quality of the workplace, or a similar problem. Generally, solving the problem could be delayed, but the level of general inconvenience would be high.

Two types of emergency maintenance can be identified depending on the initiator of the maintenance request. When the request is *guest-initiated,* it often concerns the malfunction of something in the guestroom. A prompt and courteous response which either satisfies the guest with a repair or moves the guest to another room (which everyone involved hopes will not be necessary) is called for. In this instance, the emergency will directly relate to the guest's perception of the property. When the request is *employee-initiated,* the immediate issue may not be guest satisfaction, but it is likely that the problem, if not corrected, will eventually result in guest dissatisfaction. Examples of this type of emergency maintenance could be clogged drains in the kitchen or a failed swimming pool heater.

Breakdown maintenance is generally agreed to be the most expensive form of maintenance since, in addition to the cost of the repair, there is often the potential for loss of business or production as a result. This type of maintenance results when a piece of equipment or a structural component completely fails. There is essentially no leeway in the scheduling of this maintenance—the equipment must be repaired immediately or the operation will be shut down. Examples of this would be burst pipes, ruptured water heaters, failed motors or broken belts on fans, or broken glass in windows or doors. In some instances, it may be possible to take some initial action in the breakdown mode which will allow the problem to be shifted to either emergency or scheduled maintenance. An example would be a breakdown response to shut off the water to a ruptured water heater, followed by an emergency or scheduled action to replace the water heater.

Breakdown and emergency are expensive forms of maintenance for several reasons. Because of their unpredictable nature, the labor used to effect the repair is usually costly. It is often not necessarily performed by the best person for the repair, but rather by whoever is available, and often on overtime because of the timing of the event. Also, the failure of an item often results in damage to other items. Finally, the disruption caused by the failure wreaks havoc with schedules and planning.

Guestroom Maintenance

Guestroom maintenance has a special meaning in the lodging industry. As it is used in many operations, it refers to preventive maintenance. In others, it takes on more characteristics of scheduled maintenance. In whatever category, it is an important maintenance activity.

For the guest, the guestroom is one of the most visible elements of the lodging experience. The condition and proper operation of furniture, fixtures, and equipment, the appearance of ceilings and walls (whether painted, plastered, or wallpapered), the condition of carpets and floor coverings, and the cleanliness of the exteriors of windows are all included in the maintenance and repair of guestrooms.

Simple actions in guestroom maintenance often make major contributions to the goals of the engineering department. Attention to leaks from faucets and proper caulking of sinks and tubs control maintenance costs by stopping greater problems from occurring (such as the failure of the ceiling or wall in the bath below due to such leakages). This obviously protects the physical plant investment and contributes to customer satisfaction (nobody likes a leaky faucet). Housekeeping appreciates not needing to clean up around the mess created by a failed wall or ceiling and the repair work which results.

Staff at the front desk do not have to be concerned about a room which is out of service or an unhappy customer. Leaks also waste water, affecting the energy costs of the building. And, finally, the leaking water could create an unsafe condition due to falling plaster, a slippery floor, or some other problem.

Because of the critical nature of guestroom maintenance, many lodging properties and chains have rather formal programs dedicated to this task. Some of these programs use the term guestroom preventive maintenance. Common provisions of these programs are:

- An inspection sheet to be used by the guestroom maintenance person to inspect the entire guestroom for needed maintenance.
- A guestroom maintenance cart containing all parts and supplies commonly required for the repair of the guestroom. Repairs are usually performed immediately using items on the cart. If more extensive repair is required, a note is made and a repair work order initiated.
- Dedication of one or more experienced property maintenance staff members to guestroom maintenance. Guestroom maintenance is not used as a means of new employee training. Rather, this function is considered to be so important that it is assigned to the better, more experienced employees.
- A schedule which ensures regular attention to guestroom maintenance. The frequency of guestroom maintenance is sometimes related to the cost of the room (that is, the more expensive rooms receive maintenance more frequently than standard rooms). This schedule also requires adjustment as properties age or the occupancy changes.
- Management inspections of the guestrooms after maintenance to check the quality of the work.

At a smaller property, guestroom maintenance may be one of several activities performed by a single member of the property engineering staff. In this situation, it is important to allow the individual an appropriate amount of time for this activity. Failure to dedicate this time will result in its being consumed for other activities, which in turn leads to deterioration of the guestrooms and problems for the property in terms of guest perceptions, occupancy, and the bottom line.

Contract Maintenance

The decision to perform maintenance with in-house personnel or to contract this maintenance is usually under the control of the engineering manager. There are potential advantages and disadvantages to contract maintenance services. Potential advantages include:

- Reduction of total labor costs
- Reduction of the cost of supplies and equipment
- Use of the latest techniques and methods
- Savings in administrative time
- Flexibility to meet emergencies or changes in needs
- Removal of the need to negotiate with labor unions
- Removal of the need to recruit and train employees

Potential disadvantages of contract maintenance services include:

- False labor cost savings unless staffing levels are actually reduced
- Gradual escalation in total costs without property level monitoring or control
- Managerial laziness resulting in a failure to negotiate the best price for the service or a lack of competitive bidding
- Unavailability of employees for other tasks
- Loss of control over employees (security, attitude, identity with the property)
- Loss of contact with the needs of the facility and staff

Outside contracts primarily provide three types of maintenance: routine, preventive, and scheduled. They may also handle the special needs of a property, such as those for which special equipment is required or which are infrequent and beyond the scope of the property engineering staff.

Many commercial buildings rely on contract janitorial services for all building interior cleaning. In the lodging industry, the use of contract cleaning services is usually limited to public spaces. Another common type of routine maintenance contract concerns grounds maintenance. While grounds maintenance is mostly routine, it may also present certain special needs. Among these are the necessity of licensing for the applications of certain chemicals and the need to have somewhat specialized skills if the property has unique landscaping features.

Contract maintenance services which might be classified as preventive and scheduled (we will not distinguish between the two categories when dealing with contract services) include water treatment and equipment service contracts. These examples also extend into the special needs category, since there are somewhat special skills or equipment necessary to perform these services. At small properties, the service of HVAC equipment may be handled by contract due to the small onsite workforce and the skill levels of this staff.

The special needs or skills required to calibrate building controls, charge fire extinguishers, and test and adjust building fire alarm systems all result in their becoming contracted services. The special equipment needed to clean kitchen ductwork, dispose of grease and other refuse, or remove snow from parking lots often results in these tasks being contracted.

The responsibilities of the engineering manager relative to these contracts should not be ignored. For all contracts, it is important that the contractor have appropriate insurance coverage for employees working at the property. The contract should be carefully structured to define exactly what work is to be performed. A review of the contract may identify work which the property does not require or which does not need to be performed as frequently as the contract specifies. The work performed by the contractor should be inspected to ensure that it meets the standards of the contract. The contractor's employees should have their access to the property controlled and limited to only those areas where they need to be. Finally, it is important that the contractor perform the work in a manner consistent with the safety concerns of the property, local codes, and other relevant rules and regulations. The engineering manager or his or her representative should be actively involved in all of these activities.

Maintenance Management Systems

In order to effectively manage the maintenance function, it is necessary to keep records, use certain management systems, and establish standards for the work to be done. Failure to establish correct departmental operating procedures will result in the inability to perform work in a cost-efficient and timely manner. In addition, failure to document work performed, sources of parts, modifications made to building systems, and so forth can result in future problems when ownership changes or the engineering manager leaves the property. Properly initiated and maintained maintenance management systems can contribute significantly to overall efficiency in the department as well.

Records

Records concerning the building, the equipment, and the maintenance performed on both are a major contributor to the effective management of the engineering department. While our emphasis here is on those records which relate to the maintenance function, it is important to realize that the engineering department usually stores the only copies of the building plans. These plans are one of the most important records in the hands of the department. The building plans are often referred to in the years following construction as changes occur in the building's physical layout, control systems, electrical service, and other features. Ideally, these changes will all be noted on sets of the building plans to maintain a constantly updated set of plans portraying the building as it actually exists. While this ideal is seldom attained, the more accurate the set of plans in the engineering department, the fewer surprises will occur when work is undertaken, the more cost efficient the department will be when tackling projects needing current building plan information, and the easier the transition will be for a new manager or staff person in engineering.

Exhibit 2.3 Sample Maintenance Work Order

DELTA FORMS - MILWAUKEE U.S.A.

(414) 461-0086

HYATT HOTELS®

MAINTENANCE REQUEST

1345239

TIME ______

BY ______ DATE ______

LOCATION ______

PROBLEM ______

ASSIGNED TO ______

DATE COMPL. ______ TIME SPENT ______

COMPLETED BY ______

REMARKS ______

RPHK-04

HYATT HOTELS MAINTENANCE CHECK LIST

Check (☒) Indicates Unsatisfactory Condition
Explain Check In Remarks Section

BEDROOM - FOYER - CLOSET

☐ WALLS ☐ WOODWORK ☐ DOORS
☐ CEILING ☐ TELEVISION ☐ LIGHTS
☐ FLOORS ☐ A.C. UNIT ☐ BLINDS
☐ WINDOWS ☐ DRAPES

REMARKS: ______

BATHROOM

☐ TRIM ☐ SHOWER
☐ DRAINS ☐ LIGHTS
☐ WALL PAPER ☐ PAINT
☐ TILE OR GLASS ☐ DOOR
☐ ACCESSORIES ☐ WINDOW

REMARKS: ______

Courtesy of Hyatt Corporation.

Important engineering department records and managerial tools include work orders, preventive maintenance instructions, equipment data cards, equipment history records, equipment instruction and repair manuals, maintenance schedules, parts inventory records, building plans, and equipment and system drawings.

Work orders are a key element of the engineering department operation. They document necessary work and serve as a means for all departments to communicate with engineering. Most operations use some formal work order system which usually has a numbered three-part form—one copy kept by the initiator, one copy retained in engineering, and the third copy given to the tradesperson assigned to the repair. The maintenance dispatcher or engineering manager assigns the work order to an individual who returns it to engineering when the work is completed. The individual completing the task indicates the number of hours required to complete the work, any parts or supplies required, and other relevant information. A sample work order is shown in Exhibit 2.3.

The engineering department has several responsibilities with regard to work orders. The department must be sure all work orders are taken care of in a timely manner. If this cannot be done, the initiator of the work order should be told that there will be a delay and, if possible, the reasons for the delay. The department should also follow a procedure of notifying the individual initiating the work order when the work is completed and, depending on the nature of the work, when the work will be initiated. This serves several functions. First of all, it provides a quality control check. The individual requesting the work will be able to inspect the work to ensure that it is done properly. Also, sometimes the written description of the job and what the individual really wants done are two different things. Communication helps to alleviate this problem. Another function served by the work order is that it informs people about the activities of the maintenance department. When individuals initiate work order after work order and never receive feedback that the work has been accomplished, they may develop negative feelings concerning the maintenance operation. Work order feedback shows the property's personnel that they are taken seriously and that the engineering department responds appropriately to their concerns.

Preventive maintenance instructions can be thought of as a form of work order. Rather than being initiated by an individual as a result of a problem or need, however, they are issued as a regular part of the building maintenance program. These instructions are developed as a result of a careful review of possible failure points, necessary inspection items, and the recommendations of equipment manufacturers. Since some preventive maintenance is required to maintain the warranty on equipment, it is important that clear instructions be provided for the necessary work and that records be kept of the work performed. Exhibit 2.4 is a sample of a preventive maintenance work order.

Equipment data cards contain basic information about pieces of equipment. This information can include technical data, manufacturers' information, cost, special instructions, warranty information, and references to other information as well (such as the storage location of manuals and drawings). Equipment data cards can be valuable when considering whether equipment has reached the end of its useful life, when attempting to determine whether a repair is under warranty, and when evaluating the need for spare parts or backup units. Exhibit 2.5 is a sample equipment data card.

Equipment history records are logs of the inspection and maintenance work performed on a given piece of equipment. They may be separate items or may be incorporated into the equipment data card. Their purpose is to provide a documentation of all maintenance activity on a given piece of equipment. Referral to these records can be very helpful when deciding whether to repair or replace an item. Exhibit 2.6 is a sample equipment history record card.

Virtually every piece of equipment purchased for a building will have some sort of an *instruction and/or repair manual* shipped with the product. Many of these manuals will contain troubleshooting data, schematics, part numbers, and ordering information. It is very helpful for the maintenance person assigned to repair equipment to have access to this information. This requires that some type of binder or file be maintained with this information and that the maintenance person know such a resource exists and where to find it.

Maintenance schedules are developed at the property using a number of information sources. Equipment instruction and repair manuals, preventive maintenance instructions, property occupancy statistics, climatic data, and other relevant factors are used to prepare a long-range maintenance schedule which attempts to plan property maintenance. The schedule must be developed by integrating information about necessary maintenance with staffing plans and periods when equipment or areas are accessible to maintenance. Adequate provision for breakdown or emergency maintenance should also be considered. Care should be taken to consider not only total available labor hours but also labor hours by trade, especially when a union operation makes trade issues more important. By taking a long-term view (6 to 12 months) of the maintenance scheduling process, it is possible to anticipate and adjust to problem times. For example, the department manager should use the maintenance schedule to plan employee vacation times (and vice versa). Including capital projects on the schedule will assist the manager in allocating personnel for the project or its aftermath.

The maintenance department uses a number of special parts and supplies while performing its duties. If repairs are to be made in a timely manner with minimal disruption to operations, a proper inventory of parts and supplies must be maintained. Maintaining this inventory means not only that these items must be in stock

Exhibit 2.4 Sample Preventive Maintenance Schedule

SCORE® PREVENTIVE MAINTENANCE
SCHEDULED WORK ORDER

SERVIDYNE® SYSTEMS, INC.

SERVICE ENGINEER ____________ TRADE WK

EQUIPMENT NUMBER
EQUIPMENT DESCRIPTION
MISCELLANEOUS DESCRIPTION
SEASON

FACILITY
LOCATION
MOTOR

ZONE

WORK ORDER #
TO BE COMPLETED BY
PRIORITY
TRAVEL TIME ____________

TASK NUMBER	TASKS TO BE COMPLETED	TIME TO COMPLETE		MATERIAL OR TOOL REQUIREMENTS				COMMENTS	REASON NOT DONE
		HRS.	MIN.	QTY.	UNIT	DESCRIPTION	COST		

REASON NOT DONE

1 - CAN'T STOP EQUIPMENT FOR PM
2 - NOT IN OPERATION
3 - DOWN FOR REPAIR
4 - UNNECESSARY AT THIS TIME
5 - MATERIALS NOT AVAILABLE
6 - TOOLS NOT AVAILABLE
7 - NOT ENOUGH TIME
8 - UNABLE TO LOCATE EQUIPMENT
9 - WRONG PM ACTION FOR EQUIPMENT
10 - OTHER ____________

REVIEWED BY MANAGER

/DATE/

INITIALS

RESCHEDULE WEEK

COMMENTS FOR EQUIPMENT HISTORY

YOUR SINGLE SOURCE SERVICE® COMPANY

Courtesy of Servidyne Systems, Inc.

Exhibit 2.5 Sample Equipment Data Card

EQUIPMENT RECORD

ACME VISIBLE CROZET VIRGINIA #60P05

MFG NAME		MFG ORDER NO		SERIAL NO
EQUIP. NO	TYPE OR MODEL	DRAWING NO	OUR P O NO.	
VENDOR	APPROP NO	SHOP ORDER NO		
EQUIPMENT COST	INSTALLATION COST	DATE INSTALLED	LOCATION	

EQUIPMENT DESCRIPTION

MAINTENANCE REQUIREMENTS	ELECTRICAL EQUIPMENT				
	EQUIP				
	MAKE				
	SERIAL NO				
	TYPE FRAME				
	VOLTAGE				
INSPECTION REQUIREMENTS	PHASE				
	H P				
	R P M				
	DRIVE				
	CIRCUIT				
	DATE INSTALLED				
LUBRICATION	COST				
MANUAL PAGE / LUBE PERIOD					

SPARE PARTS ON OTHER SIDE

Courtesy of Acme Visible Records.

at the property, but also that there must be a paper system which keeps track of inventory issues and receipts and a physical system which locates the inventory when needed. For example, when work orders are completed, the data on them concerning hours and materials used should be recorded to the appropriate records in the engineering office.

A proper inventory control system will avoid both frequent outages of needed supplies and overstocking of items (which raises storage costs). In larger operations, the parts room attendant should be a link in the process of dispatching any work orders requiring special parts.

Standards

Within the department, there is the need to establish various standards. Some of these standards need to be stated during employee training, since they relate to expected employee performance. Other standards are used internally by management to measure departmental performance. The rise over the past few years of quality control as an issue in the lodging industry has added emphasis to the need for standards. This is because many people active in quality control consider the establishment of standards to be one of the initial steps in a quality control program.

As they relate to employees, standards may concern the employees' physical appearance and method of addressing guests and co-workers, the physical condition of the workplace, and any topics for which management chooses not to rely solely on the employees' judgment.

Management also uses standards to measure departmental performance. Recordkeeping is a central element of this internal control. For guestroom maintenance, the manager may monitor the number of rooms maintained per week. Other items of concern could be the number of work orders processed per week or month, the

Exhibit 2.6 Sample Equipment History Record Card

HISTORY OF REPAIRS

DATE	W.O. NO.	DESCRIPTION OF REPAIRS	DOWN TIME	MAN HOURS	MATERIAL COST

TAG NO.	DESCRIPTION	WEEKLY CONTROL 1 2 3 4	MONTHLY INSPECTION CONTROL
			JAN FEB MAR APR MAY JUN JUL AUG SEP OCT NOV DEC

10 20 30 4 50 60 70 8

TYPIST PLEASE NOTE – START ALL TYPING AT SAME POINT ON SCALE. THEN REMOVE THIS STUB. BE SURE YOU HAVE A WELL INKED RIBBON. CARE USED IN TYPING WILL IMPROVE REFERENCE DURING THE ENTIRE LIFE OF THE INDEX. TRY A FEW IN THE POCKETS TO SEE HOW THEY LOOK BEFORE TYPING THE ENTIRE LIST

RE-ORDER FORM NO. 60P01

ACME VISIBLE RECORDS
CROZET VIRGINIA

PRINTED IN U.S.A.

Courtesy of Acme Visible Records.

number of work orders received, and the number of work orders backlogged. For larger operations, this information may be tabulated by craft. For operations with adequate records, it is also helpful to attempt to distinguish the distribution of labor time by major categories (such as preventive, scheduled, and breakdown maintenance).

Standards must be viewed flexibly and as tools. Property needs change with time and with systems. Recognizing the real changes and adjusting to them while monitoring and controlling those items which should not change are the manager's responsibility. For multi-unit operations, care should be taken to avoid applying performance standards too rigidly to every engineering department. However, other standards, such as employee appearance or budgetary control methods, are proper and should be enforced.

Energy Management Methods

Consumption and Cost Control

To effectively control the amount of money spent on energy, management must monitor both the consumption of energy and the cost paid for units of that energy. Watching only one of these two factors may lead to improper decisions or eliminate some cost-saving opportunities. Two examples will demonstrate this. In the first, watching only the consumption of energy would suggest switching the fuel used for heating water from natural gas to electricity. This change would lower the consumption of the units of energy at the property because electricity heats water more efficiently than natural gas. This decision would be misguided, however, because the equivalent cost of electricity is usually so much higher than for natural gas that any savings due to improved efficiency would be offset by the substantial increase in cost. In the second example, a commercial property is billed in two ways for its use of electricity: one is for the amount of energy consumed during a billing period and the other is for the maximum rate (or *demand*) at which the energy is consumed. Tracking only the amount of consumption removes management's attention from the possible savings due to reductions in demand.

Records

Effective monitoring of any situation demands accurate recordkeeping of the important variables. The control of energy expenses needs, at a minimum, monthly records for both the consumption and cost of energy. In addition, two other variables are often recorded to allow better interpretation of the consumption values. These two variables are the number of occupied rooms (or sometimes the number of people who stayed at the property) and the severity of the weather, measured in heating or cooling degree days (see Chapter 6 for a definition of degree days). Some properties record the data on energy consumption, occupied rooms, and degree days on a daily or weekly basis to permit a more timely monitoring of the operation of the property's equipment.

Standards

Standards from external sources provide a comparison for the data at your property. In the area of energy management, four different sources of information are available: (1) accounting information on lodging operations from accounting firms, (2) energy consumption data from national surveys, (3) typical costs of utilities for various locations, and (4) energy and cost information from other properties if your property is part of a chain. The information from these sources is presented in various forms (some of which have been discussed in Chapter 1). The total cost of energy may be expressed as a percentage of total revenue and in dollars per available room; the consumption of energy may be expressed in *Btu* (*British thermal units*) per square foot of floor area; and the unit costs of the fuels are generally documented in dollars per unit of consumption (for example, kwh for electricity and gallons for fuel oil).

Such data may allow a property to compare its performance with that of similar properties. Comparisons with averaged national data, however, are not very satisfying to management because it is almost impossible to find properties that are similar enough for the results to be meaningful. There are so many factors that affect energy consumption (for example, building materials, location, primary market segment, level of service, building age) that few comparisons are valid except within chains of similar properties in equivalent locations.

Monitoring Performance

Monitoring performance over a period of time offers the best potential for determining the success of an energy management program. Whether this is done for consumption or cost per unit of energy or both, the approach can be applied in three ways: (1) compare the current month's information to the same month of the previous year, (2) compare current year-to-date information with that of the previous year, and (3) compare the information using a twelve-month moving average.

The first two are easier to apply, but they also suffer from an important weakness. They assume that factors such as weather and occupancy were the same during both periods. This is usually not true, so any variation in the results could be attributed to the differences in these factors rather than to improved or reduced performance in conserving energy. This effect is most pronounced in comparisons of the data for the current month with that for the same month of the previous year. The year-to-date technique becomes more accurate during the latter portion of the year because the comparison is based on almost a full year of information. The third technique, a twelve-month moving average, shows the best stability because the comparison is always made using twelve months' worth of data.

A final approach—one that does not rely solely on observations made over a period of time—which has proven valid, but which also takes time to implement, is monitoring energy consumption using certain statistical techniques. This approach removes the variations in results caused by the lack of similarity in the periods used for the comparison. A discussion of this very complex topic is beyond the scope of this text.[2]

The Utility Bill. Often, analysis of the utility bill will reveal savings opportunities. Utilities are sold to all customers under several rate categories and utility customers may qualify under more than one rate category. Because the utility company is under no obligation to bill at (or even determine) the cheapest applicable rate, the rate category assigned to a property may not be the most advantageous for the property. A utility bill audit and rate analysis can determine whether this is the case.

The Uniform System of Accounts

Recording the financial transactions of a property using a standardized set of accounts is necessary in order to report and monitor the progress of a business. Two such sets of standardized accounts developed for the lodging industry, known as the *Uniform System of Accounts for Hotels*[3] and the *Uniform System of Accounts and Expense Dictionary for Small Hotels, Motels, and Motor Hotels*,[4] provide the structure for documenting the financial operations of a property.

The two most important financial statements at the property level are the balance sheet and the statement of income. The balance sheet presents the financial position of the business (that is, assets, liabilities, and equity) on a specific date, usually at the end of the operating year. The statement of income summarizes the results of operation of the business (that is, income and expenses) over a specific period of time, usually a month, a quarter, or a year. Exhibits 2.7 and 2.8 show one possible set of these statements for a lodging facility. The balance sheet does not differ materially from those of other businesses, while the statement of income is specialized to lodging facilities.

The engineering department is directly connected to several of the accounts on these statements. As described earlier, the department is charged for the total amounts in the accounts "energy costs" and "property operations and maintenance" on the statement of income. Further, expenditures for capital projects, such as replacement of equipment or renovations, influence the accounts "buildings" and "furnishings and equipment" on the balance sheet.

As shown in Exhibit 2.8, more detailed breakdowns of the department's expenses are found in schedules 12 and 13 for "property operation and maintenance" and "energy costs," respectively (see Exhibits 2.9 and 2.10). Each schedule contains the label for each detailed expense category as well as a description of the items that are included in each. For example, the POM expenses on schedule 12 are separated into two major categories: payroll expenses and other expenses. The latter category includes the materials and contract services necessary for the upkeep of the facility. Credits for cost recoveries and capitalized improvements (that is, improvements to the building and its equipment that must be capitalized because of tax regulations) are subtracted to obtain the net cost for property operation. Likewise, the energy expenses on schedule 13 are divided into electricity, fuel, steam, and water. The credits due to cost recoveries (that is, reimbursements from other businesses such as attached condominiums) and charges to other departments within the property are subtracted to determine the net energy cost.

The Engineering Department—An Undistributed Operating Expense

Further inspection of Exhibit 2.8 indicates that the expenses for the department are treated differently from the expenses for many of the other departments. The direct expenses incurred by departments that are major sources of revenue (for example, rooms or food and beverage) are distributed against the revenue generated. However, the expenses for departments that produce no revenue (such as engineering) are reported as undistributed operating expenses. As such, the department is viewed as a cost center that provides services to the remainder of the property for the overall benefit of its operation.

An example of each situation follows. For the food and beverage department, the accounting system summarizes all revenues generated by the department's outlets and some of the expenses incurred by the operation of the department. For example, food and beverage sales for the property's restaurants, room service, and function rooms are credited to this department, as are the rental fees for the function rooms. This

Exhibit 2.7 Balance Sheet

BALANCE SHEET

Assets

	Date 19	Date 19
CURRENT ASSETS		
Cash		
House Banks		
Demand Deposits	$	$
Temporary Cash Investments		
Total Cash		
Marketable Securities		
Receivables		
Accounts Receivable—Trade		
Notes Receivable		
Other		
Total Receivables		
Less Allowance for Doubtful Accounts		
Net Receivables		
Inventories		
Prepaid Expenses		
Other		
Total Current Assets		
NONCURRENT RECEIVABLES		
Owners and Officers		
Other		
Total Noncurrent Receivables		
INVESTMENTS		
PROPERTY AND EQUIPMENT		
Land		
Buildings		
Leaseholds and Leasehold Improvements		
Construction in Progress		
Furnishings and Equipment		
China, Glassware, Silver, Linen, and Uniforms		
Less Accumulated Depreciation and Amortization		
Net Property and Equipment		
OTHER ASSETS		
Security Deposits		
Preopening Expenses		
Deferred Charges		
Other		
Total Other Assets		
TOTAL ASSETS	$	$

BALANCE SHEET (continued)

Liabilities and Owners' Equity

CURRENT LIABILITIES		
Notes Payable	$	$
Current Maturities of Long-Term Debt		
Accounts Payable		
Federal, State, and City Income Taxes		
Deferred Income Taxes		
Accrued Expenses		
Advance Deposits		
Other		
Total Current Liabilities		
LONG-TERM DEBT		
Notes and Other Similar Liabilities		
Obligations Under Capital Leases		
Less Current Maturities		
Total Long-Term Debt		
OTHER LONG-TERM LIABILITIES		
DEFERRED INCOME TAXES		
COMMITMENTS AND CONTINGENCIES		
***OWNERS' EQUITY**		
Preferred Stock, Par Value $______		
Authorized ________ Shares		
Issued ________ Shares		
Common Stock, Par Value $______		
Authorized ________ Shares		
Issued ________ Shares		
Additional Paid-In Capital		
Retained Earnings		
Total Owners' Equity		
TOTAL LIABILITIES AND OWNERS' EQUITY	$	$

See the accompanying notes to financial statements.

*The line items of this section reflect a corporate form of business organization. For line items appropriate to proprietorships and partnerships, see the explanatory notes for this section.

Source: *Uniform System of Accounts and Expense Dictionary for Small Hotels, Motels, and Motor Hotels*, 4th Ed. (East Lansing, Mich.: Educational Institute of the American Hotel & Motel Association, 1987), pp. 4–5.

Exhibit 2.8 Statement of Income

STATEMENT OF INCOME

	Schedule	Current Period: Net Revenue	Cost of Sales	Payroll and Related Expenses	Other Expenses	Income (Loss)
OPERATED DEPARTMENTS						
Rooms	1	$	$	$	$	$
Food and Beverage	2					
Telephone	3					
Gift Shop	4					
Garage and Parking	5					
Other Operated Departments						
Rentals and Other Income	6					
Total Operated Departments						
UNDISTRIBUTED OPERATING EXPENSES						
Administrative and General	7					
Data Processing	8					
Human Resources	9					
Transportation	10					
Marketing	11					
Property Operation and Maintenance	12					
Energy Costs	13					
Total Undistributed Operating Expenses						
INCOME BEFORE MANAGEMENT FEES AND FIXED CHARGES		$	$	$	$	
Management Fees						
Rent, Property Taxes, and Insurance	14					
Interest Expense	14					
Depreciation and Amortization	14					
INCOME BEFORE INCOME TAXES AND GAIN OR LOSS ON SALE OF PROPERTY						
Gain or Loss on Sale of Property	14					
INCOME BEFORE INCOME TAXES						
Income Taxes	15					
NET INCOME						$

Source: *Uniform System of Accounts and Expense Dictionary for Small Hotels, Motels, and Motor Hotels*, 4th Ed. (East Lansing, Mich.: Educational Institute of the American Hotel & Motel Association, 1987), p. 24.

department is charged for the expenses of food, beverages, wages for its employees, and so forth, but not for the utilities or the maintenance of the building's spaces under the control of the department. In contrast, for the engineering department, the accounting system charges against its operation the expenses for the energy and the maintenance used throughout the entire facility, even though the staff of the department has no authority or control over the activities in the other departments.

This differential treatment of departments causes problems in the functioning of the property. First, an analysis of the statement of income for a revenue-producing department overstates its profit because it is not charged

Exhibit 2.9 Property Operation and Maintenance—Schedule 12

PROPERTY OPERATION AND MAINTENANCE—SCHEDULE 12

	Current Period
SALARIES AND WAGES	$
EMPLOYEE BENEFITS	______
Total Payroll and Related Expenses	______
OTHER EXPENSES	
Building Supplies	
Electrical and Mechanical Equipment	
Engineering Supplies	
Furniture, Fixtures, Equipment, and Decor	
Grounds and Landscaping	
Operating Supplies	
Removal of Waste Matter	
Swimming Pool	
Uniforms	
Other	______
Total Other Expenses	______
TOTAL PROPERTY OPERATION AND MAINTENANCE	$ ______

Property Operation and Maintenance—Schedule 12 illustrates a format and identifies line items which commonly appear on a supplemental schedule supporting the Payroll and Related Expenses and Other Expenses reported on the Statement of Income under Undistributed Operating Expenses—Property Operation and Maintenance. This format and the line items will vary according to the needs and requirements of individual properties. Therefore, the line items listed on Schedule 12 may not apply to the operations of every small hotel or motel. Individual properties should modify Schedule 12 to meet their own needs and requirements, while remaining consistent with generally accepted accounting principles.

Salaries and Wages

This expense item on Schedule 12 includes regular pay, overtime pay, vacation pay, severance pay, incentive pay, holiday pay, and bonuses for employees of the property operation and maintenance department. For a classification of employees included in this group, see Salaries and Wages—Schedule 16.

Employee Benefits

This expense item on Schedule 12 includes payroll taxes, payroll-related insurance expense, pension, and other related expenses applicable to the property operation and maintenance department. Also included is the cost of food and beverages furnished to employees of the property operation and maintenance department.

Total Payroll and Related Expenses

This total is calculated by adding Salaries and Wages to Employee Benefits. The Total Payroll and Related Expenses figure on Schedule 12 is the same figure that appears on the Statement of Income in the Payroll and Related Expenses column for Undistributed Operating Expenses—Property Operation and Maintenance.

(continued)

Exhibit 2.9 (continued)

Other Expenses

This expense item on Schedule 12 includes significant expenses of the property operation and maintenance department. Items appearing under Other Expenses vary from property to property. Examples of items which commonly appear as Other Expenses follow.

Building Supplies

This item includes the cost of materials and contracts related to the repair and maintenance of the interior and exterior of the property's buildings. Examples of repair and maintenance areas included under Building Supplies are as follows:

Ceilings	Floors	Stairways
Doors	Masonry	Walls
Fire escapes	Roof	Waterproofing
Fire hoses	Sidewalks	Windows

Electrical and Mechanical Equipment

This item includes the cost of materials and contracts related to the repair of equipment. Classifications of these costs vary from property to property. Commonly used classifications include: heating, ventilating and air conditioning, general electrical and mechanical equipment, kitchen equipment, laundry equipment, plumbing, elevators, and refrigeration. Maintenance contracts for specialized equipment, such as for telephone or data processing equipment, should be charged directly to the appropriate schedules.

Engineering Supplies

This item includes the cost of the following supplies used in maintaining the property:

Fuses	Packing	Water treatment chemicals and additives
Greases	Small tools	
Light bulbs	Solvents	
Oils	Waste	

Furniture, Fixtures, Equipment, and Decor

This item includes the cost of materials and contracts related to painting, decorating, and repairing curtains and draperies, furniture, and floor coverings for guestrooms, corridors, dining rooms, and public rooms.

Grounds and Landscaping

This item includes the cost of supplies and contracts related to the maintenance of property grounds.

Operating Supplies

This item includes the cost of printed forms, service manuals, stationery, and office supplies used by employees of the property operation and maintenance department.

Removal of Waste Matter

This item includes the cost of rubbish removal and the expense of operating an incinerator.

Swimming Pool

This item includes the cost of materials, supplies, and contracts related to the repair and maintenance of the swimming pool.

Exhibit 2.9 (continued)

Uniforms

This item includes the cost or rental of uniforms for employees of the property operation and maintenance department. This expense item also includes costs of cleaning or repairing uniforms of property operation and maintenance department employees.

Other

This item includes property operation and maintenance expenses which do not apply to line items discussed previously.

Total Other Expenses

This total is calculated by adding all items listed under Other Expenses. The Total Other Expenses figure on Schedule 12 is the same figure that appears on the Statement of Income in the Other Expenses column for Undistributed Operating Expenses—Property Operation and Maintenance.

Source: *Uniform System of Accounts and Expense Dictionary for Small Hotels, Motels, and Motor Hotels,* 4th Ed. (East Lansing, Mich.: Educational Institute of the American Hotel & Motel Association, 1987), pp. 66–68.

completely for its expenses. This effect can distort business decision-making regarding the best use of the space provided for the department. For example, food and beverage departments in many properties would not be "profitable" if all undistributed expenses were allocated to them. Analyzing the true cost of operating food and beverage departments has led to the development of several new lodging concepts that de-emphasize food and beverage outlets.

Second, the results of operation as reported by the statement of income at the departmental level do not encourage cost-saving behavior on the part of the department's employees with regard to maintenance or energy expenses. If the employees of the rooms department, for example, were especially aware of a procedure to set the room thermostat to a specified value when cleaning the room or of cleaning the room with particular care to avoid damaging the walls and furniture with the vacuum cleaner, the savings in the expenses would not affect the profitability of the rooms department. Consequently, the improvement would be unnoticed by the employees' superiors and the opportunity to offer praise or a reward would be lost.

The uniform systems address this problem in two ways. First, these documents suggest allocating a portion of the undistributed expenses to each of the revenue-producing departments. Allocation of the undistributed expenses is the only means of determining net departmental income or loss. Since management decisions may be based on the figures affected by such allocation, the allocation methods should be reasonable and fair.

A more radical approach involves the use of submetering. As the *Uniform System of Accounts for Hotels* states, "Where submetering capability exists, consideration should be given to charging costs to the various operating departments. While this is a major departure from historical practice, it will emphasize cost awareness and improve decision making in cost control."[5]

Submetering of Utilities

Two managerial practices—matching responsibility with authority and giving feedback when measuring performance—provide a rationale for allocating utility costs to the departments that are consuming the energy.[6] The engineering department has no direct authority over daily operations in many of the departments and has little direct control over the use of utilities in these areas. Consequently, engineering should not be held responsible for the consumption of these utilities.

The submetering technique has several requirements. First, the property must be divided into separate zones according to the department which has control over the consumption of utilities within the space. The restaurants would be assigned to the food and beverage department, while the guestrooms would be assigned to the

Exhibit 2.10 Energy Costs—Schedule 13

ENERGY COSTS—SCHEDULE 13

	Current Period
Electric Current	$
Fuel	
Steam	
Water	
TOTAL ENERGY COSTS	$

Energy Costs—Schedule 13 illustrates a format and identifies line items which commonly appear on a supplemental schedule supporting the Other Expenses reported on the Statement of Income under Undistributed Operating Expenses—Energy Costs. This format and the line items will vary according to the needs and requirements of individual properties. Therefore, the line items listed on Schedule 13 may not apply to the operations of every small hotel or motel. If the property submeters utilities, the costs of these utilities may be charged to appropriate departments and reported on departmental schedules under Other Expenses. These costs should then be subtracted from appropriate Energy Cost items. Individual properties should modify Schedule 13 to meet their own needs and requirements, while remaining consistent with generally accepted accounting principles.

Electric Current

This item includes the cost of light and power purchased from outside producers, and the cost of breakdown service.

Fuel

This item includes the cost of fuel consumed. Classifications of these costs vary from property to property. Commonly used classifications include: coal, oil, and gas. Energy Costs—Fuel does not include the cost of kitchen fuel. This cost is reported on Food and Beverage—Schedule 2 and listed separately under Other Expenses—Kitchen Fuel.

Steam

This item includes the cost of steam purchased from outside producers.

Water

This item includes the cost of water and sewage services purchased from outside companies. This item also includes the cost of water purchased for drinking purposes or specially treated for circulating ice water systems.

Source: *Uniform System of Accounts and Expense Dictionary for Small Hotels, Motels, and Motor Hotels*, 4th Ed. (East Lansing, Mich.: Educational Institute of the American Hotel & Motel Association, 1987), p. 69.

rooms department. Not all spaces can be assigned, however, as some are not primarily associated with only one department. Second, submeters must be installed to measure the amounts of utilities that are consumed by each zone—the master meter installed by the utility company measures only the consumption of the entire building. Third, the readings from the submeters are used to distribute the monthly utility bills on a proportional basis to the departments according to the zones assigned to them.

When implementing this technique, plan

first and meter second. Each submeter should measure the energy use in a given manager's area of responsibility to provide a clear picture of whether each manager's energy conservation efforts are effective. Matching a property's organization chart with its physical configuration will allow management to determine which manager will be responsible for energy consumption in each submetered zone. Despite the benefits of submetering, submetering the entire property may not be cost-effective because some departments' energy use is comparatively small.

In addition to the primary benefit of better cost performance, the technique has three other positive aspects. First, the records from the submeters allow the continual monitoring of the efficiency of the production equipment (for example, boilers). Second, more accurate standards for consumption on a unit basis (for example, per pound of laundry or per meal cooked in the kitchen) can be established. Third, the records provide the data necessary for after-the-fact documentation of the value of a capital expenditure associated with conserving utilities.

Personnel Management

Although our purpose is not to develop a text on personnel management (there are many resources available on this topic and many properties have standard policies in addition), there are certain unique elements of personnel management in the engineering area which should be of interest to students and practitioners as well.

The engineering department often contains a group of people who are among the most highly paid at the facility, have moderate to high skill levels, and can usually find other employment rather readily in other lodging establishments or in virtually any commercial building and most manufacturing facilities. Personnel management for such a group is quite different from that needed in housekeeping or food and beverage, where the characteristics of the average employee are very different.

One way in which the different characteristics of the engineering department personnel manifest themselves is in the issue of departmental turnover and factors affecting this issue. In a study of 17 lodging properties over a three-year period, it was noted that 13 of the 17 had low turnover rates in engineering, compared with only three with low rates in food and beverage and four in housekeeping. When the authors of this study investigated those factors affecting turnover, they found that the factors deemed important to low turnover for engineers were, first, quality of supervision, followed by management support and selection and training. Working conditions, job status, and compensation were of less importance to the engineers. The study also stated:

> The supervisory style that was perceived as most successful with engineers and technicians was one that allowed and encouraged them to work autonomously. . . . General supervision, rather than close scrutiny, often appeals to individuals in engineering who are largely self-reliant and who prefer independent operation. . . . [One] chief engineer said, "Let the skilled staff have a free hand in doing their job and make spot checks to let them know you're still in control and still interested in how they're doing." . . .
>
> Top management support was particularly important to engineering in the approval of major budget items that staff members felt were required to accomplish their job. For example, one department head said, "Morale really drops if we aren't authorized the money for parts, equipment, or renovations that the crew feels are needed to keep the place in top shape. They don't accept excuses, only solid facts as to why funds aren't available now." Since the engineering staff generally feels that much of its work has little visibility, recognition by top management was considered a boost to worker morale and stability.
>
> For proper selection and training, managers must analyze the skills, knowledge, and experience needed for vacant jobs before recruiting and hiring again. One manager said, "If all you look for is bodies, you can expect poor performance and high turnover." Another manager said that engineering jobs involving contact with guests need to be assigned to individuals who will treat such relationships with dignity and respect. Guest interaction is a factor that is often overlooked in the engineering department's recruiting. Engineers who don't come from hotel engineering backgrounds may find guests difficult to contend with and, consequently, may

leave. Conversely, those who dislike interaction with guests were considered possible candidates for discharge.

Unless they are clearly substandard, working conditions, job status, and salary apparently have little impact on turnover among engineers. One department head found that many engineers with experience in other businesses came to the hotel knowing that their salaries would be lower than before. "They do it because work here is more varied and interesting, because they have a lot of freedom, and because working conditions are generally better," he said, adding that this was particularly true of older men who had had a chance to compare various work experiences (workers from the construction industry, for example).

Failure even to consider strategies used by successful departments largely explained the plight of the three hotels with relatively high levels of engineering turnover. In one case, the supervisor contracted with outside firms for high-level jobs, leaving staff members with tasks they perceived as routine and of low status. The supervisor's meager expectations decreased job interest and productivity and increased turnover. In another hotel, specialists were hired for seasonal positions, such as pool attendant, groundskeeper, and landscaper. As winter approached, each was laid off, increasing turnover counts. Job rotation is a strategy now being considered for a portion of this crew as a more cost-effective way of handling seasonal jobs.[7]

Care in developing personnel management policies which are appropriate for these individuals should significantly improve the departmental morale and performance of these skilled and important members of the property team.

Notes

1. See Raymond S. Schmidgall, *Hospitality Industry Managerial Accounting* (East Lansing, Mich.: Educational Institute of the American Hotel & Motel Association, 1986), Chapter 14.
2. See Michael H. Redlin, "Energy Consumption in Lodging Properties: Applying Multiple Regression Analysis for Effective Measurement," *The Cornell Hotel and Restaurant Administration Quarterly*, February 1979, pp. 48–52, and Michael H. Redlin and Jan A. deRoos, "Gauging Energy Savings: Further Applications of Multiple-Regression Analysis," *The Cornell Hotel and Restaurant Administration Quarterly*, February 1980, pp. 48–52.
3. *Uniform System of Accounts for Hotels*, 8th Edition (New York: Hotel Association of New York City, Inc., 1985).
4. *The Uniform System of Accounts and Expense Dictionary for Small Hotels, Motels, and Motor Hotels*, 4th Ed. (East Lansing, Mich.: Educational Institute of the American Hotel & Motel Association, 1987).
5. *Uniform System of Accounts for Hotels*, p. ix.
6. For a more detailed treatment of this topic, see Michael H. Redlin and Lawrence M. Goland, "Submetering of Hotel Utilities," *The Cornell Hotel and Restaurant Administration Quarterly*, February 1984, pp. 44–50, on which parts of this section are based.
7. William J. Wasmuth and Stanley W. Davis, "Managing Employee Turnover: Why Employees Leave," *The Cornell Hotel and Restaurant Administration Quarterly*, May 1983, pp. 11–18.

3

Engineering Systems in Lodging Facilities

Engineering systems are installed in lodging facilities for several purposes. One major purpose is supplying guests and employees with a comfortable building offering basic services such as those provided by water systems and building HVAC systems. Some systems—for example, fire alarm systems—are installed to satisfy local code requirements or regulations and often are designed to protect the guest, the employee, or the general public from harm due to accidents, fires, or other problems. Some building systems—for example, electrical systems—primarily serve a supporting role for other systems, providing the inputs required to effectively operate these other systems. Finally, certain systems or subsystems help to create the property's image and contribute to the overall aesthetics of the grounds, building, or interiors. The lighting system is probably the primary example of this type of system.

Understanding common factors which influence the design and operation of these systems will aid the manager of a lodging facility in controlling costs, performing building modifications, adhering to safety concerns, and, in general, operating a facility which meets the needs of guests and employees. A working knowledge of the different systems which may be installed in a lodging property will prepare the manager not only for the diversity of equipment found in the industry, but also for the variety of management needs associated with different buildings and systems.

This chapter provides an overview of the types of engineering systems found in buildings, what constitutes them, why they are there, and why it is important for a lodging manager to know about them. More detailed information on some of these individual systems is presented in later chapters.

Engineering Systems: An Introduction

The systems discussed in this book are those which constitute 35%–40% of the building construction cost and generate a large fraction of both the energy and property operation and maintenance (POM) costs at the property. Major engineering systems include water and wastewater, electrical, lighting, food service refrigeration, and heating, ventilation, and air conditioning. We consider to be major those systems which significantly and daily influence guest comfort, employee productivity, safety, the operation of another major system, and building operating costs.

The components of most (but not all) major systems can be organized into four functional subgroups: *sources*, *distribution systems*, *delivery or utilization devices*, and various elements of *control and safety equipment*. The examination of systems which follows briefly outlines some of these system components and the design process for engineering systems in general. Some engineering systems (fire, security, vertical transportation, and telephone) which do not naturally divide into these four subgroups are of such a specialized nature that, with the exception of fire systems, discussion of them beyond the brief treatment in this chapter is not possible within this text. In addition, some of these systems may be solely under an outside contract for maintenance and operation.

Water and Wastewater Systems

Water systems are installed to meet the needs of guests, employees, and equipment; to conform to local codes; to contribute to building aesthetics; and to maintain the grounds. The characteristics required of the water may vary with each use. The cleanliness, quantity, and quality of the water supply can have a major impact on guest satisfaction and on the quality and quantity of the work performed by several departments in the property.

Wastewater (sewage) systems are necessary not only to remove the water brought into the property by the water system, but also to treat this water if necessary before it leaves the property. Some of these systems handle rainwater and site runoff from streams as well. Each category of wastewater system requires different design criteria. Often, the different wastewater systems at a property are physically separate from each other. Wastewater systems rely primarily upon gravity to move wastewater through the systems. This can result in special design and operational concerns.

Water and wastewater systems (that is, the building plumbing) constitute 5%–12% of the construction cost of a lodging facility. The cost of water represents 5%–15% of the energy expenditures of the typical lodging establishment. While management may seldom observe these systems directly, a well-managed operation does not ignore or neglect their role and importance in a well-run, pleasant, and safe facility.

The Systems

Exhibit 3.1 outlines the types of water systems and the loads they serve at a typical lodging establishment. The actual system design for each of these major systems can vary significantly depending on the water source and the size of the building. The potable (that is, drinkable) supply is usually provided from a local

Exhibit 3.1 Building Water Systems and Uses

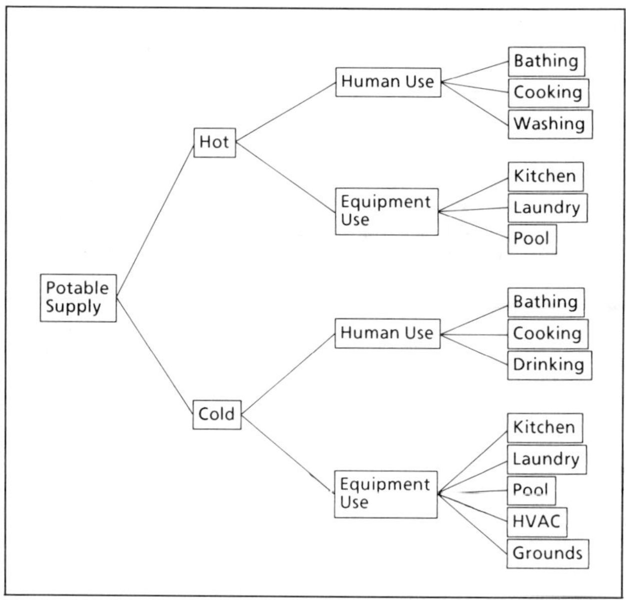

water utility, although the property may operate its own well or use other sources, in which instance potability needs to be ensured by water treatment. Distribution of water throughout the property differs for hot and cold water as well as for water provided for human use and equipment.

Exhibit 3.2 illustrates the primary subdivisions of the property wastewater systems. Note that the storm and sanitary systems are two separate systems and that the sanitary system keeps wastewater containing grease separate from wastewater without grease.

Water distribution systems for smaller properties may rely solely on the local water utility to supply adequate pressure for uses in the building. Larger buildings will need to install pumps to move water about the building and may subdivide the water system into zones within the building as well. Special systems, treatment, and components are required, depending on the end use of the water.

Major components of building water systems include pipes, valves, pumps, filters, softeners, water heaters, controls (temperature, pressure), showers, tubs, faucets, commodes, and storage tanks. Viewing these components in terms of the four major subgroups of system

Exhibit 3.2 Primary Subdivisions of Property Wastewater Systems

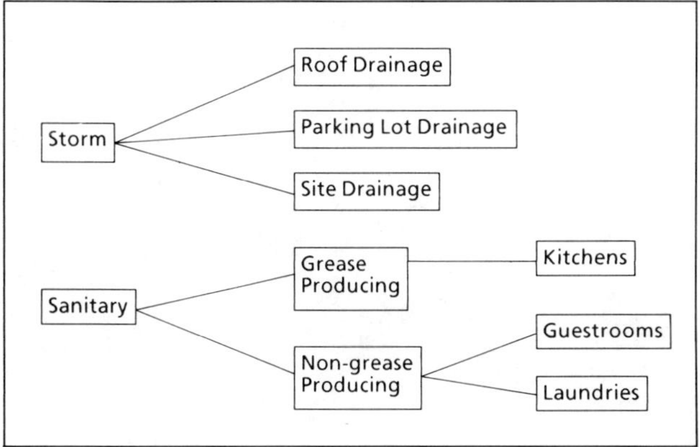

components outlined earlier can help in understanding the systems. Sources for water are not only the places the water originates (local utility, well, stream, or lake), but also the locations within the property which store water (tanks) and produce water of special characteristics (water heaters, softeners, and other filtering or treating devices). Distribution systems are composed primarily of the pipes and pumps (or drainage ditches in rainwater systems). These components move the water from the sources to the point of use. Delivery devices include all water-using appliances which are connected to the distribution system and provide water for a variety of needs. Some of these appliances have direct human contact, while others use the water to help operate equipment. Associated with the water system are various controls and safety devices such as valves, temperature controllers, and pressure regulators. These items help to ensure that the water is maintained at conditions which are suitable for the end use and safe.

Managerial Concerns

Ensuring potability of the building water supply is among the more important concerns of management. Unfortunately, this is a growing problem as more pollutants enter the water supply. Another appropriate area of attention is providing treatment suitable for the efficient operation of equipment and the performance of various cleaning tasks. For properties with pools, continual attention to the chemical composition of the pool water is needed; pool water can be particularly problematic if neglected.

Rising water rates and local shortages over the past few years have resulted in increased interest in water conservation. Possibilities for the reuse of some discharge water (sometimes called *grey water reuse*) are being considered by some lodging chains. Code issues relative to reuse and the increasing regulations and costs associated with sewage discharges of all types are motivating many properties to rethink sources and uses of water. With the retrofit of building sprinkler systems being required by more codes, there are concerns about the adequacy (quantity) of water supplies as well.

A problem area for some facilities is the quantity of water available during times of peak use. A hot water system must be able to provide sufficient hot water even when demand is at its highest. This problem and the problem of the high cost of hot water due to the cost of the energy required to heat the water result in managerial attention to and concern over the usage of hot water in particular.

Food Service Refrigeration Systems

"Cold" is needed in numerous locations in lodging properties. In the kitchen, walk-in refrigerators store raw food products before they are used and assembled dishes until they are served. In the lounge, ice machines generate the ice which is used in drinks and for the cooling of a food display. On the guestroom floors, ice machines provide the ice desired by the guests for their personal use. This "cold" is produced by removing heat from the space (for example, inside a refrigerator) or the substance (for example, water) where the cold is desired. A compressive refrigeration system removes this heat by the continuous evaporation and condensation of a fluid inside the system which absorbs heat from one location and deposits it in another.

The costs of satisfying the guests' desires for cool drinks and food and meeting the property's need for safe conditions in which to store food in various forms can be substantial. Exhibit 3.3 shows the typical costs of purchasing and operating three common types of equipment that

Exhibit 3.3 Typical Purchase and Energy Costs for Food Service Refrigeration Equipment

Type of Equipment	Purchase Cost (1986)	Annual Energy Cost *
Reach-in Refrigerator (40 cubic feet)	\$2,600 - 3,200	\$150
Walk-in Refrigerator (9.5′ x 8′ x 12′)	\$9,000 - 11,000	\$500
Ice Machine (400 lb. of ice/day)	\$2,100 - 2,700	\$600

*Electricity @ \$.08/kilowatt-hour

Exhibit 3.4 Sketch of a Walk-In Refrigerator

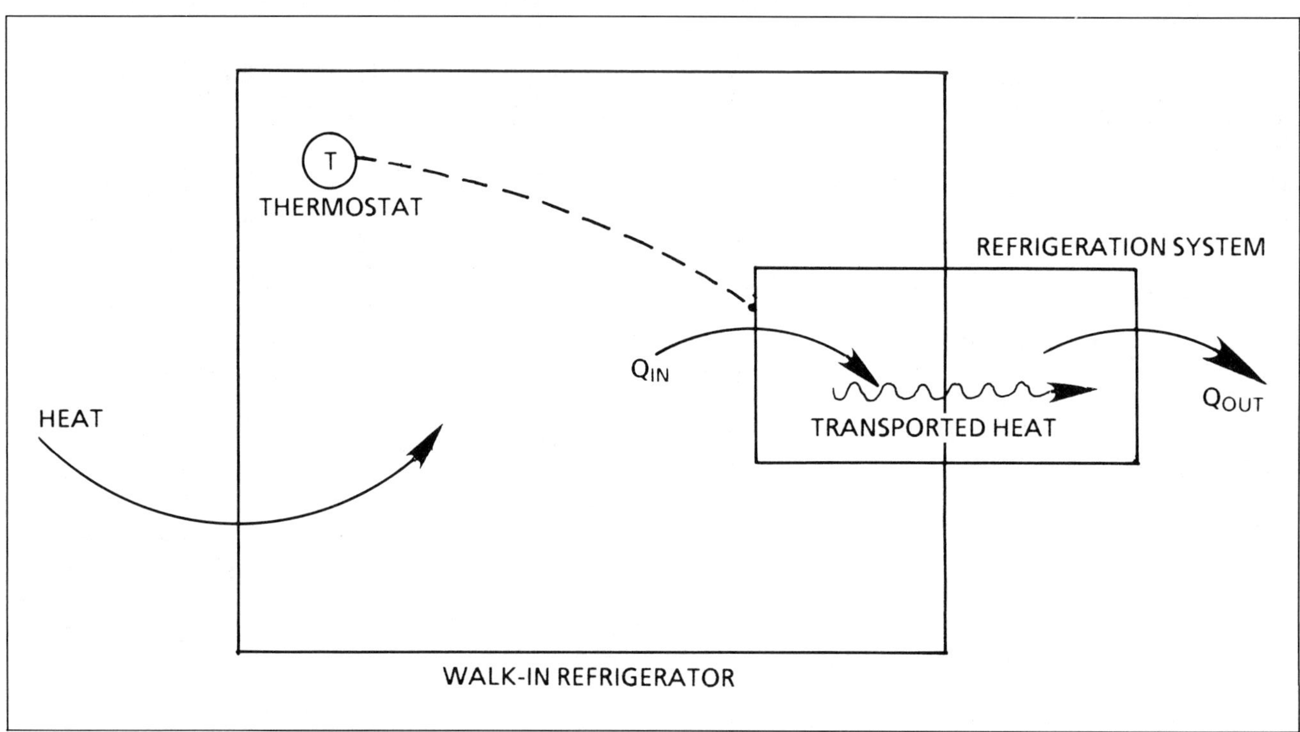

contain a refrigeration system. Further, the overall cost of operating the refrigeration systems in a restaurant represents approximately 3%–8% of the total energy consumed for food production and storage, lighting, and sanitation.[1]

Refrigeration systems exist in numerous

pieces of equipment throughout a lodging facility such as walk-in refrigerators and freezers, reach-in refrigerators and freezers, ice machines, cold bains, drinking fountains, beverage dispensing systems, and portable cold food delivery carts.

Principles of Operation

The operation of a refrigeration system is demonstrated by the sketch of a walk-in refrigerator in Exhibit 3.4. The walls of the refrigerator enclose the space that is cooled by the refrigeration system. Notice that a portion of the system is located inside the cooled space and the remainder of the system is located outside the cooled space, usually in the kitchen or in an adjacent remote location.

The primary objective of the system is to maintain the temperature of the cooled space at a specific value by removing any heat energy that enters the space. The system is under the control of a thermostat in the space. Over time, heat energy enters the space through various means such as heat transferred through the walls of the walk-in or warm food that is inserted into the walk-in for storage. This heat energy causes the inside air temperature of the walk-in to increase. When this air temperature increases above the upper limit set by the thermostat, the refrigeration system turns on and removes heat from the space until the air temperature is cooled below the lower limit set by the thermostat. At that time, the system turns off and waits for the next activation signal from the thermostat.

While activated, the system transfers heat from inside the walk-in to a location that is outside of it. First, this heat is absorbed by the portion of the refrigeration system that is inside the walk-in. The heat flow occurs because the temperature of this portion of the system is lower than the air temperature in the walk-in. The absorbed heat is then transported through the system by the refrigerant and dissipated into a cooling medium (either water or the surrounding air) by the portion of the system that is external to the walk-in. This heat flows from this portion of the system into the cooling medium because the temperature of this portion is maintained above the temperature of cooling air or water.

The system works by changing the state of its refrigerant from a liquid to a gas and then back to a liquid in a continuous cycle. The absorbed heat changes the state of the refrigerant from a liquid to a gas; the rejected heat changes the state of the same substance back to a liquid.

System Components

As shown in Exhibit 3.5, the four major components of the system are the evaporator coil, the compressor, the condenser coil, and the expansion valve. In the diagram, the refrigerant flows clockwise around the closed system. Starting at the entrance to the evaporator coil, the fluid is in the liquid state at a low pressure. As it flows through the coil, it evaporates and absorbs heat from the coil and the coil's surroundings. As the refrigerant exits the coil, it is in the gaseous state at the same temperature and pressure. In the compressor, which is driven by an electrical motor, the fluid remains a gas, but its pressure and temperature are substantially increased. The fluid then passes into the condenser coil where it is exposed to a temperature that is below its boiling point for the existing pressure. As the fluid is cooled, it condenses back into a high-pressure liquid at the same temperature and pressure and rejects heat to its surroundings. This refrigerant can now begin the cycle again by flowing back to the entrance of the evaporator coil through the expansion valve which controls the amount of the fluid flow and reduces its pressure.

Alternative Configurations

The primary characteristics which distinguish the different types of systems are the location of the condenser and the cooling medium. Either the condenser is located in the same unit as the evaporator and the compressor (classified as *self-contained*) or the condenser and compressor are located separately from the evaporator, possibly in a adjacent room (classified as *remote*). In either case, the condenser can be cooled by the air in its surrounding environment or it can be cooled by water.

Managerial Concerns

Management's interest in food service refrigeration systems is twofold. First, the systems must be selected for type and size and installed properly. With regard to type, a water-cooled system, in general, operates at a higher effi-

Exhibit 3.5 Schematic of a Compressive Refrigeration System

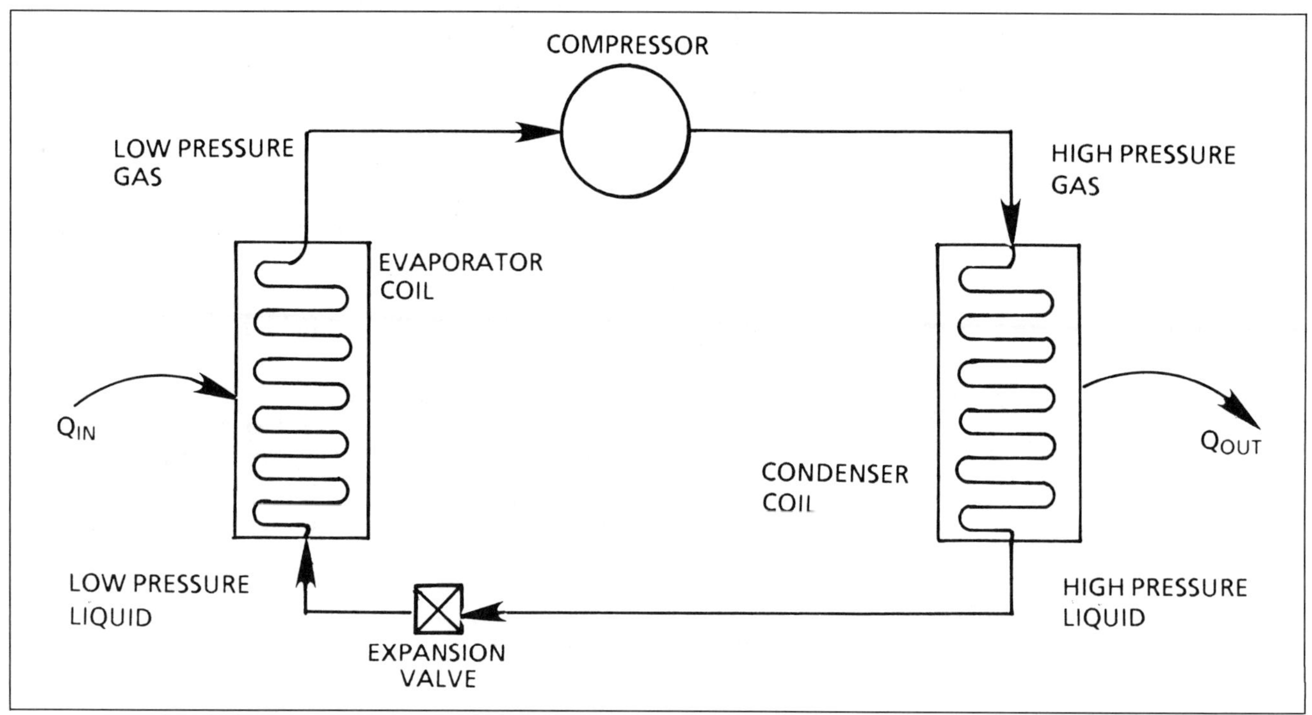

ciency than an air-cooled machine, although this advantage is offset by the additional cost of the water. Proper sizing of the equipment prevents the loss of capacity during periods of extreme operating conditions (for example, reduced production of ice from an ice machine during extremely hot weather). Proper installation includes considerations such as adequate access for easy maintenance and the availability of the necessary utilities (for example, water for water-cooled ice machines on guestroom floors and drains for the condensate which forms on the evaporator coil of walk-ins).

Second, the staff must operate and maintain the equipment so that it can provide the necessary cooling for (1) the temperatures required by the health codes for the safe storage of cold food and (2) the services and amenities expected by the guest, such as chilled water, mixers, wine, and beer. The primary concern is the reliability of the equipment. Unexpected failures can cause losses of valuable inventory or guest dissatisfaction. In addition, maintaining the operating efficiency of the systems keeps energy costs under control. This aspect includes both maintaining the efficiency of the equipment and applying heat recovery techniques to reuse the energy discarded by the condenser coil.

Heating, Ventilating, and Air Conditioning Systems

The heating, ventilating, and air conditioning (HVAC) system in a lodging property has a major impact on a guest's perception of the facility. The system must maintain the inside air at the proper temperature, humidity, and quality. Further, the design of the system must be sensitive to aesthetic concerns such as velocity of drafts, noise levels, and appearance. Last, it must operate at all times, delivering either heating or cooling upon the demand of the guest.

The system also has two important influences on the operation of the property. First, employees expect to work in conditions that are conducive to health, safety, and productivity. The kitchens, laundries, shops, and administrative offices must be kept at temperatures and humidities that are comfortable to the workers and to their sensitive equipment (for example, computers). Second, the energy and mainte-

Exhibit 3.6 Schematic of an HVAC System

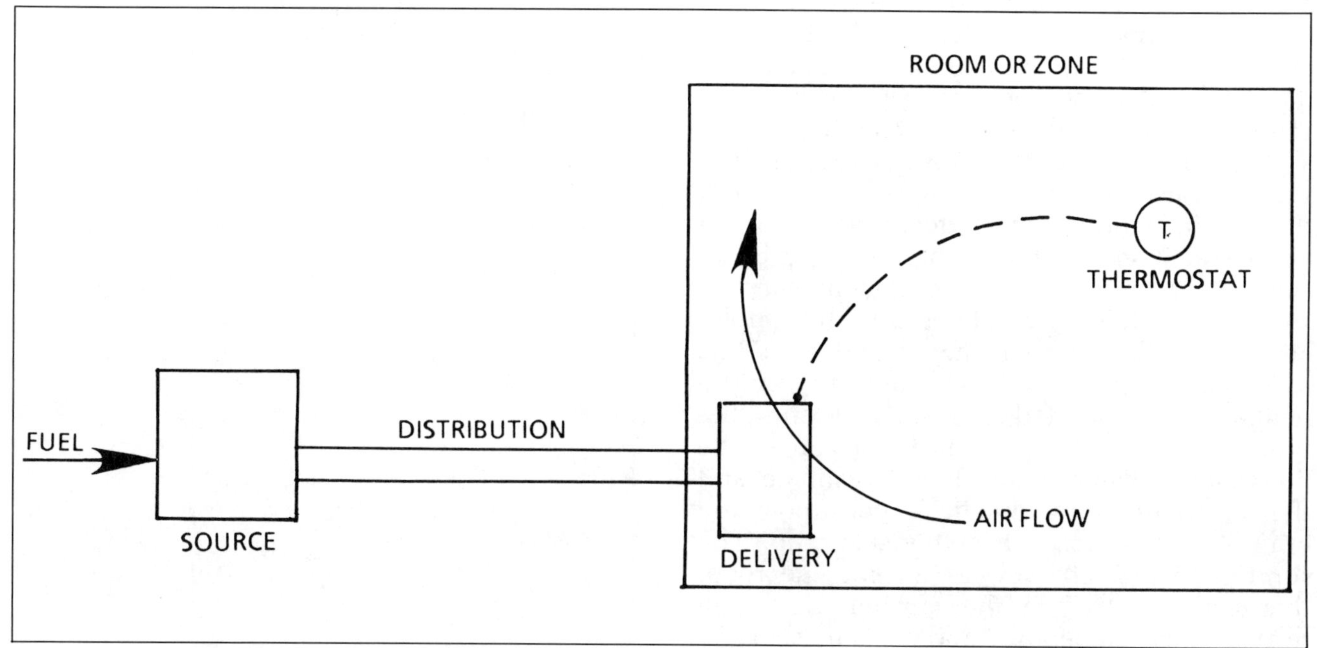

nance costs of operating the system are substantial. Its operation consumes approximately 12% of the POM budget for non-payroll items and a varying, yet large, percentage of the energy budget of the facility on an annual basis.

The HVAC system is also costly to purchase and build, typically representing 9%–16% of the cost of constructing a new property.

The system affects almost every room within the property. The front-of-the-house areas such as guestrooms, function rooms, lobby, and restaurants receive the most attention, especially with regard to their aesthetic impact. The systems in the back of the house, though not as sophisticated, still must provide acceptable conditions for temperature, humidity, and air quality.

Principles of Operation

The basic operation of the heating and cooling portions of the system is shown in Exhibit 3.6. The objective of maintaining the proper air temperature in the room or zone is accomplished under the control of a thermostat. In the heating mode, when the air temperature falls below the proper level, the thermostat activates the room unit which then provides heat by blowing hot air into the room. The heat needed to heat that air is acquired through a distribution channel from the heat source. In response to this call from the room for heat, the source (for example, water boiler, hot-air furnace, or electrical heating element) produces the heat by consuming a fuel (for example, natural gas or electricity). When the temperature of the room eventually returns to the proper level, the thermostat deactivates the room unit, which then waits for the next activation signal from the thermostat. A similar sequence of events occurs in the cooling mode when the air temperature rises above the proper level. In this case, however, cool air is delivered to the room and "cold" is produced by the source (for example, a compressive refrigeration system as described in the section on food service refrigeration).

Components

The components of this system fall into the four major subgroups of components listed earlier. The sources for the heating and cooling effects take the utilities (for example, natural gas, fuel oil, steam, electricity, and chilled water) purchased from utility companies or produced onsite and convert the utilities into either heat or cold. The components that do this are boilers, furnaces, electrical resistance elements, or refrigeration systems. Also, the fresh air that is required to maintain the indoor air quality is taken from the outside of the building through the air intake system. The distribution systems include the pipes and air ducts, with the necessary pumps and fans, which transport the heating and cooling effect and the fresh air to the zones and which remove exhaust from the room. Pieces of equipment such as steam lines, chilled-water lines, and the supply-air fan for the ballroom are included in this subgroup. The delivery systems are components that are located in the zones and that transfer the effects into the air in the zones. The hot-water radiator in the lobby vestibule and the air conditioning unit in a guestroom are examples of equipment in this subgroup. The controls and safety devices include the room thermostat, valves in the fan-coil units, fan relays, boiler temperature and pressure sensors, and pressure sensors that indicate when the air filters are dirty. All of these components contribute to the proper and safe operation of the entire HVAC system.

Alternative Configurations

The two characteristics which differentiate the various configurations of HVAC systems are (1) the relative location of the source and delivery components and (2) the medium used in the distribution components. If the source components are located directly adjacent to or inside the zone, then the system is considered a *decentralized* system. The opposite situation, in which the source components are located a substantial distance from the zones, is known as a *centralized* system.

The diagram in Exhibit 3.7 shows the positioning of the components for a decentralized system in a typical guestroom. When the system is activated, return air from the room is drawn through the filter before it is mixed with outside air. This mixed air flows over both an electrical heating element and the evaporator coil of a refrigeration system, one of which is activated depending on whether heating or cooling is desired. The supply fan blows the conditioned air into the room through a supply-air grate in the enclosing case. This air movement causes the proper distribution of the conditioned air throughout the entire guestroom. Exhaust air is removed from the room through an exhaust-air grate located in the bathroom.

Exhibit 3.7 Sketch of a Decentralized HVAC System in a Guestroom

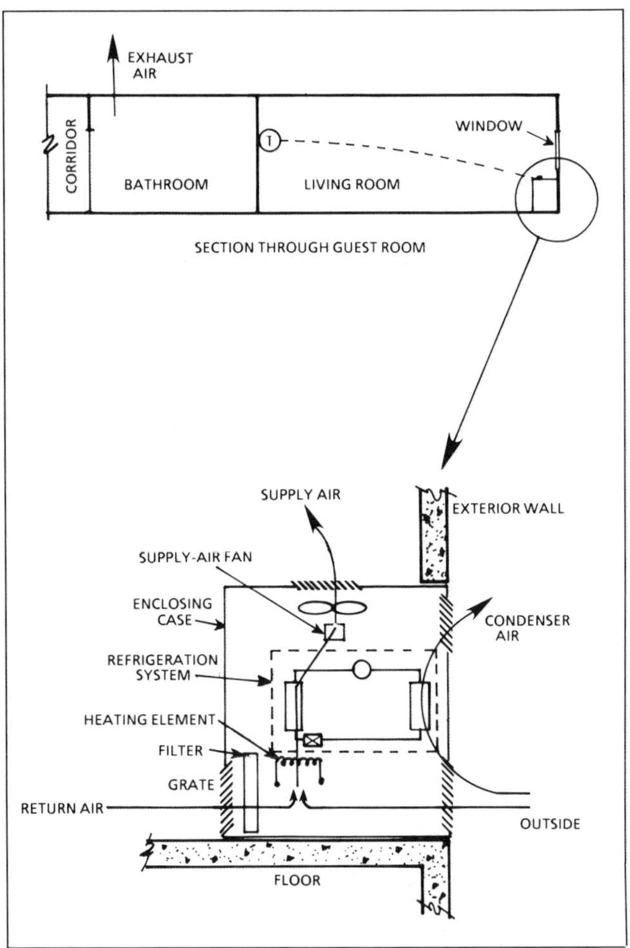

If the system is a centralized system, the heating or cooling effect must be transported from the location of the source equipment to the zone through the distribution system. Two major alternatives are available for the medium used in the distribution system: water and air. A combination system, which uses both media, also is commonly used. A third medium, steam, was often used in older buildings, but only for heating.

The diagrams for a water-based centralized and an air-based centralized system are shown in Exhibit 3.8. In both cases, the boiler and chiller are located in a central mechanical room.

Exhibit 3.8 Schematics of Centralized HVAC Systems

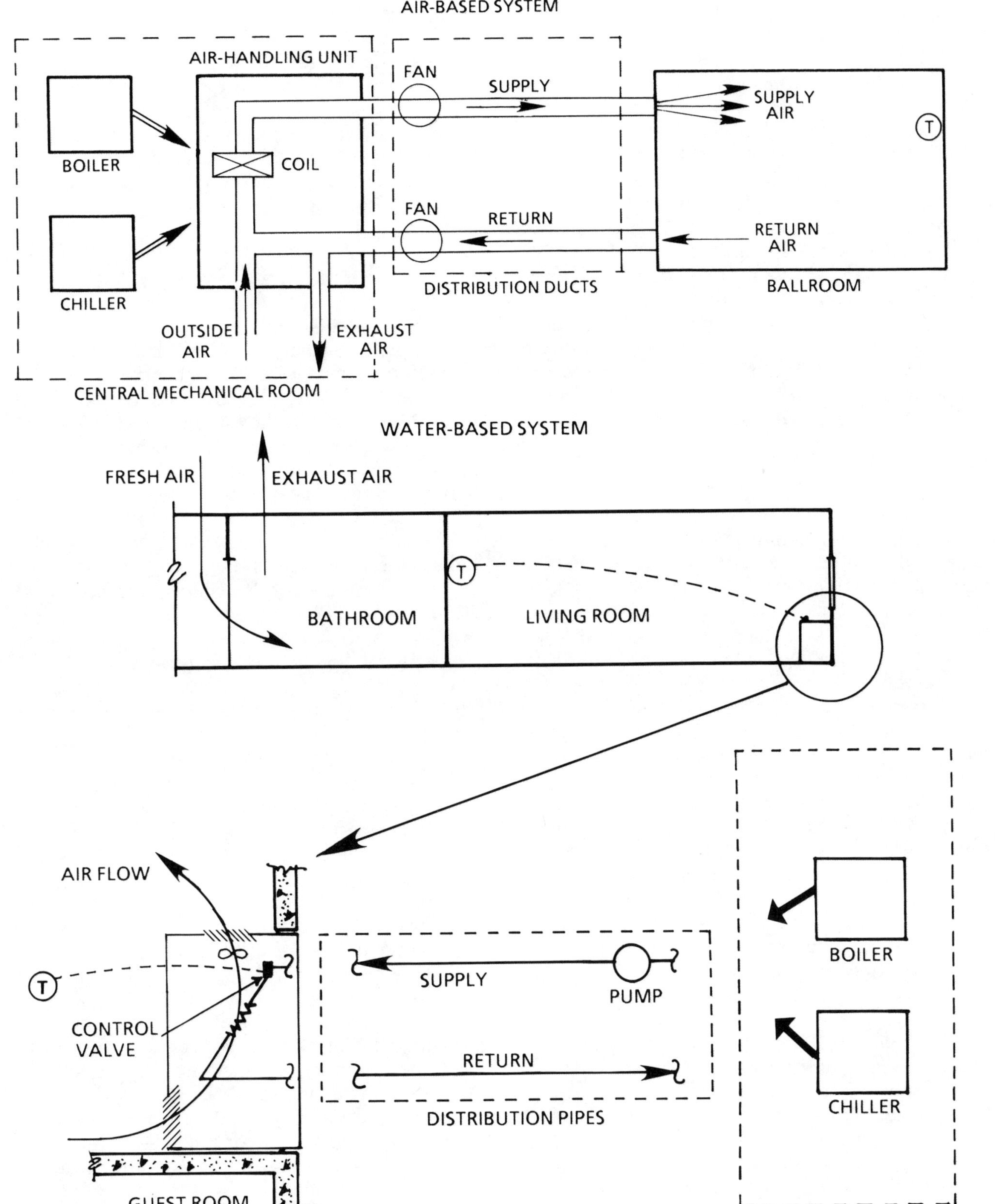

In the water-based system, the heating or cooling effect is carried to the zone by water pumped through pipes. At the room, the flow of the water through the coil is controlled by a valve that is activated by the room thermostat. The air flowing over the coil is either heated or cooled when the valve is open. A supply fan blows the conditioned air throughout the room. Fresh air is supplied to the room through the corridor and exhaust air is removed from the bathroom.

In the air-based system, the coil for transferring the effect to the air is inside an air handling unit which is usually also located in the central mechanical room. The conditioned air is then taken to and returned from the room by supply-air and return-air ducts, respectively. The air enters and leaves the room through supply-air and return-air grates. The fresh air is added to and the exhaust air is removed from the system in the air handling unit.

Managerial Concerns

Because the HVAC systems in a building are so expensive to build and to operate, they represent significant challenges for management. During the initial design of new properties or very substantial renovations of old properties, it is very important for management to select the type and size of equipment that will satisfy the guest and also meet the business objectives of the property. Decentralized HVAC equipment, for example, is usually less expensive to purchase than the corresponding centralized system. But, in general, it has a lower operating efficiency and a shorter life span, thus causing higher operating and replacement costs. Additionally, the units usually provide less guest satisfaction due to the noise levels in the room. The original selection of the fuel source also has a dramatic effect on the future energy costs for the property, especially in regions that have a substantial heating season. For these reasons, the initial cost and the operating costs of the systems for the various fuels should be analyzed.

Furthermore, management must strive to maintain the systems at their peak performance levels while assuring their reliable operation. First, guest satisfaction relies on comfortable front-of-the-house areas. Anything less than this causes guest dissatisfaction and potential loss of future business. Second, recent cases identifying the HVAC system as the source of airborne illnesses further emphasize the importance of proper operation. Third, the high cost of operating these systems will be even higher if poor maintenance allows their efficiency to drop.

Finally, upgrading or modifying these systems is often studied because of the high operating costs. Numerous new products, some that are worthwhile and some that are worthless, enter the marketplace every year. Management must be capable of prudently analyzing the costs and benefits of such products.

Electrical Systems

Electrical systems constitute approximately 10% of the construction cost of a lodging facility. The electrical system is one of the most invisible of systems, serving primarily a service role for the other systems in the building. Because of the important service role it plays, the electrical system needs to be well designed and maintained. In addition, the costs of electrical energy (75%–95% of the total energy account) and the safety concerns associated with electrical systems call for managerial interest.

For most electrical systems, the source of electricity is the local electric utility. This utility provides electricity to the property, bills the property for this service, and maintains a relatively reliable supply of high quality energy. Within the property, other locations serve as processors of the electricity supplied by the utility, becoming, in effect, subsources at the facility. These include building transformers which change the voltage of the electrical supply, battery supplies for lighting systems and computers, and emergency power systems which operate during a power failure. The property's distribution system consists of wires or similar components which move the electricity around the building to the delivery or utilization devices (the elements of the building which actually use the electricity). These include lights, motors, electric heaters, computers, and building controls of various types. Each piece of equipment requires the electrical supply to have certain characteristics, among which are voltage, type of current, phase, and amperage. In order to maintain a safe and controllable system, various controls and safety devices are installed. These range from the commonly encountered light switch to fuses and circuit breakers (which

Exhibit 3.9 Single Line or Block Diagram of a Typical Building Electrical System

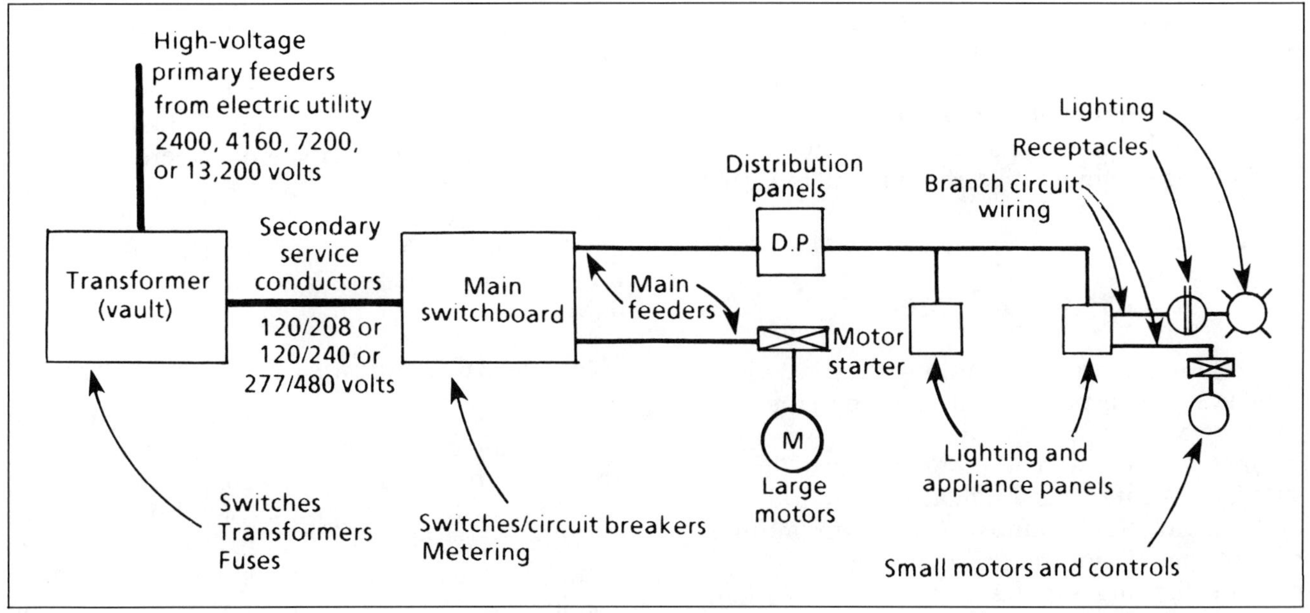

control the amount of current flowing in a circuit) to disconnects on building distribution panels (which allow circuits to be removed from service for maintenance needs).

A very basic electrical system schematic is shown in Exhibit 3.9. The system is somewhat similar to a building water system. Wires serve the same function as pipes, voltage is similar to pressure, current is analogous to water flow, and the subdivision of the system into branch circuits is similar to that which is done for water systems based on categories of usage (hot/cold, potable/non-potable). Both electrical and water system design and modifications must meet the applicable code provisions and are among the more heavily regulated aspects of building system design.

Managerial Concerns

An appropriate and reliable supply of electricity is becoming more important for lodging establishments as the facilities become more electrically intensive. One major concern at present is the electrical supply for computer systems. Because of the sensitive nature of these systems, it is often necessary to specify extensive protective provisions in electrical systems to ensure proper operation of computer systems, even during power outages. When managers do not understand the basics of electrical systems, problems may result in procuring equipment of various types. The special needs of computer equipment provide even more incentive to develop some basic grasp of electrical system fundamentals.

Increased concerns over life safety issues, especially during fires, have resulted in the need to consider the emergency power requirements of facilities, the interfacing of these emergency power systems with building systems, and the overall reliability of the systems. Safe operation of electrical systems is also a very important issue. Since 10%–20% of lodging industry fires result from electrical problems and significant guest and employee safety concerns exist with regard to electrical systems, a manager must devote attention to electrical safety in all departments.

Onsite production of electricity by lodging establishments to achieve cost savings is occurring in the 1980s and will continue to grow during the 1990s. This onsite production is known as *cogeneration*. As more lodging facilities generate electricity, lodging managers will need a broadened knowledge of electrical systems, utility billing and service requirements, and contract negotiations targeted specifically at issues relating to cogeneration.

The development of complex billing methods by electrical utilities and the large portion of the property's energy account represented by electricity make it imperative that property electrical bills be understood and managed. Lack of attention to these bills can result in unnecessary charges and higher costs for what is already one of the largest single bills received at the property.

Lighting Systems

Lighting systems are among the most visible of all systems, especially with regard to the effect they are attempting to achieve. The system may be installed for a marketing purpose (lighted signage), a safety/security purpose (parking lot lighting), to create a mood (nightclub lighting), to illuminate a workplace (kitchen lighting), or to provide lighting for the guest's needs (a lamp near the bed). Regardless of its purpose, it requires not only an appropriate design but also continued maintenance (lamp replacement and fixture cleaning), repair (switch and cord replacement), modification (changing office lighting to accommodate computer screens) and, eventually, replacement (as concepts, marketing plans, and local codes dictate).

Separating the initial and energy costs of lighting systems from the overall costs of electrical/lighting systems is difficult since there are so many elements of the electrical systems that are used by several subsystems. Lighting has been estimated as using about 20% of the total electricity consumed in a lodging facility.

Lighting systems can use a variety of sources to produce the light. The cheapest lighting source will always be sunlight, but it is unfortunately not available at all times nor is it suitable for all lighting needs. While the most commonly used artificial sources are incandescent lamps in guestrooms, hallways, and restaurants and fluorescent lamps in back-of-the-house locations, there is a growing use of fluorescent lamps in all areas. Exterior lighting (parking lots, recreation areas, and grounds) was once almost exclusively incandescent or mercury vapor, but we now find metal halide and sodium lamps becoming more common in these areas and in some interior applications. The use of more efficient distribution/delivery devices—the lamp fixtures themselves—is becoming more common as the lighting system is viewed as a system. This approach leads to consideration of the role of all the system's various components.

Major advances in light sources, distribution/delivery devices, and controls have resulted in the ability to more efficiently operate lighting systems. Advances in controllable fluorescent lamps and occupancy sensors enable lighting systems to operate at exactly the correct times and to deliver only the needed amount of light.

Managerial Concerns

Since a significant amount of a lighting system's life cycle costs are expended on energy and sometimes maintenance costs, management should encourage an analysis of lighting systems on a life cycle cost basis. Careful analysis of these issues for existing or new systems will produce the lowest cost option which still meets the property's needs.

With all the technological developments in the lighting area over the past 10 years, one of the major concerns facing managers is sorting through all the latest developments to determine whether one is appropriate for their properties. This requires a basic knowledge of the function served by the lighting system, the characteristics of the existing and proposed lighting components, the lighting needs of the facility, and the way in which the proposed modification will apply to existing circumstances. Managers should be particularly sensitive to lighting in areas where computer screens are in use, such as accounting and reservations.

Providing adequate lighting of hallways, grounds, and parking areas contributes to the overall security at the property. The purchase of exterior lighting services from the local electric utility is usually the most expensive way to provide these services. Replacement of these lights with those owned by the property will often pay back the investment in one to two years.

Fire Protection Systems

Fire protection is a major concern throughout the lodging industry. We focus here and in Chapter 12 primarily upon some of the hardware installed as part of fire protection. Also important, of course, is employee training dealing with proper actions to take to reduce the likelihood of fires and how to respond if a fire should occur.

Fire protection systems include detection, notification, suppression, and smoke control systems of various types. Detection devices include smoke and heat detectors. Notification systems make use of audible alarms, visual alarms, and telephone connection to the fire department. Suppression equipment includes portable extinguishers, kitchen hood systems, and sprinklers. Smoke control relies on fans, vents, and dampers. The local codes and regulations and the standards of the individual property will dictate which of these components will be installed.

Major managerial concerns regarding fire protection systems include maintenance and testing of all equipment, consideration of fire protection issues when performing building modifications (including simple renovations), and attention to situations which may result in arson (for example, political unrest and tense labor situations).

Security Systems

Security systems and equipment at a lodging property will vary with the type of property, the design and layout of the property, the security risks, and the management choices regarding how security issues will be handled. The equipment is only a part of a property's overall security program, the major components of which are locks and key control, guestroom security, control of persons on premises, perimeter control, protection of assets (money on hand, guests' assets, equipment, inventories), emergency procedures, communications, and security records.

Locks are obviously a major element of the building security system. Recent developments in electronic locking systems have expanded the range of locking options for guestrooms beyond those of the traditional mechanical locks. Mechanical (key) locking systems have several variations, primarily with regard to the method of changing the lock code ("re-keying") and whether a deadbolt feature is an integral element of the lock. Key control for mechanical locking systems is an essential element of a building security plan. Key control is sometimes largely the engineering department's responsibility—the department often cuts new keys and it is one of the few departments staffed at all times.

Electronic locking options vary depending on power source (internal battery or central wiring) and method of lock reprogramming (from a central computer or upon use of a new access card). The primary advantages of the electronic locking systems are the ability to continually change lock combinations (removing the possibility of reuse of a key or of readily picking the lock) and, in some systems, the ability to identify who secured access to a given room based on a record which identifies the access card used.

Other forms of security equipment include closed-circuit television systems, occupancy sensors, elevator key controls limiting guest floor access, exit alarms on fire exits, and chains on guestroom doors. Some elements of the building lighting system are major contributors to property security as well.

The engineering department plays an important role in the security of a property. In coordination with the security department or function, engineering maintains the security devices and systems on the property. Engineering should give high priority to any security or life-safety systems or devices in need of repair, maintenance, or replacement. In establishments where work orders are issued, the overprint "SECURITY PRIORITY" in red ink or security work orders printed on colored paper can be used to highlight urgency. Whenever a failure in the security systems or devices is detected, a work order form should be completed and immediately sent to the proper person for authorization and action. A copy of the work order form should also be provided to the security office for follow-up.

Telephone Systems

Guests use telephones to place personal and business calls to locations within the property and off the premises. Employees often require telephones in the performance of their daily duties. Also, both guests and employees may need to communicate with computers at external locations (for example, an employee transmitting reservation information from property to property or a guest transmitting the most recent sales figures to the district sales director).

To provide for all its anticipated phone needs, the entire property is wired with telephone cable to connect the individual telephone hand sets and any computer interface devices (that is, modems) with a central console within the property (see Exhibit 3.10). This central console is then connected to the local telephone company's central office by trunk lines for local and long distance calls.

There are two different categories of phone lines within the system: switched and dedicated. Ordinary calls from one phone to another require the switching (that is, connection) of the appropriate sets of wires and trunks in the central console. When the call is finished, the lines are disconnected to allow for use by other callers. Some situations, however, require dedicated lines which provide constant connection between the sender and receiver. Examples of these are lines for reservations, credit authorizations, the computer at headquarters, fire alarms, and telex.

If a property wishes to charge its guests for long distance and/or local calls, the property must have equipment and procedures that monitor the guests' phone use. These can be as simple as a call back from the long distance operator with time and charges when the call is complete or as sophisticated as a call accounting system (CAS) that automatically routes the long distance call in the most cost-effective way and posts charges for the call to the guest's account.

Vertical Transportation Systems

Vertical transportation systems convey people and material vertically in buildings with adequate safety protection against falling. The need for vertical transportation is as obvious as it is essential in a high-rise building, but even a two-story property needs a service elevator for efficient operation. At any given time, guests need access to their rooms; large numbers of guests may simultaneously depart a second-floor ballroom heading for the lobby; the housekeeping staff needs linen in the guestrooms from the laundry; the room service staff must deliver meals from the kitchen to the guests; and fresh food and canned goods must be transported from receiving to the kitchen.

Exhibit 3.10 Schematic of a Lodging Property Telephone System

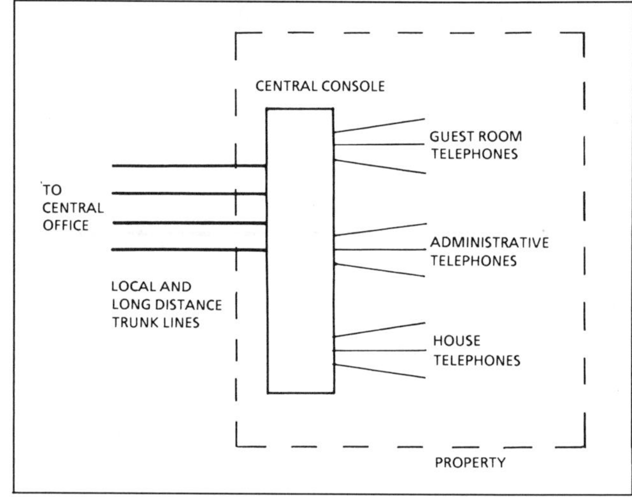

There are three groups of vertical transportation systems: escalators, elevators, and dumbwaiters. The decision on which of these is most appropriate for a specific application depends on the necessary height of transport, the volume of traffic, and whether or not people will be riding on the equipment. Escalators are used where large numbers of people want to go up or down only one or two floors. The most common application is from function floors to the lobby or to other function floors in properties with substantial meeting facilities. Elevators are installed where the volume of people traffic is small, and may be used in any building with more than one floor. Dumbwaiters are devices that are not permitted to transport people, so their application is limited to the movement of material (for example, meals in a kitchen, soiled dishes, and garbage), usually from one floor to another.

A high-rise convention hotel with a roof-top restaurant requires the most complex systems. The guests ride to their rooms on elevators which are selected for excellent ride characteristics and rapid response times to requests from the floors. A separate passenger elevator may be dedicated to the roof-top restaurant for travel to it from the lobby. Service elevators allow the housekeeping and room service staffs to reach the guestrooms from the back of the house. These same service elevators also transport employees and materials to and from the employee entrance and receiving dock. In the convention area of the property, multiple escalators provide the conventioneer with fast access to functions.

Engineering System Design

The design of all the systems installed in the modern lodging establishment requires the services of a number of specialists and input from individuals representing various special interests. A list of the individuals who will participate, directly or indirectly, in the design process for most of the engineering systems discussed in this text would include the building owner/developer, building operator, architects, interior designers, landscape architects, engineers, and special consultants. Consultants whose expertise may be required for some or all of these systems include mechanical engineers, electrical engineers, structural engineers, lighting consultants, acoustical consultants, food service consultants, laundry consultants, elevator consultants, audio-visual specialists, telecommunications consultants, security consultants, code consultants, safety consultants, and a construction manager. Some of these consultant specialties may be a part of the project architect/engineer group. Others will most likely be retained from outside this group specifically for the project.

Each individual involved in the design will bring specific expertise and a group of concerns to this process. The building owner will always be concerned with costs, the various specialists will have an interest in providing the best systems, and the building operator will be concerned with a facility which is easy and cost-effective to operate. Resolving the conflicts and interrelationships among the systems and the people is a major requirement for a successful building. Communication among all those involved in the design process is very important, especially when dealing with those specialists providing services who are not directly connected with the primary building architect or engineer.

In the following discussion, we develop some of the steps and concerns which exist when designing engineering systems. The discussion is not exhaustive. Its purpose is to convey some understanding of important issues in this design process. Whether your role is in the design, development, or management of a hospitality facility, some understanding of concerns in system design should prove helpful in accomplishing your tasks and understanding those of others. Well-designed engineering systems result in facilities which meet or exceed guest expectations and in reasonable maintenance costs. Such systems also produce a working environment for the staff which enhances their productivity, while providing a safe environment for all within the building.

Stages in the System Design Process

There are several steps or stages in the design of building systems. The more quantitative portions of the design process are:

1. Load analysis
2. Preliminary system and equipment selection
3. Annual energy usage estimation
4. Life cycle costing
5. Consideration of equipment interconnections and interactions
6. Final design

While not all the steps are necessarily performed in the design of each system, this list is a reference for the discussion which follows.

For most systems designed by the engineers, the starting point for the system design is a load analysis. A load is a calculated quantity of required capacity or need, sometimes with a factor of time involved—that is, how much over what amount of time. Each system in the building will have the load defined in a different way. For structural elements of the building, the load will be all forces acting upon the structure. This will include the weight of the building itself, its contents, and the effect on the building of such things as wind. Other systems will require different information in order to develop the load. The load analysis is usually a worst-case or peak-load analysis because the system which is installed must be able to meet the highest possible demand which will be placed on it.

The peak load estimate for some systems is derived by subdividing the building into components (for example, guestrooms, public space, kitchen, and so forth) and determining the system requirements for each of these components. The individual requirements are then accumulated to determine some overall peak value, often taking into account other concerns such as the timing of the loads, concurrent needs, or other issues.

Once the peak requirements of the system are known, it is possible to make preliminary system and equipment selections. Due to inherent inefficiencies and losses in equipment and systems (that is, the usable output is less than what you start with because no machine or system runs at 100% efficiency), it is necessary to consider the additional needs and loads imposed by the equipment itself. For example, the heat produced by fan motors in a building ventilation system must be added to the overall heat to be removed by the HVAC system.

After determination of the peak load, there may be an attempt to determine the annual usage of energy for a particular system. This attempt will consider information about the annual hours of system operation and the fraction of the peak load that the system will use during each hour of system operation.

Following the peak load estimation, equipment selection, and annual energy use calculations, there may be some estimation of life cycle costs for the systems, especially when various options are under consideration for the equipment. This may be followed by negotiation between the owner/developer, engineer, architect, and operator concerning which systems to install. Once these issues are resolved, further design takes into consideration equipment interconnections and interactions. Many pieces of equipment require inputs from other systems and influence the design of these systems. This process can be very involved and may result in repeating part or all of the design process.

At each phase of the design process, each individual involved will apply design criteria representing his or her specific expertise and interests. The engineer must eventually produce a design which is satisfactory to all concerned. This final design is then used to develop specifications for the systems and equipment which will be purchased as well as to develop the mechanical, electrical, structural and other plans for the building itself.

Objective Design Criteria

Some design criteria are relatively objective, meaning they can be expressed in numbers of some type. Some broad categories of objective criteria are initial cost, capacity (equipment or system output), space requirements, and energy consumption. When defining the conditions which major engineering systems are to maintain or supply, it is possible to identify objective design criteria for specific systems. A partial list of the possible objective design criteria which could be established for the types of engineering systems includes:

- Water systems: pressure, temperature, flow rate, and quality
- HVAC systems: interior air conditions (temperature, humidity, quality, quantity, velocity)
- Electrical systems: voltage, frequency, signal purity, number of phases
- Lighting systems: light levels, color rendition
- Refrigeration systems: operating temperatures
- Fire protection systems: water pressure, flow, loudness of alarms

Besides the specific objective criteria, there are many additional items of concern in the design process. These other items may be considered to be historical and/or subjective.

Historical and Subjective Design Criteria

Historical criteria may be objective, but are derived from experience or knowledge concerning systems and equipment. Information relating to expected maintenance, component life, and expected repair (down) time is historical in nature and is generally developed from experience rather than from information in design manuals or supplier expectations.

Subjective criteria are numerous and an all-encompassing list is difficult to develop since individual systems will have unique subjective concerns. A partial list of subjective design criteria for building systems includes appearance, maintainability, reliability, flexibility, fire and smoke control, pollution control, liquid leakage hazards, space suitability, public relations features, additional life safety features, and noise.

Balancing these criteria in the design process can be complex. The architect and the owner will have certain expectations concerning appearance which may not be compatible. When these concerns are matched against the types of systems proposed by the engineer, further differences of opinion may result. For example, the use of through-the-wall HVAC units in guestrooms may not be compatible with the proposed architectural design. Access to building equipment may require modifications in building floor plans or interior design which constrain the interior designer. One of the authors of this text visited a resort property where maintenance access to the guestroom HVAC unit required a virtual disassembly of the bathroom ceiling and lighting system, turning what should have been a 15-minute repair job for one person into nearly an hour-long task for two people.

Codes and Standards

All buildings are subject to numerous regulations which are often grouped under the heading of codes. Some of these codes concern zoning, plumbing, fire, health, electrical systems, the environment, and energy. Each of these regulations imposes restrictions or requirements on the system designer. One type of code is the *specification code,* which is quite specific in what shall or shall not be used—for example, a plumbing code which prohibits the use of plastic piping or an energy code which specifies storm windows. Another type of code is the *performance code,* which specifies the required result but allows the designer latitude in how to achieve this result—for example, an energy code based on energy use per square foot of building area, but with no specific requirements regarding how this usage level is to be achieved. Each aspect of codes will be encountered during both building construction and operation and will require building and system modifications to achieve compliance.

Since the development of codes requires considerable expertise, much consultation with experienced practitioners, and a great deal of time and involvement, code development has been undertaken by a number of industry and technical agencies and societies. The codes developed by these agencies are usually then adopted in whole or in part by the local governmental body. Some of the agencies whose codes are particularly important for the systems discussed in this text and the operation of the engineering department are:

- ANSI—American National Standards Institute
- ARI—Air-Conditioning and Refrigeration Institute
- ASHRAE—American Society of Heating, Refrigerating and Air Conditioning Engineers
- BOCA—Building Officials and Code Administrators International
- NEMA—National Electrical Manufacturers Association
- NFPA—National Fire Protection Association
- NSF—National Sanitation Foundation
- UL—Underwriters Laboratory

Since the codes are usually adopted and enforced at the level of the local governmental body, it is common to hire one or more local code consultants during system design. In the chapters which follow, we will cite several common code requirements when discussing various systems to illustrate the role of codes in system design and operation.

Besides codes and regulations which have the power of law in the community, it is very common for lodging companies to have their own standards for building systems as well. These companies will certainly meet the local codes, but they may go beyond the code in certain areas for which they believe it is important to do so. One example of this could be in the fire code, where many locations do not currently require the installation of sprinklers, but where some lodging companies have mandated their installation in all properties, code or not. Setting standards for building systems can become one of the first steps in the quality assurance process for building systems and the maintenance and engineering department.

System Interactions

So far in this chapter, the building systems have been treated as separate entities for ease of understanding. In fact, they are integrally connected into one system—the building—and they must operate effectively with one another. The first type of interaction is due to the fact that a by-product of the operation of one system must often be considered as a load for a second system. For example, the waste heat generated by the lighting system affects the design of the HVAC system. The second type of interaction occurs when the operation of one system requires the output of another system. For example, a decentralized air conditioning unit in a guestroom requires electricity to operate.

Load Interactions

The interaction of the loads is due to two by-products: waste heat and wastewater. Therefore, the only two major systems that are affected by these loads are the HVAC system and the wastewater system. The HVAC system must accommodate the waste heat generated by the other systems in the building, while the wastewater system must be able to remove the wastewater produced by the other systems.

Heat affecting the HVAC system is discarded from lights, distribution equipment in other systems (fans, pumps), kitchen equipment (broilers, fryers, dishwashers), laundry equipment (washers, dryers), computers, the telephone central console, elevators and escalators, and food service refrigeration systems.

Water which adds to the load of the wastewater systems is discarded from the following:

- Potable and non-potable water systems (which provide water that, except when used for landscaping, evaporated in pools, and so forth, must eventually be removed from the property)
- Cooling water from water-cooled condensers in air conditioning and food service refrigeration units
- Condensate removal from air conditioning and food service refrigeration units

Output Interactions

Two of the major systems in the building exhibit one characteristic that differentiates them from the rest. Almost all of the output of the electrical system and a large portion of the output of the water system are provided to other systems for their use rather than directly to the guests or employees. All systems rely on at least one of these two systems for their operation, and may rely on others as well. For example, the HVAC system relies on the following systems for its operation:

- The electrical system, which operates source equipment (refrigeration systems, heating elements), distribution and delivery equipment (fans, pumps), and control equipment (thermostat, valves)
- The water system, used with humidification equipment, water-cooled refrigeration systems, and evaporative cooling systems such as cooling towers
- The wastewater system, used with water-cooled refrigeration systems and for condensate removal
- The fire protection system, which may signal the HVAC system to go into emergency operation (that is, turning on exhaust fans on fire floors, closing off ventilation ducts to non-fire floors, and so forth)

The lighting system relies on the electrical system to power the lights and various controls (such as photoelectric sensors). The water and wastewater systems rely on the electrical system to power source equipment (for example, water heaters), distribution equipment (such as pumps), and various controls. The fire protection system relies on electrical controls and on the water system as a source for an extinguishing agent. The vertical transportation, telephone, and security systems rely on electricity for production and control. In addition, the fire protection system may signal for emergency operation of elevators.

These interactions demonstrate how interconnected the operations of the building systems really are. Separated, they are ineffectual. Together, they are the building.

Notes

1. This figure is derived from information presented in Mazzucchi, R. P., "The Project on Restaurant Energy Performance End-Use Monitoring and Analysis" in *Energy Use in Commercial Buildings: Measurements and Models*, Annual Meeting of American Society of Heating, Refrigerating, and Air-conditioning Engineers, Portland, Ore., June 1986, p. 21 and in *Summary Report of Energy Usage/Consumption Analysis for Six Hotels/Motels* (New York: Hospitality, Lodging and Travel Research Foundation, Inc., 1981), p. IV-43.

4

Water and Wastewater Systems

Water Usage and Sources

Water is used at all lodging establishments for bathing and sanitary purposes in guestrooms, for drinking, and for cleaning activities in and about the facility. In addition, water may be used for sanitizing purposes and cooking in restaurants, for cleaning in laundry operations, for recreational purposes such as in pools, and as a cooling medium for various pieces of equipment. Most of the water "used" at the property is disposed of through the sewage system at the property. Exceptions to this are the makeup water used in cooling towers and swimming pools and the water used on the grounds of a property to water lawns and shrubs.

The American Hotel & Motel Association (AH&MA) surveys water usage in properties to provide some information regarding basic water consumption rates. Exhibit 4.1 indicates the variation in water use by size of property, showing a tendency toward somewhat higher water use per occupied room as the property size increases.

The AH&MA Technical Services Center offers the following guidelines for water usage at various types of properties:[1]

- Transient Budget Property—This type of property is composed primarily of guestrooms, with a laundry, but no pool or restaurant. The use of 60 to 100 gallons per guest per day represents a range of excellent to acceptable.
- Transient Property—Here, a laundry and swimming pool are common, but a restaurant is not. The excellent to acceptable range of water per guest per day is 75 to 130 gallons.
- Convention/Resort Property—This type of property has laundry, pool, restaurants, landscaping, and a high ratio of public to guest space. The excellent to acceptable daily rate would be 120 to 200 gallons per guest.

An important subcategory of water usage is hot water usage, which costs the property not only for the water but also for the energy used to heat the water. Depending on the fuel source used for water heating, the cost of the heat can range from 4 to 20 times the cost of the water itself.

The Technical Services Center of AH&MA has collected some data on domestic hot water consumption. Exhibit 4.2 illustrates the collected data for summer and winter periods. Note that there is a rather large variation in the usage of hot water as a function of the number of guests, especially for the Woodstock property. There is a significant variation among properties in their hot water usage and a slight seasonal variation as well.

Some variations in hot water consumption are due to site geographic circumstances, while other variations can be attributed to the operating temperature selected for the hot water supply system. Sites with a cold supply water

Exhibit 4.1 Average Water Use per Occupied Room—By Property Size

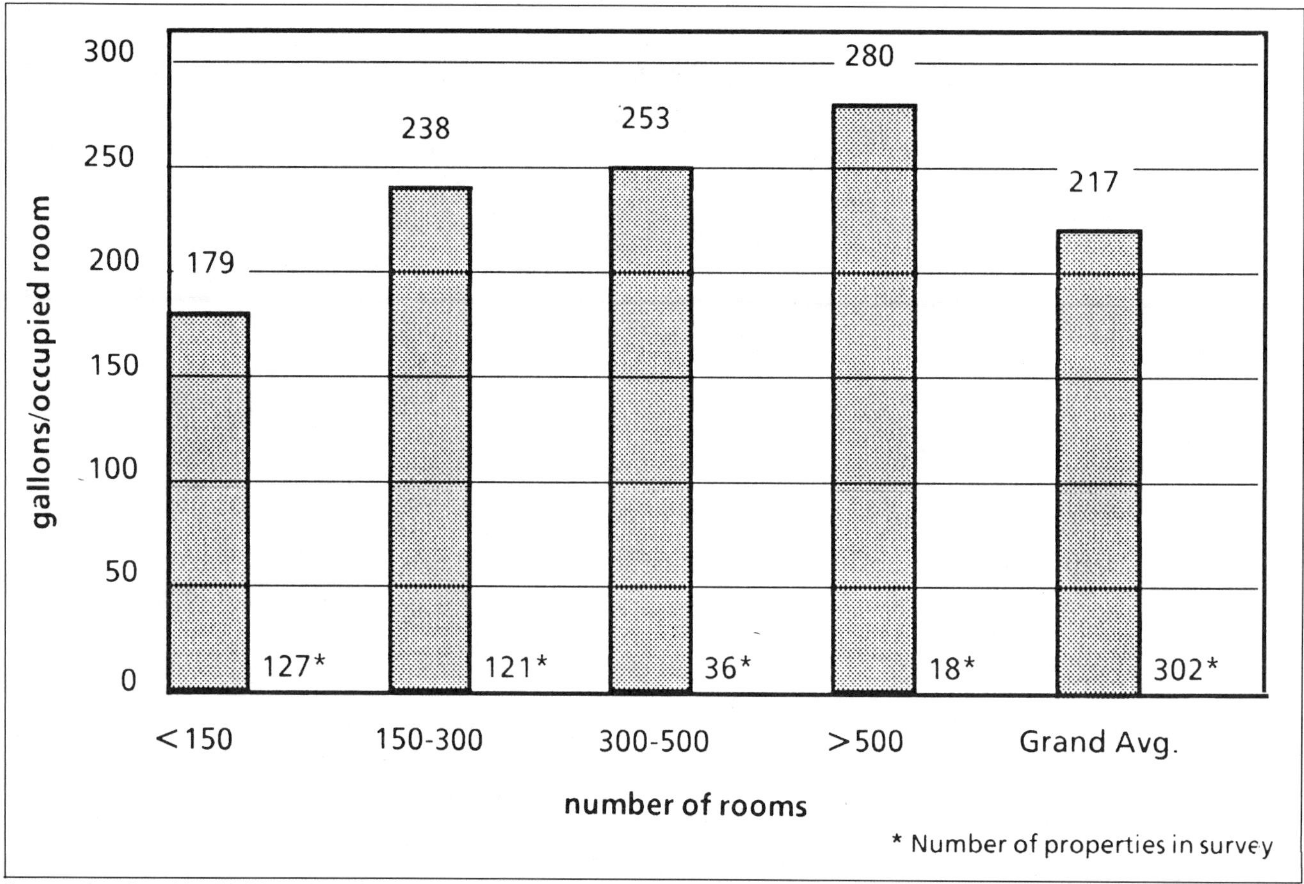

Source: American Hotel & Motel Association, Technical Services Center, The Hospitality, Lodging & Travel Research Foundation, Inc., *Survey of Energy and Water Use in Hotels and Motels—1984* (New York: American Hotel & Motel Association, 1985).

temperature or relatively low hot water temperature are likely to use somewhat greater amounts of hot water than sites with warmer hot water and supply water temperatures. Further variations in property hot water consumption can be due to the type of shower head installed and the presence of onsite laundry and food service facilities.

Purchased Water Sources

Most hospitality properties purchase water from a local water utility. This utility may use a well, lake, stream, river, or reservoir as its actual water source. The utility will typically remove suspended solids via coagulation, sedimentation, and/or filtration and disinfect the water supply by chlorination. This water is then delivered to the property through underground pipes. The quantity of water used by the property is metered at the point the utility pipe merges with the property water system.

It is common practice for the local water utility to meter consumption of potable water (either in cubic feet or in gallons) and to base both the water and sewage billing on the quantity of potable water consumed. Due to the large quantities of water being recorded by the meter, it is common practice to register usage in hundreds of cubic feet or gallons. Actual consumption may be shown directly on the meter dial in the correct units or the meter may have a constant which needs to be applied to the meter reading in order to reach the actual level of consumption.

Rates for potable water vary widely. One source cites a typical price range of $.50 to $4.50 per 1,000 gallons, with values as high as $28.00 per 1,000 gallons possible in locations where desalination plants are used.[2] Rates for sewage

Exhibit 4.2 Daily Domestic Hot Water Usage Per Guest

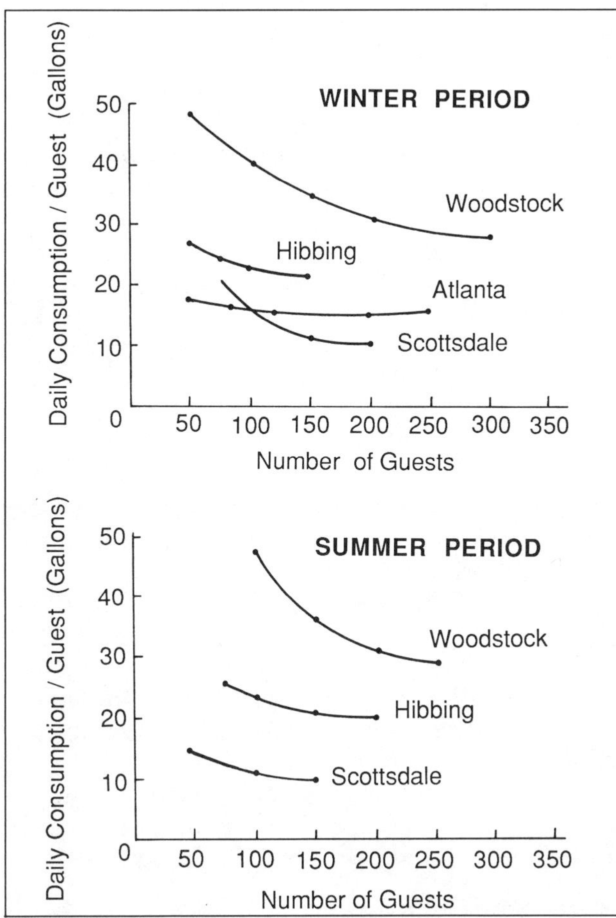

Source: The American Hotel & Motel Association, The Hospitality, Lodging & Travel Research Foundation, Inc., *Summary Report of Energy Usage/Consumption Analysis For Six Hotels/Motels* (New York: American Hotel & Motel Association, 1981).

may depend somewhat on the overall characteristics of the discharge (temperature, grease content, and so forth). Rates ranging from $.20 to $1.20 per 1000 gallons can be found across the United States.

In 1985, United States lodging properties averaged approximately $110 per available room per year for water and sewage[3] (meaning a 400-room hotel could have an annual water and sewage bill of $44,000). Based on the consumption data in Exhibit 4.1, a 400-room property operating at 70% occupancy could have an annual water consumption of about 26 *million* gallons. Larger properties may spend 7%–8% of their energy budget for water and sewage costs. Smaller motel properties may spend up to 15% of their energy budget on water and sewage.

Since water which is used in the swimming pools and cooling towers and for grounds irrigation does not enter the sewer system, it may be desirable to install submeters (sometimes called deduct meters) on the supply lines for such applications and negotiate an appropriate credit from the local utility. In a warm weather location, the cooling tower and irrigation water consumption at a resort property may account for 30%–40% of total water needs, offering the potential for significant reductions in sewage charges through submetering.

Produced Onsite

Onsite water production may be required at island resorts and other remote locations. Depending on the quality of the water source, various levels of treatment may be required. At an island location surrounded by saltwater, the only reliable option may be desalination using either distillation or reverse osmosis. This source may be supplemented with deliveries of water from ocean-going tankers and by the capture of rainwater.

Properties at other remote locations may rely on wells, streams, or lakes as their water source. Various levels of treatment may be required to ensure both potability and cleanliness. All water produced onsite should probably be chlorinated to reduce the possibility of disease transmission.

When onsite water production is necessary, the reuse of water (sometimes called gray water reuse) should be considered, especially when a costly method such as reverse osmosis is used. Relatively clean wastewater, such as that produced from certain laundry cycles and the effluent from wastewater treatment systems, can be used to supply needs for landscape watering and similar non-potable uses. These wastewater flows become, in effect, water sources reducing overall water needs. Depending on the cost and scarcity of water, further gray water reuse may be considered.

Water Quality Problems and Treatment Methods

Water quality refers to the bacteriological cleanliness of the water, the guests' perceptions of the water (color, odor, taste, clearness, and so forth), and the effect of the water on the operation of equipment. For the property operating its own water supply system, water quality and treatment are obviously of constant concern. However, the property purchasing water from a community supply system is not immune from the need to treat its water and to oversee its quality. The engineer is concerned with the quality of water as it relates both to the needs of the guest and to the effective operation of all the property's equipment.

From 1971 to 1980, there were 121 documented cases of waterborne disease in community water systems and another 157 cases in non-community systems (such as those installed at institutions, camps, parks, and some motels).[4] In both types of systems, the major contributors to the outbreaks were deficiencies in treatment and the use of untreated groundwater. The hotel or motel engineer given the responsibility of operating a water supply system must conscientiously uphold high standards if the quality of the supply is to be maintained.

Besides pollution- or contamination-caused health problems (which sometimes can be prevented through chlorination with sodium hypochlorite or chlorine gas), there are other problems which can have an adverse effect on the perceived quality and overall operation of the property. Water quality problems which may affect lodging operations include hardness, taste and odor, color, turbidity, and corrosion. These water quality problems can be treated at the property level if they are not handled by the utility company.[5] Data from a survey of water utilities indicates that utility control of turbidity is in general probably satisfactory, but that iron and manganese concentrations are frequently high.[6] Over-chlorination of the drinking water supply is also likely to be encountered, resulting in taste and odor concerns. If questions arise concerning the water quality at a property, water samples may be sent to a test lab for analysis.

Hardness

Caused by high concentrations of dissolved minerals and/or salts, hardness can reduce linen life, require the use of additional detergents in laundry operations, cause scaling in steam boilers (and possibly in hot water boilers), and result in potential guest dissatisfaction when bathing (due to soap scum and difficulty in soap lathering). Hardness in a water supply will make housekeeping functions more difficult by increasing the probability of soap scum buildup on bathroom fixtures and spotting on walls, mirrors, and chrome.

Hardness is a common problem with a relatively simple solution. The cation (positively charged ion) exchange method used for softening replaces the Ca^{2+} (calcium) or Mg^{2+} (magnesium) ions in the hard water with Na^{+} (sodium) ions. The exchange takes place when the hard water passes through a material known as a zeolite (which we will denote by a Z). For calcium, the process may be represented by the chemical equation

$$Ca^{2+} + 2\,NaZ \rightleftharpoons CaZ_2 + 2\,Na^{+}$$

After the zeolite column has been in use for some time, its ability to remove the calcium or magnesium is reduced. When this occurs, it is necessary to flush the zeolite, usually with a strong solution of sodium chloride (salt). The high concentration of sodium forces the reaction in the opposite direction and restores the ability of the zeolite to remove calcium or magnesium salts. Water softened by this method should not be used for drinking since the high sodium levels which result are not desirable, especially for people on low salt diets.

Taste and Odor

Taste and odor problems are generally caused by the presence of organic material or hydrogen sulfide in the water. Such problems may be present in any water supply. The taste of beverages (especially coffee and tea) can be affected by these problems. Guests may perceive the taste and odor problems to be due to pollution, which is usually not the case.

Hydrogen sulfide also causes corrosion of iron and other metals and stains fixtures. This gas may be removed by chlorination followed by filtered removal of the sulfur particles which precipitate. If smaller amounts of hydrogen sulfide are present, an iron removal filter may suffice. Very low levels of hydrogen sulfide and most other tastes and odors can generally be effectively removed with activated carbon filters.

Color

The color of the water supply can be affected by the presence of iron or manganese in the water supply. If these minerals are present, there will be staining of linens and bathroom fixtures. The use of chlorine bleach will accentuate the problems with linens.

Color problems due to iron and manganese can be solved by several methods. When low to moderate amounts of these materials are present, an ion exchange water softener will remove them from the water. However, if the iron or manganese is precipitated, it may clog the softener, requiring periodic cleaning or the use of additives with the regeneration salt. If the iron and manganese concentration is too high, if much of the iron is already precipitated, or if only iron removal is desired, iron removal filters may be used. These filters oxidize dissolved iron or manganese to an insoluble state and remove the precipitate. The filters are backwashed periodically to flush the accumulated deposits and regenerated with potassium permanganate to restore their oxidizing power.

If the iron and manganese problems are associated with organic matter, if iron or manganese bacteria are present, or if the concentration is exceptionally high, chemical treatment using a solution of household bleach may be used. This treatment would then be followed by carbon filtering to remove the precipitate and eliminate the chlorine taste and odor. Another method for treating water with high iron and manganese levels is the use of food-grade polyphosphate compounds. These compounds cause the iron and manganese ions to stay in solution, reducing staining and deposits in pipes and water-using equipment.

Turbidity

Turbid water contains suspended solids and is cloudy or murky, which can negatively influence perceptions of quality. In addition, water heaters may collect the suspended solids and filters may clog on some pieces of equipment. The collected material may occasionally break free, resulting in quite significant short-term turbidity problems. Turbidity may be treated with filtration.

Corrosion

Acidity due to entrained oxygen or carbon dioxide in some water supplies may accelerate the corrosion of piping and water-using equipment. The result will be higher maintenance costs and possibly early replacement of the equipment.

Corrosion can be treated once its cause is determined. If the prime cause of corrosion is acidity (a low pH), the treatment is neutralization of the acidity. This may be done by the installation of a neutralizing filter containing materials such as calcite (calcium carbonate) or magnesia (magnesium oxide). Since these filters function as mechanical (particulate) filters as well as chemical filters, backwashing is required. Another treatment method involves mixing a solution of soda ash (sodium carbonate) into the water supply to neutralize the acid.

Potable Water Supply and Distribution

The supply and distribution of potable water within a property will vary depending on the location, size, and physical layout of the building or buildings. In addition, the intended uses will influence the design of the system. The discussion which follows specifically applies to water supplied by a local water utility, but many points also apply to water supplies produced onsite.

Methods of Supply

To improve potential reliability, the supply of water to a building may be provided by more than one supply line from the local utility. The water pressure within the building may rely solely upon the pressure present in the supply pipes or pumps may be used. Storage tanks combined with pumps may also be used to meet the specified quantity and pressure needs.

The water supply from the local utility is usually between 50 and 100 psi (pounds per square inch). Most water usage requirements have pressure needs of 5 to 20 psi. To the extent that the water main pressure from the local utility exceeds these nominal requirements, the excess pressure may be used to move water about the building. This excess pressure usually allows the supply of water to a height of four to six stories. Supplying water to greater heights will require a pumped system.

The supply of water may use either an *upfeed* or *downfeed* method. Upfeed is used when the system relies on the utility main pressure only. For high-rise buildings, an upfeed design may be used with pumps providing the necessary pressure and flow. The flow of water in upfeed systems is from lower levels in the building to upper levels. Downfeed systems use water storage tanks on the roof or top floor of the building which are fed via pipes and pumps from the basement. These tanks then supply water to the floors below. In a high-rise structure, there may be several zones, each served by a tank, and possibly a lower zone which is served by an upfeed system relying on the main pressure.

Exhibit 4.3 illustrates a downfeed design of a water supply system for a moderate high-rise building. This figure illustrates several other features of such a supply system. The suction tank in the basement reduces the instantaneous demand on the water utility, allowing for a smaller service line. The tank also ensures that the building water pump will always have a supply of water. The fire reserve in the storage tank helps to ensure an adequate supply of water for the fire protection system. The vertical hot water flow in the building may rely on natural convection to avoid cool hot water. The individual floors in the building will often have a looped hot water system with circulating pumps to ensure immediate hot water availability in all guestrooms.

There are often at least three identifiable water systems within a building: cold water, hot water, and fire. Separation of these systems is accomplished by separate piping and by check valves (devices which allow water to flow in only one direction). The systems may be further subdivided depending on usage. The cold water system is generally divided into water for consumption and use by people (guestrooms, public spaces, kitchens) and consumption and use by equipment (laundry, grounds, cooling towers, boiler makeup, pools). Hot water of 120°–140°F may be consumed and used by or for people, guestrooms, public spaces, and kitchens. Hot water of 140°–180°F is generally consumed and used by equipment (for example, laundry and dishwashing). The fire system may divide into sprinkler systems and building standpipes and fire hoses.

Water used by equipment may require special treatment due to unique quality needs of the equipment being served. This treatment may render the water non-potable, resulting in the need to avoid the reintroduction of this water into the potable system.

Controls

Control in water systems is accomplished by several devices. Major items of concern are water pressure, flow rate, and contamination. Water pressure is controlled by the installation of pumps (to increase the pressure), expansion tanks (to allow for changes in water volume within the system without causing high pressure or a vacuum to form), and pressure reducing (regulating) valves. Pressure reducing valves may be installed on the building water service as well as on water lines within the building. Contamination (or mixing) of water streams is controlled by backflow preventers and sound piping practices.

The type of pump will vary depending on the application. Relatively inexpensive pumps may be used for circulation of potable water. Pumps to move water from lower floors of the building to upper levels must have high flow rates and operate under high pressures (several hundred psi) and may be relatively expensive. Submersible pumps are installed in wells to pump water out of the well. These may be controlled by pressure or by a float in a tank which activates the pump when the tank level drops below some preset level. Sump pumps are designed to operate based on water level in the sump and cycle to keep the water below some preset level. Pool pumps must be constructed of special materials to resist corrosion by the pool water.

Pressure regulating valves are installed to keep the supply pressure to fixtures and equipment within a range which allows for proper operation. They are a necessity in high-rise buildings where the water pressure at certain locations in the building can exceed 100 psi due to the design of the piping system. Equipment such as dishwashers will also have these devices installed on the water supply line to keep the supply water pressure under about 25 psi under flow conditions (that is, during operation).

Backflow preventers may be installed wherever non-potable water could backflow into the potable water system. Anywhere the potable water system is connected to a piece of equipment or an application where the equipment is capable of creating a pressure greater than that in the supply line, a backflow preventer of some

Exhibit 4.3 Downfeed Design for a High-Rise Building

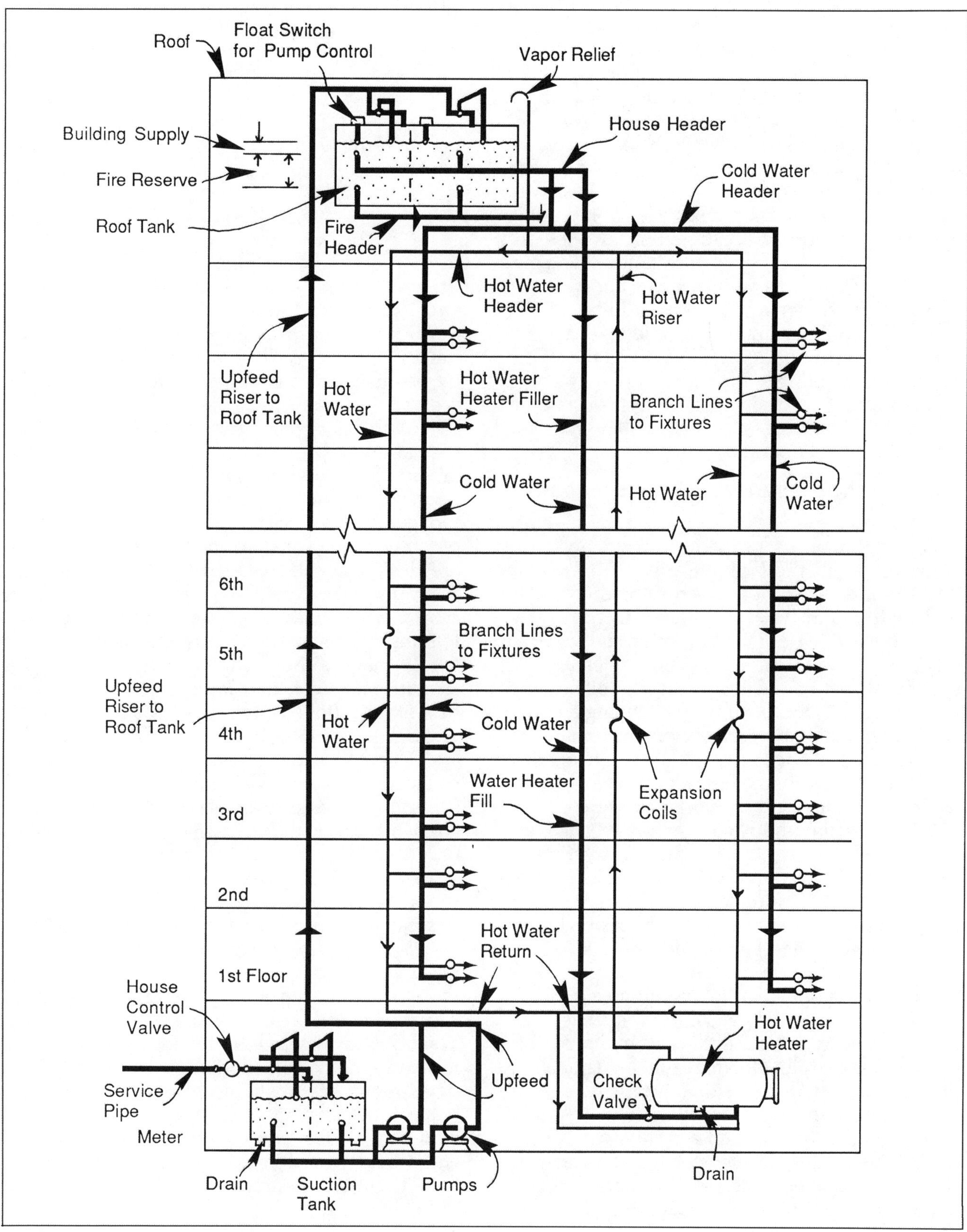

type is needed. In addition, at locations where the water pressure drops suddenly, back siphonage can occur (that is, water next to the pressure drop can be sucked back into the system). Backflow may occur at locations where a pump exists (such as laundry or dishwashing operations) and when makeup water is supplied to boilers or cooling towers. Back siphonage should be guarded against when supply faucets extend below overflow drains, flexible hoses are attached to sinks, and uses for non-potable water are connected upstream from uses for potable water such as in irrigation systems. While check valves can inhibit backflow, a backflow preventer will have the additional feature of an integral drain that relieves the pressure causing the backflow and vents the water which is attempting to flow backwards. The vent line is piped to a drain with an appropriate air gap to avoid backpressure and to allow for easy inspection of its operation.

Repair and Maintenance Considerations

The building water system is a potentially large consumer of property maintenance expenses. Should the building piping deteriorate due to either corrosion or erosion, the cost to replace it would be very high since it is essentially "buried" within the building. The repair of other minor (and more accessible) elements of the water system, such as faucets, toilets, and shower heads, can consume an amazing amount of time and money. Neglect of the repair and maintenance of these items can result in other problems for property interiors due to leaking water and will result in higher utility costs for purchased water and water heating fuel as well.

Since some of the need to repair water systems is directly traceable to problems with water quality, attention to adequate treatment is an essential element of water system preventive maintenance. Prompt repair of any leaking faucets, valves, and pumps is also important if additional problems are to be minimized.

The failure to design or retrofit water systems to eliminate or reduce water hammer (that is, clanging in pipes) can result in damage to piping and valves. Water hammer is caused by the abrupt stopping of rapidly flowing water, such as might occur when a dishwasher's solenoid valve is closed. A water hammer arrester should be installed to absorb the energy present in the moving water, thereby stopping the transfer of this energy to the valves or piping system. Installation of such a device is an example of how a well-designed system can contribute to reduced maintenance costs over the system lifetime and, in this instance, a quieter system operation.

Storm and Sanitary Sewer Systems

All of the water purchased or produced by the property must be disposed of in accordance with local regulations and codes. In addition, rainwater runoff from parking lots and buildings must be provided for. These two needs are met by the installation of sewer systems at the property.

One major characteristic of sewer systems is that almost all flow in such systems relies on gravity. The only locations where pumped flow occurs are where a sewage lift pump is employed, such as a sump pump. The implications of gravity flow are substantial. When systems are designed and installed, it is important that the piping size be adequate. Sewage system piping is generally much larger than water system piping. Some of this increased size is necessary to handle the wastes which may be in the system. However, the slower flow which occurs in a gravity flow system means the pipes must be larger.

The storm sewer system is dedicated to the collection and removal of rainwater. Drains on roofs and in parking areas collect this water and connect with a municipal storm sewer system or, in rural locations, a storm water drainage system. Water collected in a storm sewer system is not subject to treatment and is allowed to flow to some receiving location such as a lake or river.

The sanitary sewer system receives all the wastewater from within the building, collects this water, and pipes it to the municipal sanitary sewer or to the onsite sewage treatment facility. This system may be subdivided into two separate systems. All kitchen equipment capable of developing greasy liquid waste may be connected to a separate piping system which includes a grease interceptor or trap. All other equipment would be connected to another system. These two systems may join at a point after the grease trap.

The grease trap prevents grease from leaving the building and contaminating the sanitary sewer system where it creates maintenance problems and may interfere with the operation of sewage treatment facilities. Periodic cleaning of the grease trap is required if it is to continue to function properly and with an unimpeded flow of wastewater. Such cleaning may be performed by in-house personnel or by an outside firm. In any event, the grease which is removed must be disposed of in a manner consistent with local codes.

Disposal Costs and Regulations

As stated earlier, the cost of sewage disposal is usually based on consumption of potable water. Therefore, one method of reducing the sewage cost is deduct metering of water usage which does not enter the property's sewage system (for example, cooling towers).

Another method of reducing costs is making changes in the waste stream which result in billing at a lower rate. Disposal costs for sewage will vary in some communities depending on the composition of the waste. Among the factors which may influence the charges for sewage levied against commercial buildings, the one most likely to affect a hospitality facility is an additional charge for waste containing grease. Depending on the billing method used, it may be advisable to separate water usage for the kitchen areas from the water system for the rest of the property to avoid having all water usage at the facility assessed at the higher rate.

Most sewage disposal regulations now prohibit the discharge of storm runoff into the sanitary sewer system because of the surges which result in the system. Hospitality properties should therefore separate their storm and sanitary sewer systems. Since storm sewer discharges are not treated, the property should never discharge wastes of any kind into the storm sewers. In addition, the discharge of certain wastes into the sanitary sewer system, such as paints and oils, is often prohibited. These wastes should be disposed of at approved disposal locations, some of which also serve as recycling sites.

Packaged Waste Treatment Systems

Onsite waste treatment may be necessary for locations without access to municipal sewage services. Such locations include restaurants at highway sites, resorts, and some private clubs. The treatment required and the system necessary to perform this treatment will vary from location to location.[7]

For small restaurants or lodging establishments, a simple septic system may be adequate. These systems utilize a septic tank in which nondecomposable solids accumulate and a tile drainage field which distributes wastewater. Periodic pumping of the septic tank is required and the drainage field needs to be replaced every 10 to 15 years. Some sites have poor soil conditions which preclude the effective use of such systems.

Larger restaurants, motels, and resorts will need to install packaged waste treatment plants. These plants process wastewater in order to render it less objectionable and therefore suitable for discharge to a river, lake, ocean, or other location. Treatment consists of two elements: aerating the waste material to oxidize it and settling the solid material present in the oxidized effluent. The plant will probably use significant amounts of electricity during aeration, which involves spraying the sewage water into the air or forcing air through the water. Various levels of treatment will be required, depending upon the local codes. The sewage plant should *always* be located on the leeward side of the property based on the prevailing winds.

Water Heating—Fuel Sources and Equipment

Water heating is of interest to lodging managers for several reasons. First of all, the cost of water heating can be substantial. A 400-room property spending $44,000 per year on water and sewage charges could easily exceed that cost just to heat water. When this relatively large cost concern is combined with the hot water supply problems at some properties, the motivation should be present for managers to develop some understanding of water heating for their facility.

Conventional Water Heating Equipment

Conventional water heating equipment may be either directly fired or indirectly fired. Directly fired equipment (see Exhibit 4.4) uses as a

Exhibit 4.4 Directly Fired Water Heater

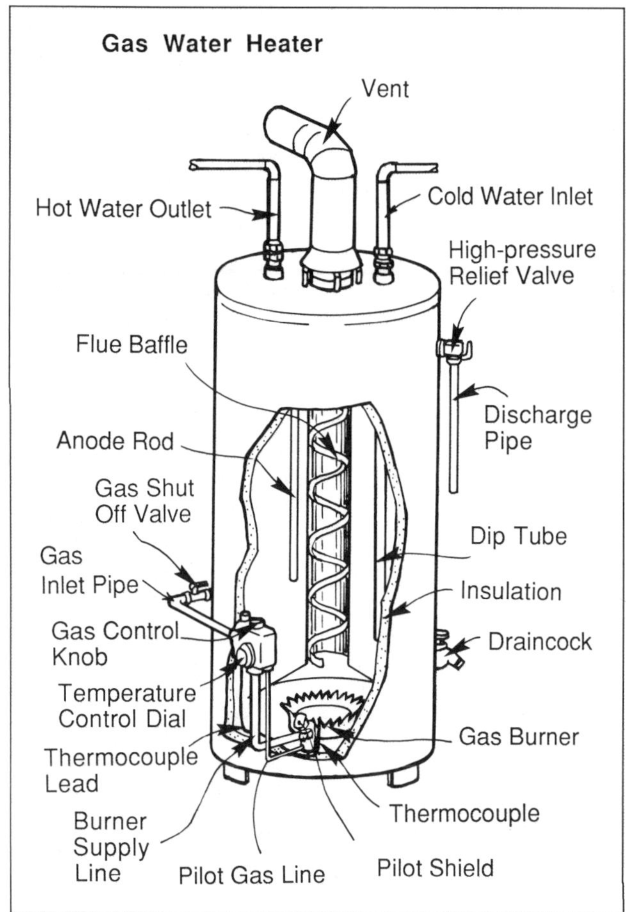

Exhibit 4.5 Indirectly Fired Water Heater

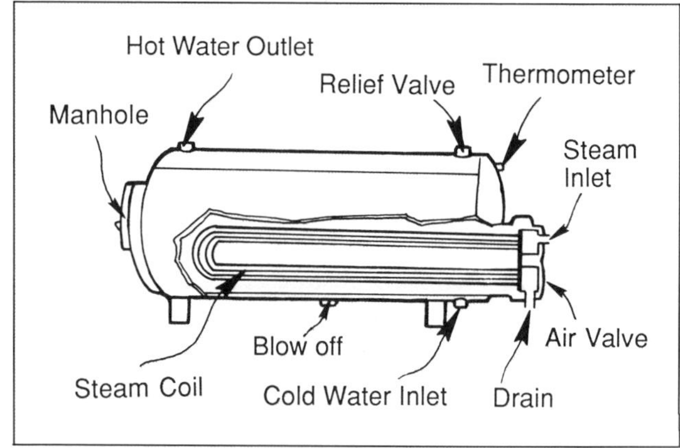

fuel source either oil, natural gas, liquified petroleum gas (LP gas), or electricity. The fuel is burned (or, in the instance of electricity, flows through a heating element) and the resulting heat is transferred to the water. Indirectly fired equipment (see Exhibit 4.5) relies on thermal contact in a heat exchanger between a hot fluid (water or steam) and the water which is to be heated. Water may also be heated by blending, which is direct injection of steam or hot water into the water to be heated.

When water heating equipment is selected, major concerns should be the operating cost of the equipment (basically a function of the fuel cost and efficiency of fuel combustion/heat transfer), the recovery rate (defined as the number of gallons per unit of time which can be raised a fixed temperature difference), and the storage capacity of the equipment.

The operating cost of the equipment (neglecting storage tank standby losses) can be calculated from the following equation:

$$\text{Operating Cost per 1000 gal} = \frac{1\ \text{Btu}}{\text{lb-°F}} \times 1000\ \text{gal} \times \frac{8.34\ \text{lb}}{\text{gal}} \times \Delta\text{T} \times \text{FC} \times \frac{1}{\text{ECF}} \times \frac{1}{\text{EFF}}$$

where *Operating Cost* is the cost of fuel required per 1000 gallons of water delivered from the water heating equipment; ΔT is the temperature rise of the water in Fahrenheit degrees; *FC* is the Fuel Cost per normal unit of purchase (for example, per kwh for electricity); *ECF* is the Energy Content of the Fuel in Btu per normal unit of purchase (for example, 3412 Btu per kwh); and *EFF* is the efficiency of the equipment (Btu of energy transferred to the water in the equipment divided by the Btu of energy contained in the fuel burned in the equipment).

The efficiency of commercial fossil fuel water heating appliances is affected both by the completeness of the combustion process and by the efficiency of heat transfer between the flame and combustion by-products and the water. These water heaters require an adequate supply of, and proper mixing of the fuel with, combustion air. Smaller water heaters installed in restaurants are similar to units purchased for residential usage. These smaller units usually use atmospheric burners. Larger water heating appliances are more likely to have power burners which use a fan to supply the combustion air. Periodic adjustment and cleaning of the burner on water heating equipment helps to maintain optimal combustion efficiency.

Among the most efficient water heating appliances are the instantaneous heaters, which have operating efficiencies in excess of 90%. The instantaneous heaters rely on a very efficient combustion and heat transfer process. These units have essentially no inherent storage, so the standby losses (that is, heat losses from the exterior of a storage tank) from such devices do not exist. These units may supply a load directly (with no additional storage) to, for example, a room or a small group of rooms. The units may also be installed individually or in multiples and connected to a well-insulated storage tank where their high efficiency (but low recovery rate) is integrated with separate storage in order to optimize the overall water heating system. The instantaneous heaters may use electricity or gas.

Heat transfer efficiency for water heating equipment can be affected by the cleanliness of the heat transfer areas on both the heat and water sides. On the heat side, periodic cleaning of soot from the surface may be required, especially for oil-fired units. Since the hot water supply system is not a closed loop system (as are most heating systems), the quality of the water supply is a significant factor in maintaining efficient heat transfer on the water side. Hardness in the supply water can contribute to a significant scale buildup in the water heater.

The recovery rate of a water heating appliance defines the rate at which water can be heated by the appliance. The recovery rate is usually stated in gallons per minute for a specified temperature rise. The temperature rise is typically 90F° for residential appliances and 100F° for commercial equipment.[8] The recovery rate is important when the appliance will be under a sustained demand for hot water. The recovery rate and the storage volume determine the amount of hot water available from the water heating system in any time period. Failure to put together a water heating system with the correct combination of recovery rate and storage volume may result in an inadequate supply of hot water for property needs.

The storage volume may be an integral element of the water heating equipment (as in residential and small commercial water heating equipment) or may be provided by a separate storage tank. The storage volume serves as a buffer between the demands of the load and the recovery capacity of the water heater. Hot water storage allows the installation of a water heater with a lower recovery rate, which generally means a smaller investment both in the water heater and in the utility service necessary to supply the fuel.

When either an indirect method of water heating (a steam-to-water or water-to-water heat exchanger) or blending is used, the efficiency of the overall water heating system will depend primarily upon the efficiency of the boiler producing the steam or hot water. Indirect methods may be chosen when production of hot water is desired at a site remote from the fuel source (such as on an upper floor). An indirect water heating system using steam is capable of providing about 1,000 Btu of energy to the water for each pound of steam used in the system. The capacity of an indirect water heating system using a hot water source varies, depending on the temperature of the hot water source.

Blending (or direct injection methods of water heating) results in the need to produce potentially significant quantities of makeup water for the boiler. For this reason, its usage in the hospitality industry is usually somewhat limited. Some dishwashers have steam injected into the wash water for heating. If a direct injection water heating method is used, careful selection of the water treatment chemicals used in the boiler system is particularly important. Some chemicals used in the treatment of boiler water are not suitable for use in potable water supplies. Before using direct injection water heating equipment, it is advisable to check with the supplier of your boiler water treatment chemicals to determine whether the chemicals are compatible with such usage.

Heat Pump Water Heaters

The heat pump water heater (HPWH) is a relatively recent entry into the water heating equipment market. The HPWH is generally an air source heat pump which has a water-cooled condenser. Water source devices are also available. The water is heated in the water-cooled condenser. A water temperature of up to 140°F can be obtained with these units. Exhibit 4.6 is a schematic for a typical HPWH installation.

The air source HPWH uses as its heat source either outside air or the air within the building.

Exhibit 4.6 Schematic of a Typical Heat Pump Water Heater Installation

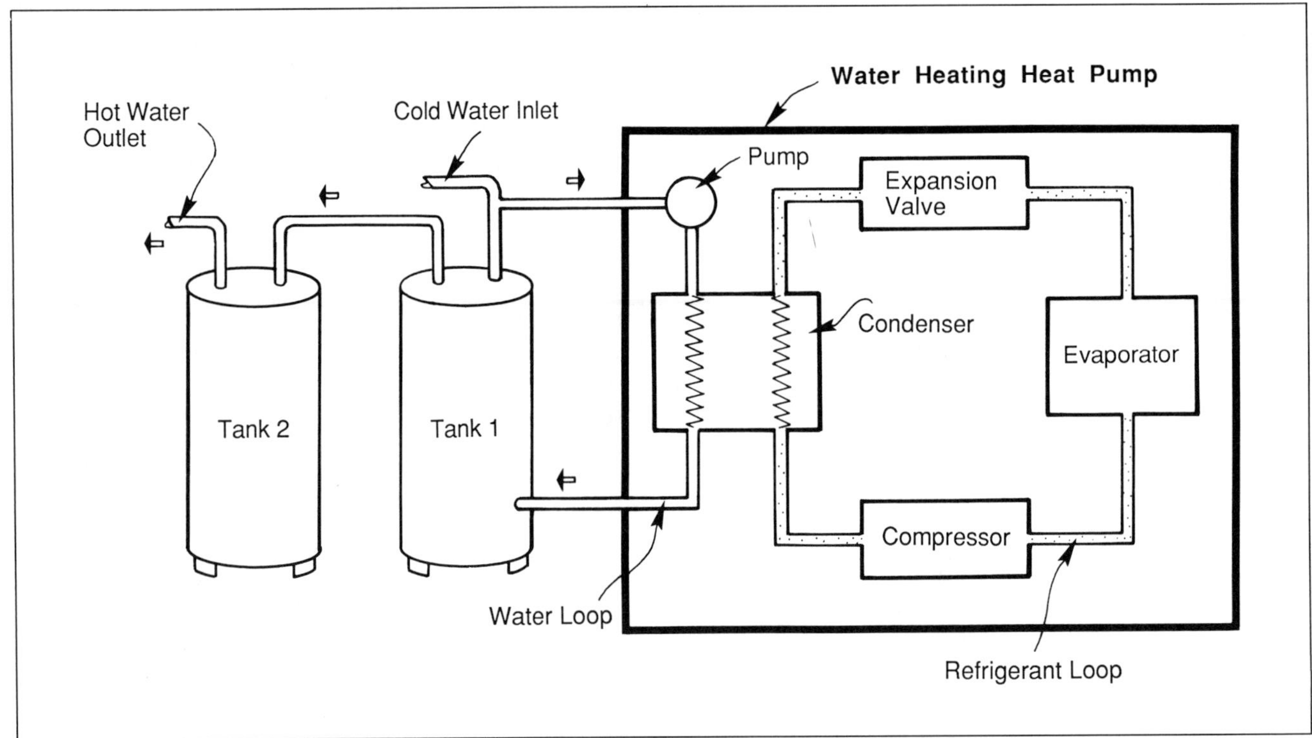

The water source units may use well water or the return chilled water line in the building. The efficiency (*coefficient of performance* or *COP*[9]) of an HPWH is higher with higher temperature heat sources. Therefore, the operation of an HPWH using outside air sources will be most effective in areas where the average ambient air temperature is high. However, since such locations will usually also have a significant need for space cooling, the HPWH is often located within the building using the interior air as the heat source. In this way, the cooling of the air resulting from the removal of heat by the heat pump water heater will reduce the load on the space cooling equipment. Besides the heat removed from the air in the process of changing its temperature, the HPWH also removes latent heat (moisture) from the air. For this reason, the HPWH must usually be installed with a condensate drain line to allow for the removal of the water condensed during latent heat removal.

The HPWH can provide a cost-effective alternative to electric resistance water heating and may be a less costly method of water heating than fossil fuel under some circumstances. When operated with a 75°F air source, one brand of HPWH can operate with a COP of 2.7 when heating water from 55° to 135°F. This unit would have an operating cost which is 37% (1/2.7) that of an electric resistance water heater (which has a COP of approximately 1.0)—a potentially significant savings.

Most commercial HPWHs must be connected to separate water storage tanks since the HPWH does not generally have an integral storage tank. This lack of an integral storage tank allows the HPWH to be more readily installed in locations where either cooling is needed (such as a laundry or kitchen) or where waste heat is available (such as a boiler or compressor room).

Several companies offer HPWHs which can heat swimming pool or spa water. These units offer the added benefit of reducing the humidity in the vicinity of indoor pools if the HPWH uses the pool area air as a heat source. This reduced humidity can reduce maintenance costs in the pool area and contribute to comfort. The use of an HPWH in a pool area as a means of humidity

Exhibit 4.7 Lodging Industry Waste Heat Recovery Potential

	Energy Consumed by Air Conditioning (10^9 Btu/yr)[a]	Energy Consumed for Water Heating (10^9 Btu/yr)[b]	Recoverable Energy Using WHR (10^9 Btu/yr)[cd]	Occupancy (percent)[e]
Alabama	213	204	107	65
Florida	2,177	1,647	1,090	80
Georgia	305	346	153	65
Kentucky	192	228	96	65
Louisiana	265	224	133	65
Mississippi	145	156	73	65
North Carolina	421	500	211	65
South Carolina	231	261	116	65
Tennessee	300	356	150	65
Southeast	4,249	3,922	2,129	67
Nation	15,030	17,846	7,526	65

[a]Air conditioning is based on 1 ton per room and 0.25 diversity (site visits)
[b]Assumes 50 gal/day of 140°F water for each occupied room (R.H. Perry)
[c]Assumes 50% of air conditioning is with window units; these were neglected because applying waste heat recovery is difficult. Assumes remaining 50% air conditioning is well suited for waste heat recovery. Assumes R-12 systems, EER = 8.0, negligible absorption units (interviews with managers)
[d]Assumes refrigeration is negligible (site visits)
[e]U.S. Fact Book, 1978

control instead of venting the pool area can also significantly reduce the cost of air heating in the pool area during the winter months.

Heat Recovery Water Heating

An HPWH often capitalizes on the fact that refrigeration equipment rejects a substantial amount of heat which can potentially be recovered and used. Existing refrigeration equipment can also be retrofitted for heat recovery. This heat recovery can supply a substantial portion of the water heating needs of a lodging facility. Two options which will generally reduce costs and require a minimal amount of maintenance are refrigeration heat recovery and laundry wastewater heat recovery.

The operation of any refrigeration cycle requires that significant quantities of heat be rejected from the refrigeration system. This heat rejection occurs in the condenser where the heat is rejected to either air or water, depending on the design of the equipment. If the heat rejection is to water, the water is usually then circulated to a cooling tower where the heat is removed by evaporation. All heat rejection methods cost the property not only the operating cost associated with the methods, but also the loss of potentially usable energy. Refrigeration heat recovery for water heating recovers and uses a significant fraction of the rejected heat.

Studies conducted for the U.S. Department of Energy have identified the lodging and restaurant industries as possessing a significant potential for the use of refrigeration waste heat recovery for water heating.[10] This potential exists in those properties which have centralized cooling equipment and a centralized building hot water supply system. Exhibit 4.7 indicates the potential for hotels and motels in nine southeastern states and a nationwide estimate. The payback period for waste heat recovery equipment in the lodging and restaurant sectors was estimated at less than three years. If the nationwide potential were achieved in U.S. lodging markets, the dollar savings would amount to $45 million (at a conservative estimate of $6 per million Btu).

Restaurants and lodging properties were identified as having "extensive" uses for recovered heat and an "excellent" potential for the integration of the heat recovery option into their operations. "A serious barrier to the implementation of refrigerant heat recovery is the lack of knowledge of this very valuable technology among management personnel. Most are familiar with similar technologies, such as solar energy conversion, but do not understand the inner workings of the refrigeration cycle sufficiently to see the benefits of heat recovery."[11] Application 4.3 at the end of this chapter provides a more detailed discussion of refrigeration heat recovery devices and their operation and economics.

Properties with an onsite laundry have the opportunity to significantly reduce the cost of water heating for the laundry by recovering heat from the laundry wastewater to preheat the incoming water. The incoming water can typically be heated to within 10–15F° of the exit water. Installation of such a system involves some of the same considerations as refrigeration heat recovery, especially timing of the needs for hot water and sizing of storage tanks. Payback periods on laundry wastewater heat recovery are typically three years or less.

Solar Water Heating

Using solar energy has emerged as a possible method of providing both space and water heating. Since solar equipment is capital intensive, the use of solar energy for water heating—a year-round load—is probably the most practical application. Solar water heating systems are generally installed to serve as pre-heaters for the service hot water with the fossil or electric water heater serving in either a topping or backup mode.

Exhibit 4.8 shows the key components and basic configuration of a typical solar water heating system. The solar collectors are the most visible component of the system. When the pump controller senses that the collectors are warmer than the storage tank by some preset amount, the pump is activated and the heat is removed from the collectors and transferred to the water in the storage tank. While some systems attempt to heat water directly in the collectors, most commercial systems use some sort of heat transfer fluid in the collectors and transfer the heat to the water to be heated through a heat exchanger. The most common heat transfer fluid is a mixture of antifreeze and water, although distilled water and various heat transfer oils may be used as well. The volume of the storage is determined by the collector area and the daily water load. Storage of 1 to 1.5 gallons per square foot of collector area is typical.

The amount of solar energy delivered from a solar water heating system will depend primarily on the efficiency of the solar collectors, heat losses from the piping and storage tanks, the collector area, the size of the storage tanks, and the amount of solar energy available at the site. The expected performance of solar water heating systems in various climates can be estimated using data from the Solar Rating Certification Corporation (SRCC).[12] In addition, the suppliers of solar energy equipment should be able to provide an estimate of a system's performance using one of the commonly used computer programs developed for this purpose.

Exhibit 4.8 Basic Configuration of an Antifreeze-Based Solar Water Heating System

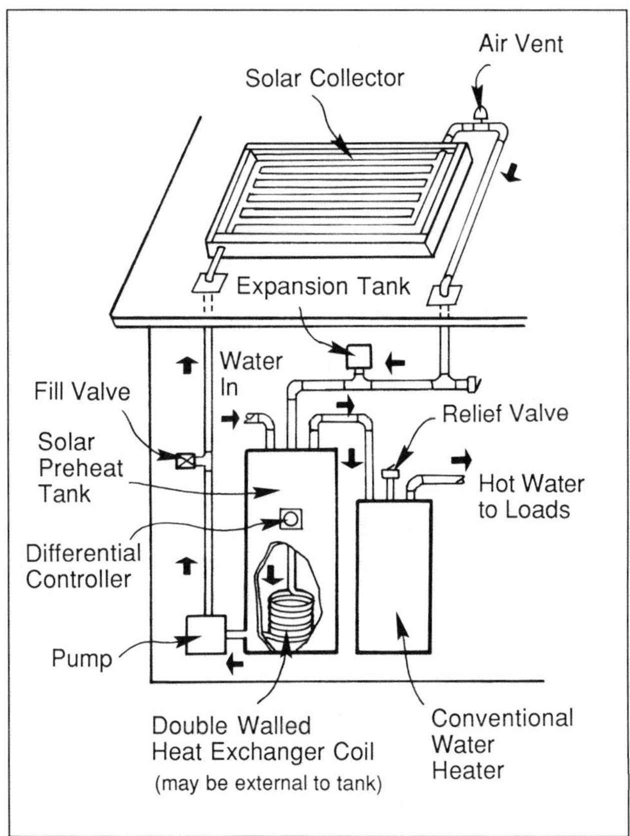

Controls

Water heating systems use controls and safety devices to limit the pressure in water heaters and at usage points, control the water temperature, reduce the potential for back siphonage of contaminated water into the potable water system, and reduce the possibility of a vacuum forming in the system during cooling of the heated water. The actual installation of any water heating device should follow the recommendations of the manufacturer and the local building codes. The American Society of Mechanical Engineers (ASME)[13] and the National Fire Protection Association (NFPA)[14] have codes and standards which have special significance in water heating applications. The National Sanitation Foundation has a standard for hot water supplies to dishwashing machines.[15] Local health codes and OSHA regulations must also be adhered to.

Since the heating of water results in an expansion of its volume, it is important that an upper limit be placed on the pressure of a water heating storage tank. A pressure release valve is usually installed to limit the pressure in the tank. This valve should be provided with adequate vent piping to direct discharge hot water to a drain. Periodic testing of this valve is necessary.

Water temperature can be controlled both at the water heating appliance and near the user. At the water heating appliance, a spillage temperature release valve can be used to vent water or steam from the tank when the temperature exceeds a preset value (typically 210°F). Another form of temperature control discontinues the supply of fuel to the burner or electricity to the element when a temperature set by the user is reached. This is the primary method used to control the burner operation. Manufacturers may build redundancy into the appliance by installing an additional high limit control which will discontinue the fuel supply when the high limit set by the manufacturer (in accordance with the physical limits of the system design) is reached. Nearer to the user, the control generally consists of a mixing valve set to maintain a fixed discharge water temperature—for example, a mixing valve on the guestroom hot water line that lowers the guestroom hot water temperature to 115°F while maintaining the main circulating water line at 140°F.

Backflow preventers (discussed earlier) may also prevent the loss of hot water from the water heater by backflow through the cold water inlet—a situation which is more likely when a building plumbing system has had several modifications over the years.

Repair and Maintenance Considerations

The water heating system is generally a once-through system, with heated water exiting the system at various usage points. As the quantity of water moving through the system increases, so does the possibility of scale buildup on the heat transfer coils of the heating appliance. Softening of water supplies is often needed, especially for the water needs of laundries or ware washing. Periodic de-liming of the water heater or chemical cleaning of heat transfer surfaces may be required. An exhaust stack thermometer can provide a clue to the need for cleaning. If the stack temperature during operation is recorded, the need for cleaning can be identified by an increase in the stack temperature (signaling decreased heat transfer from the fuel to the water). Another obvious sign of decreased heat transfer is an inability to supply the load as equipment ages.

Pressure relief valves are among the most important and often most neglected items of a repair and maintenance program. Failure of these valves to perform, installation of the wrong valve, or blockage of the valve discharge can result (and has resulted) in the explosion of water heaters, causing significant property damage and injury and death to employees and guests. A property maintenance program should include the periodic checking of these valves and the replacement of valves which have failed. In addition, the piping system should be checked following any work near the water heater to ensure that the valve has not been bypassed or otherwise made inoperable.

Directly fired water heaters will require draining at regular intervals and after they are chemically cleaned. Deposits of dirt and minerals will build up at the bottom of water heater tanks and should be removed. Removal will help to ensure that the hot water supply is maintained at a high quality and that the heat transfer from the fuel source to the water occurs efficiently.

Hot water valves are more likely to require repair than cold water valves. When water systems are in electrical contact with metals different from the water system piping, corrosion can occur. This problem is accelerated by higher temperatures. In water heaters, corrosion protection is sometimes provided by the use of a sacrificial anode, usually made of magnesium or another anodic metal, immersed in the tank. This active metal reduces the corrosion of other metallic components. Periodic inspection and replacement of this anode is required. Corrosion problems can be severe in municipal water systems, depending on the source. Boston, for example, has water which is relatively acidic and soft and, consequently, corrosive to piping. Under such circumstances, increasing the alkalinity of the property hot water supply through chemical treatment could result in decreased requirements for piping system maintenance—a good example of preventive maintenance.

In locations where a fossil fuel water heater is used, the possible production of carbon monoxide is a concern. Carbon monoxide will form if the water heater is not supplied with a sufficient amount of oxygen and/or the exhaust gases are not completely removed from the space. Ensuring that the water heater is supplied with an adequate supply of oxygen is a key element in the proper operation of this equipment. Carbon monoxide monitoring equipment is relatively inexpensive and should be considered when the water heating appliance is near an area frequented by employees or guests.

Applications

4.1 Ice Machines and Water Quality Problems

The water quality problems encountered in ice machines include sediment, lime scale, cloudy or "milky" ice, and objectionable odor and taste. Basic water treatment methods can be applied to solve these problems.

Sediment problems may be solved by the installation of appropriate filters. Besides solving the visible problems associated with sediment, the problems with valves and solenoids which result when dirt clogs these devices will be reduced.

Lime scale problems (caused by dissolved minerals) are solved by adding a slowly soluble food-grade polyphosphate to the water entering the ice machine. This chemical keeps minerals in solution and limits scale formation. It also helps prevent mineral deposits in the sump of the unit.

Cloudy or "milky" ice results from high levels of mineral content in the supply water. The ultimate solution to this problem is demineralization or distillation of the supply water. The latter is an expensive process.

An objectionable odor and/or taste may be due to high levels of chlorine or other substances in the supply water. A carbon filter is often used to reduce or eliminate these problems.

An ice machine which has had inadequate water treatment should be thoroughly cleaned before the initiation of any of the treatment methods discussed above. This treatment should be done with a mild acid to remove scale formation. All water distribution holes should be cleaned. In addition, all loose scale and dirt should be flushed from the unit and the unit thoroughly rinsed.

4.2 Water Systems for Swimming Pools

Data from a recent survey indicates that approximately 61% of the lodging establishments surveyed have an outdoor swimming pool, 27% have an indoor pool, and 35% have health club facilities.[16] Given these figures, it is quite likely that a lodging manager will be faced with responsibility for a water system for a swimming pool and, possibly, for a Jacuzzi or other similar amenity.

Exhibit 4.9 is a typical swimming pool piping, filtering, and heating schematic. The equipment is installed to maintain the bacteriological cleanliness of the pool, remove debris, and maintain the pool temperature at a comfortable level. The bacteriological cleanliness of the pool water is maintained by the addition of a chemical disinfectant, usually chlorine, but sometimes bromine or iodine. The chemical may be added in liquid, gas, or dry form. The dry form may be granular or tablet. The chemical level should be maintained at .6 to 1.9 parts per million (ppm) of residual chlorine. In order for this residual chlorine to be effective at reducing bacteriological contamination, the pool water must be maintained at a pH level of 7.2 to 7.6 (7.0 is neutral and values above 7.0 indicate increasing alkalinity). Since the normal tendency of pool water is to increase in pH, muriatic acid or sodium bisulfite may be added to reduce the pH. In outdoor pools, cyanuric acid may be added since it stabilizes the chlorine and reduces the rate of chlorine breakdown by ultraviolet rays.

Bromine may be used in place of chlorine. Its lack of an unpleasant odor, its effective sanitization and retention of this sanitizing ability over a range of pH values, and its somewhat higher stability when subjected to ultraviolet rays have made it attractive for pool water

Exhibit 4.9 Typical Swimming Pool Piping, Filtering, and Heating Schematic

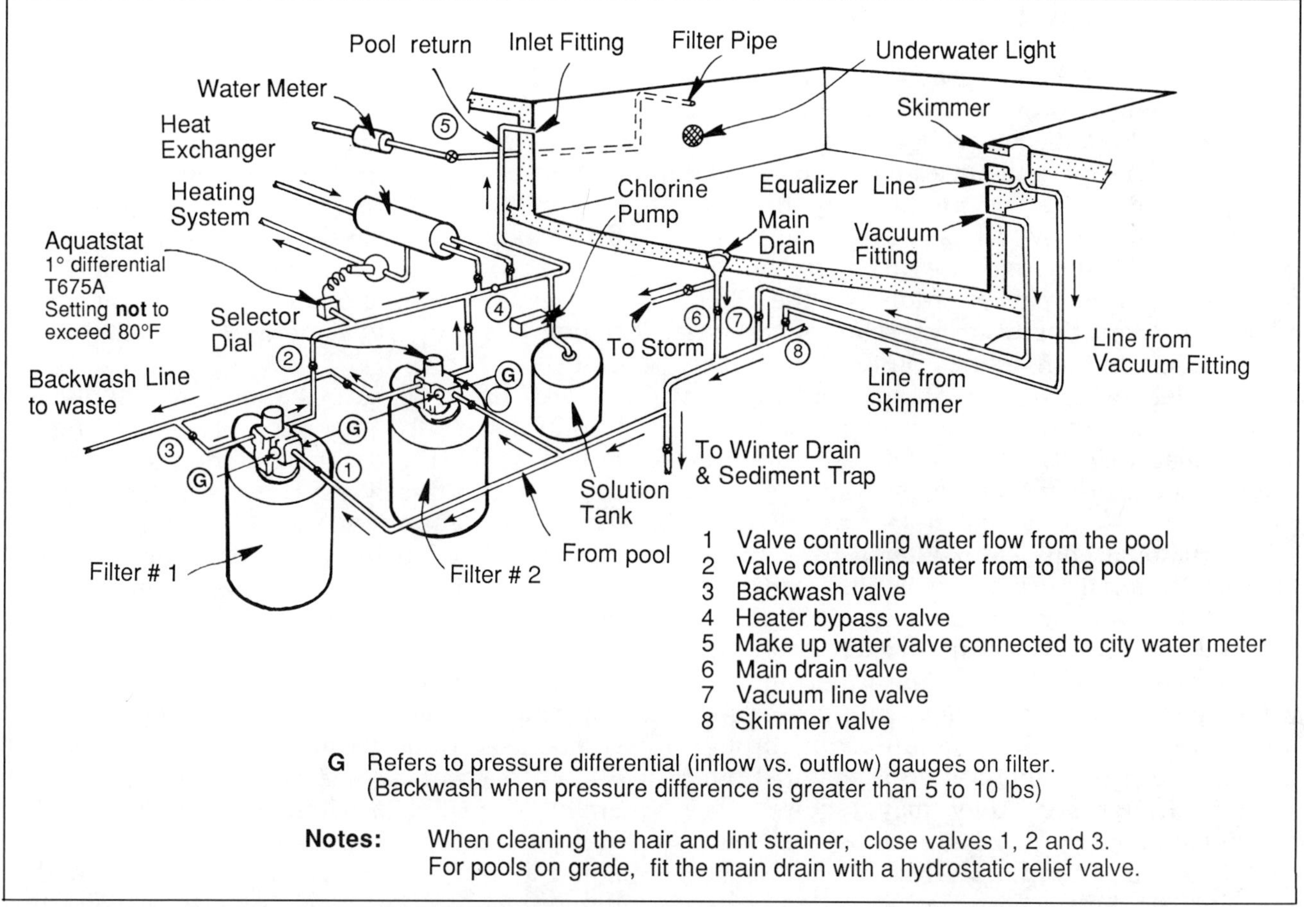

Source: Mel A. Shear, *Handbook of Building Maintenance Management* (Reston, Va.: Reston Publishing, 1983), p. 318.

treatment. However, there is no ultraviolet stabilizer for bromine.

Ozone is very effective in destroying bacteria and bad odors. Since it lacks any residual level, it is used in conjunction with chlorine or bromine.

There has been recent discussion on the appropriateness of using free chlorine as a measure of the ability of a pool to maintain basic bacteriological quality.[17] Free chlorine levels are measured by many standard pool test kits. Operators may find, however, that oxidation reduction potential (ORP or Redox)—a measure of the oxidizing properties of the sanitizer in water—will become the standard of the future for bacteriological control. The control of pH will probably also continue to be necessary, since the pH affects the comfort of the swimmers, corrosion of metal pool parts, and leaching of plaster pools.

Algae growth, a perennial problem in pools, produces a disagreeable odor or taste, clogs pool filters, and interferes with the action of chlorine and other sanitizers. While proper chlorine levels can inhibit algae growth, an algicide must be added to the water regularly. It may also be necessary to periodically "shock" the pool with high levels of algicide to kill the algae. The pool must be closed to all use during this treatment. Pool temperatures above 80°F, a pH above 7.8, and high levels of sunlight will encourage the growth of algae.

Filters serve to remove debris from the pool. Water is circulated through the filters and back to the pool. A strainer is often installed in front of the filter to remove larger debris. Filters may use sand, sand and gravel, or diatomaceous earth, or may be synthetic. All filters must be cleaned. Perhaps the best indicator that cleaning is needed occurs when the water pressure through the filter drops below a specified point.

Sand or sand and gravel filters rely on gravity pulling pool water through the sand or gravel bed. Periodic inspection of the filter is needed to determine the need for cleaning. The filter performance can be enhanced by the addition of a filter aid which serves to trap small particles on the surface of the sand. To clean the filter, a chemical may be added to the filter, allowed to stand for 12 or more hours without circulation, and then drained off to a sewer. The filter is cleaned by backwashing (applying the flow of water from bottom to top). Although sand replacement may be required as often as every year, a lifetime of several years is more likely.

A diatomaceous earth filter uses a special filtering material applied to a filter cartridge. These filters are smaller than sand filters and weigh less. They clean the water faster and require less disinfectant for the water and less water for backwashing. They use more pumping energy due to the pressure drop through the filter, consume more filtering material, and have a shorter life. They may require more maintenance since they are somewhat more complex than sand/gravel filters.

Since pool water is treated and often heated water, it should not be used to backwash filters. Such a use wastes a relatively costly item. Water from the building distribution system should be used to backwash filters and the effluent should be piped to a drain.

Pool heating is necessary in many locations. A temperature range of 75°–80°F for pool water and air conditions of 75°–85°F and 50%–60% relative humidity are comfortable to most people. The pool heating system should be installed based on considerations of operating efficiency, especially when long heating seasons are involved. Over one half of the heating requirement of an outdoor pool is due to the water which evaporates from the pool. Pool heating requirements can be reduced substantially by the use of a pool cover. In addition, the cover will decrease maintenance, chemical, and water costs by a substantial amount.

The accidental discharge of chlorine gas may result in chlorine poisoning. For this reason, if chorine gas is stored, use of a chlorine gas sensor and alarm may be desirable to detect leaks before they pose problems.

4.3 Refrigeration Heat Recovery for Water Heating

In light of the significant potential of refrigeration heat recovery and the interest shown in this method of water heating by hospitality firms, a further discussion of this topic may be of interest to certain managers. Refrigeration heat recovery can make a relatively significant contribution to a property's energy management program.

See Exhibit 3.5 in Chapter 3 for an illustration of a standard vapor compression refrigeration cycle. Heat recovery is accomplished at the condenser in this cycle. The gaseous refrigerant leaves the compressor and enters the condenser at relatively high temperatures. For air cooled equipment, these temperatures are necessary if heat is to be rejected from the condenser to warm or hot air (such as the air on the roof of a restaurant on a warm summer day). The high temperatures which exist at the compressor exit can be used to heat water.

Refrigerant leaving the compressor will generally be heated to a temperature significantly above that at which the refrigerant turns from a liquid to a vapor. The energy which is added to the refrigerant vapor in order to achieve this higher temperature is known as *superheat*. Within the condenser, this superheat must be removed along with the heat of condensation (that is, the energy which must be removed from the refrigerant in order to change its state from a vapor to a liquid).

Refrigeration heat recovery devices may be purchased to recover only the higher temperature heat (superheat) rejected from the refrigeration system or they may be installed to recover all the rejected heat. If all the rejected heat is recovered, over 15,000 Btu/hour can be recovered per ton (12,000 Btu) of refrigeration. Since recovery of all the heat can result in more hot water than is needed, some properties install devices which recover only superheat (desuperheaters) and retain the air cooled condenser to reject the excess heat not needed for water heating. Desuperheaters are capable of recovering 15%–25% of the total heat rejected from a piece of refrigeration equipment.

Exhibit 4.10 illustrates a refrigeration heat

Exhibit 4.10 Refrigeration Heat Recovery Design for a Motel

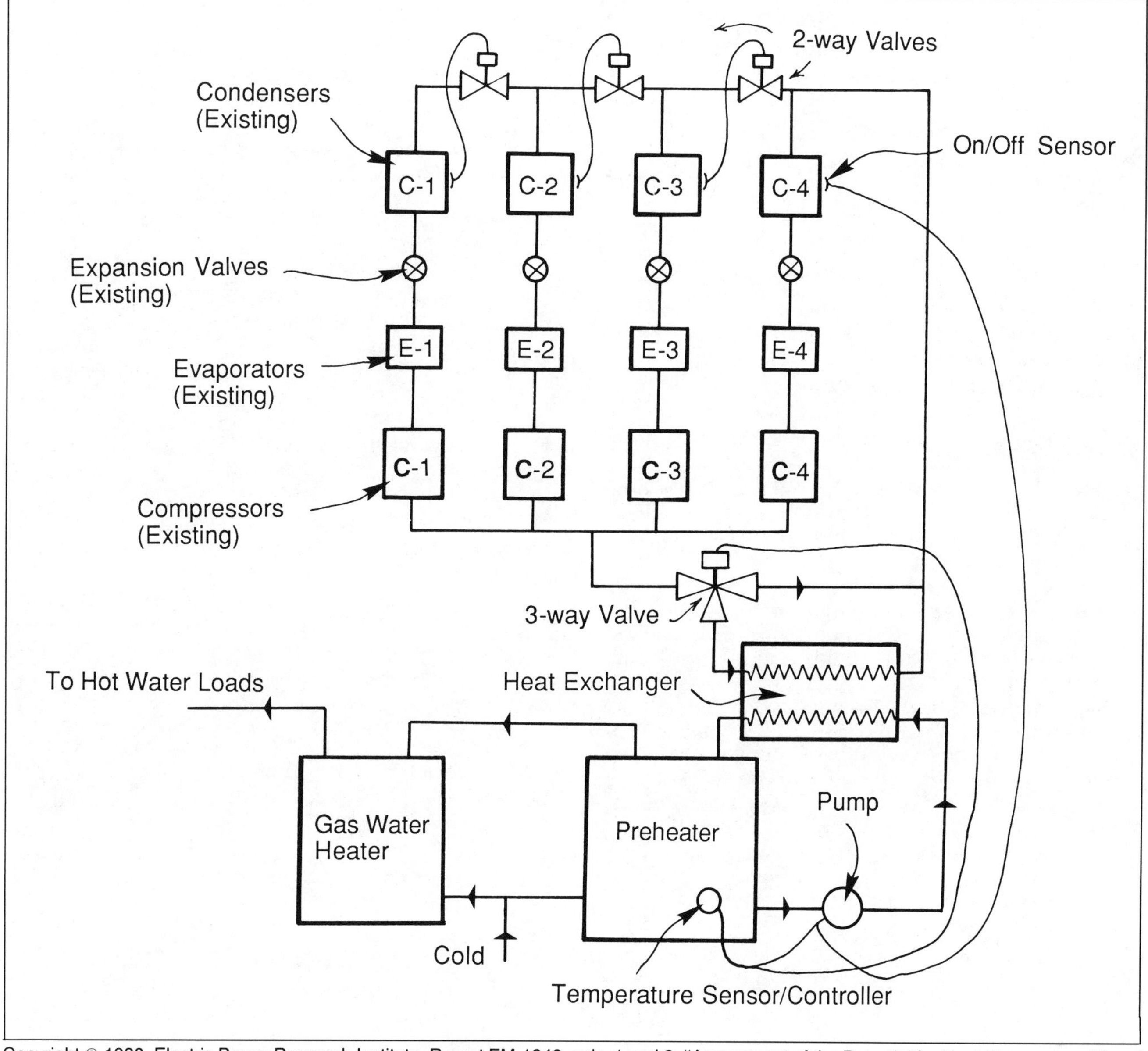

recovery design for a motel. The motel has four existing air cooled condensers which are connected to four stage reciprocating chillers rated at 60 tons (720,000 Btu/hr) each. Installed in series with these condensers is one heat exchanger and the necessary piping and valving required for refrigerant flow to be either piped through the heat exchanger and then to the air cooled condenser *or* for the refrigerant to be piped only through the air cooled condensers. Refrigerant would be piped through the air cooled condensers when the water had been heated to 140°F.

Water is pumped to the heat exchanger from the bottom of the storage tank (the location of the coldest water) and is returned to the tank after being circulated through the refrigeration heat recovery exchanger. Water is returned to the tank at approximately one third of the way from the top of the tank to enhance tank stratification. Data from the motel indicated that a 200 gallon preheater storage is required. The existing gas water heater serves to top off the preheated water if necessary. The payback on this system was estimated at two years.

Notes

1. Jack Wolfe, "Water Management Guidelines: Study Usage, Stop Waste," *Lodging*, July 1984, p. 55.
2. Valentine A. Lehr, "Gray Water Systems," *Heating/Piping/Air Conditioning*, January 1987, pp. 103-113.
3. *U.S. Lodging Industry—1986* (Philadelphia: Laventhol & Horwath, 1986).
4. Edwin C. Lippy and Steven C. Waltrip, "Waterborne Disease Outbreaks—1946-1980: A Thirty-Five-Year Perspective," *Journal of the American Water Works Association*, February 1984, p. 60.
5. Several undated publications of the Water Quality Association discuss many of these problems. See *Hardness; Corrosion; Turbidity, Color, Odor and Taste;* and *The Stainers—Iron and Manganese* (Lisle, Ill.: Water Quality Association, all undated).
6. Report of the 1977-1978 Disinfection Committee of the American Water Works Association, "Disinfection, Water Quality Control, and Safety Practices of the Water Utility Industry in 1978 in the United States," *Journal of the American Water Works Association*, January 1983, p. 51.
7. A detailed discussion of the operation of wastewater treatment plants is beyond the scope of this text. A large amount of information on this topic is available from the Water Pollution Control Federation, 2626 Pennsylvania Avenue N.W., Washington, D.C. 20037. Of particular interest in this regard is their text titled *Operation of Extended Aeration Package Treatment Plants* (Washington, D.C.: Water Pollution Control Federation, 1985).
8. Throughout this text, we cite absolute temperatures in degrees Fahrenheit (*x*°F)—for example, water freezes at 32°F. We cite temperature *differences* in Fahrenheit degrees (*x*F°)—for example, the difference between water's freezing (32°F) and boiling (212°F) points is 180F°; water heated from 50°F to 140°F has been raised 90F°.
9. The coefficient of performance is derived by dividing the usable heat delivered by the electrical energy input.
10. U.S. Department of Energy—Office of Building and Community Systems, *Proceedings of the Conference on Waste Heat Recovery for Energy Conservation—Residential and Light Commercial Heat Pumps, Air Conditioning, and Refrigeration Systems* (Springfield, Va.: National Technical Information Service, 1980).
11. U.S. Department of Energy, *Proceedings*, p. 152.
12. The Directory of SRCC-Certified Solar Water Heating Systems Ratings is available from SRCC, 1001 Connecticut Ave. N.W., Suite 800, Washington, D.C. 20036.
13. *ASME Boiler and Pressure Vessel Code* (New York: American Society of Mechanical Engineers, 1983).
14. *NFPA Standard 31—Oil Burning Equipment* (Quincy, Mass.: National Fire Protection Association, 1987) and *NFPA Standard 54—National Fuel Gas Code* (Quincy, Mass.: National Fire Protection Association, 1984).
15. *Commercial Gas & Electrically Heated Hot Water Generating Equipment for Food Service Establishments Using Dishwashing Machines*, Std. No. 5 (Ann Arbor, Mich.: National Sanitation Foundation, 1959).
16. *U.S. Lodging Industry—1986* (Philadelphia: Laventhol & Horwath, 1986).
17. Jacques M. Steininger, "PPM or ORP: Which Should Be Used?" *Swimming Pool & Spa Merchandiser*, November 1985, pp. 103-107.

5

Electrical Systems

Sources and Uses of Electricity

Purchased from Local Utility

The most common source of electricity in the United States is the local electric utility. This utility may serve an urban area (such as Consolidated Edison in the New York City area) or a significant portion of a state (such as Pacific Gas and Electric in California). The utility provides electrical service at a specified voltage to customers who pay a monthly fee based on usage. The fee generally includes a customer fee, a charge based on energy usage (cost per kilowatt-hour or kwh), a charge based on peak demand (cost per kilowatt or kw), and sometimes other charges. Each electric utility has its own method for bill determination.

There is significant variation in the cost of electricity from electric utilities across the United States. Low cost locations (such as the Pacific Northwest) may have electric rates which average $.03 per kwh, while the more expensive locations (such as New York City, Boston, and San Diego) may have rates which average $.10 to $.12 per kwh.

Produced Onsite

Properties that do not have access to a reliable source of electricity or that consider the local electricity source to be too expensive (such as island resorts and properties located in developing countries) may produce their own electricity onsite. Also, some United States properties have installed cogeneration systems (engine driven generators producing electricity and a usable thermal output) within the past few years. Whether cogeneration becomes widespread in the industry or remains limited to locations with expensive electricity will be determined by energy prices and tax legislation over the next few years.

The onsite production of electricity at resorts and properties in developing countries differs from the cogeneration at U.S. properties. The U.S. cogeneration installations generally rely on the local electric utility for backup power. The others rely upon themselves for backup. A failure of the onsite system at a U.S. property is potentially economically costly, but generally will not result in the loss of electric power. In a resort or developing country, loss of the onsite power system results in a loss of power and a potentially significant problem in operating the facility.

Onsite production of electricity places more responsibilities upon the engineering staff than does the purchase of electricity from the local utility—for example, the responsibility for voltage stability, correct phase relationships, elimination of current surges, and maintenance of the engine generator set.

Lodging Facility Electricity Usage

Lodging properties use electricity to power a variety of equipment. Large users of electricity include fans, space cooling equipment (chillers and/or air conditioners), lighting, elevators, much kitchen equipment, and possibly (in properties with electric resistance heating or heat pumps) the building space heating and water heating equipment.

On a Btu basis, electricity accounts for about one half of total hotel/motel energy usage. Data compiled by the American Hotel & Motel Association indicates that U.S. properties not using electricity for heating applications consume an average of about 19 kwh of electricity per square foot per year. Regions of the country with high cooling loads averaged a higher kwh usage (about 22 kwh per square foot per year in the Southern U.S.). All-electric properties averaged about 28 kwh per square foot per year.[1] A study by the Department of Energy which used computer modeling to estimate the energy consumption of a larger hotel (315,000 square feet) using fossil fuel for space and water heating concluded that such a property's electrical energy usage would be 20 to 25 kwh per square foot per year depending on location, with southern sites having the highest values.[2]

Electric Bills

Electric bills constitute approximately 75% of the average lodging property's total utility bills (excluding telephone). For the all-electric property, the figure may be 90% or more. Although electric utility tariffs can be rather complex, making their analysis somewhat difficult, the significant portion of total utility costs attributable to electricity justifies the effort required to understand the nature of electric utility billing. The starting point for understanding the billing process is understanding the items which are metered (measured) by the electric utility.

Electrical Metering

The electric utility installs a meter at the property which measures several factors used to calculate the electric bill. Factors measured include electrical energy consumption (kwh), peak electrical demand (kw), and reactive kilovolt amperes (rkva or kvar).

The energy consumption is simply a tally over the billing period (usually a month) of the kwh used in the period. The consumption is recorded by a series of dials on the meter. It is sometimes necessary to multiply the actual number shown on the meter by a constant since the meters may be recording consumption to the nearest 100 or even 1,000 kwh in large properties. Since the meter provides a running sum of consumption, the consumption in a billing period is determined by subtracting the meter reading from the end of the previous period from that for the current period.

The peak demand (kw) is actually a measure of the peak average demand over some specified period. The local utility will divide the billing period into 15-, 30-, or even 60-minute periods and the demand meter will measure the average demand in each period. The largest value measured during the billing period is recorded by the meter as the peak demand and read by the meter reader.

Reactive kilovolt amperes are a measure of the amount of reactive power used by the building. Reactive power performs no useful work at the property and, from the utility company standpoint, represents production and distribution costs for which billing based on kwh and kw alone does not provide adequate cost recovery. Measurement of rkva may not be done at all properties and variations in the use of this billing method are great from utility to utility.

Consumption Charges

Consumption charges are those charges based solely on the quantity of electricity required. These charges are expressed as cost per kwh in some form or another. These charges may have a uniform charge per kwh for all units of consumption or, as is more common, may have a declining block structure in which the charge per kwh decreases as the amount of consumption increases. A declining block structure schedule might charge $.10 per kwh for the first 10,000 kwh, $.05 per kwh for the next 90,000 kwh, and $.04 for all kwh over 100,000 (within any single billing period).

Demand Charges

Demand charges multiply the measured peak average demand by a charge per kw. This charge may include a fixed charge as well as a charge per kw and may have a declining block feature similar to that for the consumption (kwh) charge. An example might be $70 per month for the first 10 kw of billing demand, $7 per kw per month for the next 90 kw of billing demand, and $5 per kw per month for all demand over 100 kw.

Some utilities incorporate the concept of a demand ratchet in their demand billing. The utility bases the demand billing on the peak demand during the past year, a percentage of this peak demand, or the actual peak demand during the month, whichever is greatest. Under such a billing structure, a large peak demand achieved in one month can affect the electric bill for the following 11 months. With ratcheted demand billing, if the peak average demand during the past 11 months was 1,000 kw and the utility billing is based on the current month's demand or 80% of the 11-month peak, the property will pay as if the demand were 800 kw any time actual demand is 800 kw *or less;* if the measured demand is more than 800 kw, the demand charge will be based on the actual measured demand.

Demand charges vary significantly from utility to utility. Charges as high as $15 per kw and as low as $2 per kw can be found.

Load Factor Based Billing

Load factor based billing incorporates the metered demand *and* energy consumption in the determination of the rate which will apply to the energy consumption. This method may be applied in addition to a consumption charge or may be the only actual "consumption" charge. A separate demand charge also exists in most instances. The term *load factor* refers to the ratio of the actual kwh in the month to the maximum possible kwh in the month given the measured peak demand. In equation form, the load factor can be written as follows:

$$\text{Load Factor} = \frac{\text{Actual kwh}}{\text{Max Possible kwh}} = \frac{\text{Metered kwh}}{\text{Metered Peak Demand} \times \text{Hours in Billing Period}}$$

A property using 200,000 kwh in a month with a peak demand of 500 kw would have a load factor of 200,000/(500 × 24 × 30) or 56% (assuming a 30-day month).

Load factor based billing reduces the average cost per kwh as the load factor of the customer increases. Load factors increase when the value of the above ratio increases—such as when kwh consumption goes up while peak demand remains the same or decreases, or when peak demand decreases while kwh consumption remains the same or rises. For example, assume a rate of $.06 per kwh for the first 10,000 kwh and $.05 per kwh for all kwh over 10,000 except $.04 per kwh over 10,000 kwh and over 350 hours' use of metered demand. For a rate such as this, the resulting cost for 200,000 kwh of energy usage and a 500 kw peak demand would be:

$.06/kwh × 10,000 kwh = $600
$.05/kwh × 165,000 kwh = $8,250
(the 165,000 is 350 hrs × 500 kw minus 10,000 kwh)
$.04/kwh × 25,000 kwh = $1,000
(the 25,000 is 200,000 minus 350 hrs × 500 kw)

In this case, any kwh consumption above 200,000 (which would increase the load factor) will be charged at the cheapest rate ($.04), thereby lowering the average cost per kwh. Similarly, a lower peak demand would reduce the number of kwh in the second equation—for example, a 400 kw peak demand multiplied by 350 hours minus 10,000 would mean that only 130,000 kwh would be charged at $.05/kwh instead of 165,000. The 35,000 kwh difference would be charged at $.04/kwh, again increasing the proportion of the total energy bill charged at the cheapest rate and thereby reducing the average cost per kwh.

Power Factor Adjustment

The electric utility may impose some additional charge on a customer which has a low power factor. Power factor is the ratio between the real and apparent power required by the customer. Real power is the value measured by the demand meter. Apparent power is the value obtained by taking the product of the supply voltage to the property and the peak current flow. An equation for the power factor for a three phase service is:

$$\text{Power Factor} = \text{Measured W}/(\text{V} \times \text{A} \times \sqrt{3})$$

where *Measured W* is the real power (in Watts); *V* is the supply voltage to the building; *A* is peak amps drawn by the building; and $\sqrt{3}$ is 1.732 (the square root of the number of phases). If the property has a peak demand of 500 kw (500,000 watts), is supplied with power at 480 volts (three phase), and has a peak current draw of 600 amps, the power factor would be 1.0.

The additional charge imposed by some electric utilities for a poor power factor is usually levied when the customer's power factor drops below some level, typically in the range of .8 to .9. The additional charge can take many forms, including an increase in the effective demand charge, an increase in the effective energy charge, or a surcharge on the entire bill. The charge imposed may increase as the power factor decreases.

Fuel Adjustment Charge

During the 1970s, electric utilities experienced dramatic variations in fuel prices due to the fluctuating world oil market. The results of these variations were financial instability for the utility and a potential bureaucratic nightmare for utility regulatory bodies as they attempted to respond to continual requests for rate changes. The fuel adjustment charge (sometimes called the energy cost adjustment) was implemented as a means of handling variations or fluctuations in fuel or purchased energy costs. The fuel adjustment charge is a charge or credit applied to the bill based on the cost to the utility of fuel or purchased power during the period covered by the bill. The charge is usually applied to the kwh consumption metered for the customer.

Fuel adjustment charges may be a very small part of the total bill or may constitute as much as 25% of the bill, depending on the utility. In areas where hydroelectric power is available, the fuel adjustment may be credits during periods of high water availability at the hydroelectric sites and additional charges when less water is available.

Rate Schedules

Electric utilities will usually establish classes of customers based on levels of energy and demand usage and the service voltage. Commonly used classifications are (1) residential, commercial, and industrial or (2) residential and general. Each customer classification will have a different rate schedule and, within a given classification, there will often be subclasses.

Restaurants are generally billed on the commercial or small general rate schedule since their usage of energy typically does not qualify them for the industrial or large general service rate. Lodging properties having more than 100 rooms usually fall into the industrial or large general service categories.

The industrial or large general service rate is almost always the lowest rate. Further reductions in the industrial or large general service rate are often available for service at primary (high) voltage. This type of service requires the customer to own and maintain its own transformer and switchgear. Sometimes the rate differential for primary service is so significant that the purchase of the transformer and switchgear can be repaid within a few years from the resulting electric bill savings.

A relatively recent modification to electric utility billing practices is the introduction of time-of-use rates. These rates establish various times of the day or periods of the year and vary the rates charged depending on when the energy use or demand occurs. Such rates may require the installation of special meters capable of recording energy use and demand during various periods of the day. In general, the time-of-use rates assign higher charges to consumption occurring during the normal business day and significantly lower charges to usage during night and/or weekend periods.

While the local utility will periodically review the rate class at which a customer is billed and change this class if it is appropriate, the property shares the responsibility for ensuring that charges are made at the correct rate. It is particularly important to review this issue when a major addition is made to the building or when usage changes for some reason, since a change in rate class may be appropriate.

Distribution and Supply Within the Property

Code Regulations

The local governmental body usually has an electric code which must be followed in the wiring and installation of all electrical devices and circuits. This code usually follows the National Electrical Code® (*NEC®*) developed by the National Fire Protection Association (NFPA).[3] The *NEC* defines basic electrical wiring and circuiting design and safety measures established to protect people and property from hazards arising from the use of electricity. The *NEC* has been incorporated into the Occupational Safety and Health Act (OSHA) and therefore has, in effect, the force of law. The local governmental body may make additions to the *NEC* which must also be complied with. Failure to follow the applicable codes can result in potentially unsafe electrical installations and the need to redo electrical work in a manner which meets the code requirements.

Exhibit 5.1 Electrical Circuits

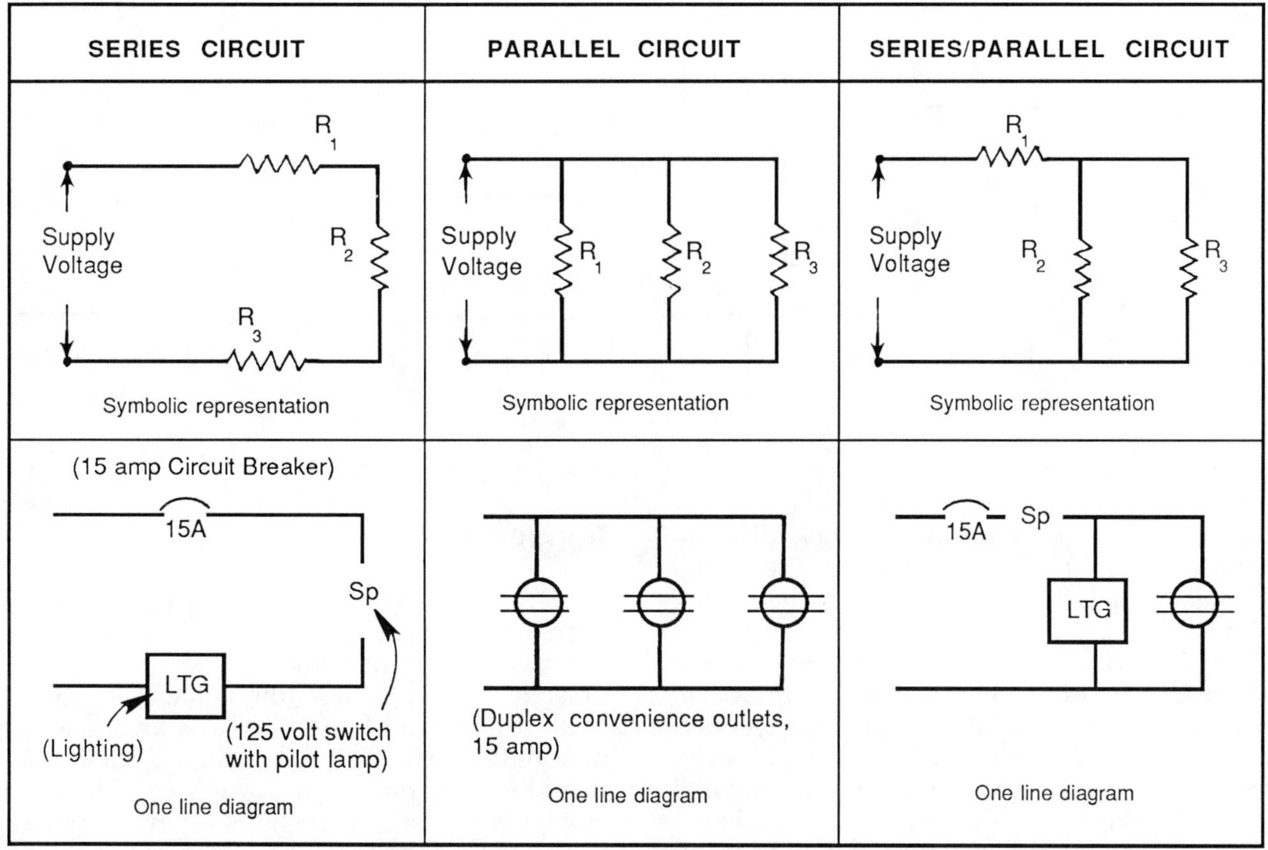

NOTE: "R" denotes a load or control device

A brief discussion of several elements of the *NEC* which pertain to guestrooms is found in Application 5.1 at the end of this chapter.

Basic Circuits

Electrical circuits provide "an arrangement of electrical equipment with electrical conductors interconnecting all of the component products. The function of the entire connected system is to provide for safe and effective transfer of electrical energy from a source of power (such as an electric utility line or a generator) to lamps, motors, appliances, machines, and any other functional or utilization equipment that performs a useful purpose when supplied with electric current."[4]

Electrical circuits are configured in series, in parallel, or combinations of the two. Series circuits are commonly used for control and equipment protection where switches, fuses, and/or starters are wired in series with the device or load. Parallel circuits are commonly used to connect equipment to the electrical supply. Exhibit 5.1 illustrates these basic configurations and, using symbols for common electrical system components, shows how they would appear in electrical drawings of a building electrical service.

The design of an electrical supply system requires the calculation of expected power and current requirements for the installed equipment. Basic power relationships between current and voltage in single and three phase circuits are discussed in Appendix A. Application 5.2 at the end of this chapter describes some details of the electrical supply for single and three phase circuits commonly encountered in commercial buildings.

Exhibit 5.2 Block Diagram of the Electrical Service to a Commercial Building

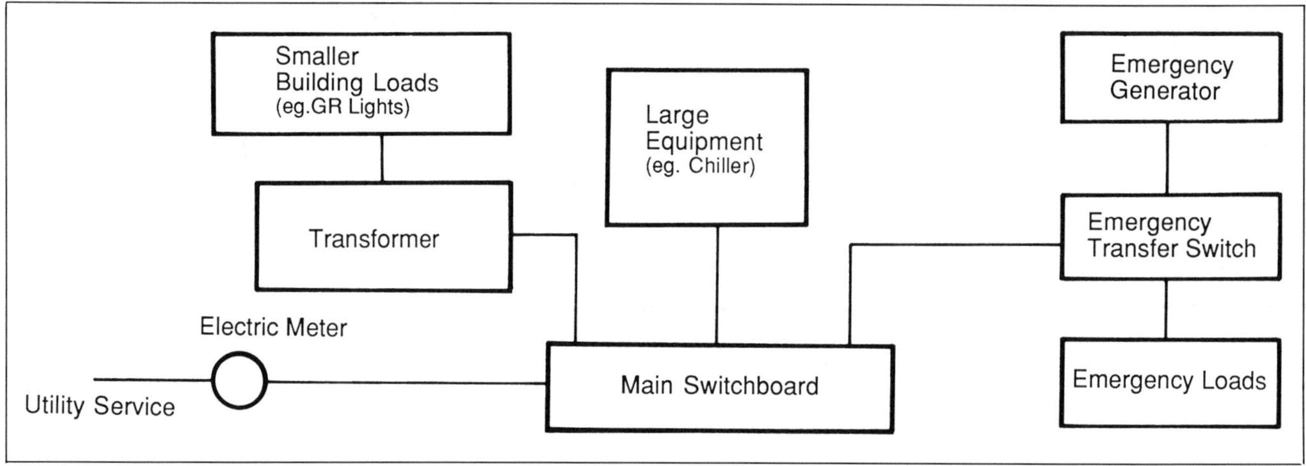

Exhibit 5.2 is a single line (or block) diagram of the electrical service to a commercial building such as a hotel. The lines represent the wiring connecting the components. Shown are the major components of the electrical supply system within the building and the utility interface. Components after the electric meter are generally owned and maintained by the property, while components before the meter are owned and maintained by the electric utility. Large loads (such as the chiller shown in the diagram) are supplied at a higher voltage than is supplied to lighting circuits or guestrooms and are generally three phase rather than single phase. High voltage three phase supply results in more efficient equipment operation and a reduced cost for wiring and protective equipment.

For larger commercial buildings, it is common for the local utility to supply electrical service using multiple feeds from separate circuits. With this arrangement, the loss of one circuit from the utility, whether for maintenance or due to a malfunction, will not result in a loss of electricity at the building.

The property wiring system may be configured so that the supply of electrical power to a location will also flow through or be utilized by other locations. Under many circumstances this will pose few problems. However, electronic equipment and computers may not function properly under this arrangement. Application 5.3 discusses some of the design concerns for electrical systems supplying computers and point-of-sale devices.

Transformers

Transformers in electrical systems serve to change the voltage at which electrical energy is supplied. A transformer would typically be present to "step down" the voltage of the electrical supply from the utility to a level used for distribution within the building. Transformers would also be present to further step down the voltage for circuits such as lighting or wall outlets in guestrooms.

Transformers are specified based on voltage, phase, power, sound level, and insulation class. The voltage specification indicates the voltage level available from the transformer and the voltage level at which the transformer is to be supplied. The phase specification refers to whether the transformer is single or three phase. The power rating is given in kva (kilovolt amperes) and is the product of the supply voltage and the rated full load current. The transformer sound level is given in decibels (db), with a higher value indicating a noisier transformer. The insulation class (A, B, F, and H) specifies the type of insulation used in the transformer and the maximum operating temperature of the transformer.

Transformers may be classified as wet or dry, depending on the medium used to remove heat from the transformers. Wet transformers use askarel, oil, or silicone as the cooling medium and reject heat to the ambient air by circulating this fluid through external air-cooled exchangers. Dry transformers circulate air past the transformer elements to remove heat.

Because the operation of a transformer results in heat production, the ventilation of a transformer room (or vault) is necessary. It is important that ventilation air flow freely. Poor ventilation can result in operation of the transformer at higher than rated temperatures, resulting in premature failure, higher operating power losses, and possibly fires. The *NEC* (Article 450) establishes numerous design requirements for rooms and vaults containing transformers, among which are prohibitions against placing transformers in rooms containing combustible materials and requirements that vaults be kept locked. Transformer rooms and vaults are *not* to be used as storage areas.

During the past few years, concern has emerged over transformers using askarel as a coolant. Askarel is 50%–70% polychlorinated biphenyl (PCB), which can produce highly toxic dioxin and dibenzofuran when burned. In 1982, the Environmental Protection Agency (EPA) classified all transformers with coolant containing more than 500 ppm (parts per million) of PCB as "PCB transformers." These transformers are subject to stringent regulations requiring, among other things, their labeling as "PCB transformers," compliance with strict regulations governing their disposal, and the reporting to the EPA of any major leak or spill of transformer oil. In addition, a relatively recent EPA ruling:

- Has prohibited the installation of PCB transformers in or near commercial buildings since October 1985
- Requires marking of PCB transformer locations
- Requires removal of all combustible materials stored within or near a PCB transformer enclosure
- Requires registration of all PCB transformers with fire departments
- Prohibits the continued use beyond 1990 of higher secondary voltage (480 volts or above) PCB transformers interconnected in a series of three or more
- Requires the installation by Oct. 1, 1990, of additional electrical protective devices on PCB transformers

Transformers with coolant containing 50 to 500 ppm are classified as "PCB contaminated" and subject to less stringent regulations.[5]

Since the building contamination which could result from a PCB transformer fire could close the building indefinitely, the presence of such transformers in the building is a definite risk for the building owner/manager.

Riser Diagrams

Electrical riser diagrams illustrate vertical sections of the electrical supply system of a building. All panels, feeders, switches, switchboards, and major components are shown up to, but not including, branch circuiting. They provide an overview of the electrical service within the building while omitting much detail. Exhibit 5.3 is a riser diagram for a typical commercial building. The lower portion of the diagram denotes the main service panel with the risers denoted by numbers on the panel. On each floor, the individual panels are denoted by numbers and letters.

Fuses and Other Protective Equipment

Certain equipment is installed in electrical circuits to protect equipment and people from malfunctions (including shorts), overloads, and other hazardous incidents. Equipment which protects electrical equipment does not necessarily protect people.

Overloads of electrical circuits are avoided or controlled by the use of fuses and circuit breakers. Fuses are non-resettable devices which melt if circuit current exceeds their rating. The fuse or fuse element is then replaced. Fuses may have a time delay feature to allow for momentary current surges required to start electric motors. A separate fuse must be installed on each "leg" of a three phase supply. This type of protective installation is vulnerable under the loss of a single phase. Motors lacking phase failure and unbalance protection can be damaged or destroyed if a phase is lost.

Circuit breakers provide resettable protection. Excessive current will "trip" the circuit breaker, causing a loss of power on the load side. When the source of the problem is corrected, power can be restored by manually resetting the circuit breaker. Since the circuit breaker will interrupt all circuits connected through it, a circuit breaker will not continue to

Exhibit 5.3 Typical Power Riser Schematic

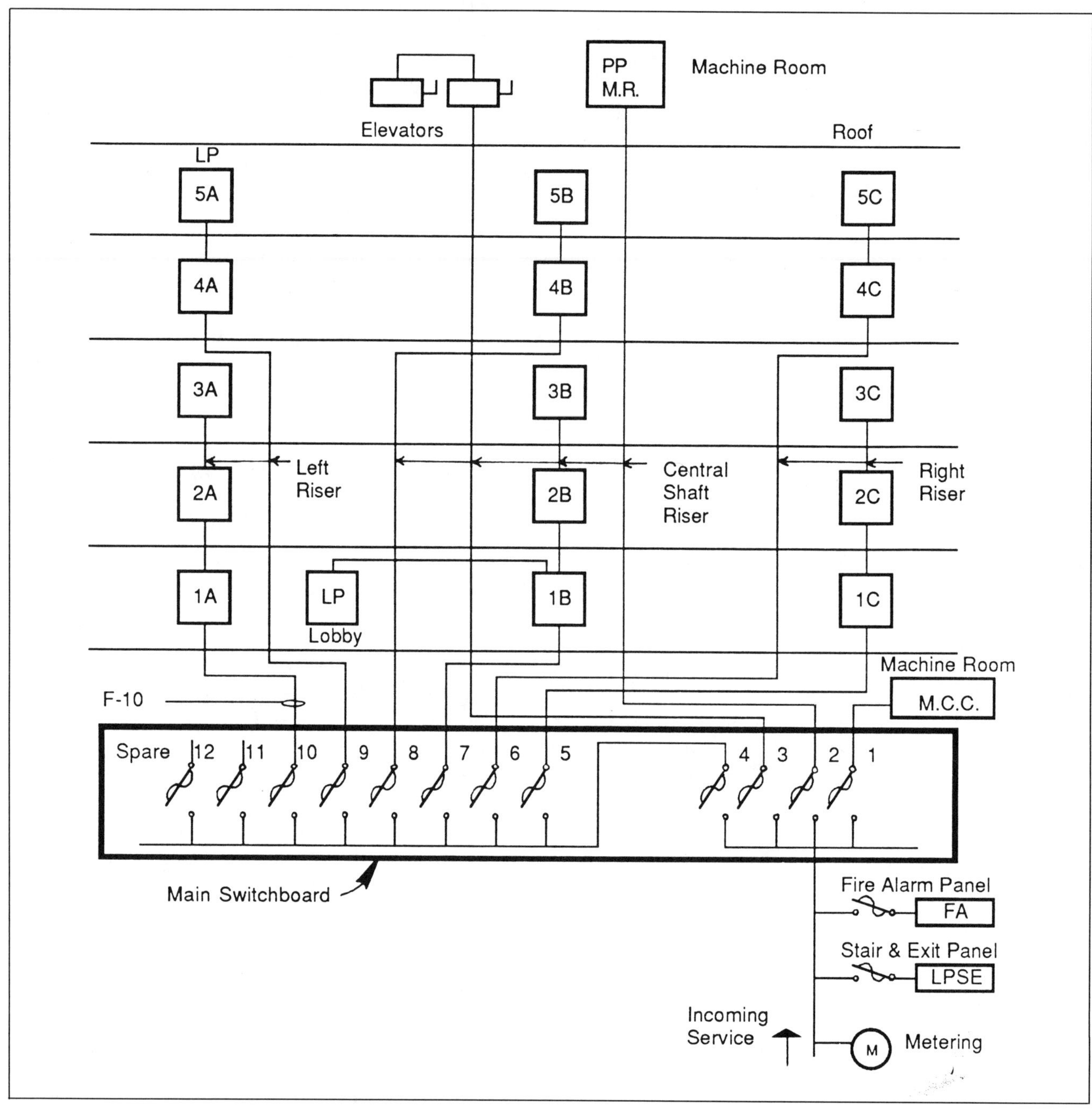

supply electricity in the other phases if excess current occurs in one phase. Circuit breakers are more expensive than fuses and are more likely to be found at locations where human interaction with the electric system is likely, such as in the distribution panels for the kitchen or guestrooms. Circuit breakers require periodic cleaning and maintenance. As mechanical circuit breakers age, their sensitivity and response time change. For this reason, consideration should be given to the replacement of older circuit breakers with newer solid state components in order to maintain adequate protection.

One type of circuit breaker, the ground fault

circuit interrupter or GFCI (sometimes called the ground fault interrupter or GFI), provides special protection to humans. This device responds more rapidly than a typical circuit breaker to a surge in current or a high current flow on the neutral line. The quick response of this device results in a greater level of protection against brief flows of high levels of electric current which could have serious effects on humans. See Application 5.4 for a further discussion of GFCIs and their applications.

Low Voltage Circuits

Low voltage circuits, typically 24 volt, are used for control wiring in various applications, HVAC control being among the most common. Circuits operated at this lower voltage require smaller wire sizes and are inherently safer to humans than the use of line voltage control wiring. These circuits will generally function in an on/off mode, controlling relays which turn equipment on and off, open and close valves and, when more sophisticated control systems are used, may also convey information to processing units which are involved in environmental control. Low voltage circuits are also used with some lighting designs.

Maintenance and Upkeep

Electrical equipment maintenance should be part of an overall building maintenance program. Because most aspects of the electrical system are fixed in place and hidden in walls, breaker boxes, and conduits, the maintenance of electrical equipment sometimes is neglected. Such neglect can result in major problems for the property.

As with any maintenance program, the maintenance instructions of the equipment manufacturers should be kept on file in the engineering office, included in the building preventive and scheduled maintenance activities, and updated as circuits and equipment are modified, added, and removed. Since major portions of the electrical system are assembled onsite using components from many manufacturers, the development of an electrical equipment maintenance program is somewhat challenging. The National Fire Protection Association has issued a publication that can aid managers in developing electrical equipment programs.[6] This publication is the basis for the discussion which follows.

Transformers

Since transformers are relatively expensive items in the electrical system ($200 per kva for dry transformers), serve large and potentially sensitive loads, are subject to various forms of breakdown, are often difficult to remove and replace quickly, and are often located in areas which are not subject to day-to-day contact by the staff, they require special attention from the engineering manager with regard to maintenance.

Measurements of load current, voltage, operating temperature, and insulation resistance are recommended for all transformers. Oil-filled transformers are recommended to have measurements of liquid level and liquid temperature, operating pressure, and dielectric (liquid) tests.

In dry transformers, cleaning of the air passages and windings is recommended to maintain correct operating temperatures and to reduce the possibility of short circuits. The startup of idle dry transformers should include special attention to manufacturers' instructions for prestartup drying of the transformer. Attention to these instructions will minimize the potential for arcing or other failure due to moisture in the transformer.[7]

Substations and Switchgear

Substations are composed of transformers, regulators, air switches, circuit breakers, and lightning arrestors. These may be owned by the electric utility or, at large properties and resorts, by the property. *Switchgear* includes equipment for switching, interrupting, control, and metering; protective and regulating devices (and their supporting structure); and enclosures, conductors, electric interconnections, and accessories. Switchgear is generally owned and maintained by the property.

Since substations may be located outdoors, it is particularly important that fences or other security enclosures be adequate and secured. Atmospheric contamination in urban or coastal areas may necessitate relatively frequent inspection of substation components and periodic cleaning. Infestations by birds or other animals should be removed, since they can short-circuit this equipment.

Switchgear is long lived (20 to 30 years) and requires only basic maintenance in order to function properly. Inspections of the switchgear for signs of condensation, dirt, and cracked or discolored ceramic parts are generally sufficient. Attention should also be given to infestations of rodents or birds nesting in switchgear, since these have resulted in shorts which have either temporarily removed equipment from service or resulted in equipment failure.

Electrical Wiring

While the majority of the electrical wiring installed in a building is contained in conduits and requires no maintenance, there are several instances where the wiring does require periodic maintenance. Some of this maintenance occurs as a part of guestroom maintenance, some is associated with equipment used by the staff, and some is necessary where wiring interconnects with controls and protective equipment.

Guestroom maintenance should include the inspection of all exposed electrical wiring, including lamp cords, wall outlets, and switches. Frayed cords, broken plugs, and cracked or broken outlet and switch covers should all be repaired as part of guestroom maintenance.

All portable electrical equipment used by the staff should periodically be checked and maintained. These appliances often last longer when periodically cleaned and lubricated. All extension cords used in the building should be inspected on a regular basis and faulty cords either repaired or replaced. Kitchen equipment should also be cleaned and checked for proper operation. Kitchen maintenance requires checking of plugs and ground connections to ensure that all equipment is properly grounded and that protective devices are properly sized.

Loose electrical connections are an important concern. Besides the obvious problem of electrical shock which may occur if electrical wires separate from connections in switchboards, wall outlets, motors, and elsewhere, loose electrical connections can lead to overheating and possibly fire. In order to diagnose loose connections, many commercial and industrial facilities periodically scan their electrical systems with infrared cameras. These cameras display a picture of the area being scanned with hot spots (loose connections, overloaded equipment, and so forth) highlighted. In this manner, potential problems can be identified and corrective action taken. Infrared scanning of electrical systems is one recent addition to preventive maintenance programs.

Emergency Power

Code Regulations

The building/electrical codes in many cities require emergency power systems. The code requirement is often based on the requirements established in the *NEC* and the Life Safety Code.[8] The *NEC* states:

> Emergency systems are generally installed in places of assembly where artificial illumination is required for safe exiting and for panic control in buildings subject to occupancy by large numbers of persons, such as hotels, theaters. . . . Emergency systems may also provide power for such functions as ventilation when essential to maintain life, fire detection and alarm systems, elevators, fire pumps, public safety communication systems, industrial processes where current interruption would produce serious life safety or health hazards, and similar functions.[9]

The Code allows the local authority to accept a second power service separate from the normal service to serve as the emergency power source. While such an emergency power provision may be *acceptable* to the local authority, it generally is not a substitute for an onsite emergency power system. Any property which attempts to substitute a second power source for an emergency power system should realize that such an arrangement does not usually help much during a major power outage and sometimes offers little real protection even during minor outages.

Emergency Power Circuits

With certain exceptions, emergency power circuits are designed using the same criteria used for other circuits. The major exception concerns the location of emergency circuits. Because of the sensitive nature of these circuits, they are not to be wired in the same raceway, cable, box, or cabinet with other wiring except where such co-location is unavoidable, such as in transfer switch locations and in exit or emergency lighting fixtures supplied from two sources.

Battery Systems

Battery systems generally consist of small, wall-mounted units used for lighting. These units have rechargeable batteries, a charger, a switch to energize the lights upon loss of power in the building, and the lights themselves. They are connected to and charged by the electric supply system of the building. The Life Safety Code (Chapter 5, Section 5-9) requires that emergency systems installed for lighting be capable of supplying not less than one footcandle of lighting for a period of not less than 1.5 hours in the event of normal lighting failure.

While it is possible to operate large battery systems to provide emergency power for larger building loads, the cost and operational problems with such installations result in their seldom being used. Battery systems are installed to provide an uninterruptible power supply (UPS) for computers and other electronic data processing or communications equipment. UPS systems are installed to provide a power supply for this equipment which is "clean," that is, which does not have the surges, dips, transients, and other potential problems associated with the building electrical supply. The systems are also installed to allow for either continued operation of the equipment during a power failure or to allow for the orderly shutdown of the equipment following a failure. Application 5.3 discusses some of the concerns in the design of electrical power supplies for computers and other electrical equipment.

Generator Systems

In larger properties and locations with more frequent electric power interruptions, natural gas- or diesel-driven engine generator systems will generally be found. These systems are wired through an automatic transfer switch which, upon sensing a loss of power from the electric utility, fires the engine powering the generator and switches the power source for the connected loads to the engine generator. A time delay occurs during this switching which allows the engine to come nearly to full speed and power prior to the connection of the loads.

The *NEC* (Article 700) and *Emergency and Standby Power Systems*[10] discuss various requirements for emergency systems. The *NEC* requires that the systems be periodically tested under load conditions and that a written record of these tests be kept. Identification of the state of the system (connected/not connected, operating/not operating) by means of signaling equipment and other provisions are specified in the Code. One feature of particular importance is the requirement for onsite storage of at least two hours' fuel at the full-demand fuel consumption rate. Since the use of natural gas to satisfy this requirement is not allowed by the Code unless local authorities permit, onsite fuel storage must be considered as part of the design of the systems.

Generator systems are required due to the large electrical needs of the emergency systems of modern lodging facilities. Requirements to pressurize areas of the building in case of fire and to supply power for selected elevators, pumps in various areas, and other equipment in building emergency systems result in significant electrical consumption during emergencies. Emergency generator systems are typically sized at approximately 1 to 1.5 kw per room (an emergency generator at a 500-room hotel would be 500 to 750 kw) with variations resulting from differing electrical loads. It is relatively rare for food service refrigeration equipment or space cooling equipment to be connected to the emergency power system. As a result, a prolonged power outage will generally result in a loss of stored food and a rather large cleanup effort.

Electric Motors

One of the major uses of electricity in a commercial building is as the energy source for electric motors. These motors power building HVAC equipment, kitchen equipment, pumps in water systems, and more. Understanding some basic elements of electric motor terminology and maintenance is crucial for an adequate managerial overview of building electrical systems.

Types of Electric Motors

Equipment motors may use direct current, single phase alternating current, or three phase alternating current. Direct current motors are most likely to be found powering elevators because they are highly suitable for variable speed applications. Single phase alternating current motors are generally used in small, stationary appliances, portable cleaning appliances, and room-size HVAC equipment. Three phase motors will generally be found connected to larger loads such as HVAC fans, pumps in water systems, and the compressor on large chillers. Most three phase motors are induction motors (often called "squirrel cage motors" because of the motor's interior design).

While induction motors operate at a speed which is almost constant from no load to full load, the development of adjustable frequency drives permits these motors to be used in adjustable-speed applications. These drives have seen retrofit application to building HVAC fan motors and to condensing/cooling and chilled water pumps. Adjustable or variable speed results in more efficient operation of the motor at partial loads.

An understanding of electric motor ratings and applications is helpful when contemplating motor replacement or maintenance. Application 5.5 presents information concerning electric motor nameplate data.

Energy Conservation and Electric Motors

In recent years, there has been great interest in reducing the amount of energy consumed by electric motors. One method suggested to reduce this consumption has been the use of energy efficient motors. Since the lifetime operating cost of a motor can easily exceed its purchase price by a factor of 10 or more, the increased initial cost of these more efficient motors can often quickly be paid back. A typical 7.5 horsepower TEFC (Totally Enclosed Fan Cooled) motor manufactured in 1965 had an efficiency of 84%. An energy efficient motor manufactured in the 1980s has an efficiency of 91%, requiring 7.7% less operating power than the 1965 motor. In addition to energy savings, these energy efficient motors have lower electrical demands and generally higher power factors and contribute less heat to the building to be removed by ventilation or space cooling. The lower operating temperatures and improved design of these motors should result in longer motor lifetime and lower maintenance costs. These motors have other advantages as well, among which is a design which is better suited for use with energy management systems which use motor cycling as a management strategy.[11]

The following formula can be used to calculate the annual motor operating costs:

$$\text{Annual Motor Operating Cost} = 0.746 \times HP \times C \times N \times 100/EFF$$

where *0.746* converts *HP* to kw; *HP* is the rating of specified load in horsepower; *C* is energy cost per kwh; *N* is running time (hours per year); and *EFF* is the efficiency of the motor. Performing the calculation twice to determine the operating costs for two similar motors operating at the same specified load but having different operating efficiencies reveals the potential annual cost savings of using the more efficient motor.

When a motor winding fails, the maintenance manager must decide whether to have it rewound or to replace the motor. The above equation can be used to calculate the potential advantage of replacing the motor with a more efficient one. Motor rewinding generally results in a motor which has an efficiency which is *lower* than the original motor's. Therefore, the savings associated with replacement by an energy efficient motor should be somewhat greater than those calculated using the formula.

When replacing a motor, the manager should carefully evaluate the motor size (HP) required. If the initial motor sizing was incorrect or the loads have changed, the required motor HP can sometimes be reduced. Such reduction results in a lower replacement cost and lower operating costs due to both a lower power requirement and a higher efficiency, since the motor will be operating closer to its rated output and, therefore, more efficiently.[12]

Another method of reducing electric motor energy usage (as well as building HVAC energy usage) is cycling HVAC and refrigeration equipment motors on and off. The energy savings achieved with cycling must be balanced against the possible shortening of the life of the motor and its starting equipment. This concern has resulted in the establishment of a maximum number of starts per hour for motors and a minimum time between starts. These standards are set forward in a publication of the National Electrical Manufacturers Association (NEMA).[13] NEMA establishes these standards based on the motor design and the inertia of the motor and the driven equipment. Loads such as fans have high inertia and will require longer times between starts than loads such as a centrifugal pump with its discharge valve closed.[14] Equipment manufacturers have their own standards which may be more stringent than the NEMA standard. Failure to adhere to the manufacturer's standards can result in voiding of equipment warranties.

Applications

5.1 Guestrooms and the National Electrical Code

The *NEC* generally does not consider guestrooms in lodging establishments to be dwelling units and subject to the same code provisions as homes. According to the *NEC*, a dwelling unit must have "permanent provisions for cooking and sanitation." Most hotel and motel rooms would not meet the cooking criterion, although some suite hotels would and would, therefore, be subject to all the Code provisions applicable to homes.

The use of ground fault circuit interrupters (GFCI) is required in hotel and motel bathrooms as well as dwelling units, even though the "typical" guestroom is not classified as a dwelling unit. Other variations exist as well. For example, while the use of voltages in excess of 150 volts is prohibited for screwshell lampholders, receptacles (wall outlets), or appliances in guestrooms (unless the appliances are permanently connected and are rated over 1380 watts), the use of voltages as high as 240 volts for splitwired duplex outlets within the guestroom is not prohibited. Another exception allows the use of voltages in excess of 150 volts when supplied to permanently connected appliances in dwelling units or hotel or motel guestrooms. This provision allows permanently installed room HVAC units to be wired at voltages higher than 120, resulting in savings in wiring costs and slight improvements in operating efficiency.

5.2 Single and Three Phase Circuit Wiring

Electric circuits will vary in their design depending on the application. The following discussion briefly addresses some of the key variations in design in order to provide you with a deeper understanding of electrical systems.

Most lodging facilities and many restaurants are served by three phase electric service. Within the property, individual loads may be three phase or single phase depending on size. A common wiring arrangement is the 120/208 volt, three phase, four wire system. A schematic of such a system is shown in Exhibit 5.4. In this system, a 120 volt supply is available for loads such as lighting, receptacles, and small motors, while a 208 volt supply is available for larger motors and equipment. The 208 volt supply is available in both a single and a three phase supply. Exhibit 5.5 illustrates the flexibility of the 120/208 system and schematically identifies the interconnection of the loads with the electrical system (this drawing omits the protective devices and the panel which would also be present).

At larger properties, the electrical supply for central chillers, pumps, and air-handling equipment may be supplied at 480 volts (three phase) with 277, 240, 208, and 120 also available. Exhibits 5.6 and 5.7 illustrate such a service. Transformers distributed throughout the property make it possible to match supply voltages to the various connected loads.

Exhibit 5.8 illustrates receptacle configurations for various types of electrical service and the related wiring diagrams.

5.3 Power Supply Considerations for Computers and Other Electronic Equipment

The lodging industry uses computers for applications ranging from reservations to accounting and word processing to maintenance recordkeeping. The sensitivity of some of these applications requires attention to the impact of electrical power system disturbances on computer operation.[15] The various types of disturbances on electrical power systems may originate both within and outside the building. Disturbances are characterized by voltage aberrations and include sags, surges, voltage transients or impulses, low or high voltage, and power outages.

Sags are instances of short duration (usually a few cycles) when the voltage on the power line decreases below the nominal level for one or more cycles. *Surges* are instances of short duration (usually a few cycles) when the voltage on the power line increases above the nominal level for one or more cycles. *Voltage transients or impulses* are brief high frequency spikes appearing on top of the 60-cycle wave. They are very brief in duration, existing for only a fraction of a cycle. *Low or high voltage* refers to situations when the voltage level is above or below the

Exhibit 5.4 120/208 Volt, Three Phase, Four Wire System

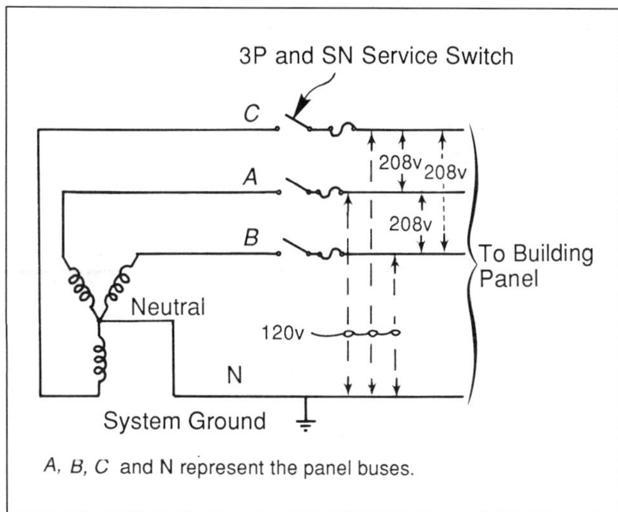

A, B, C and N represent the panel buses.

Exhibit 5.5 Schematic of Loads in a 120/208 Volt System

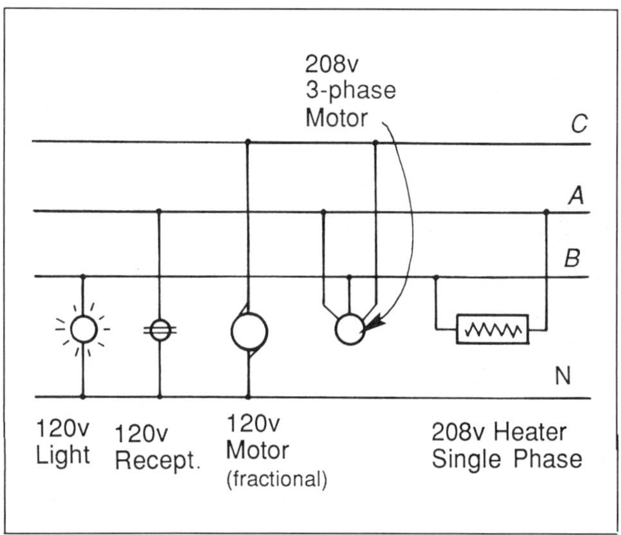

Exhibit 5.6 277/480 Volt, Three Phase, Four Wire System

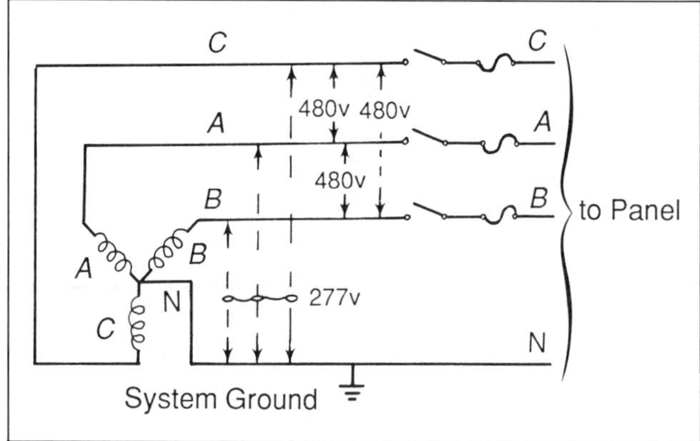

Exhibit 5.7 Normal Load Arrangement for a 277/480 Volt, Three Phase, Four Wire System

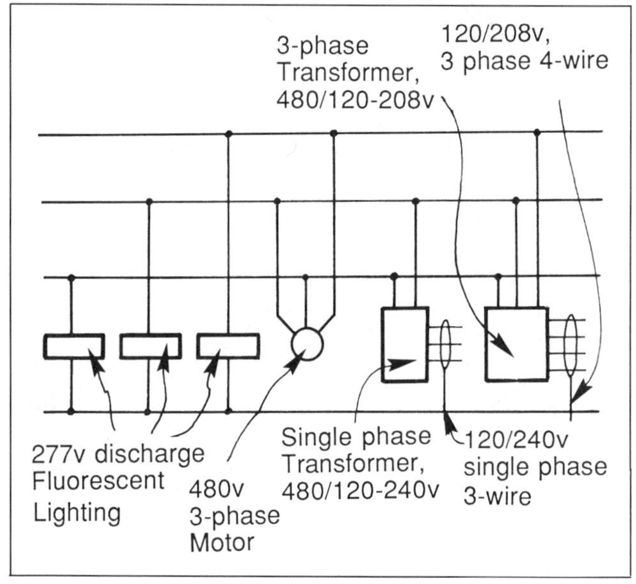

nominal level for an extended time, usually for several minutes or hours. During *power outages*, the electrical supply to the computer is terminated due to a failure outside the property (the electric utility) or within the property (an overloaded circuit, transformer failure, and so forth).

Each of these problems requires a somewhat different solution. The frequency of occurrence of the various problems and the severity of the resulting computer problem will dictate which solution is selected in a given instance. Methods include the use of dedicated lines, transient suppressors, voltage regulators, shielded isolation transformers, rotary filters or motor-alternator sets, and uninterruptible power supplies.

Dedicated lines are electric lines supplied directly to the computer from the building transformer. These lines shield out electrical noise (stray signals introduced into the electrical distribution system by other equipment, usually of

Exhibit 5.8 Selected Receptacle Configurations and NEMA Designations

RATING and POSSIBLE APPLICATION	RECEPTACLE CONFIGURATION	RECEPTACLE WIRING DIAGRAM
15A, 125v 2 pole, 3-wire grounding Guest Room Duplex Outlet	NEMA 5-15R 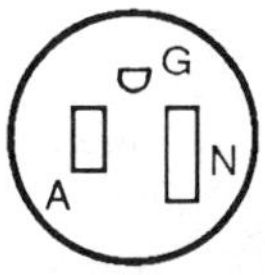 G A N	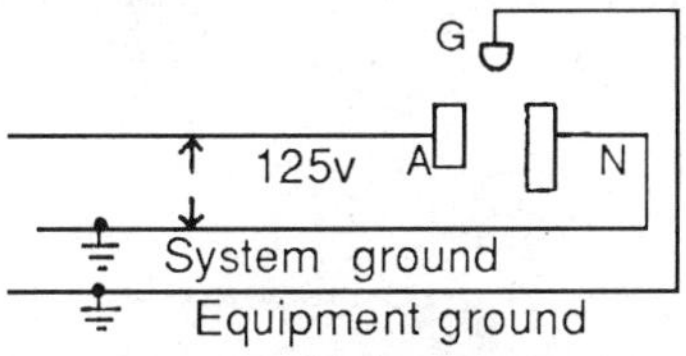 G 125v A N System ground Equipment ground
30A, 125/250v 3 pole, 3-wire New Marina	NEMA 10-30R  N B A	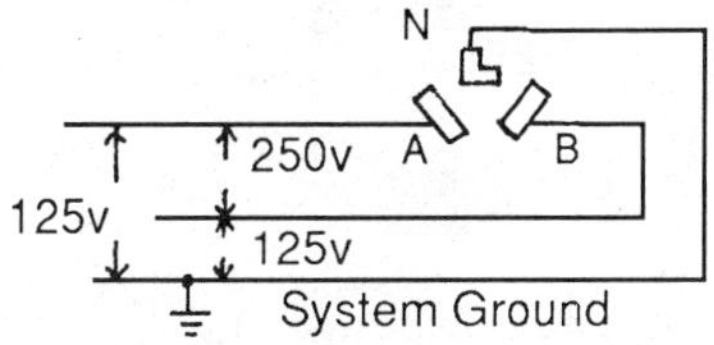 N 250v A B 125v 125v System Ground
50A, 125/250v 3-pole, 3-wire Floor Machine or Dryer 208 VAC	NEMA 10-50R  N B A	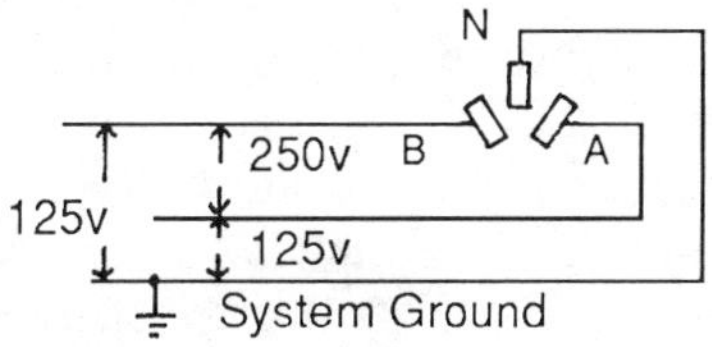 N 250v B A 125v 125v System Ground

NOTE: "N" denotes system ground or neutral, "G" denotes equipment ground, and "A" and "B" denote "hot" legs of electrical service.

non-60-cycle frequencies, but sometimes high or low voltages as well) which may be introduced by the operation of other equipment on the circuit with the computer equipment. They also reduce the potential for voltage problems on the line supplying the computer.

Transient suppressors serve as line filters to suppress surges or spikes of voltage and/or frequency on the power line. Lower cost units function primarily to protect from large surges such as may be caused by lightning.

Voltage regulators maintain voltage output within specified limits and are effective in solving high or low voltage problems.

Shielded isolation transformers serve to isolate the computer from electrical noise produced within the building or entering the building from the outside.

With *rotary filters or motor-alternator sets,* a motor fed from the electrical system drives an alternator which feeds power to the computer. These devices are capable of solving most commonly encountered power problems except for a prolonged outage.

An *uninterruptible power supply (UPS)* is a system which consists of a rectifier/charger, solid-state inverter, battery bank, and other necessary equipment. UPS systems are capable of solving virtually all power supply problems, including outages. Different configurations of the equipment exist which address various concerns. This is a relatively expensive solution.

Electrical power supplies for electronic cash registers (ECR) must be configured separately from the electrical power supply to other equipment. Electrical noise in the power supply circuit must be minimized if problems with garbled transactions, scrambled memory, and unit component failure and downtime are to be reduced. At a minimum, a dedicated circuit should be used. Under many circumstances, an isolated ground circuit is the best choice. A dedicated circuit, with or without an isolated ground, allows the equipment to be protected from outages, surges, or transients which could be introduced on these lines by the operation of other equipment on the same circuit. With no other equipment connected on the circuit, the breaker on this circuit is very unlikely to trip and cause problems.

A dedicated isolated ground circuit combines the benefits of the dedicated circuit with separation of the ground from ground fault and harmonic currents originating elsewhere. In addition, the conductors usually found in such installations provide greater isolation from induced voltages such as radio frequency interferences.

The power source for isolated ground circuits should never serve heavily inductive loads, such as motors or fluorescent lighting. Use of a duplex receptacle when a single ECR is installed is not recommended since the possibility will then exist that the unused outlet will become a plug-in location for potentially problem-causing equipment. The conductors supplying the receptacle should not run in conduits with other circuits to avoid induced transients. The ECR manufacturer may have other recommendations that should be followed.

Installation of a dedicated isolated ground circuit may not provide adequate protection if the power from the local utility is not clean enough. Under these circumstances, it will be necessary to install additional protective equipment. This may include the UPS systems described earlier or a combination of UPS and emergency power. See Application 5.6 for an example of such a system.

5.4 Ground Fault Circuit Interrupters

In order to protect people from potential electrocution, requirements have been established for the use of ground fault circuit interrupters. These devices measure the currents going through the hot and neutral wires of a circuit and compare these measurements. As long as the currents passing through each conductor remain equal, the device remains in a closed position. If one conductor comes in contact with a grounded object, some of the current will bypass the neutral wire and the current measurements will no longer be equal. The unbalanced current is registered and the circuit is "tripped out." This protects the individual from a high flow of current and potential injury.

GFCIs are available as permanent outlet devices as a part of the duplex (or similar) receptacle or as circuit breaker-type interrupters. They are also available as a plug-in device which can be inserted into a receptacle; the appliance is then plugged into the GFCI. Each will have a test and reset button to allow for periodic testing.

Besides the requirement for the use of GFCIs in guest bathrooms as discussed in Application 5.1, the devices are also required in temporary wiring situations, such as construction sites, according to OSHA regulations.

5.5 Electric Motor Nameplate Data

NEMA specifies that the following data should be stamped on every motor nameplate: manufacturer, type, frame, horsepower, time rating, ambient temperature, RPM, frequency, phases, rated load amps, voltage, locked rotor code letter, design letter, service factor, and insulation class. An understanding of the motor nameplate data is important when considering motor replacement or maintenance. The following is a brief explanation of some of the terms found on the nameplate.

Ambient temperature is specified in °C or °F and indicates the maximum ambient temperature at which the motor can safety deliver rated horsepower. *RPM* (rotations per minute) refers to the speed of the output shaft when delivering rated horsepower to the driven device (with rated voltage and frequency applied to the terminals of the motor). *Frequency and phases* specify the rated frequency (hertz) for the motor's electrical supply system and the number of phases for which the motor is designed. *Rated load amps* refers to the current drawn by the motor at rated voltage and frequency with full rated horsepower delivered to the load. *Voltage* refers to the design value of the voltage as supplied to the terminals of the motor, rather than the voltage of the supply line. *Locked rotor code letter* (F,G,H,I,J,K or L) refers to the locked rotor kva per HP of the motor, with later letters indicating a greater starting current surge. The *design letter* specifies certain technical characteristics of the motor such as minimum torque, maximum inrush current, and maximum slip. The *service factor* is generally in the range of 1.0 to 1.15 and designates a multiplier to be applied to the rated horsepower. Operation of the motor

Exhibit 5.9 UPS Schematic

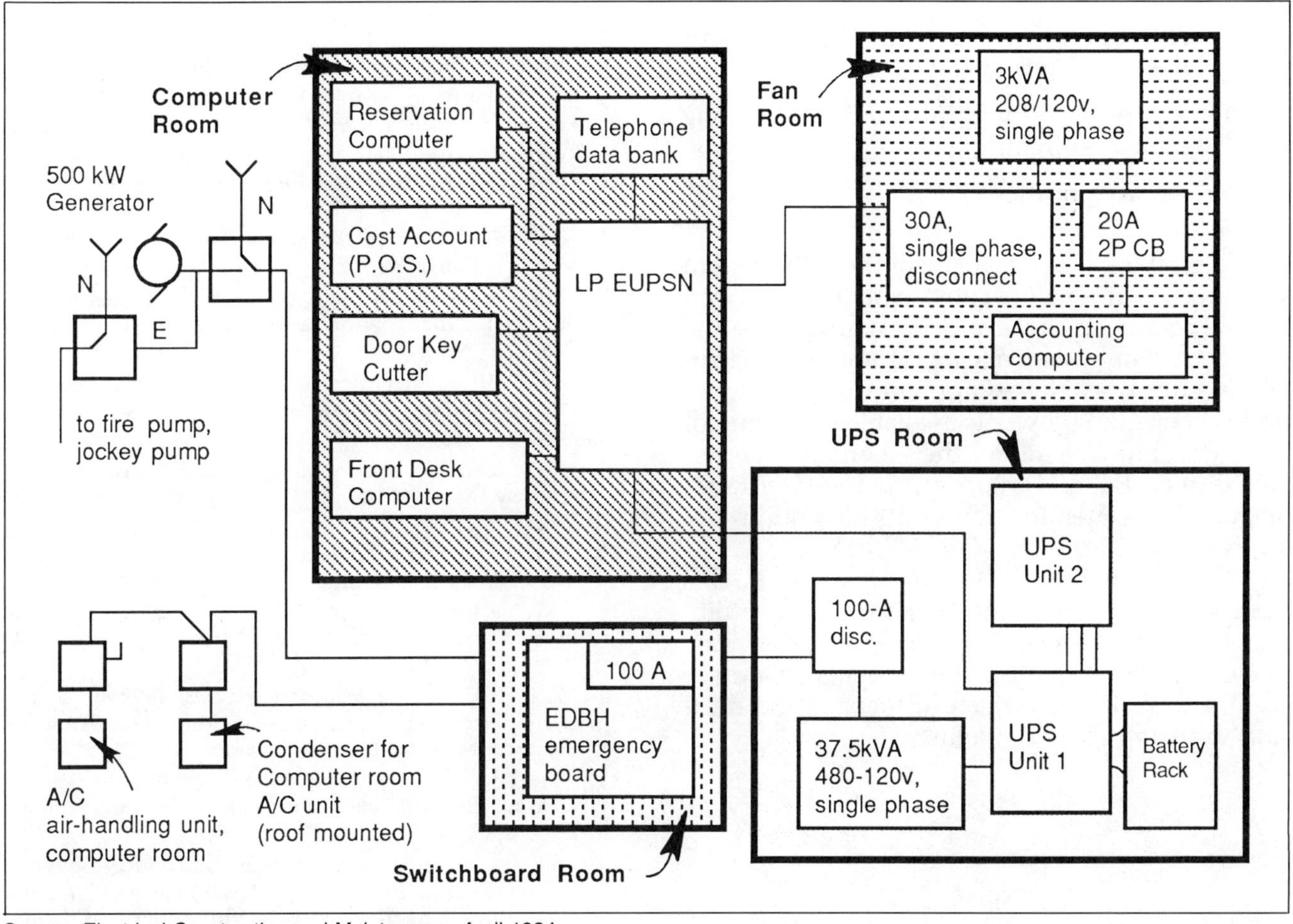

Source: *Electrical Construction and Maintenance*, April 1984.

at a load greater than the service factor times the rated horsepower will damage the insulation. Operation of the motor above the rated horsepower but below service factor times rated horsepower results in a shortened life for the insulation. The *insulation class* is related to the type of materials used for insulation and is linked to the operating temperature range for the motor. The *frame* identifies the dimensions of the motor. A NEMA frame identification number would specify the mounting dimensions (requiring reference to NEMA publication MG1-1987[16]). When replacing a motor, the selection of a replacement with the same frame will ensure that the replacement motor will fit the mounting used for the old motor. *Horsepower* refers to the rated horsepower the motor was designed to deliver at its shaft with rated frequency and voltage applied to the terminal with a service factor of 1.0.[17]

5.6 UPS System at Hilton Hotel, Lake Buena Vista

The 814-room Hilton Hotel, Lake Buena Vista, Florida, has installed an uninterruptible power supply (UPS) which provides reliable power to the following facilities:

- A national reservations computer system
- A point-of-sales (POS) terminal system (cost accounting use)
- A key-card cutter system (a cardboard card that a guest uses instead of a metal

key is encoded with a non-duplicated pattern of small holes)

- A property management system (front desk CRT terminals)
- A private multipurpose telephone branch exchange system (data bank)
- An accounting system

Exhibit 5.9 is a schematic of the UPS system showing its interconnection with the serviced loads and the emergency power supply for the property. This system allows for not only a clean power supply to the equipment during the period when utility power is available (by virtue of the UPS), but also allows the emergency generator to feed the UPS during prolonged outages or for the generator to feed the equipment directly should the UPS fail.

The frequency of power outages at this location and the requirement of the local utility that the hotel annually de-energize the electric power system to check the emergency power system were factors which influenced the decision to install such a system.[18]

Notes

1. Technical Services Center, The Hospitality, Lodging and Travel Research Foundation, Inc., *A Survey of the Energy and Water Use of Selected Hotels and Motels—1983* (New York: The American Hotel & Motel Association, 1984).
2. U.S. Department of Energy, National Technical Information Service, *Recommendations for Energy Conservation Standards and Guidelines for New Commercial Buildings, Volume III: Description of the Testing Process*, PNL 4870-7, Report # DOE/NBB-0051/6 (Washington: Government Printing Office, 1983).
3. NFPA 70, *National Electrical Code* (Quincy, Mass.: National Fire Protection Association, 1987).
4. J. F. McPartland, "Basic Design of Electrical Circuits," *Electrical Construction and Maintenance*, May 1985, p. 53.
5. Terry Michaud, "Electrical Transformers—The 'PCB' Dilemma," *Building Operating Management*, Dec. 1982, pp. 42-44, 46.
6. NFPA 70B, *Electrical Equipment Maintenance* (Quincy, Mass.: National Fire Protection Association, 1983).
7. Other maintenance activities and a suggested frequency for their performance can be found in NFPA 70B.
8. NFPA 101, *Life Safety Code* (Quincy, Mass.: National Fire Protection Association, 1985).
9. *NEC*, p. 645.
10. NFPA 110, *Emergency and Standby Power Systems* (Quincy, Mass.: National Fire Protection Association, 1985).
11. "Selecting Energy-Efficient Motors," *Electrical Construction and Maintenance*, March, 1984, pp. 38, 44, 175.
12. A. T. Nestor, "What Price Efficiency? Evaluating Motor Efficiency Economics," *Plant Engineering*, August 4, 1983, pp. 70-71.
13. MG10-1983, *Energy Management Guide for Selection and Use of Polyphase Motors* (Washington, D.C.: National Electrical Manufacturers Association, 1983).
14. Alfred Berutti, "Cycling of Motors For Energy Conservation," *Electrical Construction and Maintenance*, January 1984, pp. 68-69.
15. This discussion is based in part on David E. Shapiro, "Hints on Installing Electronic Cash Registers," *Electrical Construction and Maintenance*, June 1986, pp. 80-83. See this reference for additional ECR wiring guidelines.
16. MG1-1987, *Motors and Generators* (Washington, D.C.: National Electrical Manufacturers Association, 1987).
17. E. J. Feldman, "Motor Facts—Nameplate Data—For Better Motor Installation and Maintenance," *Electrical Construction and Maintenance*, Dec. 1983, pp. 36, 40.
18. Joseph Knisley, "UPS System Serves Luxury Hotel Computers," *Electrical Construction and Maintenance*, April 1984, pp. 74-77.

6

Heating Systems

The heating system and its components are part of the HVAC system as described in Chapter 3. The purpose of the system is to provide heat energy to each room to replace the heat energy that is lost to the outdoors during cold weather. The fuel consumption of the system is directly related to the heat losses from the building.

The importance of the system—measured in installation costs, hours of operation, and operating costs—is directly dependent on the climate of the property. In cold climates, the heating system often operates for more than half of the operating hours in a year and consumes utilities that represent a substantial portion of the energy expenses. In a temperate climate, the system operates throughout the day and night during a few cold months and sometimes at night during the rest of the year. Even in warm climates, the system must be available to operate during the brief spells of cold weather.

System Configuration

As stated in Chapter 3, there are two common configurations for HVAC systems: decentralized and centralized. Due to code regulations concerning the burning of fossil fuels in inhabited spaces, the most common utility for a decentralized system is electricity because it produces no poisonous products of combustion as do fossil fuels. In a centralized system, the least expensive utility, measured in cost per usable Btu, is usually selected, so the choice is often a fossil fuel.

System Diagrams and Components

Exhibit 6.1 shows a schematic of the major components of a decentralized electrical heating system as they might be installed in a guestroom. The system includes an enclosing case, an electrical resistance element, and a fan for the forced circulation of the air.

An electrical resistance heating element converts electricity into heat energy. The efficiency of conversion for this type of equipment is 100%, so 3,413 Btu/hr of heat are produced for every kilowatt of power consumed by the element. The specific size of the element, measured in kw, is determined by the maximum heating load at design conditions.

The heat must be transported throughout the room in order to maintain the guest's comfort in all locations in the space. The heat produced by the element is transferred directly into the surrounding air inside the enclosure. The fan circulates that warmed air around the room while drawing other cooler air over the element. The intake and diffuser grates are positioned to enhance the circulation of the warmer and cooler air to prevent cold spots from developing near the windows or in corners of the room.

The enclosing case contains all of the components of the heating system and often the components of the air conditioning system to form an integrated system as discussed briefly in Chapter 3 and in more detail in Chapter 9.

Exhibit 6.2 contains the schematic diagram of the major components of a centralized system using a natural gas boiler and a hot water distribution system as they might be installed in a similar guestroom. The portion of the system that is in the guestroom includes an enclosing case, a heating coil, and a circulation fan. The remaining portion of the system includes the boiler as well as the piping and circulation pumps for the hot water.

The pieces of equipment that convert the natural gas into heat energy and distribute it around the building are installed in a central location. The natural gas is burned in a boiler with the useful heat being stored in hot water. The waste products of combustion and some heat are exhausted to the outdoor environment through a flue. The conversion efficiency for this process is usually around 80% for a well-regulated boiler. The hot water is circulated throughout the building in two pipes, one supplying the heated water to the rooms and the other returning the water from the rooms after it has lost some of its heat. This circulation is forced by pumps which operate whenever the boiler is producing hot water.

In the guestroom, the operation of this type of system is very similar to that of the decentralized system except that a hot water coil replaces the electrical heating element. The circulation patterns of the air caused by the fan and the placement of the intake and diffuser grates are the same. The thermostat activates the system to deliver heat into the air surrounding the heating coil by controlling a valve that allows hot water to flow through the coil. The enclosure also often contains the components of an air conditioning system as part of an integrated system.

Exhibit 6.1 Schematic for an Electrical Decentralized Heating System

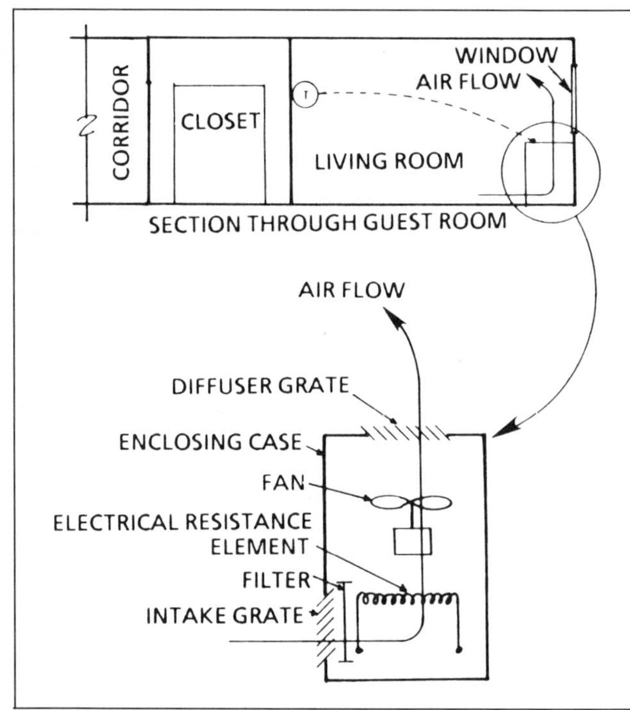

System Operation

The primary goal of the system in either configuration is to maintain the temperature of the heated space at a specific value by supplying heat energy to replace the heat that is lost from the space. Over a period of time, heat energy leaves the zone through various paths. For example, heat flows through the exterior wall to the colder outdoor air, warm air is lost inadvertently to the outdoors through cracks around windows and through doors when they are open, and warm air is exhausted to the outdoors when fresh air for human comfort is brought into the building. When the air temperature in the zone decreases below the desired temperature, the thermostat activates the heating system. When the desired temperature is again achieved, the system is deactivated and waits for the next signal from the thermostat.

In a decentralized system, the operation of the components is straightforward. The signal from the thermostat controls a relay which allows electricity to flow through the heating element and activates the circulation fan to move the air through the system and into the room.

In a centralized system, the operation is more complex. In a water-based system, for example, the signal from the thermostat controls a valve in the heating coil. When activated, the valve opens and water flows from the hot water supply line through the coil to the return line. At the same time, the circulation fan draws air over the hot coil and distributes the heated air around the room. The operation of the centrally located source component, however, is not directly related to the signal from the thermostat. Instead, the boiler has its own thermostat that measures the temperature of the water in the hot water supply line just as it leaves the boiler. This thermostat controls the burner in the boiler so that the boiler maintains a constant output temperature for the water.

Exhibit 6.2 Schematic for a Centralized Heating System with Natural Gas Boiler and Hot Water Distribution

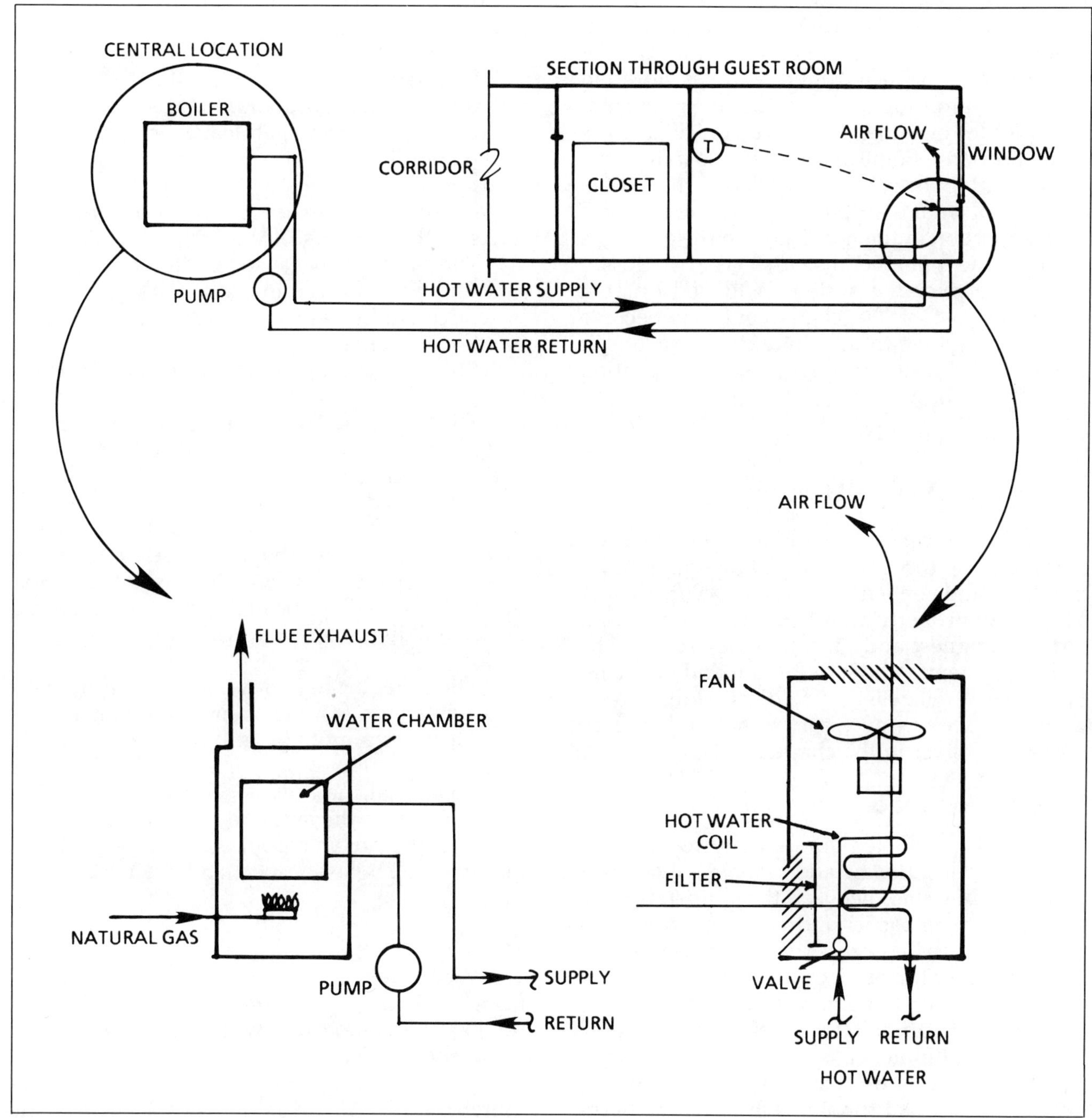

The boiler is turned on whenever it is likely that the building will have a demand for heat. This demand may not come from all of the rooms at the same time. Even in cold weather, only some of the rooms are being heated at any specific time. In mild weather, some of the rooms are being heated while others are being cooled because of heat that has entered the room through such sources as lights or the sun. Therefore, the component that is the heating source must operate at any time of the year when there is a need for heating in rooms, even if only a small percentage of the total rooms need it.

An important implication follows from this. When this component is operating, it is burning fuel. Some of the heat from that fuel is stored in the distribution medium (water, in the current example) for eventual transport to various parts of the property. Some of the heat is lost from the component to the surrounding room (that is, the mechanical room around the boiler becomes hot). A portion of the heat is lost to the outdoors through the flue. Because the last two losses occur whenever the system is turned on, the operating cost of the component can become very high relative to the amount of heat that is actually used in the property, especially during periods of mild weather.

Heating Loads

The heat losses or loads for a building are classified into three categories: transmission, infiltration, and ventilation. They all occur in every hospitality property and they all affect the comfort of the guest and the cost of energy for the heating system. A brief definition and an example for each follows. A very detailed discussion of the calculations necessary to determine loads is provided later in the chapter.

Transmission Load

Heat is conducted through physical barriers (that is, walls, floors, and ceilings) whenever there is a difference between the temperature on one side of the barrier and the temperature on the other side. In a property, this causes a heat loss whenever the outdoor temperature is lower than the indoor temperature. The lost heat is "transmitted" through the barrier because of the temperature difference.

Three factors determine the rate at which heat is transmitted through a barrier: the barrier's area, its construction materials, and the size of the temperature difference. Some walls (for example, single-pane windows) transmit heat rapidly, while others (for example, well-insulated masonry walls) lose heat slowly. A colder outdoor temperature means there will be a larger temperature difference, which causes more heat to flow.

Any exterior surface in a property—guestroom wall, restaurant window, swimming pool enclosure—is an example of a transmission load.

Infiltration Load

Whenever air leaks from the inside of a building to the outdoors, heat is lost. The warmer, inside air which leaves is replaced by colder, outdoor air. This loss of heat is considered an infiltration load if the loss is unintentional, such as leaks due to cracks around windows or the opening of the lobby doors.

The air leaks are caused by differences in air pressure between the inside and the outdoors. Whenever and wherever the pressure inside the building is higher than it is outside, air leaks out. If the indoor air pressure is lower, then air leaks in.

These pressure differences are caused primarily by wind and the density difference between warm and cold air. When wind blows against the side of a building, it causes a high pressure region on the windward side and a low pressure region on the opposite side. When warm air inside a tall building rises to the top floors, it creates indoor high pressure at the top of the building and indoor low pressure at the bottom.

The rate of heat loss due to infiltration depends on the volume of air flow (measured in cubic feet per minute or cfm) and the difference between the indoor and outdoor temperatures. The volume of the flow is controlled by several factors, such as the size and type of the opening (for example, an open door or a crack around the perimeter of a closed door) and the wind velocity.

Ventilation Load

Whenever air is intentionally exhausted from the building and replaced by outside air, the heat loss associated with the transfer of the air is considered a ventilation load. This air is exhausted from the property because codes require the HVAC system to deliver specific amounts of fresh air to occupied spaces. As with infiltration loads, the rate of heat loss is dependent on the volume of air flow and the difference in temperature. The minimum air flow is determined by the codes (see Appendix B for examples).

As shown in the diagrams for the HVAC system in Chapter 3, fresh air is circulated to a

Exhibit 6.3 Typical Outdoor Temperature Variations for a Cold Climate

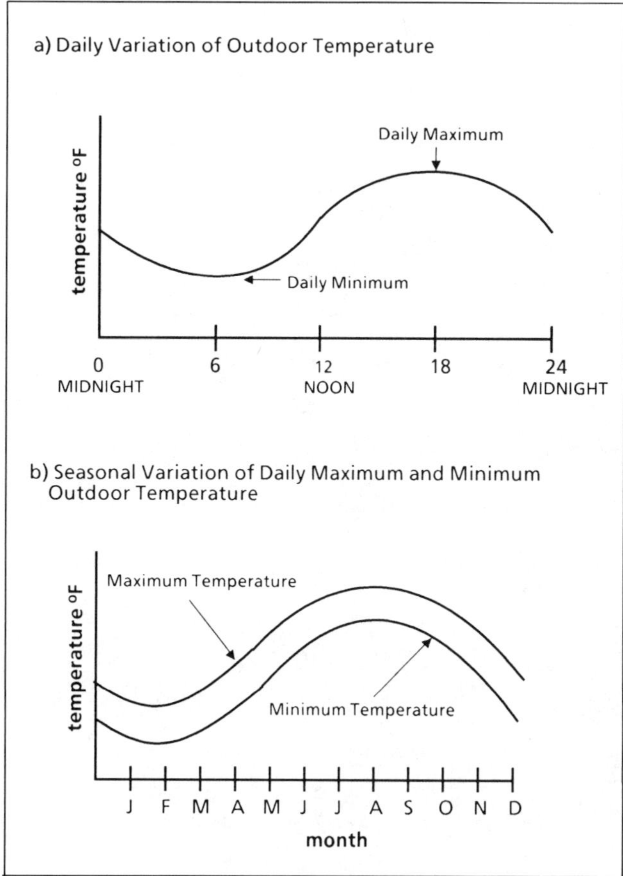

guestroom either directly from the outdoors or through the corridor, while a similar volume of air is exhausted from the room. Fresh air must be heated, thus causing a load on the heating system.

Profiles

The discussion in this section presents general profiles for variations in the three heating loads. These profiles do not represent variations that actually occur in a specific location on any given day.

All of the three heating loads vary hour by hour over the entire year. The variations, however, fall into several patterns based on their causes. The two major causes for the hourly fluctuations are the changes in outdoor temperature and in the activity of the guests and employees. The first cause dramatically affects the size of all three loads, while the second cause influences only the infiltration load.

There are two major types of outdoor temperature variations: daily and seasonal. The daily temperatures vary over the 24-hour period from midnight to midnight between the maximum and minimum temperatures for the day. The minimum temperature usually occurs just before sunrise, while the maximum occurs late in the afternoon. The magnitude of the daily maximum and minimum temperatures varies seasonally. Exhibit 6.3 shows typical profiles for these two categories of variation for a location in a cold climate in the Northern Hemisphere.

The hour-by-hour variations in the size of two of the heating loads, transmission and ventilation, depend totally on these temperature profiles under the assumption that the ventilation is constantly on. The third load, infiltration, is also affected by these profiles, though not to the same degree. Exhibit 6.4 shows the effect of daily temperature variations on these loads. Notice that the ventilation load has its peak and valley at exactly the same time as the minimum and maximum temperature. The transmission load profile has the same shape as the ventilation load profile, but it is delayed slightly because of the thermal storage capacity of the building materials in the exterior surfaces. The heavier the material and the thicker the wall, the longer is the delay. Notice also that there are no loads at all when the outdoor temperature is greater than the inside temperature.

The hour-by-hour variation in the size of the infiltration load is affected by two simultaneous influences. The temperature profile determines a profile for the infiltration load that is very similar to the ventilation load profile if we assume that the volume of infiltration is constant during the day at the maximum volume. The variation of the actual load occurs as the volume of infiltration changes due to less wind or fewer door openings.

Characteristics of Fuels and Systems

Fuels

The source components of the heating system consume a utility in order to produce heat.

A resistance heating element consumes electricity; a water boiler often also uses natural gas, fuel oils of various weights, or LPG (liquified petroleum gas); a hot air furnace might use any of them.

These fuels have different physical characteristics. The fossil fuels (natural gas, fuel oil, and LPG) are either liquids or gases when supplied to the property. Natural gas is provided through a pipeline as a gas under pressure. LPG is delivered by a vehicle as a liquid under pressure, but is a gas as used because it is evaporated before it is burned. Fuel oil is delivered by a vehicle as a liquid under no pressure and is consumed as a liquid. Electricity is delivered as electrical power through power lines. Steam is provided as a high-pressure gas through a steam pipe.

The choice of which fuel to use has a major impact on several aspects of the heating system: its design, its initial cost, its operation, and its cost for energy.

Design. The influences on the design of the system are twofold. First, according to present codes, electricity is the only fuel that can be used in a decentralized system for a guestroom. If any other fuel is used, then the combustion of the fuel must occur outside the space. Second, the delivery and storage of the fuel must be considered. For electricity, no storage is necessary, but the electrical system in the building must be increased in size to accommodate the extra power requirements. Natural gas and steam require pipes from the local utility company, but do not require any storage. Fuel oil and LPG are delivered periodically and stored in onsite tanks. Easy access to the tanks for delivery is essential and the tanks must satisfy very detailed code requirements in order to ensure safe storage. The requirements for LPG are especially restrictive.

Initial Cost. An electrical heating system, especially if it is a decentralized system, is often less expensive to construct than systems for the other fuels. The systems are less complex because no additional distribution system is necessary and because the source component does not need sophisticated control or safety devices. Also, no storage equipment must be built.

Operation. As is the case with design and initial cost, the implications of choosing any of the fossil fuels are very similar, while those of choosing electricity are substantially different. In general, electrical systems are easier and less expen-

Exhibit 6.4 Typical Profiles for Ventilation, Transmission, and Infiltration Loads

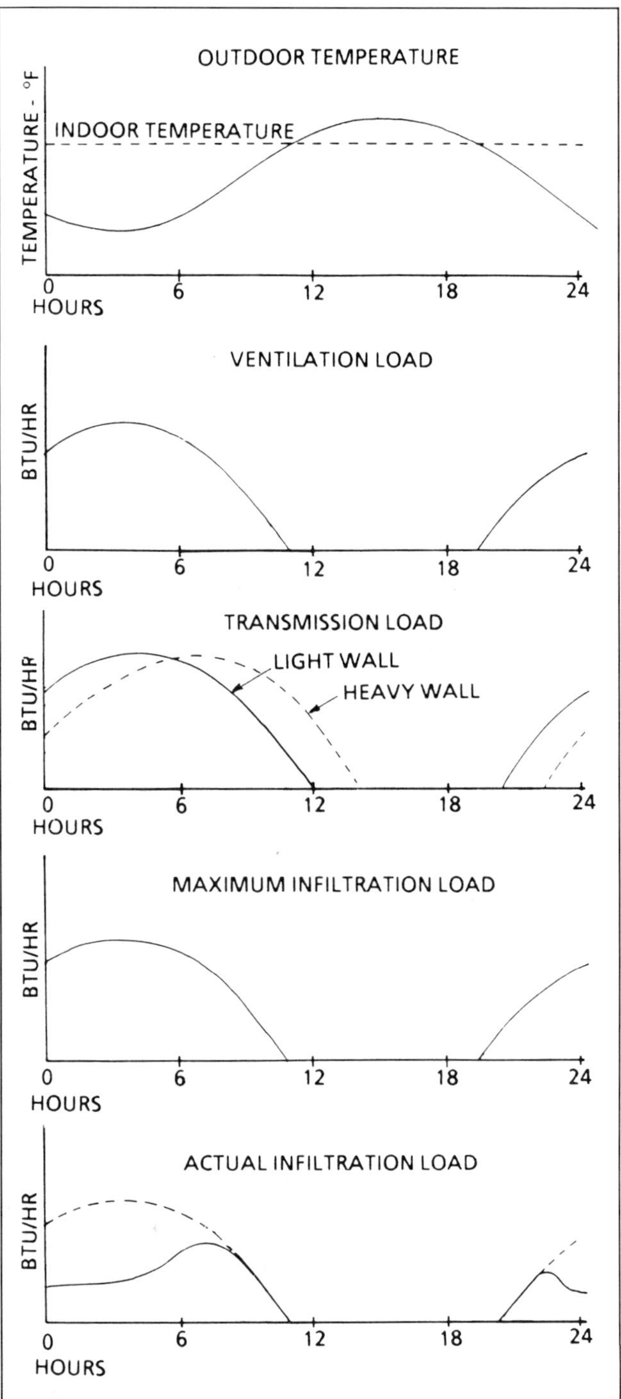

sive to maintain than fossil fuel systems. Of fossil fuels, systems using natural gas and LPG are usually less expensive to maintain than systems using fuel oil.[1]

In some locations, natural gas offers a unique opportunity for cost reductions for the heating system. Some utility companies offer "interruptible" natural gas as a fuel at substantially reduced costs. The property must, however, be prepared with a backup system for when the utility company interrupts the supply of gas in periods of high demand. Often this is accomplished with a dual burner boiler or furnace which uses fuel oil as the secondary fuel.

Cost for Energy. The fuels are purchased in different units. Electricity is supplied in kwh; fuel oil and LPG are purchased by the gallon; natural gas is supplied in therms (that is, 100,000 Btu) and hundreds or thousands of cubic feet (ccf or mcf, respectively); and steam is purchased by the pound. Each of these units contains a different amount of energy. It is very important to compare the effective cost of different fuels in order to determine which is the most desirable. A section following shortly presents a method which accomplishes the comparison.

System Size

The size of the heating system depends primarily on two factors: (1) the size and type of construction of the building and (2) the weather for the location. First, larger buildings require larger heating systems and buildings which are designed and constructed with energy efficient exterior surfaces may use smaller systems. Second, the system is designed to respond to the weather conditions for the location. Therefore, the size of the system is directly dependent on the extreme cold temperatures for the specific location. Two identical buildings would have different system sizes if they were located in two different climatic zones. Exhibit 6.5 shows typical system sizes for the same building in various locations.

Consumption of Energy

As Exhibit 6.5 shows, the relative importance of the heating system to the HVAC system and the proportion of the energy expenses that it generates are extremely dependent on the location of the property. In very cold climates, the heating system's effect is major, while in very warm climates, the effect is minimal. Consequently, the importance of studying the consumption of the heating system depends on the location of the property.

Exhibit 6.5 Typical Sizes and Consumptions of Heating Systems for Guestroom Areas

Size: Btu/hr-ft²	Consumption: Btu/ft²-yr	Location
21	48,500	Syracuse
27	61,200	Minneapolis
20	56,450	Denver
13	31,700	Seattle
8	17,000	San Francisco
14	23,600	Memphis
8	9,400	Los Angeles
9	8,300	Phoenix
11	12,000	San Antonio
7	3,600	Miami

Source: Armand Domanic Iaia, *Computer Modeling of Building Criteria to Determine Their Efficiency in Different Climates*, Monograph, School of Hotel Administration, Cornell University, 1983.

Separating the consumption of the heating system from that for other systems is almost impossible using just the utility meter readings. This separation can be accomplished, however, if detailed metering is installed which separates heating system consumption from that for other purposes or if a separate fuel is used only for heating. Another alternative is to estimate the consumption of heating energy and fuel using detailed equations that describe the flow of heat in a building. A section later in this chapter presents several techniques for performing the estimates. Exhibit 6.6 shows a sample property's consumption of energy for heating in comparison to the total.

Economics of Selection

There are two economic criteria for selection: the initial installation cost and the annual cost of operation for energy and maintenance. The estimates for the two components are determined separately and then combined using capital budgeting techniques to determine which type of fuel has the lowest total cost over the expected life of the system.

Estimating the annual energy cost is a two step process. First, the amount of energy to be used must be estimated. Then, the effective cost

Exhibit 6.6 Computer Model of Energy Consumption in a Property

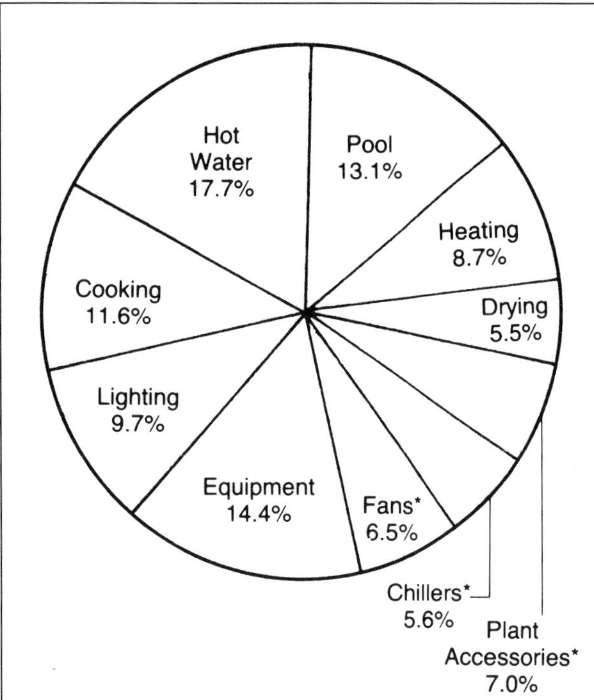

* Items from each of these categories are used in air conditioning which accounts for approximately 12% of the energy consumption in a property.

Source: Robach Inc., Torrance, Calif., 1977.

of that energy must be determined. An estimate for the amount used requires a detailed analysis (as shown later in this chapter). An estimate for the effective cost is performed as follows.

Although the different fuels are purchased in different units containing differing amounts of heat energy, it is possible to compare their effective cost by using a common basis of measurement. This basis is measured in MMBtu (1,000,000 Btu) of output energy from the system; that is, the efficiency of production is included in the analysis. The equation that determines the effective cost of the heat-producing capability of a utility is

$$COST_{MMBtu} = COST_{UNIT} \times 1{,}000{,}000/(k \times V)$$

where $COST_{MMBtu}$ is the effective cost of the fuel per MMBtu; $COST_{UNIT}$ is the actual cost of the utility per unit (gallons of fuel oil, kwh of electricity); the constant (1,000,000) converts the units to MMBtu; *k* is the efficiency of energy production for the system; and *V* is the heat content of the fuel in units consistent with the units for the utility.

Certain data is necessary for the equation. Exhibit 6.7 shows representative values for *k* in various types of systems. Notice that electricity has an efficiency that is substantially higher than any of the fossil fuels and that the values for the fossil fuels are relatively similar. Exhibit 6.8 shows the heating values for several common fuels. Using the equation and the information from Exhibits 6.7 and 6.8, Exhibit 6.9 calculates the effective cost of three common fuels at typical unit costs.

In general, the answer that is arrived at after balancing the initial and operating costs has one common theme. Assuming that the relative effective costs of the fuels in the specific location are similar to the national averages and that the availability of the fuels is the same, the severity of the climate primarily determines the choice of the fuel. Cold climates suggest a fossil fuel, while warm climates suggest electricity. This is because the effective cost of the fuel is most important to the decision in cold climates and

Exhibit 6.7 Typical Values of k, the Efficiency of Energy Production

Type of System	k
Electric	.95-1.0
Natural Gas	.80
Fuel Oil	.75
LPG	.80
Steam	.95-1.0

Exhibit 6.8 Heating Values for Various Fuels

Fuel	Approximate Heating Value
Electricity	3,413 Btu/kwh
Natural Gas	103,000 Btu/ccf
Fuel Oil (#2)	140,000 Btu/gal
Fuel Oil (#6)	150,000 Btu/gal
LPG	95,000 Btu/gal
Steam	1,000 Btu/lb

the initial cost of the system is most important in warm climates.

System Design

The process of designing and selecting the heating system has four steps: (1) determine the magnitudes of the three heating loads, (2) combine the separate loads to determine the size of the system, (3) estimate the consumption of the system for various fuels, and (4) select the best system based on the design criteria and the total cost of the system over its lifetime.

The following sections present an overview of the details for accomplishing the analysis.

Load Calculations

As described before, the three loads on a heating system are transmission, infiltration, and ventilation. The methods for determining each load are as follows.

Transmission Loads. The amount of heat (Q_T) which flows through a specific wall depends on three parameters: the construction of the wall (including types and thicknesses of materials), the difference in temperature of the environments on the two sides of the wall, and the surface area of the wall.

The tendency of a composite wall, which is constructed from several layers of materials, to conduct heat is summarized in a variable designated as the *U factor* (discussed in Appendix A). This variable, which is measured in Btu/hr-ft^2-F°, combines the thermal resistances of all the layers in the wall, including the interior and exterior films of air that form on the surfaces, into an overall heat transfer coefficient for the assembled wall. The larger the U factor, the more easily the wall transmits heat. Buildings that are designed to conserve energy are built with exterior walls, floors, and ceilings that have very low U factors to minimize the amount of energy that flows to the outdoors. Exhibit 6.10 shows values for the U factors of several common walls.

The temperature difference between one side of a wall and the other side has a fundamental effect on the amount of heat that flows through the wall. The larger the temperature difference, the larger is the flow of heat. The difference in temperature is determined by subtracting the air temperature of the space on one side of the wall from the air temperature of the space on the other side. When the air temperatures in two adjacent rooms are the same, no heat flows through the intermediate wall. When the inside air temperature of a guestroom is higher than the outdoor air temperature, as it is during the winter season, heat flows from the guestroom air through the exterior wall to the outdoor air. In this case, the temperature difference is calculated as

$$TD = T_I - T_O$$

where T_I is the temperature of the inside air and T_O is the temperature of the outside air.

The effect of the area of the wall, the third parameter, is directly proportional. The larger the surface area of the wall, the larger is the amount of heat flow.

These three parameters are combined into an equation that expresses the total heat flow through a specific building wall as follows:

$$Q_T = U \times A \times TD$$

where Q_T is the total heat flow in Btu/hr; U is the U factor for the wall in Btu/hr-ft^2-F°; A is the surface area in ft^2; and TD is the temperature difference between the environments on the two sides of the wall in F°. The form of the equation matches a common sense understanding of heat

Exhibit 6.9 Effective Cost of Various Fuels

Data:

Fuel	Cost
Electricity	\$.08/kwh
Natural Gas	\$.40/ccf
Fuel Oil (#2)	\$.60/gal

What is the effective cost per MMBtu?

Calculations:

Basic equation:

$$COST_{MMBtu} = COST_{UNIT} \times 1{,}000{,}000/(k \times V)$$

Electricity:

$$\$.08 \times 1{,}000{,}000/(1.0 \times 3{,}413) = \$23.44/MMBtu$$

Natural Gas:

$$\$.40 \times 1{,}000{,}000/(.8 \times 103{,}000) = \$4.85/MMBtu$$

Fuel Oil:

$$\$.60 \times 1{,}000{,}000/(.75 \times 140{,}000) = \$5.71/MMBtu$$

Exhibit 6.10 U Factors for Typical Walls

Wall Construction	U Factor (Btu/Hr-Ft²-F°)
Construction 1. Outside surface (15 mph wind) 2. Siding, wood, 0.5 in., 8 in. lapped (average) 3. Sheathing, 0.5-in. asphalt impregnated 4. Nonreflective air space, 3.5 in. (50° F mean; 10F° temperature difference) 5. Nominal 2-in. x 4-in. wood stud 6. Gypsum wallboard, 0.5-in. 7. Inside surface (still air)	Without insulation .206 With insulation .081
Construction 1. Outside surface (15 mph wind) 2. Common Brick, 8-in. 3. Nominal 1-in. x 3-in. vertical furring 4. Nonreflective air space, 0.75 in. (50° F mean; 10F° temperature difference) 5. Gypsum wallboard, 0.5-in. 6. Inside surface (still air)	Without insulation .257 With insulation .127
Construction 1. Outside surface (15 mph wind) 2. Face brick, 4-in. 3. Cement mortar, 0.5 in. 4. Concrete block, cinder aggregate, 8-in. 5. Reflective air space, 0.75 in. (50° F mean; 30F° temperature difference) 6. Nominal 1-in. x 3-in. vertical furring 7. Gypsum wallboard, 0.5-in., foil backed 8. Inside surface (still air)	.171

Reprinted by permission from *1981 ASHRAE Handbook—Fundamentals.*

flow. First, the overall heat flow increases proportionally with increases in U factor, surface area, and temperature difference. Second, the units on the variables match, as they must.

The application of this equation for estimating the transmission heat loss for a single room or an entire building requires specific information regarding the construction of the building, the weather conditions for the building site, and the interior conditions necessary for human comfort. The American Society of Heating, Refrigerating, and Air-conditioning Engineers (ASHRAE) publishes tables of values for thermal properties of individual building materials and values of U factors for wall assemblies.[2] Values for a few building materials are shown in Appendix A. ASHRAE also publishes weather information on numerous locations throughout the United States and Canada as well as selected locations for other countries to be used as data for this equation.[3] Finally, ASHRAE suggests interior design conditions in several of its publications,[4] a summary of which is presented in Appendix B. Exhibit 6.11 shows an example of a transmission calculation.

Infiltration Loads. Three characteristics determine the size of the infiltration load: (1) the

Exhibit 6.11 Sample Transmission Load Calculation

Data:

Temperatures
  Outdoor = 34°F
  Indoor = 70°F
Wall Construction
  Type 1 from Exhibit 6.10, without insulation
Area is 100 ft^2

What is the transmission load?

Calculation:

$Q_T = U \times A \times TD;\ TD = T_I - T_O$
$= .206 \times 100 \times (70 - 34)$
$= 742$ Btu/hr

Exhibit 6.12 Infiltration Rates for Various Window Frames

Key to window infiltration chart

Leakage Between Sash And Frame			
Type	Material	Weatherstripped?	Fit
1) All Hinged	Wood Metal	Yes Yes	Avg. Avg.
2) All Hinged	Wood Metal	No No	Avg. Avg.
Double Hung	Steel	No	Avg.
3) All	Wood	Yes	Loose
Double Hung	Steel	Yes	Avg.
4) Casement	Steel	No	Avg.
5) All Hinged	Wood	No	Loose

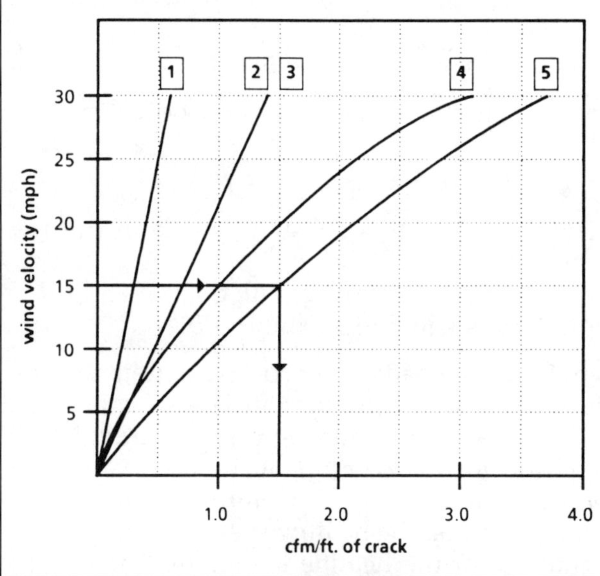

Reprinted by permission of Dubin-Bloome Associates, East Norwalk, Conn.

amount of air flow measured in cubic feet per minute, (2) the difference in air temperature between the interior air (T_I) and the outdoor air (T_O), and (3) physical properties of air at typical room temperatures—that is, specific heat (.24 Btu/lb-F°) and density (.075 lb/ft^3). These three characteristics are combined into one equation that determines the amount of heat necessary to heat dry air from one temperature to another as follows:

$$Q_I = 1.08 \times \text{cfm} \times \text{TD}$$

where Q_I is the load in Btu/hr; *1.08* is a constant that combines the specific heat, the density, and a conversion from minutes to hours; *cfm* is the amount of air flow in ft^3/min; and *TD* is the temperature difference ($T_I - T_O$) in F°.

Applying this equation requires knowledge of the volume of air flow. This information comes from various sources[5] in which two methods are used to determine the flow: the crack method and the air change method.

Exhibit 6.12 shows data representative of the crack method in which the infiltration for a window is determined for the type of window on the basis of cfm of flow per lineal foot of crack. The total amount of flow is then determined by multiplying the length of the cracks by the cfm/ft from the chart. Another example of the data is shown in Exhibit 6.13, in which the flow rate in cfm is given for three configurations of entrance doors. This data is for one door and should be extended for multiple doors.

For properties with construction similar to residential construction, a simpler approach—the air change method—may be used. Although the number of air changes per hour varies, a typical value of .5 air changes per hour is often used as an estimate. The total amount of infiltration air flow is determined by multiplying the air changes per hour by the volume of the space measured in cubic feet. This technique is very easy to use, but is subject to error when the

Exhibit 6.13 Infiltration Rates for Various Types of Doors

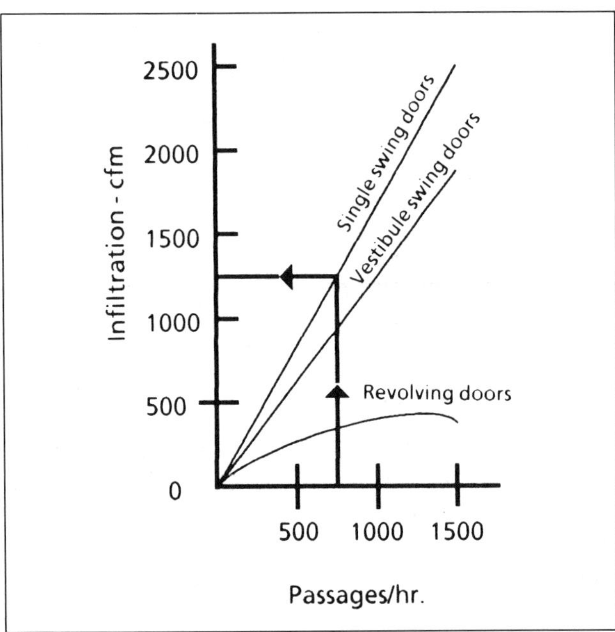

Reprinted by permission of Dubin-Bloome Associates, East Norwalk, Conn.

Exhibit 6.14 Sample Infiltration Load Calculation

Data:

Vestibule door into lobby, swing type, 500 passages per hour
Cubic feet/minute = 650 (from Exhibit 6.13)
Temperatures
Outdoor = 34°F
Indoor = 70°F

What is the infiltration load?

Calculation:

$Q_I = 1.08 \times \text{cfm} \times \text{TD}; \text{TD} = T_I - T_O$
$= 1.08 \times 650 \times (70 - 34)$
$= 25{,}272$ Btu/hr

construction differs substantially from the residential type.

An example of the calculation for an infiltration load is shown in Exhibit 6.14.

Ventilation Loads. Forced circulation of fresh outside air is mandatory in commercial buildings, where a minimum amount of outdoor air is required for the comfort of the occupants. This outdoor air, like the air from infiltration, represents a load on the heating system. Likewise, the equation for the heating load is the same:

$$Q_V = 1.08 \times \text{cfm} \times \text{TD}$$

where the variables are the same except that cfm is now the amount of ventilation air required rather than the amount of infiltration air.

The information necessary for the application of this equation is available in resources previously cited. The data on the amount of necessary ventilation air is documented in Appendix B.

System Size

When adding the separate loads to determine the size of the heating system, two factors must be considered. What weather should be used to represent the design conditions and how should the separate loads be combined?

First, although the load equations can be used to estimate the heat flow any time of the day or year, they are usually applied at "design conditions" in order to determine the maximum loads. An outside design temperature for the heating season is determined for each location for which ASHRAE publishes weather data. Selected data of this type is shown in Exhibit 6.15. The outside design temperature is not the coldest temperature ever recorded for a location. Heating systems usually have a factor of safety designed into them; also, other internal sources of heat, such as lights and people, contribute to the heating of the space. Therefore, the design transmission load is not calculated with an extreme temperature, but rather with a temperature that includes either 97.5% or 99% of the temperatures, with a preference for the 97.5% temperature.

Second, the maximums of the separate loads usually occur at the same time early in the morning of the coldest day of the year. Therefore, the sum of the three loads at their individual maximums represents the total heating load (Q_{Lmax}) and is the basis for determining the size of the system.

$$Q_{Lmax} = Q_{Tmax} + Q_{Imax} + Q_{Vmax}$$

Heat from internal sources (Q_{INT}) such as

Exhibit 6.15 Selected Winter Climatic Conditions for the United States

Location	Design Dry-Bulb 99%	97.5%
Phoenix, Ariz.	31	34
Los Angeles, Cal.	41	43
San Francisco, Cal.	35	38
Denver, Colo.	−5	1
Washington, D.C.	14	17
Miami, Fla.	44	47
Atlanta, Ga.	17	22
Chicago, Ill.	−8	−4
Wichita, Kans.	3	7
Boston, Mass.	6	9
Minneapolis, Minn.	−16	−12
New York, N.Y.	12	15
Syracuse, N.Y.	−3	2
Memphis, Tenn.	13	18
San Antonio, Tex.	25	30
Seattle, Wash.	21	26

Reprinted by permission from *1985 ASHRAE Handbook—Fundamentals.*

lights, equipment, or people is included when performing this determination because such heat warms the building, reducing the heat required from the heating system. The system size is

$$SIZE = Q_{Lmax} - Q_{INT}$$

where the units for all three variables are Btu/hr.

Calculations are performed to estimate the total heating load for each zone of a building. In a decentralized arrangement, a decentralized unit is specified which has a heating capacity that is the size just greater than the calculated size for the zone. In a centralized arrangement, the total heating loads for all of the zones are added together to determine the grand total for the building. Often an estimate for the losses of heat in the distribution system is added to this grand total to ensure that the necessary heat can be delivered to the zones.

The choices for the applicable conditions for the determination of the size of the heating system are as follows. The outdoor design temperature is chosen (typically from ASHRAE data) for the specific location; the indoor design temperature is selected either from within the comfort zone (as described in Appendix B) or in accordance with the recommendation of 72°F taken from ASHRAE Standard 90A-1980; the ventilation rate is determined based on maximum occupancy (again, see Appendix B); and the infiltration rates are determined from data such as that in Exhibits 6.12 and 6.13 using the winter wind (15 mph). The physical descriptions of the building which affect the heating loads—U factors and surface areas for the transmission load and types of windows and doors for the infiltration load—are determined from either the building plans or the actual building.

System Consumption

As with the size of the system, the required energy production of a heating system depends on the construction of the building and the weather for its location. In order to predict this energy production over a specified period of time, the effects of these two factors, including their variations over the period of time, must be determined. There are three types of methods for performing such an estimate: single-measure, simplified multiple-measure, and detailed simulation. In the order presented, the methods are increasingly accurate at the cost of being increasingly complex in their calculations and requirements for information. In this section, only the single-measure methods are discussed.[6]

In the single-measure methods, the configuration of the building is assumed to remain constant and only the variation of the weather is accounted for. The logic of this approach can be seen by observing the equation for the total hourly heat loss for a building, $Q_L = Q_T + Q_I + Q_V$. The three components of the loss (transmission, infiltration, and ventilation) can be represented by two forms: (1) $U \times A \times TD$ for transmission and (2) $1.08 \times cfm \times TD$ for infiltration and ventilation. When these substitutions for the three losses are made into the total equation, the expression for the total hourly heat loss has the form

$$Q_L = U \times A \times TD + 1.08 \times cfm \times TD$$

where $U \times A$ represents the combined effects of all the building surfaces and *cfm* is the combined total circulation of air for infiltration and ventilation. This equation can be factored into two parts as follows:

$$Q_L = (U \times A + 1.08 \times cfm) \times TD$$

where the expression inside the parentheses describes the overall effect of the building and the variable *TD* describes the effect of the weather. This reconfiguration of the equation indicates the approach for the single-measure methods, which assume that the building configuration is constant and estimate only the effects caused by the variation in the weather as measured by the temperature difference between the indoor and outdoor temperatures.

The equation for the total hourly heat loss can be extended to apply to any time period. By using the concept of an average daily temperature, the energy requirements for an entire day can be written as

$$LOSS_{DAY} = (U \times A + 1.08 \times cfm) \times TD_{AVE} \times 24$$

where $LOSS_{DAY}$ is in Btu; TD_{AVE} is the temperature difference between the inside temperature and the average outdoor temperature for the day in F°; *24* is a constant for the number of hours in the day; and the other variables are as described in the equation for the total hourly heat loss. The energy requirements of any number of days can be determined by summing the requirements for the individual days in the period. As all of the terms in the equation for the daily requirements are constant except for TD_{AVE}, the energy requirements for any period (for example, a month or a heating season) can be expressed as

$$LOSS_{PERIOD} = (U \times A + 1.08 \times cfm) \times 24 \times (TD_{AVE1} + \ldots + TD_{AVEn})$$

where $LOSS_{PERIOD}$ is in Btu and TD_{AVEn} is the average temperature difference for the nth day in F°.

The average temperature difference in a specific location for one day is counted in *degree days*. Using the most common base of 65°F as a reference, the number of degrees that the average outdoor temperature for the day is below 65°F is the number of heating degree days that occurred on that day. When the average outdoor temperature is 25°F, then the heating degree days for that day are 40. When the average outdoor temperature is above the base temperature, then no heating degree days occurred on that day.

With this definition of heating degree days, an estimate for the energy production of the heating system can now be expressed as

$$LOSS_{PERIOD} = (Q_{Lmax}/TD_{max}) \times 24 \times DD_{PERIOD}$$

where DD_{PERIOD} is the number of heating degree days for the period of time for which the estimate is desired; and Q_{Lmax}/TD_{max} is a different form of the expression U × A + 1.08 × cfm (by reference to the factored form of the equation for total hourly heat loss). The result of the calculation is Btu of energy produced by the heating system.

Often it is desirable to estimate the annual energy production of a heating system during the design stages, as shown in Exhibit 6.16. In order to accomplish this, data on the annual heating degree days for various locations is necessary. One source of the information is ASHRAE.[7] Exhibit 6.17 includes a sample of the data.

The most common form of the heating degree day data uses the base of 65°F. This base has valid historical significance as the temperature at which a typical older building begins to require heating. When the outdoor temperature is greater than 65°F, then internal heat sources provide enough heat to keep the building warm

Exhibit 6.16 Sample Calculation for the Required Energy Production of a Heating System

Data:

Location: Syracuse, New York
Degree days for the heating season = 6,756 (base 65°F)

Q_{Lmax} = .93 MMBtu/hr
T_I = 70°F
T_O = 2°F
TD_{max} = 68F°

What is the required energy production for the heating system?

Calculation:

Basic equation:

$$LOSS_{PERIOD} = (Q_{Lmax}/TD_{max}) \times 24 \times DD_{PERIOD}$$
$$= (.93/68) \times 24 \times 6,756$$
$$= 2,218 \text{ MMBtu/heating season}$$

Exhibit 6.17 Selected Data for Heating Degree Days

Station	Avg. Winter Temp	July	Aug.	Sept	Oct.	Nov.	Dec.	Jan.	Feb.	Mar.	Apr.	May	June	Yearly Total
Phoenix, Ariz.	58.5	0	0	0	22	234	415	474	328	217	75	0	0	1765
Los Angeles, Cal.	57.4	28	28	42	78	180	291	372	302	288	219	158	81	2061
San Francisco, Cal.	53.4	81	78	60	143	306	462	508	395	363	279	214	126	3015
Denver, Colo.	37.6	6	9	117	428	819	1035	1132	938	887	558	288	66	6283
Washington, D.C.	45.7	0	0	33	217	519	834	871	762	626	288	74	0	4224
Miami, Fla.	71.1	0	0	0	0	0	65	74	56	19	0	0	0	214
Atlanta, Ga.	51.7	0	0	18	124	417	648	636	518	428	147	25	0	2961
Chicago, Ill.	35.8	0	12	117	381	807	1166	1265	1086	939	534	260	72	6639
Wichita, Kans.	44.2	0	0	33	229	618	905	1023	804	645	270	87	6	4620
Boston, Mass.	40.0	0	9	60	316	603	983	1088	972	846	513	208	36	5634
Minneapolis, Minn.	28.3	22	31	189	505	1014	1454	1631	1380	1166	621	288	81	8382
New York, N.Y.	43.1	0	0	27	223	528	887	973	879	750	414	124	6	4811
Syracuse, N.Y.	35.2	6	28	132	415	744	1153	1271	1140	1004	570	248	45	6756
Memphis, Tenn.	50.5	0	0	18	130	447	698	729	585	456	147	22	0	3232
San Antonio, Tex.	60.1	0	0	0	31	204	363	428	286	195	39	0	0	1546
Seattle, Wash.	44.2	56	62	162	391	633	750	828	678	657	474	295	159	5145

Reprinted by permission from *1981 ASHRAE Handbook—Fundamentals.*

even though heat losses are occurring. The energy consumption of the system is proportional to the number of degrees of temperature below 65°F, hence the use of heating degree days measured from a base of 65°F.

Variable Base Degree-day Technique. Today's buildings, however, are designed to be much less wasteful of energy, so many of them do not need heat from the heating system until the outdoor temperature drops below a much lower base than 65°F. Consequently, an estimate of the energy requirements using heating degree days with a 65°F base overstates the usage.

Another single-measure approach to estimating the energy production is to determine the actual temperature below which the building requires heat from the heating system. The number of heating degree days that cause the production of energy is then determined using that base temperature. Data for the heating degree days at various base temperatures in various locations is available.[8] The application of this technique requires the calculation of the building's *balance temperature*, the temperature at which the production of heat from internal sources just offsets the total hourly heat losses.

The balance temperature is determined by first finding the temperature difference, TD_B, that puts the production of heat from internal sources and the heat losses of the building in balance. This value is determined as follows:

$$TD_B = Q_{INT}/(U \times A + 1.08 \times cfm)$$

where Q_{INT} is the total heat generated from internal sources such as lights, people, and equipment in Btu/hr and the expression in the

Exhibit 6.18 Sample Calculation for the Required Energy Production of a Heating System Using Variable Base Degree Days

Data:

Location: Syracuse, New York
Q_{Lmax} = .93 MMBtu/hr
TD_{max} = 68
Q_{INT} = .182 MMBtu/hr
DD_{PERIOD} (base 57°F) = 4,500

What is the required energy production for the heating system?

Calculation:

Basic equation: $TD_B = Q_{INT}/(U \times A + 1.08 \times cfm)$
with $U \times A + 1.08 \times cfm = Q_{Lmax}/TD_{max}$
$= 182/(930/68)$
$= 13.3F°$
$T_B = T_I - TD_B$
$= 70 - 13.3$
$= 56.7°F$
$LOSS_{PERIOD} = (Q_{Lmax}/TD_{max}) \times 24 \times DD_{PERIOD}$
$= (.93/68) \times 24 \times 4{,}500$
= 1,477 MMBtu/heating season

parentheses represents the entire building's effect on the heat loss as shown in the equation for the total heat loss. The balance temperature, T_B, is then calculated from TD_B as follows:

$$T_B = T_I - TD_B$$

where T_B is in °F and T_I is the interior design temperature for the building.

The final equation for estimating the energy production using this method is

$$LOSS_{PERIOD} = (Q_{Lmax}/TD_{max}) \times 24 \times DD_{PERIODb}$$

where the important change from the previous technique is the use of $DD_{PERIODb}$, heating degree days with a base of the balance temperature, instead of DD_{PERIOD}, heating degree days (base 65°F). See Exhibit 6.18 for a sample calculation using this technique.

The application of either of these single-measure methods must be done with knowledge of the assumptions and limitations of the calculations. The configuration and operation of the building are assumed to be constant throughout the period of analysis. For example, the installation of a thermostat with night setback would not be acknowledged by this approach. Further, the effect of weather other than the outdoor temperature (for example, sunlight entering the building's windows) is not considered. With all of these limitations, however, the techniques offer an "easy" estimate of the requirements for heating energy.

Exhibit 6.19 Sample Calculations for Consumption of Three Utilities

Data:

$LOSS_{PERIOD}$ = 2,218 MMBtu per heating season

What is the required consumption of electricity, natural gas, and fuel oil?

Calculations:

Basic equation: $FC_{PERIOD} = LOSS_{PERIOD}/(k \times V)$
Electricity = $2{,}218/(1.0 \times 3{,}413)$ = 649,870 kwh
Natural gas = $2{,}218/(.8 \times 103{,}000)$ = 26,920 ccf
Fuel oil #2 = $2{,}218/(.75 \times 140{,}000)$ = 21,120 gal

Consumption of Fuel. The estimate of the required energy production of the heating system should be extended to include an estimate of the amount of fuel consumed by the heating system and the cost of that fuel because a manager is usually more interested in the consumption of utilities than in the output of the system.

The amount of the fuel consumption for any period is expressed using the equation for the required energy production for the period as developed in the previous section:

$$FC_{PERIOD} = LOSS_{PERIOD}/(k \times V)$$

where FC_{PERIOD} is the consumption of the utility for the period in its appropriate units; $LOSS_{PERIOD}$ is the required energy production calculated as described in the previous section in Btu; k is the efficiency of heat production for the system; and V is the heat content of the fuel in units consistent with the units for the utility. Exhibit 6.19 includes sample calculations comparing the consumption of three different utilities for the same property.

This estimated amount of utility consumption may be converted into the amount of the utility bill for the period by multiplying by the average cost of a unit of the utility.

Applications

The concepts and equations developed in this chapter can assist in understanding and analyzing various common situations which can be organized into the following four categories: (1) the effect that location has on the design and operating cost of the heating systems for two similar buildings in different locations, (2) estimates of the costs of operation of the heating system caused by individual components of the building, (3) estimates of the reductions in energy consumption attained by energy conservation procedures, and (4) comparison of the amounts of utility bills from period to period.

6.1 Location Effects

The location of a building has an effect on two aspects of the heating system—size and consumption. The size of the system is dependent on the value of the design temperature difference for the specific location, and the annual utility consumption of the system is dependent on the number of heating degree days for that location. Given this information, the experience gained from operating a building in one location may be extended to operating a similar building in a different climatic zone. This extension is particularly valuable to companies that construct standard buildings in various locations.

Forming a ratio of the heating system sizes for two buildings with the same design in two different locations suggests how the extension of the system size from one location to another should occur. As shown earlier, the equation for the system size is $Q_L = (U \times A + 1.08 \times cfm) \times TD$. Forming the ratio

$$Q_{L2}/Q_{L1}$$

where the subscript indicates the location, and canceling the identical expressions inside the parentheses leaves the relationship as follows:

Exhibit 6.20 The Effect of Building Location on the Heating System

A. Data:

Size of heating system in Syracuse is 930 MBtu/hr*

$T_I = 70°F$

$T_O = 2°F$

For Minneapolis:

$T_I = 70°F$

$T_O = -12°F$

What is the system size for the same building in Minneapolis?

Calculation:

Basic equation: $Q_{L2} = Q_{L1} \times (TD_2/TD_1)$
$= 930 \times (82/68)$
$= 1{,}121$ MBtu/hr*

B. Data:

Syracuse consumption = 2,218 MMBtu

DD = 6,756 (base 65°F)

Minneapolis DD = 8,382 (base 65°F)

What is the system consumption for the same building in Minneapolis?

Calculation:

Basic equation:

$$LOSS_{PERIOD2} = LOSS_{PERIOD1} \times (DD_2/DD_1) = 2{,}218 \times (8382/6756) = 2{,}752 \text{ MMBtu}$$

*MBtu = 1,000 Btu

$$Q_{L2} = Q_{L1} \times (TD_2/TD_1)$$

The conclusion is that the size of the system is proportional to the design temperature difference. The size of the second system is estimated by multiplying the known size of the first system by the ratio of the design temperature differences of the two locations. Exhibit 6.20a shows an example of this calculation.

The relative consumption of two similar buildings in different locations may similarly be determined. Forming the ratio of the required heat productions for the two buildings using the same subscripting and canceling of identical terms leaves the following relationship:

$$LOSS_{PERIOD2} = LOSS_{PERIOD1} \times (DD_{PERIOD2}/DD_{PERIOD1})$$

The form of the equation is identical to the previous equation for system size, with degree days replacing the design temperature difference. Therefore, the conclusion is the same: the relationship is proportional. Specifically, the consumption of energy for two similar buildings in different locations is proportional to the ratio of the heating degree days for the locations. Exhibit 6.20b shows an example of this calculation.

6.2 Effects of Individual Building Components

The equations and calculations that culminate in an estimate of the total cost of operating the heating system may be applied selectively to individual components of a building in order to ascertain their effect on the overall utility bill. Selective application is possible because the hourly heating losses are added together to form the total hourly heat loss for the building. The equation for the annual energy production requirements for the building is

$$LOSS_{ANNUAL} = (Q_{Lmax}/TD_{max}) \times 24 \times DD_{ANNUAL}$$

This is the loss due to all of the components and surfaces of the building.

The annual loss due to just the transmission of heat through one surface could be determined by applying the form of this equation to the transmission loss, $U \times A \times TD_{max}$, at the design temperature difference. Inserting this into the equation for the annual loss of energy gives the loss due to just the transmission load:

$$LOSS_{TRANS} = U \times A \times 24 \times DD_{ANNUAL}$$

Similarly, the annual loss due to ventilation air may be determined by:

$$LOSS_{VENT} = 1.08 \times cfm \times 24 \times DD_{ANNUAL}$$

Multiplying the annual energy loss by the effective cost of the utility provides an estimate of the effect that the building component has on the utility bill. A sample calculation is shown in Exhibit 6.21.

Exhibit 6.21 The Effect of Various Building Components on Utility Consumption

Data:

Location: Ithaca, New York
DD = 7,000
Fuel: Electricity at $.08/kwh ($23.44/MMBtu)

1. What is the yearly cost of heat lost through a 1 ft^2 window with a U factor of 1.0?
2. What is the yearly cost of heat lost because of 1 cfm of ventilation air?

Calculation 1:

Basic equation:

$$\begin{aligned} LOSS_{TRANS} &= U \times A \times DD_{ANNUAL} \\ &= 1 \times 1 \times 24 \times 7{,}000 \\ &= .168 \text{ MMBtu} \\ \text{Cost} &= .168 \text{ MMBtu} \times \$23.44/\text{MMBtu} \\ &= \$3.94 \end{aligned}$$

Calculation 2:

Basic equation:

$$\begin{aligned} LOSS_{VENT} &= 1.08 \times cfm \times 24 \times DD_{ANNUAL} \\ &= 1.08 \times 1 \times 24 \times 7{,}000 \\ &= .181 \text{ MMBtu} \\ \text{Cost} &= .181 \text{ MMBtu} \times \$23.44/\text{MMBtu} \\ &= \$4.25 \end{aligned}$$

6.3 Effects of Energy Conservation Procedures

A prudent manager determines the priority of and benefits that could be received from any actions before making the decision to proceed. Implementing energy conservation procedures is no exception. The numerous possible opportunities[9] must be put into a list by priority, and the costs and benefits of each reasonable opportunity determined. The equations developed in this chapter are the bases upon which the estimates of the savings can be made.

As in the previous Application, the equation for the annual energy production requirements may be selectively applied to changes in the building construction. For example, the effect on the annual utility bill of a decrease in the U factor of a window due to replacing the single-pane glass with double-pane may be estimated by performing two calculations, one with the old U factor and the other with the new U factor. The difference in the amount of the bill is due to the change in the U factor. The calculation may also be done in just one step, using the difference between the two U factors in the equation. The value of the equation then represents the change in the amount of the utility bill. A similar analysis could be performed on a reduction in the infiltration of air due to the installation of vestibules on the entrance doors.

A change in building operation may also be analyzed. For example, performing preventive maintenance and periodically cleaning the heater improves the efficiency (k) of operation. The impact of the improvement in k may be determined by forming the ratio of the old k to the new k and scaling the present utility consumption for heating by this ratio.

These equations do not, however, provide the basis for determining the effects of all energy conservation opportunities. Since the equations assume that the operation of the building is constant during the entire heating season, the effects of altering the setting of thermostats or periodically shutting off function rooms cannot be predicted. Therefore, judgment must be used when applying these concepts. However, their careful application does provide the owner and the manager with the ability to analyze important situations.

6.4 Comparison of Utility Bills from Period to Period

The interaction that relates the heating degree days during a specific period to the expected heating utility consumption during the same period is linear. The predictability of the relationship offers a manager a method for monitoring the heating bills for a property. In Exhibit 6.22, data for the daily consumption of heating energy is plotted versus the daily heating degree days. The data points are grouped closely around a straight line, as is suggested by the theory.

This straight line can be used to monitor the continuing performance of the heating system or to document the benefits received from the implementation of energy conservation steps that should affect the consumption of heating energy. Once the line has been plotted for historical data (that is, data for a past period), the data for future periods can be compared to the line to determine whether the same relationship between the heating energy consumed and the heating degree days still exists.

Exhibit 6.22 The Relationship of Heating Consumption to Heating Degree Days

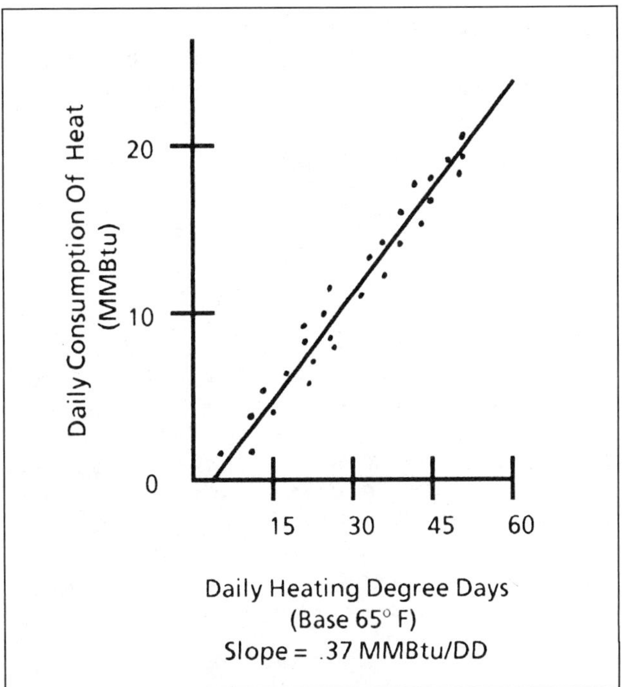

In the first case, when the system is just being monitored, there should be no change in the future periods and, therefore, the plot of any future data points should fall close to the line. If the data points begin to fall substantially above the line, then the operation of the system has deteriorated. This is a signal for further investigation into the situation.

In the second case, where a change has been made for the purposes of conserving energy, a reduction in the consumption of energy is expected. Therefore, the plot of any future points should fall substantially below the line. The amount of the deviation from the line is a measure of the benefits received from the conservation procedures. If no deviation is observed, then the steps were not effective. The implementation of the steps should be investigated further to determine why they were not effective.

In either case, the plotting of new data points against the historical data points provides management with a tool to monitor the performance of the system or the people who maintain the system. This technique works because the theoretical relationship between the consumption of heating energy and heating degree days is linear. A deviation from this linear behavior indicates that the performance of the system has changed. Implementing this monitoring procedure requires the collection of periodic data on the consumption of the heating energy and on the outdoor temperature. This data for a historical period must be collected before the monitoring can begin.

Notes

1. ASHRAE Technical Data Bulletin, *Energy Use in Commercial Buildings: Measurements and Models* (Atlanta: American Society of Heating, Refrigerating, and Air-conditioning Engineers, 1986), p. 116.
2. See *1985 ASHRAE Handbook—Fundamentals* (Atlanta: American Society of Heating, Refrigerating, and Air-conditioning Engineers, 1985), Chapter 23.
3. *1985 ASHRAE Handbook—Fundamentals*, Chapter 24.
4. See, for example, *1985 ASHRAE Handbook—Fundamentals*, Chapter 8, and *1982 ASHRAE Handbook—Applications* (Atlanta, Ga.: American Society of Heating, Refrigerating, and Air-conditioning Engineers, 1982), Chapter 3.
5. See *1985 ASHRAE Handbook—Fundamentals*, Chapter 22, and Fred S. Dubin et al., *How to Save Energy and Cut Costs in Existing Industrial and Commercial Buildings* (Park Ridge, N.J.: Noyes Data Corporation, 1976), Sections 4 and 13.
6. If further information is desired, see *1985 ASHRAE Handbook—Fundamentals*, Chapter 28, for a complete discussion of the other two methods.
7. *1980 ASHRAE Handbook—Systems* (Atlanta: American Society of Heating, Refrigerating, and Air-conditioning Engineers, 1980), Chapter 43.
8. *Degree Days to Selected Bases for First-Order Type Stations* (Asheville, N.C.: U.S. Department of Commerce, National Climatic Center, 1973).
9. For a discussion of many opportunities, see Dubin et al., *How to Save Energy and Cut Costs in Existing Industrial and Commercial Buildings; Energy Conservation Manual—Volume I*, and *Energy Maintenance Manual—Volume II* (New York: American Hotel & Motel Association, 1977); Stephen L. Baron, *Manual of Energy Saving in Existing Buildings and Plants—Volumes I & II* (Englewood, N.J.: Prentice-Hall, Inc., 1978); and Robert E. Aulbach, *Energy Management* (East Lansing, Mich.: Educational Institute of the American Hotel & Motel Association, 1984).

7

Food Service Refrigeration Systems

System Configuration

The four components of a compressive refrigeration system as described in Chapter 3 are the evaporator coil, the compressor, the condenser coil, and the expansion valve. These components are installed in a refrigerator as shown in Exhibit 7.1, with the evaporator coil located in the refrigerated space and the other components located outside the space.

The primary effect of the system is to absorb into the evaporator the heat (Q_{IN}) that enters the refrigerator, thus keeping the space at a constant temperature which is cooler than its surroundings. The absorbed heat is stored in the gaseous refrigerant and transported through the compressor to the condenser coil, where heat (Q_{OUT}) is discarded. The input (Q_{COMP}) into the system is the power to run the compressor.

Theory of Operation

In order for the heat transfer to occur, four important temperatures must have the proper relationship. The temperature of the evaporator coil (T_E) must be lower than the temperature of the inside of the refrigerated space (T_I), with a typical temperature difference of 10 to 15F°. Likewise, the temperature of the condenser coil (T_C) must be higher than the temperature of the surrounding environment (T_O), with a similar temperature difference of 10 to 15F°. Of course, the temperature of the condenser coil is higher than the temperature of the evaporator coil.

Energy balances on the refrigerated space and the refrigeration system also provide insight into the operation of the equipment. At a theoretical level with no losses, an energy balance on the refrigerated space shows that the energy absorbed into the evaporator is equal to the amount of heat (Q_L) that enters the refrigerator, because the temperature of the space remains constant over time. Likewise, an energy balance on the refrigeration system indicates that the relationship between the energy that flows into and out of the system is

$$Q_{OUT} = Q_{IN} + Q_{COMP}$$

because the temperatures of components in the system remain constant over time.

The heat absorption and rejection that is caused by the system occurs through two changes of state. This process can be better understood by comparing it to everyday occurrences. Ice (solid water) cools its surroundings (for example, food on a salad bar) by melting, thereby absorbing the heat that is required for the change of state. This process occurs at 32°F, the melting point of ice at standard atmospheric pressure. Dry ice (solid carbon dioxide) cools its surroundings (for example, a food display requiring the illusion of fog) by changing to the gaseous state. At standard atmospheric pressure, this process occurs at −109°F.

In a refrigeration system, liquid Freon (a fluorocarbon liquid refrigerant) cools its surroundings (for example, the cooling coils in a

Exhibit 7.1 Schematic of a Walk-In Refrigerator

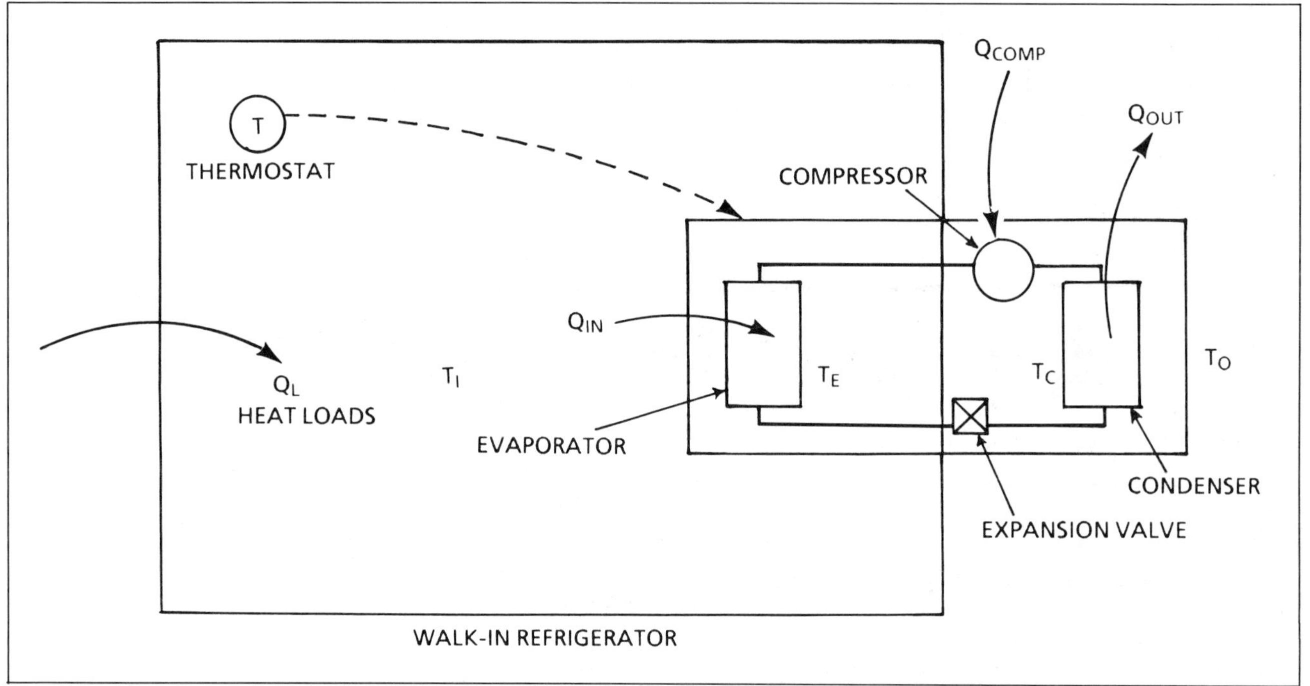

walk-in refrigerator) by boiling and absorbing the heat that is required for the vaporization of the liquid. For R-12, a common version of Freon, this process occurs at −21.6°F at standard atmospheric pressure and at 28°F at a pressure of 46.2 psi (pounds per square inch) inside the coils of the refrigerator.

The fluid refrigerant that flows through the system components is formulated to have boiling points at the working temperatures of the refrigerator or freezer at pressures that can be tolerated by the system equipment. Exhibit 7.2 shows the relationship between the boiling points of a refrigerant (R-12) and its operating pressures.

The transfer of heat into the refrigerant in the evaporator and out of the refrigerant in the condenser is accomplished by having the refrigerant undergo changes of state at two different temperatures. It is boiled in the evaporator at T_E and is condensed in the condenser at T_C. These changes of state at two different temperatures can occur because the compressor changes a low pressure in the evaporator to a high pressure in the condenser.

The system is divided into two sides. The low-pressure side begins at the outlet of the expansion valve, includes the evaporator coil, and ends at the inlet to the compressor. The high-pressure side begins at the outlet of the compressor, includes the condenser coil, and

Exhibit 7.2 R-12 Boiling Points

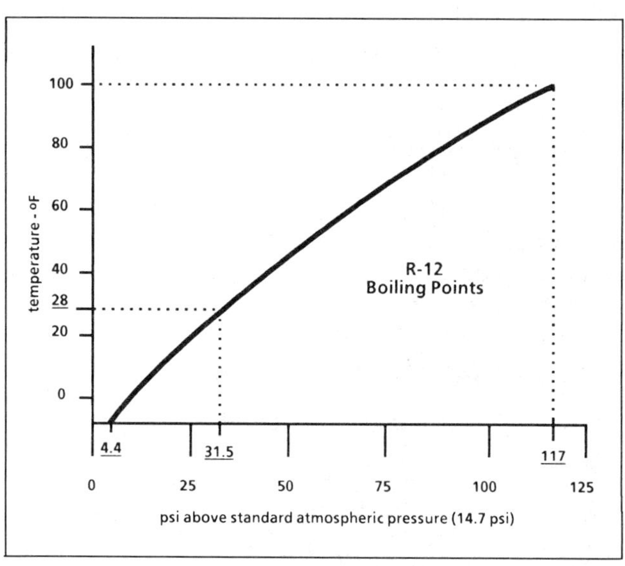

ends at the inlet to the expansion value. The pressure in the low pressure side is constant throughout at a value associated with the boiling point of the fluid at the temperature of the evaporator. Likewise, the pressure in the high pressure side is constant at a value associated with the boiling point of the fluid at the temperature of the condenser.

Description of Components

The following descriptions provide insight into the fundamental elements that make the system work properly.

Evaporator Coil. Exhibit 7.3a shows the construction of an air-source evaporator coil. A serpentine section of tubing, usually fabricated from copper for good heat conduction, is connected to surrounding flat plates of metal called fins. The refrigerant flows through the tubing as air from the refrigerated space is drawn over the fins by an evaporator fan. The heat is absorbed by the fins from the air and conducted into the fluid inside the tubing, causing the fluid to boil. The refrigerant enters as a liquid and leaves as a gas.

A water-source evaporator is constructed by enclosing the tubing and fins inside another container in which water flows (see Exhibit 7.3b). Thus, the energy is extracted from water that flows over the fins instead of air for an air-source coil. This type of coil has application in ice machines and equipment for cooling drinking water.

Condenser Coil. An air-cooled condenser coil basically resembles an air-source evaporator coil. The refrigerant condenses inside the tubing as heat is conducted to the external fins. Air is drawn over these fins by a condenser fan and the heat is dissipated into the air. The refrigerant enters as a gas and leaves as a liquid.

A water-cooled condenser coil basically resembles a water-source evaporator coil. A shell contains the water and tubing with its fins. The refrigerant flows inside the shell over the fins and tubing. The water flows inside the tubing, but the two fluids never contact or mix with each other.

Compressor. Three basic types of compressors are used in compressive refrigeration systems: reciprocating, rotary, and centrifugal.

Exhibit 7.4a shows the basic configuration of a reciprocating compressor. Notice that although

Exhibit 7.3 Construction of Air- and Water-Source Evaporators

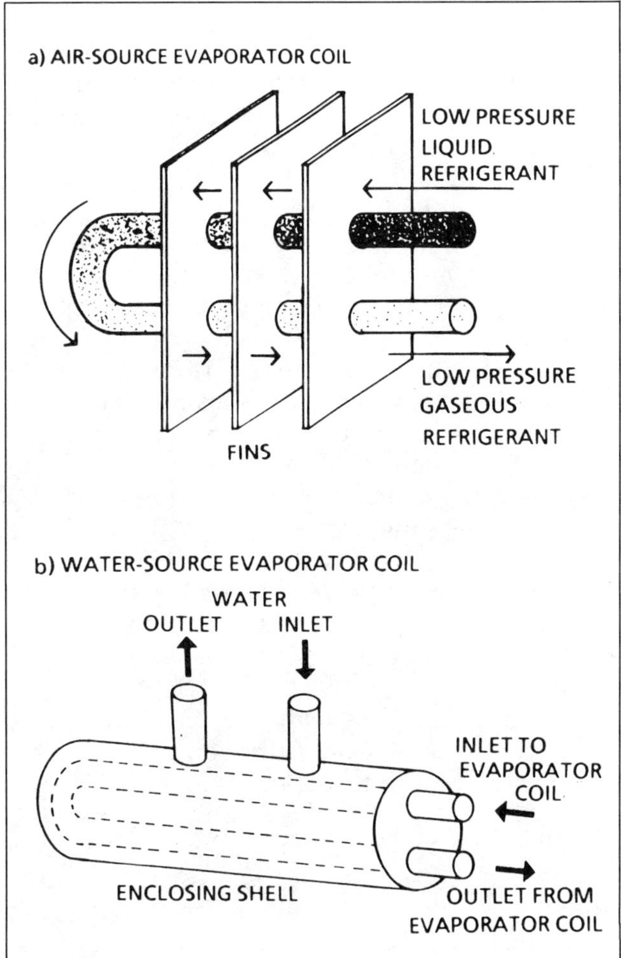

the basic components are very similar to a piston engine in a car, the operation is exactly the opposite. In a car, the expansion of the hot, burning air-gas mixture forces the piston out of the cylinder, thus providing power to the crankshaft to turn the wheels of the car. In a compressor, the power source (an electric motor) turns the crankshaft which forces the piston into the cylinder, thus compressing the gaseous fluid.

The opening and closing of the intake and exhaust valves must be timed with the rotation of the crankshaft and the direction of movement of the piston. When the piston is moving out of the cylinder, the intake valve is open and the exhaust valve is closed so that low pressure gas is drawn into the cylinder. When the piston is moving into the cylinder, the intake valve is closed and the exhaust valve is open. The gas is forced out of the exhaust port at a higher pressure.

This equipment is most commonly found in small refrigeration systems for reach-in and walk-in refrigerators and freezers and in ice machines and small air conditioners. It is easy to maintain, although the frequency of maintenance is often high.

Exhibit 7.4b details the important elements of a rotary compressor. Rotary compressors are identified by their circular, or rotary, motion. The circular piston rotates inside a circular housing, displacing the refrigerant from the cavity between the piston and the housing. This positive displacement of the refrigerant compresses the gas and exhausts it from the compressor into the line to the condenser.

The operating characteristics of, and the areas of application for, this type of compressor are very similar to those for small reciprocating compressors. Rotary compressors, however, are used more frequently in very small systems such as reach-in refrigerators.

Exhibit 7.4c presents the essential parts of a centrifugal compressor. Although its operation is very similar to a turboprop engine in that air flows over the blades of a rotating turbine, the overall effect is the opposite. In a turboprop engine, the expanding hot gas rotates the turbine and the propeller. In a compressor, the motor turns the turbine blades which compress the gas as it flows by the blades, thus producing a high pressure gas at the outlet of the turbine. These types of compressors are usually found in very large systems. They are usually not appropriate for food service refrigeration applications, but they do apply to systems that provide central air conditioning for buildings. They are often driven by electric motors, steam turbines, gas engines, or diesel engines. Their primary operational advantages are a higher efficiency of operation and lower maintenance requirements.

Expansion Valve. This component of a refrigeration system is the simplest in operation. In theory, the valve is only a constriction in the refrigerant line that inhibits the flow of the fluid. In this way, the high pressure fluid cannot flow around the system so fast that the compressor cannot keep up with the process. In practice, the valve also meters the amount of refrigerant to

Exhibit 7.4 Three Types of Compressors

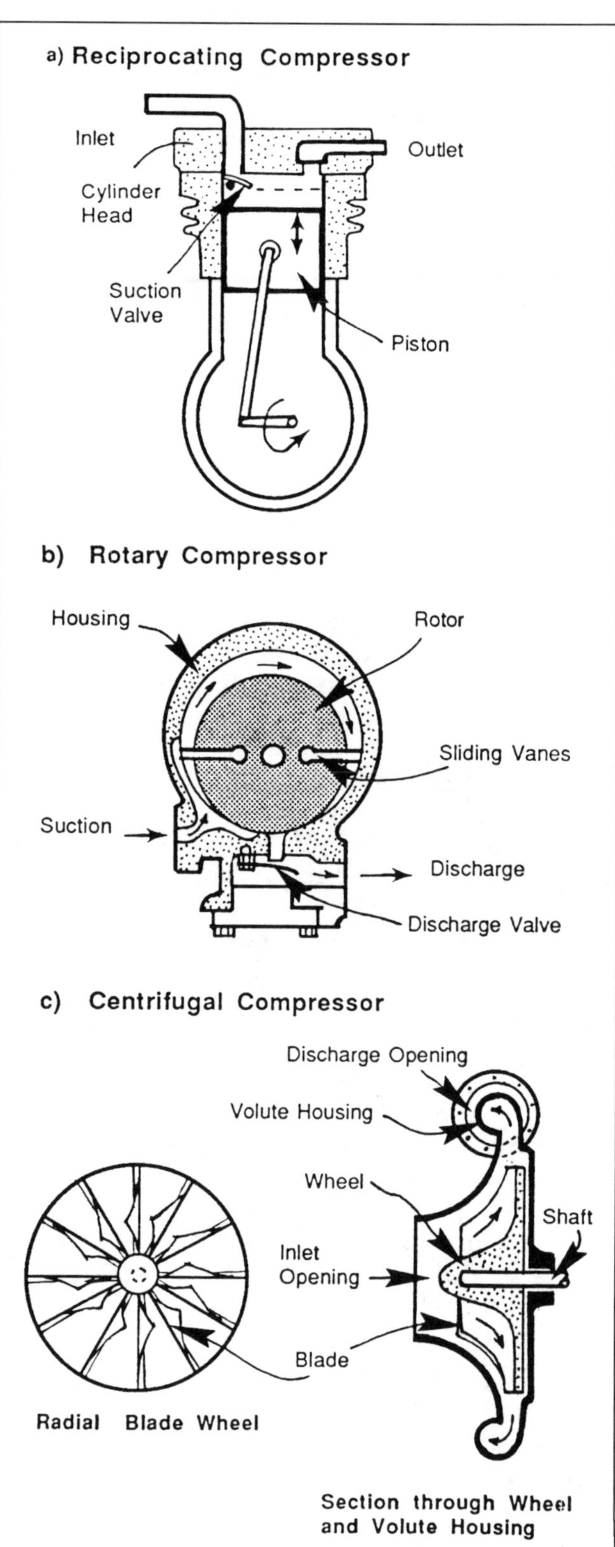

match the cooling needs of the evaporator, so that the system operates at the correct temperature and a high efficiency. Exhibit 7.5 indicates the basic parts of the valve.

Description of Operation

The thermostat in the refrigerated space initiates the operation of the refrigeration system when the temperature in the space rises above the specified desirable temperature. The compressor starts the flow of refrigerant around the loop, thus starting heat absorption in the evaporator and heat dissipation in the condenser. Refrigerant flow and heat transfer continue until the heat loads on the refrigerated space are absorbed and the temperature of the space has decreased. The thermostat then signals the system to turn off to prevent overcooling the space. Even though a refrigerator is turned on during all 24 hours of a day, the refrigeration system only operates a portion of the day. During the 24-hour day, the system is cycling on and off as the cooling is needed.

On-Off Cycling. An example of this operation is shown by the graph in Exhibit 7.6. The vertical axis is temperature in °F and the horizontal axis is time marked in ten-minute increments. Initially, three temperature profiles (internal air temperature, evaporator coil temperature, and the differential temperature between the two) are shown in the upper section of the graph and the state of the compressor is shown in the lower section.

At the start of the graph, the walk-in refrigerator is operating at its normal temperature of 38°F and the door remains closed. The only heat that enters the cooler is the heat that flows through the walls (a transmission load). As this heat enters the cooler, its inside air temperature increases. After approximately twenty minutes, the thermostat senses this increase and activates the refrigeration system. The evaporator quickly absorbs the heat from the inside air and the temperature of the air decreases. The thermostat senses this decrease and deactivates the refrigeration system. Notice that the state of the compressor switches from off to on and back to off during this cycle. This cycling would continue as long as there is a transmission load on the refrigerator.

One hour (six time increments) after the start of the graph, the refrigerator door is

Exhibit 7.5 Thermostatic Expansion Valve

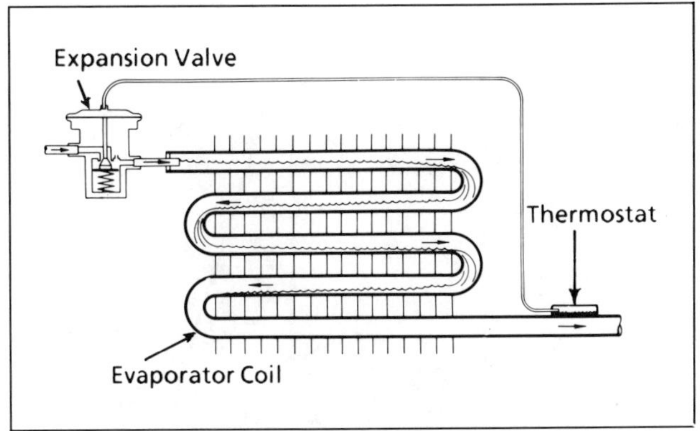

Reprinted by permission from *1983 ASHRAE Handbook—Equipment.*

opened, warm outside air enters the space (an infiltration load), and a product at room temperature (product load) is inserted into it. The air temperature immediately increases, the thermostat turns the system on, and the cooling of the inside air begins. After approximately 50 minutes, the inside air temperature is cooled sufficiently and the compressor is turned off. However, the inside air warms again quickly because the warm product is dissipating its heat into the air. In a short time, the compressor is again activated. This extended cycling continues until the product is completely cooled and then the normal cycling resumes to respond to only the transmission load. During this extended cycling, the amount of time the compressor is on in each cycle decreases from a maximum just after the door is opened until the normal cycling resumes.

Controls. The specific equipment that controls cycling is shown in Exhibit 7.7. The electricity for the compressor passes through a relay controlled by the thermostat. When the thermostat is actuated, the electricity activates the motor that drives the compressor and the fan motors for the evaporator and condenser fans. The sensor in the expansion valve opens the valve, allowing the refrigerant to flow around the system and to provide the desired cooling. Two pressure sensors provide protection for the system in case of a malfunction. The sensor on the inlet side of the compressor turns the system off if a very low pressure is sensed because of lack of refrigerant. The sensor on the outlet side turns

Exhibit 7.6 Box and Load Curves for a Walk-In Cooler

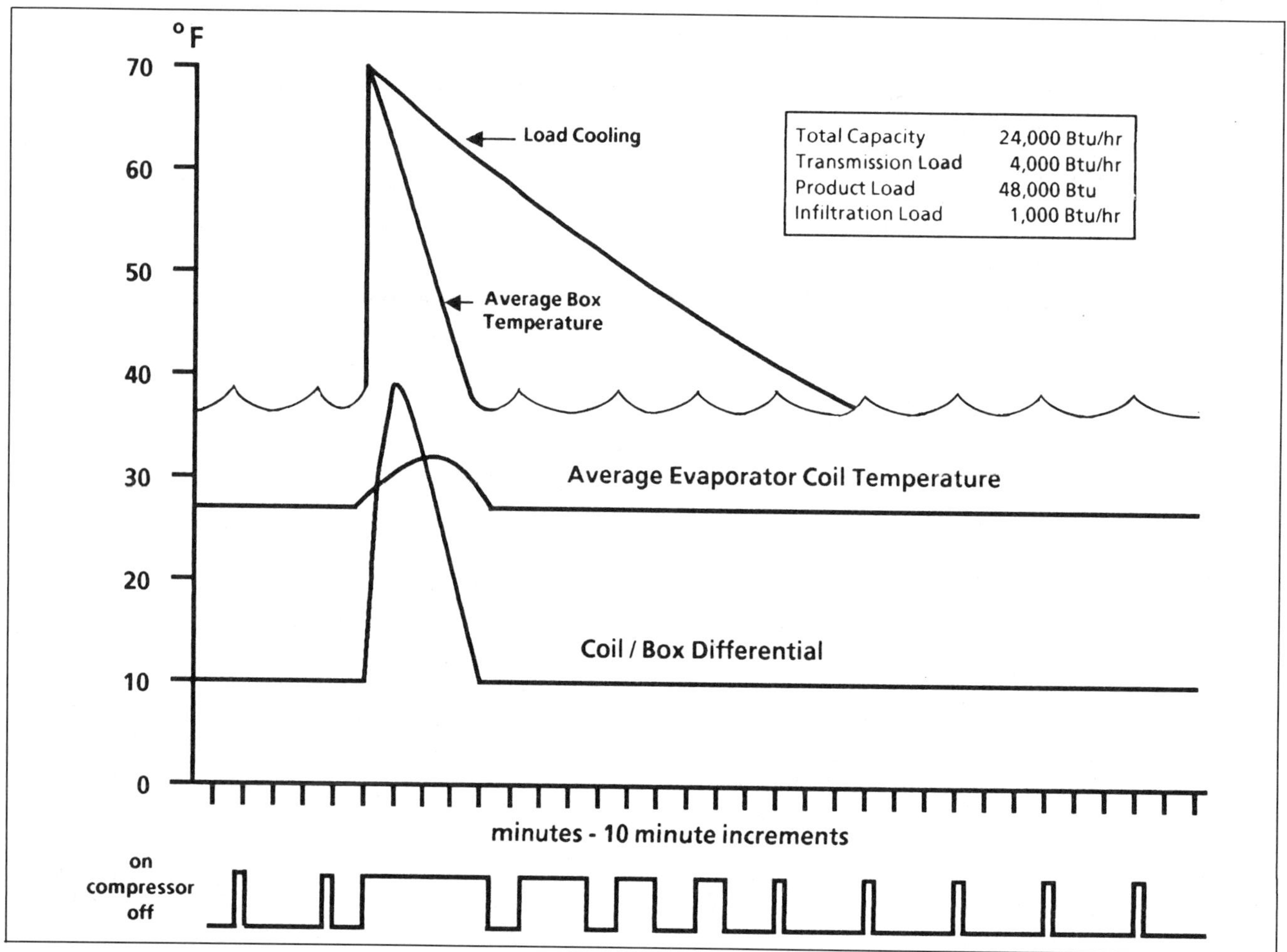

the system off if a very high pressure is sensed because of excessive condenser temperatures. Continued operation at this pressure would damage the compressor and its drive motor.

Air Flow and Humidity. The flow of the inside air is very important to the effective operation of the refrigeration system because the inside air of the space absorbs the loads from the product, walls, and lights (internal loads) and transfers this heat to the evaporator coil. An evaporator fan provides forced air circulation throughout the space and over the evaporator coil so that the rate of heat transfer can be maximized and localized hot spots can be avoided.

A larger rate of air flow coupled with a larger coil size for the evaporator decreases the temperature difference between the inside air and the evaporator coil. This lower temperature difference reduces the amount of moisture that is condensed out of the inside air at the evaporator coil, thus allowing the refrigerator to maintain a higher inside humidity. Therefore, food products that are stored exposed to the inside air maintain their quality longer because they do not dehydrate as rapidly.

Defrosting. When the temperature of the evaporator coil is below 32°F, as it is for most refrigerators and for all freezers, the moisture in the air that does condense on the evaporator coil forms a layer of ice on the coil. This layer of ice continues to build as more moisture condenses and increasingly inhibits the heat transfer from the inside air to the coil, thus reducing the overall capacity of the system and its operating

Exhibit 7.7 Cycling Control Equipment

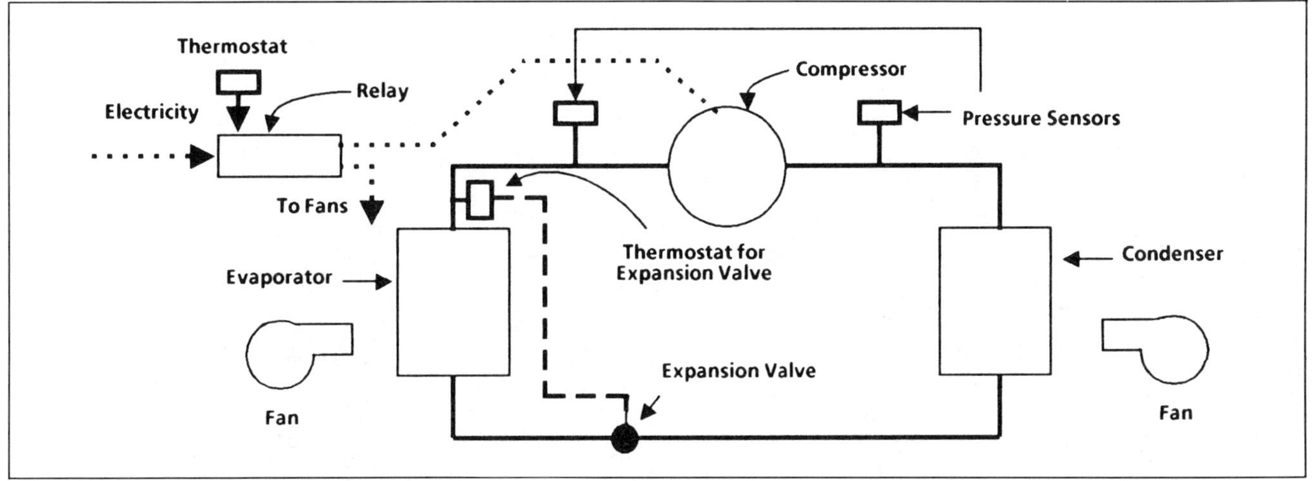

efficiency. Therefore, the coil should be periodically defrosted.

Three different types of defrost systems are commonly used: off-cycle, electric heating, and hot gas. These systems are usually under an automatic controller which initiates the cycle at timed intervals. Some systems, however, have controllers that activate the cycle after the door has been opened a specified number of times because the amount of moisture condensed on the coil is directly related to the number of times the door is opened.

The off-cycle method is the simplest to implement, but it only works for systems in which the inside air temperature is greater than 32°F. In this case, the compressor is turned off, but the fan continues to blow the inside air over the coil, thus melting the frost that has formed. This is satisfactory for refrigerators, but does not work for freezers.

The most expensive method for defrosting freezers is to energize electric heating strips that have been installed around the coil. The cost of installing these strips is low compared to the next alternative, but the operating cost is high because of the electrical consumption.

The third method is to have the "hot" refrigerant temporarily bypass the condenser and enter directly into the expansion valve before it dissipates its heat. The high temperature of the gas causes the evaporator coil to warm up and melt the frost. This method requires a bypass valve and extra tubing in the system at an additional initial cost, but the additional operating cost is minimal because less new energy is used to melt the frost.

In all of the above cases, the water that is removed from the coil must be eliminated by either an indirect connection to an external floor drain or a connection to an external condensate pan from which the water evaporates.

Refrigerant. Specialized non-toxic and non-irritating refrigerants are used for most refrigeration applications in the hospitality industry. The most common of these are Freon refrigerants, originally developed by DuPont, such as R-12, R-22, and R-502. These refrigerants are clear liquids when they are below their boiling points. They also are almost odorless.

R-12 is the most widely used in commercial refrigeration systems because it is suitable for high-, medium-, and low-temperature applications. R-22 is often used in situations where high performance is necessary and where size and capacity are important factors. R-502 is generally applied in low-temperature applications where the evaporating coil temperature is below 0°F. It is also very satisfactory for extra low-temperature systems, such as blast freezers.

The efficient operation of a refrigeration system depends on the system being completely filled with clean refrigerant. Thus, a filter and sight glass are always installed in the refrigerant loop so that impurities such as water and oil can be continuously removed and so that the operator can tell whether there are air bubbles, indicating a loss of refrigerant.

Coefficient of Performance

The efficiency of a refrigeration system is measured by comparing the amount of desired effect that is produced to the energy required for operating the system. The desired effect is the rate of heat absorbed by the evaporator. The energy required for operation is the electrical power used by the compressor motor and other auxiliary components such as fans. The ratio of these two quantities is called the *coefficient of performance* (*COP*) for the refrigeration system.

When determining the value of the COP for a specific system, the evaporator capacity in Btu/hr is divided by the rated power requirement for the compressor motor and other auxiliaries after it has been converted from kilowatts to Btu/hr. Thus, the ratio has no dimensions. Typical values of the COP for refrigerators and freezers are approximately 3 and 1, respectively. This means that 3 units of energy can be removed from a refrigerated space for every unit of energy that is used to run the compressor.

Although the size of these numbers seems to violate the principle that nothing can be more than 100% efficient, a careful look shows why this is not the case. In a water heater, electric energy is converted into heat energy with the limitation that the amount of heat produced cannot exceed the amount of energy originally in the electricity. If this did occur, it would violate the law of conservation of energy. In a refrigeration system, however, the electric energy put into the compressor is not converted into heat energy. Rather, it moves heat (existing energy) from one location (the refrigerated space) to another. Although energy cannot be created at greater than 100% efficiency, it can be transported at greater than a one to one ratio.

The COP of a refrigeration system is shown in Exhibit 7.8 as a function of the temperatures of the refrigerated space and the environment surrounding the condenser. An air-cooled condenser is used as the example for the initial portions of this discussion. The upper line represents the COP for a refrigerator with an inside temperature of 35°F and the lower line represents the COP for a freezer with an inside temperature of 0°F.

For a refrigerator, the efficiency of operation of the refrigeration system is extremely dependent on the temperature of the air surrounding the condenser. An increase in the temperature of the air near the condenser from 70°F to 100°F reduces the COP from 1.7 to 1.0—a 41% reduction in operating efficiency that results in a 70% increase in operating costs.

Exhibit 7.8 Representative COP for Refrigeration Systems

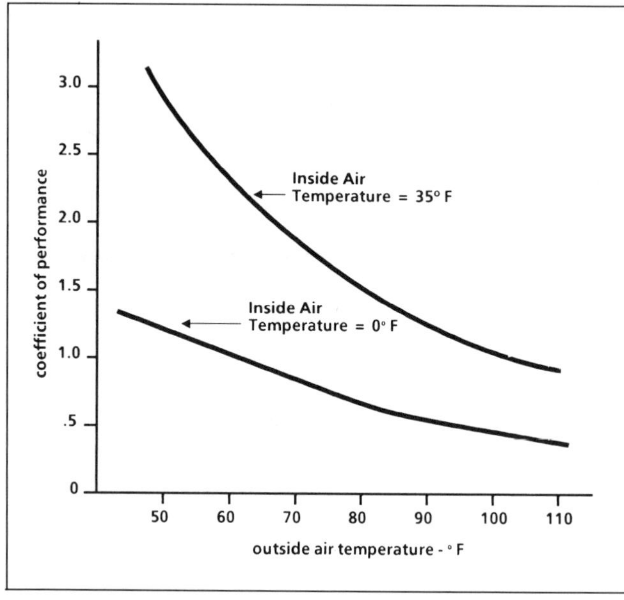

This effect can be understood by comparing the energy associated with a temperature scale to the energy associated with the height of a hill. Heat flows from a region of high temperature to a region of low temperature just as a ball rolls down a hill. Conversely, when a Btu of heat energy is removed from the refrigerated space and transferred to the air surrounding the condenser, it is being moved "uphill" against the temperature scale just as the ball must be carried uphill against the force of gravity. When the condenser is at a higher temperature, more work is necessary to move the Btu to that higher level. As more work is required for the transport of the Btu, the efficiency of the process becomes lower. Thus, the COP decreases as the temperature of the condenser air increases.

A comparison of the COP of a refrigeration system used for a freezer to that of the same refrigeration system used for a refrigerator shows two important effects. First, the general slope of the line is the same as for the refrigerator for the reason described before. Second, the COP in the freezer is always lower than that for the refrigerator for any given condenser air temperature, because a Btu absorbed in the freezer must be moved "uphill" 35F° farther than a Btu absorbed in the refrigerator.

Overall System Characteristics

Types of Systems

As stated in Chapter 3, the primary characteristics which distinguish the different types of systems as they are installed in the industry are location and type of cooling for the condenser. The systems are classified as either self-contained or remote and as either air-cooled or water-cooled. These two characteristics markedly affect the total cost of operation of the system because the energy cost is directly dependent on the COP of the system and the cost of maintaining the system is related to the ease of maintenance and the mechanical life of the equipment.

Water-Cooled Vs. Air-Cooled Condenser. A water-cooled condenser is usually very desirable because of its efficiency and maximum capacity. The efficiency is improved because the temperature of the water that cools the condenser is usually lower than the temperature of the air. As indicated in the discussion of Exhibit 7.8, the COP of the refrigeration system increases as the temperature surrounding the condenser decreases. Reducing the temperature of the operating environment of the condenser from 100°F air to 60°F water would increase the COP of a refrigerator from 1.0 to 2.2. This improvement in COP represents a 55% reduction in the consumption of energy to operate the system.

The system's capacity is increased because the improved efficiency allows more heat to be transferred from the space for the same amount of compressor input. The system is more capable of overcoming extreme conditions because there is a larger safety factor; or, if the extra capacity is excessive, a smaller compressor can be specified, thus saving money in the initial purchase price and in operating costs.

The capacity of the system is particularly important for equipment that usually operates under extreme temperature conditions. Food service refrigeration and ice machines are two very prominent examples. The cooling loads on these two types of equipment are usually the highest when the air temperature and humidity are the highest. These are precisely the conditions that have the most detrimental effect on the operation of the equipment. Thus, the systems operate at their worst when the best performance is needed.

A water-cooled condenser helps to solve this situation in two ways. First, as the cold water temperature is usually more constant than the air temperature, the operation of water-cooled equipment is more predictable and constant throughout the year. Second, as the fluid pressures in the system are not as extreme, the equipment has a longer life and it requires fewer and less expensive repairs.

The only major disadvantages of a water-cooled condenser are the extra consumption of the cooling water and the need to install a drain to remove the water. In many geographic locations, the savings received from reducing electrical consumption more than offset the increased water costs. In locations with very high water cost, however, the overall cost is higher with water-cooled condensers. The extra cost for the installation of a drain for a walk-in refrigerator in a kitchen would be nothing because the floor drain must exist to drain the condensate from the large evaporator coil. The extra cost for the installation of a drain in every guestroom for an in-room refrigerator, however, would be prohibitive, since the drain would be required just for the water-cooled condenser.

Self-Contained Vs. Remote. It is common and very desirable to locate in a remote mechanical room the compressors and condensers for large walk-in refrigerators and freezers installed in the long-term storage areas of kitchens. The advantages are threefold. First, the equipment is more accessible, making its maintenance more frequent and less costly. Second, the equipment is removed from the extreme air temperatures that usually occur in the locations where the condensers are alternatively installed (such as near the ceiling on top of the walk-in). Third, water-cooled condensers are more likely to be installed when all condensers are located in a common location which can be served by one major water line and one drain.

Self-contained units do have their place, however. When numerous small units such as

Exhibit 7.9 Common System Sizes for Various Applications

Application	Evaporator Size (Btu/hr)	Motor Size (HP)	Maximum Electrical Power	COP
Walk-in refrigerator 8′ × 12′ × 9.5′	6,600	1	1,611w	1.2
Walk-in freezer 8′ × 12′ × 9.5′	7,900	2	2,822w	.82
Reach-in refrigerator 40 ft³	2,500	1/3	734w	1.0
Reach-in freezer 40 ft³	3,100	3/4	1,194w	.76

reach-in refrigerators or small ice machines are needed in various distant locations, the self-contained unit is more desirable because the cost of running the refrigerant lines over the long distances would be too high.

Common System Installations and Size

Refrigeration systems are everywhere in today's hospitality properties. The kitchens are filled with reach-ins, walk-ins, ice machines, ice cream freezers, cold bains in the cold-food serve-out sections, undercounter storage near the main range bank, and beverage refrigerators in the service bars. The guests see the effects of refrigeration in the food and beverage outlets as salad bars, displayed wine storage, and cold-food pickup counters in cafeterias. The guests expect ice machines and vending machines for beverages in the service areas on the guestroom floors.

For each application of refrigeration equipment, there is a typical equipment size range. Each application requires a refrigeration system of a particular evaporator capacity, which then affects the necessary size of the electrical drive motor, the efficiency of operation for the overall system, and the consumption of electricity at maximum load conditions. Exhibit 7.9 includes typical information about these characteristics for various common applications.

In general, there are several trends evident in the characteristics. First, the applications that require a lower evaporator temperature necessitate equipment that is larger in capacity, has a larger motor, operates at a lower efficiency, and consumes more electricity than applications that require a higher evaporator temperature. Second, for equipment operating at similar evaporator temperatures, the efficiency of operation increases as the size of the system increases. Third, the consumption of electricity at maximum load conditions increases as the size of the system increases, but at a rate that is less than proportional to the size. This increase at less than the proportional rate is due to the increase in efficiency.

Cost of Operations for Energy

The electric motor in the refrigeration system consumes electricity whenever the system is actually circulating refrigerant. This occurs when the system is running continuously at maximum capacity or when the system is cycled on during a period of less than maximum load. The cost of operation can be estimated for either condition, although the process for the maximum-capacity situation is easier than for the partial-load situation.

The method for estimating the operating cost for an hour of running at maximum capacity is shown in Exhibit 7.10. The size of the system is taken from the manufacturer's specifications; the COP for operation is taken from the specifications or estimated from Exhibit 7.8 for the specified operating conditions or, alternatively, the input power requirements are taken from the specifications; and the cost of electricity is obtained from the utility rate schedule. The cost of operating at maximum capacity will vary from hour to hour as the temperature of the environment surrounding the condenser varies.

Although this operating cost is easy to estimate, it has relatively little significance in the day-to-day operation of the refrigeration system. The load on the system is rarely at the maximum so the actual operating costs are lower than the value previously determined. By estimating a load factor—the percent of time on the average that the system is on—the estimate for the cost of operation at maximum load can be scaled

Exhibit 7.10 Estimating Maximum Capacity Operating Cost per Hour

Data:

Size of evaporator: 2,500 Btu/hr
Operating conditions of evaporator: 35°F
Operating conditions of condenser: 90°F
Cost of electricity: $.08/kwh
Estimated COP: 1.1 (from Exhibit 7.8)

What is the operating cost per hour at maximum capacity?

Calculation:

$COP = Q_{IN}/Q_{COMP}$

$Q_{COMP} = Q_{IN}/COP = 2{,}500/1.1 = 2{,}273$ Btu/hr

Conversion to electrical units:

$Q_{COMP} = (2{,}273\ \text{Btu/hr})/(3{,}413\ \text{Btu/kwh}) = .67$ kw

$$\begin{aligned}\text{Cost per hour} &= Q_{COMP} \times 1\ \text{hour} \times (\text{cost/kwh})\\ &= .67\ \text{kw} \times 1\ \text{hour} \times (\$.08/\text{kwh})\\ &= \$.0536\end{aligned}$$

down to an estimate for the cost of actual operation. The annual energy cost (at $.08/kwh) for operating a reach-in refrigerator and a reach-in freezer is approximately $150 and $250 respectively. For a walk-in refrigerator and walk-in freezer, the figures are approximately $500 and $735 respectively.

System Design

The size and operating costs of a refrigeration system are directly related to the magnitude and timing of the heat loads from the four commonly identified sources: (1) transmission, (2) infiltration, (3) food products, and (4) equipment and people inside the refrigerator.

In the design process, the designer first determines the maximum of the four loads on the space. Then, when determining the necessary size of the refrigeration system, the sum of the extremes of the four different loads is used in order to design a system capable of responding to the most extreme conditions. Finally, the designer estimates the cost of energy for operations using average values for the loads in order to represent the effect of the loads over the year.

Exhibit 7.11 U Factors for Refrigerator Walls

Application	U Factor ($Btu/hr\text{-}ft^2\text{-}F°$)
Walk-in refrigerator (4 inches thick)	.03
Walk-in freezer (4 inches thick)	.03
Reach-in refrigerator (2 inches thick)	.06
Reach-in freezer (2 inches thick)	.06

Load Calculations

Transmission Loads. During the operation of a refrigerator, heat flows from the kitchen air through the refrigerator wall into the air inside the refrigerator because the temperature of the kitchen is higher than the inside temperature of the refrigerator.

As described in Appendix A, the equation that defines this flow of heat energy is

$$Q_T = U \times A \times TD$$

where Q_T is the heat flow into the cooled space in Btu/hr; U represents the U factor for the refrigerator walls in Btu/hr-ft^2-F°; A represents the surface area of the refrigerator in ft^2; and TD represents the difference in air temperature between the environment surrounding the refrigerator and the inside storage area in F°.

Typical values for U factors of refrigerator walls are shown in Exhibit 7.11. Observing the relative magnitudes of the values shows two interesting effects. First, the magnitude of the factor is usually smaller for walk-in refrigerators than for reach-in refrigerators because the walls of the former are generally thicker. Second, although the purchaser might expect that walls of a freezer would be designed to have a lower U factor than the walls of a refrigerator, this is not the case. The manufacturers of freezers and refrigerators usually use the same basic shell for both and just increase the size of the refrigeration system to accommodate the higher transmission load due to the larger TD in a freezer application.

The construction of a typical refrigerator

wall is shown by the cross-section diagram in Exhibit 7.12. The typical refrigerator wall built according to current industry standards has a solid interior made primarily from an insulating material such as urethane or fiberglass. The two surfaces of the walls are constructed from strong, easy-to-clean materials such as aluminum, stainless steel, or molded fiberglass in order to protect the physical integrity of, and to prevent the penetration of water into, the insulation.

The process of calculating the maximum transmission heat load involves determining the values for the variables in the equation. The inside temperature (T_I) of the cooled space is determined by the operational requirements for the equipment. Common temperatures are 35 to 40°F for refrigerators, 0°F for normal freezers, and −10°F for blast freezers.

The "outside" temperature (T_O) is chosen to represent the warmest condition for the air surrounding the cooled space. For a kitchen location, the indoor temperature during the summer is used; for a location in a lounge or bar, the indoor design temperature of the air conditioning system is used; and for remote storage outside the building, the design temperature of the summer air is used.

The determination of the U factor is performed separately for each different surface of the cooled space (that is, the four walls, the ceiling, and the floor). If the surface is in contact with another building wall or floor, the overall effect of both on the transmission of heat is determined by adding the thermal resistances of the two surfaces (see the discussion in Appendix A).

In determining area, the outside (that is, larger) dimensions of the surfaces are usually used, thus providing a safety factor in the calculation.

An example of a complete calculation for the transmission heat load for a walk-in is shown in Exhibit 7.13.

Exhibit 7.12 Cross Section of a Typical Refrigerator Wall

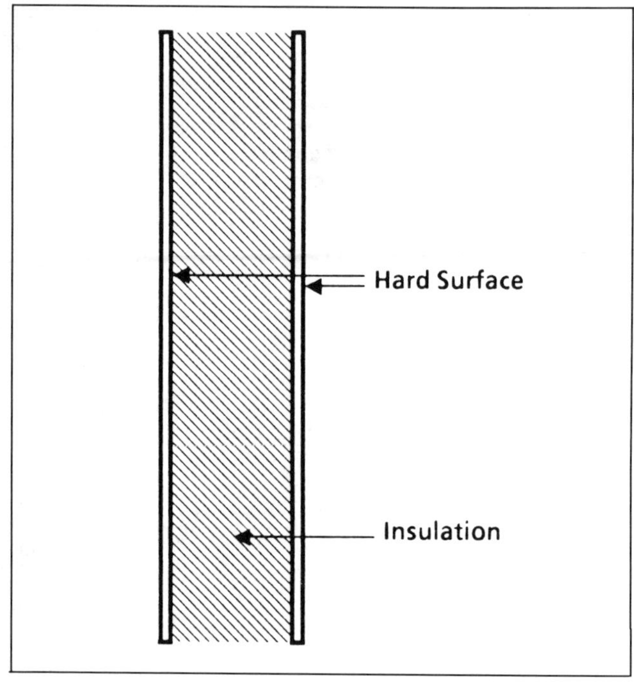

Exhibit 7.13 Sample Calculation for a Transmission Load

Data:

Size of walk-in: 8′ × 12′ × 10′
U factor: .03 Btu/hr-ft²-F°
Inside temperature: 35°F
Outside temperature: 90°F

What is the transmission load?

Calculation:

Basic equation: $Q_T = U \times A \times TD$
$A = 2 \times (8 \times 12) + 2 \times (8 \times 10) + 2 \times (12 \times 10) = 592\ ft^2$
$TD = 90 - 35 = 55$
$Q_T = .03 \times 592 \times 55 = 977$ Btu/hr

Infiltration Loads. Heat energy is exchanged from a location of high temperature to a location of low when air flows from one location to the other. Heat enters a refrigerator as the warm air in the kitchen replaces all or a portion of the air inside the refrigerator when the door is open. The equation that defines this flow of heat energy is

$$Q_I = 1.08 \times cfm \times TD$$

where Q_I is the heat flow into the cooled space in Btu/hr; *1.08* is a constant that accounts for various properties of air; *cfm* is the volume of air exchanged in ft³/min; and *TD* represents the difference in air temperature in F° between the environment surrounding the refrigerator and the inside storage area.

Although this equation is appropriate for the heating of a building, it does not completely explain the energy transfer because it does not include the effect of the moisture in the air. This limitation is not an important aspect of heating because the humidity in not usually considered, but in a refrigerator, a major portion of the load is due to the moisture in the air.

An equation which does include the effects of moisture in the air is

$$Q_I = 4.5 \times \text{cfm} \times \text{HD}$$

where Q_I and *cfm* are as before; *4.5* is a different constant that accounts for the properties of air; and *HD* is the difference in the specific enthalpies of the air in the environment surrounding the refrigerator and the air inside the storage area in Btu/lb of dry air (refer to Appendix B for the definition of specific enthalpy or the total energy in air).

An example for a typical walk-in refrigerator in Exhibit 7.14 shows the importance of using the "wet air" version of the equation rather than the "dry air" version. In this example, the former equation predicts an infiltration load that is only 50% of the true infiltration load because the equation does not account for the effect of the water vapor that must be condensed from the air in the process of cooling it.

The values of the specific enthalpy of air at various conditions (which are necessary for the application of the equation) can be found in the psychrometric chart in Appendix B. The typical conditions for the inside air of refrigerators and freezers and the corresponding specific enthalpies are 35°F at 80% rh (relative humidity) with 12.09 Btu/lb; 40°F at 80% rh with 14.11 Btu/lb; and 0°F at 80% rh with 0.67 Btu/lb. The conditions of the outside air are so variable that the chart must be consulted for the specific application. As an example, a common condition and its corresponding specific enthalpy is 90°F at 60% rh with 42.21 Btu/lb.

The remaining variable in the equation—the flow rate of the infiltration air—is very difficult to estimate because the frequency of door openings is so dependent on the operational setting of the refrigerator and the actual flow of the air is affected by parameters such as the dimensions

Exhibit 7.14 Sample Calculation Showing the Effect of Wet Air on the Infiltration Load

Data:

Inside air conditions: 35°F; 80% rh
Outside air conditions: 90°F; 50% rh
Volume of air: 10.0 cfm
Inside enthalpy: 12.0 Btu/lb
Outside enthalpy: 38.6 Btu/lb

Compare the infiltration loads using the dry air and wet air equations.

Calculation:

Basic dry air equation: $Q_I = 1.08 \times \text{cfm} \times \text{TD}$
$Q_I = 1.08 \times 10 \times (90 - 35)$
$= 594$ Btu/hr

Basic wet air equation: $Q_I = 4.5 \times \text{cfm} \times \text{HD}$
$Q_I = 4.5 \times 10 \times (38.6 - 12.0)$
$= 1{,}197$ Btu/hr

Ratio of wet air equation to dry air equation:
1,197/594 = 2.02

of the door, the temperature difference between the inside and outside air, and the time the door is open. Common practice uses one of three methods to estimate this air flow rate: air changes per day, simplified air flow, and estimates from practical field experience.

The first method uses information such as that found in Exhibit 7.15, which shows the number of air changes that are predicted to occur during a 24-hour period as a function of the volume of the refrigerator. The values in the figure decrease as the volume of the refrigerator increases for two reasons. First, a smaller refrigerator used for point-of-use storage is usually opened more frequently than a larger refrigerator used for long-term storage. Second, a smaller space is more easily emptied of its inside air than a larger space in the same amount of time for the open door. The figure also provides correction factors for heavy usage and long storage effects. The amount of air flow in cfm is then calculated from this value as follows:

$$\text{cfm} = \text{AC} \times \text{V}/1440$$

where *cfm* is ft^3/min of air flow; *AC* represents

the number of air changes in 24 hours; *V* represents the volume of the refrigerator in ft^3; and *1440* is a constant that accounts for the minutes in a day. This method applies only to refrigerators and should be used for freezers with caution because they are usually not opened as often as a refrigerator of similar size.

The second method assumes that air enters the upper half of a refrigerator door at an average velocity of 75 feet per minute and flows out of the lower half of the door at a similar rate. With information on the dimensions of the door and the number of minutes that the door is open during the hour, the desired value of the cfm can be calculated as follows:

$$\text{cfm} = 75 \times h \times w \times t/120$$

where *h* and *w* represent the height and width of the door respectively in feet; *t* represents the time in minutes the door is open in an hour; and the two constants (75 and 120) account for the average air velocity and the number of minutes in an hour times two, respectively. This method is valuable because it applies to freezers as well as refrigerators and because the effect of different operating conditions can be shown.

The third method relies on the information shown in Exhibit 7.16, which includes not only an estimate of the volume of air flow, but also the value in Btu/hr of the infiltration load that results from the flow. The table assumes several parameters in its presentation, and the notes indicate how to correct these values for other conditions. This is the easiest method to use (as no calculations are necessary), but it is also the easiest to misuse because of the inherent assumptions.

Exhibit 7.17 shows the results of infiltration load calculations for a common size walk-in refrigerator in a banquet area using the three methods.

Exhibit 7.15 Average Air Changes per Day for Storage Rooms Due to Door Openings and Infiltration

Volume (cu.ft.)	Air Changes per Day
200	44.0
300	34.5
400	29.5
500	26.0
600	23.0
800	20.0
1,000	17.5
1,500	14.0
2,000	12.0
3,000	9.5
4,000	8.2
5,000	7.2
6,000	6.5
8,000	5.5
10,000	4.9

Note: For heavy usage, multiply the above values by 2. For long storage, multiply the above values by 0.6.

Reprinted by permission from *1981 ASHRAE Handbook—Fundamentals.*

Product Loads. The product that is stored in a refrigerated space contributes to the cooling load for that space in two ways. When the product is first placed in the space, its temperature is usually higher than its eventual storage temperature. Therefore, this heat must be removed from the product in a "cool down" step. Additionally, some products such as fruits and vegetables continue to generate heat after this initial cooling step due to biological processes occurring inside them. This heat is called a respiration load. In most applications in the hospitality industry, only the cool-down load is considered; the respiration load borders on being insignificant.

For a product with an initial temperature that is above freezing when it is placed in a *freezer*, the cool-down load has three distinct components: (1) heat from cooling the product from its initial temperature down to its freezing temperature, (2) heat from the freezing of the product, and (3) heat from cooling the product down to its final storage temperature. The determination of the size of the cool-down load for a specific food product is accomplished by totaling the contributions from the three components, with the calculations for each component performed as follows.

The amount of heat removed in the first component depends on the product's weight, specific heat (see Appendix A for definition), and degrees of temperature in excess of its freezing temperature. The equation that expresses this calculation is

$$q_1 = W \times C_{p1} \times (T_1 - T_f)$$

Exhibit 7.16 Refrigeration Load Due to Door Openings, Walk-In Refrigerators

Refrigeration Load Due to Door Openings, Walk-In Refrigerators [a]

Application		cfm	Infiltration for One 36-in. Swinging Door [c d] Load, Btuh [e] 35° F room		0° F room		0° F room with a cooled vestibule	
			sensible	latent	sensible	latent	sensible	latent
Small retail and wholesale refrigerators up to and including 5000 ft³ volume	average usage	14	990	610	1580	980	660	410
	heavy usage[b]	22	1560	960	2470	1530	1040	640
Large wholesale refrigerators from 1000 ft³ and up		14	990	610	1580	980	660	410
Warehouse (long carry) refrigerators protected by vestibule		12	850	530	1350	830		

[a] Estimated from practical field experience.

[b] Chain stores, except those in small towns or city sections of limited purchasing, come under this classification. Downtown independent stores depending largely on transient trade, and stores without sales display counters, usually come under this classification.

[c] Based on 36 in. door in use at time: (1) for two doors, each on adjacent walls and in use at the same time, total load equals load for one door times 1.75; (2) for two doors each on opposite wall and in use at the same time, total load equals load for one door times 2.5; (3) for doors larger than 36 in., increase infiltration proportionately, i.e., 48 in. door average usage = 14 cfm × 48/36 = 18.5 cfm.

[d] *Doors Open in Summer:* A 36-in. swinging door standing open will pass 900 cfm when there is only one door open and no wind. This infiltration is due only to a difference in density between air outside and in the refrigerator for normal maximum summer conditions.

Two open doors on adjacent or opposite walls should not be tolerated. A slight pressure or wind will have an indeterminate effect on infiltration. Applications involving open doors are infrequent. They are usually confined to wholesale refrigerators using a single door for loading and unloading, backed up by inner lightweight, "flip" type doors.

[e] Average Btuh for quick estimating is assumed equal to load when outdoor temperature is 95° F db and 78° F wb, and when relative humidity in the refrigerator is 85%. The vestibule is assumed to be 40° F db and 75% rh.

Reprinted by permission from *1977 ASHRAE Handbook—Fundamentals.*

where q_1 is the heat in Btu; W is the weight in pounds; C_{p1} is the specific heat; T_1 is the initial temperature in °F; and T_f is the freezing temperature in °F.

The amount of heat removed in the second component depends on the product's weight and its latent heat of fusion (see Appendix A for definition). The equation that expresses the heat extraction for the freezing process is

$$q_2 = W \times h_f$$

where q_2 is in Btu and h_f is the latent heat of fusion in Btu/lb.

The equation that defines the amount of heat removed in the third component is very similar to the equation for the first component, except that the temperatures and the value of the specific heat are different. The equation is

$$q_3 = W \times C_{p2} \times (T_f - T_3)$$

where q_3 is in Btu; C_{p2} is the specific heat of the product in the frozen state; and T_3 is the final storage temperature in °F.

The actual values of the specific heat, latent heat of fusion, and freezing temperature for sample foods are shown in Exhibit 7.18. As most food products contain a high percentage of water, the values for these properties for food are very similar to the values for water. Most food products freeze at a temperature slightly below water's freezing temperature. The latent heat of fusion for water at standard atmospheric pressure is 144 Btu/lb; the latent heat of fusion for food can be estimated by multiplying its percentage of water content by the value for water. The specific heats for water are 1.0 and .5 for the liquid and frozen states respectively; the values for the two specific heats for a food product are usually slightly below the values for water.

The total cool-down load for a product inserted into a freezer is the sum of q_1, q_2, and q_3. For a product inserted into a *refrigerator*, the total cool-down load includes a partial contribution for only the first component; no calculations are necessary for the other two components. In the equation for the first component, the freezing temperature is replaced by the final storage temperature and the value calculated for q_1 is the total cool-down load.

Notice that at this point the total cool-down load is expressed in Btu, or units of energy, and not in Btu/hr, or units of energy flow, as the other loads are expressed. The final step in determining the total cool-down load is specifying the time frame over which the heat must be extracted from the product, so the amount of energy may convert to the rate of heat flow. A common assumption is a cool-down time of 24 hours. Shorter times might be necessary for rapid cooling in order to maintain the quality of the food product (for example, food texture, sanitary conditions). The final cool-down load is the total of the loads from the three components, if applicable, divided by a time. In equation form, this is expressed as

Exhibit 7.17 Sample Calculations for an Infiltration Load

Data:

Walk-in dimensions: 12′ × 15′ × 10′
Inside air conditions: 35°F; 80% rh
Outside air conditions: 90°F; 50% rh
Door openings per hour: 10
Inside enthalpy: 12.0 Btu/lb
Outside enthalpy: 38.6 Btu/lb

Determine the infiltration load using each of the three methods.

Calculations:

Method #1:
Volume of box: 12′ × 15′ × 10′ = 1,800 ft^3
Air changes (from Exhibit 7.15): 12.0
cfm = (AC × V)/1,440
= (12 × 1,800)/1,440
= 15 ft^3/min
Q_I = 4.5 × 15 × 26.6 = 1,796 Btu/hr

Method #2:
Door dimensions: 3′ × 6′
Open time: 2.5 minutes (.25 minutes/opening)
cfm = 75 × h × w × t/120
= 75 × 6 × 3 × 2.5/120
= 28 ft^3/min
Q_I = 4.5 × 28 × 26.6 = 3,351 Btu/hr

Method #3:
From Exhibit 7.16
cfm = 22 ft^3/min
Q_I = 1,560 + 960 = 2,520 Btu/hr

$$Q_P = (q_1 + q_2 + q_3)/n$$

where Q_P is in units of Btu/hr, the three loads are in units of Btu, and n is expressed in hours.

Exhibit 7.19 contains a complete sample calculation for the freezing of a beef product. Notice that the predominant component for the cool-down load is from the freezing process.

Internal Loads. Any electrical device (light bulb, fan motor) that is in the refrigerated space contributes to the heat load when the device is operating. For any electrical energy that is directly dissipated into the space, the contribution to the load is 3.41 Btu for every watt-hr. For electrical motors, the approximate heat contributed to the load on a per horsepower basis is shown in Exhibit 7.20.

Exhibit 7.18 Storage Requirements and Properties of Selected Perishable Products

Commodity	Storage Temp °F	rh	Approx. Storage life	Water content	Highest Freezing °F	Specific Heat above Freezing Btu/lb-F°	Specific Heat below Freezing Btu/lb-F°	Latent Heat Btu/lb
Asparagus	32-36	95	2 wks	84	29.9	.87	.45	120
Avocados	45-55	85-90	2-4 wks	65	31.5	.72	.40	94
Tuna	32-36	95-100	14 days	70	28.0	.72	.39	92
Shrimp	31-34	95-100	12-14 days	76	28.0	.81	.43	109
Beef, fresh average	32-34	88-92	1-6 wks	62-77	28-29	.7-.84	.39-.43	89-110
Poultry, fresh average	32	85-90	1 wk	74	27.0	.80	.42	106

Reprinted by permission from *1986 ASHRAE Handbook—Refrigeration Systems and Applications.*

Exhibit 7.19 Sample Calculation for Freezing a Beef Product

Data:

Amount of beef: 100 lbs
Initial temperature: 45°F
Storage temperature: 0°F
Values for specific heat, latent heat, and freezing temperatures taken from Exhibit 7.18

What is the amount of heat that must be removed to freeze the beef?

Calculation:

$q_1 = W \times C_{p1} \times (T_1 - T_f)$
$= 100 \times .75 \times (45 - 29)$
$= 1{,}200$ Btu

$q_2 = W \times h_f$
$= 100 \times 95$
$= 9{,}500$ Btu

$q_3 = W \times C_{p2} \times (T_f - T_3)$
$= 100 \times .4 \times (29 - 0)$
$= 1{,}160$ Btu

Total $= q_1 + q_2 + q_3 = 11{,}860$ Btu

Exhibit 7.20 Approximate Heat Equivalent of Electric Motors

Motor HP	Connected Loads in Refr. Space[a] Btu/HP-hr	Motor Losses Outside Refr. Space[b] Btu/HP-hr	Connected Load Outside Refr. Space[c] Btu/HP-hr
1/8 to 1/3	4600	2545	2100
1/2 to 3	3800	2545	1300
5 to 20	3300	2545	800

[a]For use when both useful output and motor losses are dissipated within refrigerated space; motors driving fans for forced circulation unit coolers.
[b]For use when motor losses are dissipated outside refrigerated space and useful motor work is expended within refrigerated space; pump on a circulating brine or chilled water system; fan motor outside refrigerated space driving fan circulating air within refrigerated space.
[c]For use when motor heat losses are dissipated within refrigerated space and useful work expended outside of refrigerated space; motor in refrigerated space driving pump or fan located outside of space.

Reprinted by permission from *1985 ASHRAE Handbook—Fundamentals.*

When employees are in the refrigerated space, they also contribute heat to the load. The amount is shown in Exhibit 7.21.

Exhibit 7.22 shows the calculation for the load (Q_E) from equipment and people for a typical walk-in freezer.

System Size

Although refrigeration equipment can operate continuously without any detrimental effect, the system capacity is usually selected so that the total heat load for an entire day can be extracted over a 16- to 18-hour period. This provides time for defrosting the evaporator coils, if necessary, and a safety factor for when loads exceed the design conditions.

There are two ways to determine the system capacity: reliance on material published by the equipment manufacturers and direct calculation using the results of the previous load determinations from the four different sources. The manufacturer's recommendations are usually acceptable for average conditions of ambient air

Exhibit 7.21 Heat Equivalent of Occupancy

Refrigerated Space Temperature—°F	Heat Equivalent/Person Btu/hr
50	720
40	840
30	950
20	1050
10	1200
0	1300
−10	1400

Reprinted by permission from *1985 ASHRAE Handbook—Fundamentals*.

Exhibit 7.22 Sample Calculation for Internal Loads

Data:

Lights: 100 watts
People: 1
Evaporation fan: 1/15 HP
Storage temperature: 35°F
Various values from Exhibits 7.20 and 7.21

Determine the internal loads for the walk-in refrigerator.

Calculation:

Q_E = lights + people + equipment
= 100w × (3.4 Btu/hr-w) + (1 × 900) + (1/15 × 4,600*)
= 1,547 Btu/hr

*If HP is outside the range of data in Exhibit 7.20 (as 1/15 is here), it may be necessary to choose the closest applicable load.

Exhibit 7.23 Typical Manufacturer's Recommendations for 9′6″ and 10′6″ High Walk-Ins

Refrigeration recommendations are shown below for some Bally Walk-Ins. Btu/hr load shown is computed for 9′6″ heights. Although the usage factor is slightly more for 10′6″ heights, recommendations remain the same. Recommendations are only for Walk-Ins using prefab insulated floor panels or built-in urethane insulated floors. Note: Walk-Ins with non-insulated floors are not applicable.

Walk-In Size	Storage Temp. 35°F Btu/hr load	Storage Temp. 0°F Btu/hr load
7′9″ × 11′7″	6,648	7,951
9′8″ × 13′6″	8,681	9,391
11′7″ × 15′5″	10,101	12,061

Recommendations are "average" and do not take into consideration factors such as ambient temperatures exceeding 90°F, the use of sliding glass or hinged reach-in doors or excessive opening of entrance or service doors. "Average" installation means a normal load requirement for the general storage of food products, either in a normal or low temperature Walk-In.

When Walk-Ins are to be used for sharp or quick freezing or if large quantities of warm food are to be cooled quickly, larger refrigeration systems are required. Specific size recommendations will be made by Bally's Engineering Department based on the volume and temperature of the food product to be handled.

All recommendations include air-cooled condensing units.

Working Data Catalog, Bally Case & Cooler, Inc., Bally, Penn., 1981. Used by permission.

temperature and humidity as well as for moderate amounts of product and air infiltration. See Exhibit 7.23 for a typical manufacturer's recommendation on a walk-in refrigerator or freezer. Note that there are numerous qualifying statements regarding the recommended system sizes.

For other situations or as a check on the manufacturer's recommendations, the system size can be calculated directly. The determination of the system size is accomplished by

$$Q_S = Q_{Lmax} \times 24/n$$

where Q_S is the system size in Btu/hr; Q_{Lmax} is the sum of the loads from the four different categories (Q_T, Q_I, Q_P, and Q_E) in Btu/hr; and n is the number of hours the system is to operate per 24-hour period. Exhibit 7.24 contains the calculations for the system size of a typical walk-in refrigerator.

System Consumption

Estimates of energy operating costs that are more accurate than those provided by the simple method suggested earlier in this chapter can be made. If the profiles for the loads on the system can be approximated on an hour-by-hour basis for a typical day and a representative operating temperature for the condenser can be approximated for each day of the year, accurate esti-

Exhibit 7.24 Sample Calculation for System Size

Data:

Transmission load: 2,000 Btu/hr
Infiltration load: 500 Btu/hr
Product load: 1,000 Btu/hr
Internal load: 500 Btu/hr
Working time: 18 hours/day

Determine the size for the refrigeration system.

Calculation:

Basic equation:
$$Q_{Lmax} = Q_T + Q_I + Q_P + Q_E$$
$$= 2{,}000 + 500 + 1{,}000 + 500$$
$$= 4{,}000 \text{ Btu/hr}$$
$$Q_S = Q_{Lmax} \times 24/n$$
$$= 4{,}000 \times 24/18$$
$$= 5{,}333 \text{ Btu/hr}$$

mates for the cost of operation for a day can be made and then extended into a year.

Exhibit 7.25 indicates the appropriate procedure for estimating the annual operating cost of a refrigeration system. For ease of calculation, the profiles for the four loads and the operating temperature of the condenser are assumed for the typical day. The operating cost for this day is then extended to an entire year to determine the annual costs.

If a more accurate approximation is desired, the values for the loads and the condenser's operating temperature could be varied throughout the year. Month-to-month or week-to-week variations provide reasonably accurate results. Performing the calculations on a day-to-day basis is rarely required.

Applications

The factors that affect the energy consumption of a refrigeration system may be organized into two categories: those that affect the size or the duration of the loads on the system and those that influence the operating efficiency of the system. This statement can be verified by observing the procedure for estimating the operating costs of a system. The only two aspects of the calculation that affect the total energy consumed for the year are the loads and the COP.

Exhibit 7.25 Calculation for Estimating Annual Operating Costs

Data:

Transmission load: 2,000 Btu/hr for 24 hours
Infiltration load: 500 Btu/hr for 16 hours
Product load: 1,000 Btu/hr for 6 hours
Equipment load: 500 Btu/hr for 24 hours
COP: 1.2
Cost of electricity: $.08/kwh

Estimate the annual operating costs for the walk-in refrigerator.

Calculation:

Daily energy into refrigeration
$$= (2{,}000 \times 24) + (500 \times 16) + (1{,}000 \times 6) + (500 \times 24)$$
$$= 74{,}000 \text{ Btu}$$
$$Q_{COMP} = Q_{IN}/COP$$
$$= 74{,}000/1.2$$
$$= 61{,}670 \text{ Btu}$$

Convert to electrical units
$$Q_{COMP} = 61{,}670/(3{,}413 \text{ Btu/kwh})$$
$$= 18 \text{ kwh/day}$$
$$\text{Annual Costs} = 18 \text{ kwh/day} \times 365 \text{ days/yr} \times \$.08/\text{kwh}$$
$$= \$525$$

Determining how to conserve energy in a refrigeration system requires investigating the factors that determine the loads or the COP. Reducing the size of the loads, shortening the duration of the loads, and/or increasing the COP conserve energy. Many references offer detailed lists of energy conservation procedures.[1] Several examples follow.

The transmission load can be reduced by reducing the U factor for the refrigerator, the outside surface area of the refrigerator, or the temperature difference between the inside and the outside of the refrigerated space. The U factor can be reduced by purchasing a refrigerator with thicker walls or better insulation. The outside area of the refrigerator can be reduced by using a reach-in to store food instead of a small walk-in in which a major portion of the space is for the aisle. The temperature difference can be lowered by increasing the storage temperature to its maximum allowable value or by placing the refrigerator in the coolest location in the property.

The infiltration load can be decreased by

Exhibit 7.26 Load Contributions to Overall Consumption

	Contribution to Consumption	%
Transmission	48,000	65
Infiltration	8,000	11
Product	6,000	8
Internal	12,000	16

lowering the amount of air infiltration when the doors are opened and decreasing the energy in the incoming air. The amount of infiltration can be controlled, for example, by either minimizing the number of times the door to a walk-in is opened during operating hours or installing plastic curtains to reduce the rate of air infiltration. The energy in the incoming air can be reduced by installing the refrigerator in the coolest and driest location.

The product load can be lowered by purchasing products at the lowest possible temperature and storing them in original or other tight containers to minimize the loss of water. Food that is to be stored in a refrigerator should be purchased at approximately 40°F and food that is to be frozen should be purchased in that state.

The load from people and equipment can be minimized by reducing the amount of time people spend in the refrigerated space and the amount of time internal lights are on.

The COP of the system can be increased by lowering the condenser's operating temperature and maintaining efficient heat transfer into the evaporator and out of the condenser. The condenser's operating temperature can be lowered, for example, by locating an air-cooled condenser away from the hot air near the ceiling of a kitchen or by using a water-cooled condenser. The efficient transfer of heat can be maintained by periodic cleaning of the evaporator and condenser coils or by defrosting the evaporator coil frequently if frost forms on it.

Implementing any of the previous suggestions would save energy, but how much is saved and is the effort and possible expense worth it? An analysis of the overall contribution from each load and of the effect the COP has on the annual consumption indicates the answer. Using data from Exhibit 7.25, Exhibit 7.26 shows that the four loads (Q_T, Q_I, Q_P, and Q_E) contribute 65%, 11%, 8%, and 16% respectively to the overall consumption. The transmission load is the largest contributor and, therefore, offers the greatest potential for savings. A 10% reduction in the transmission load saves 6.5% in annual operating costs, while a 10% reduction in the infiltration load would save only 1.1%. Notice, however, that an increase in COP would apply to all of the loads at all times. Therefore, a 10% increase in the efficiency of operation saves 10% in operating costs.

If a complete analysis of the costs and benefits of implementing certain energy conservation steps is needed, then the application of the procedure illustrated in Exhibit 7.26 would provide an estimate of the savings that result from the steps. The calculation would be completed twice. First, use data that represents the situation before the steps are taken. Second, use data that represents the situation after the steps are taken. The difference in operating costs is an estimate of the benefits received. Finally, a capital budgeting technique should be used to determine whether or not the benefits are appropriate to the costs.

Notes

1. For example, see *Energy Cost Reduction Plan* (Washington, D.C.: Restaurant Association of Metropolitan Washington, 1978); Arthur C. Avery, *A Modern Guide to Foodservice Equipment*, Revised Ed. (New York: CBI/Van Nostrand Reinhold, 1985); Carl Scriven and James Stevens, *Food Equipment Facts—A Handbook for the Food Service Industry* (New York: Wiley and Sons, 1982); and Sandra J. Ley, R.D., *Foodservice Refrigeration* (Boston: CBI, 1980).

8

Air Conditioning Systems

Like the heating system, the air conditioning system is part of the HVAC system as described in Chapter 3. The purpose and overall effect of the system is to remove heat and humidity from the building to maintain the proper comfort conditions.

The importance of the air conditioning system is dependent on the climate of the property. In warm climates, the cooling system often operates for substantially more than half of the operating hours in a year and consumes utilities, usually electricity, that represent a large portion of the total energy consumed by the property. In a temperate climate, the system operates around the clock during the few hot months and throughout the daylight hours during the remainder of the year. Even in cold climates, a system must be available to operate during brief hot spells. For large function areas such as ballrooms, the system often operates whenever the room is occupied, regardless of the outdoor air temperature.

Typical System Configuration

There are two common configurations for HVAC systems: decentralized and centralized. The configuration dictates the choice of utility for operating the system. Decentralized systems use only electricity. Centralized systems primarily use electricity, but sometimes use steam or some other form of heat.

Diagram for a Basic System

The system has the same basic structure and typical components regardless of whether it is installed in a decentralized or centralized arrangement. This basic structure is shown in Exhibit 8.1. The operation of the system is best described by following the air flow through the structure. Starting at point (a), the system draws return air from the zone. At point (b), some of this return air is exhausted to the outdoors in order to remove the contaminants (for example, odors, smoke) that have accumulated in the air; the remainder of the air is routed through the system. At point (c), the remaining return air is mixed with a stream of fresh outdoor air that is required by building codes. At point (d), this mixed air is passed over a set of cold cooling coils which absorb heat from the air stream. This heat absorption lowers both the temperature and the humidity of the air. This conditioned air is directed back into the zone as supply air at point (e). The supply air circulates throughout the zone and picks up the heat that is entering the zone as loads (point f). The cycle begins again when this air is taken from the room as return air at point (a).

The conditions of the air at various points in the system are well defined. At point (a), the air must be at the correct temperature and humidity to provide human comfort. (The necessary conditions are defined by the comfort zone as described in Appendix B.) The same conditions also hold for point (b). At point (c), the return air stream is mixed with the air stream from the outdoors. The outdoor air conditions depend on the weather. As a result of the mixing, the conditions of the mixed air fall between the conditions of the outdoor air and the conditions of the return air, with the exact values depending on the relative amounts of outdoor and

Exhibit 8.1 Basic Structure of an Air Conditioning System

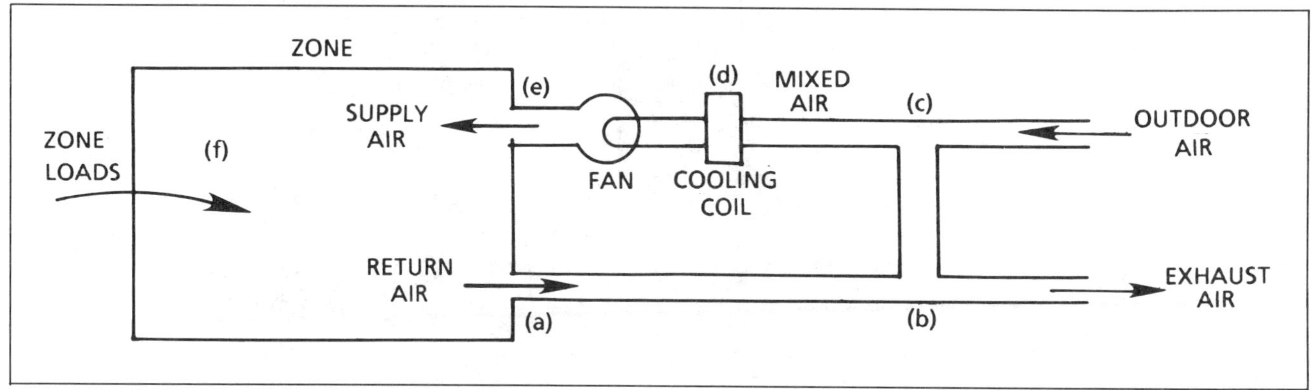

return air. As this mixed air passes over the cooling coils, the temperature and the humidity of the air are lowered. This relatively cool and dry air is supplied back into the room. The conditions of the supply air are controlled so that when the room loads are absorbed by the cool and dry air, the temperature and humidity of the room air rise just to the values required for comfort. Typical temperature differences between the return air and the supply air are 10 to 15F°. Values greater than these make the supply air too cold for comfort and values smaller than these require very large duct work because of the increase in air flow.

The energy flows into and out of the system are also well defined. Heat enters the zone in the form of loads which raise the temperature and humidity in the room. There are various sources for these loads: heat transmitted through the exterior walls, heat and humidity entering in air leaking through doors, heat and humidity given off by the occupants in the zone, and heat and/or humidity from equipment such as lights and coffee pots. Some of the energy in the return air is exhausted to the outdoors and is replaced by the energy in the ventilation air. The cooling coils extract energy from the mixed air and dissipate it to the outdoors through the refrigeration unit connected to these coils.

The volumes of air flows are also known. First, the necessary amount of supply air depends on its conditions and the size of the zone's loads. Higher loads require larger amounts of supply air, while a colder supply air temperature allows smaller amounts of supply air. The temperature and maximum amount of supply air are determined by the design of the system, while the actual values during operation are determined by the controls for the system. Second, the volume of return air is usually the same as or slightly lower than the volume of the supply air. If the volumes of the two air flows are identical, then the pressure of the air in the room stays the same as the pressure outdoors. If the air flow for the supply air, however, is greater than that for the return air, then the pressure in the room is higher than the pressure outdoors. This is desirable because air then leaks out of the building through exterior doors rather than into the building, thus avoiding uncomfortable air conditions near the entrance. Third, the volume of the ventilation air is determined by code regulations, usually on the basis of the maximum number of occupants for the space. Fourth, the volume of the exhaust air is usually the same as or slightly less than that of the ventilation air. Sometimes, as described previously, less air is returned from the room than is supplied to the room. Finally, the amounts of the mixed air and the supply air are the same.

System Components and Operation

Exhibits 8.2, 8.3, and 8.4 show by schematic diagram how this basic structure might be installed in a building for three situations: (1) a decentralized configuration in a guestroom, (2) a centralized system with a chilled water distribution system in a guestroom, and (3) a centralized system with a cold air distribution system in a meeting room.

Decentralized Configuration. According to Exhibit 8.2, the air flows for the decentralized system all occur either inside or just outside the guestroom. The return air is collected near the bottom of the enclosing case inside the room and the ventilation air is captured through the outside surface of the case. These two air streams are mixed just before the air flows over a self-contained refrigeration unit, which is very similar to the refrigeration units for food service applications. The air is cooled, dehumidified, and supplied to the room as it passes over the refrigeration unit and through the fan. The heat that is extracted from the air enters the refrigerant and the water that is removed from the air is collected in a condensate pan below the unit for removal by a drain or by evaporation to the outdoors. Air is exhausted from the room by an exhaust duct from the bathroom.

The refrigeration unit has the normal components for a compressive refrigeration system. An evaporator coil absorbs the heat from the surrounding (mixed) air; a compressor compresses the refrigerant and pumps it into the condenser coil; the condenser coil dissipates the absorbed heat in the refrigerant to the surrounding air (that is, the outdoor air); and the expansion valve controls the flow of the refrigerant.

Exhibit 8.2 Schematic of a Decentralized Air Conditioning System

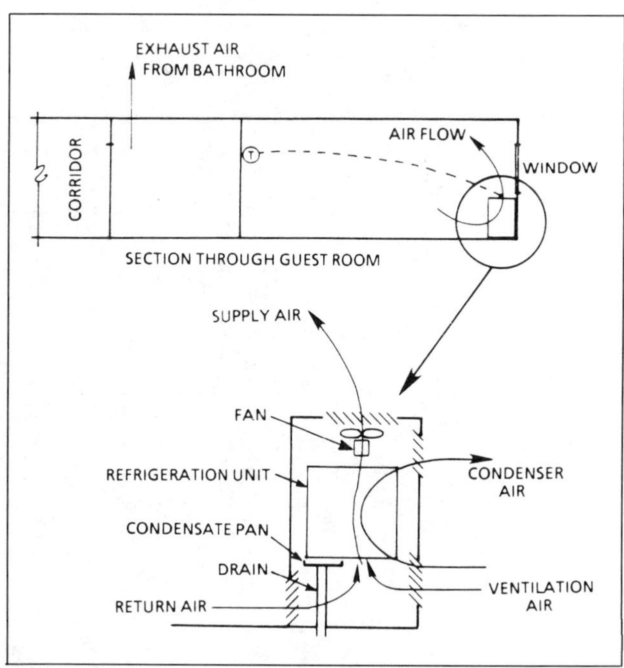

Centralized Configuration with Chilled Water Distribution. In the guestroom as shown in Exhibit 8.3, the return air is collected from the inside surface of the enclosing case near the floor, but there is no outdoor ventilation air. Instead, the ventilation air, which is already conditioned, is provided into the corridors from which it can leak into the room underneath the door. Therefore, no mixing occurs between return and ventilation air. The return air flows over a cooling coil that is cooled by the chilled water produced by the central system. The chilled water enters the coil from a supply line, picks up heat from the air stream, and returns at a higher temperature to the central location through a chilled-water return line. The water that condenses from the return air is collected in a condensate pan which allows the condensate to flow down a drain. Exhaust air is extracted from the room by the exhaust duct normally located in the bathroom.

In the central location, the chilled water is produced and distributed by a chiller (which is another name for a large refrigeration system used in cooling systems) and a circulation pump in the chilled-water system. The chilled water is produced by cooling it with a refrigeration system that often is similar to the compressive refrigeration systems described for food service applications, with the only fundamental differences being the size of the systems and the type of evaporator and condenser coils. Systems for food service applications are usually small (less than 5 HP motors) and the coils are often, but not always, air-cooled. Chillers, however, are usually large, with motors in the 100-to-200-HP range, and the coils are usually water-cooled.

The operation of a water-cooled chiller is as follows. The warmed chilled water returning from the room passes through a water-cooled evaporator coil that is part of the chiller's refrigeration system. Heat is absorbed from the chilled water by the refrigerant in the evaporator coil. The cooled chilled water is supplied back to the room for further cooling of the room. The heat absorbed in the refrigerant is transferred through the compressor to the condenser coil of the refrigeration system. The heat is discharged from the coil into water, called condenser water, which cools the coil. The condensed refrigerant

Exhibit 8.3 Schematic of a Centralized Air Conditioning System with a Chilled Water Distribution System

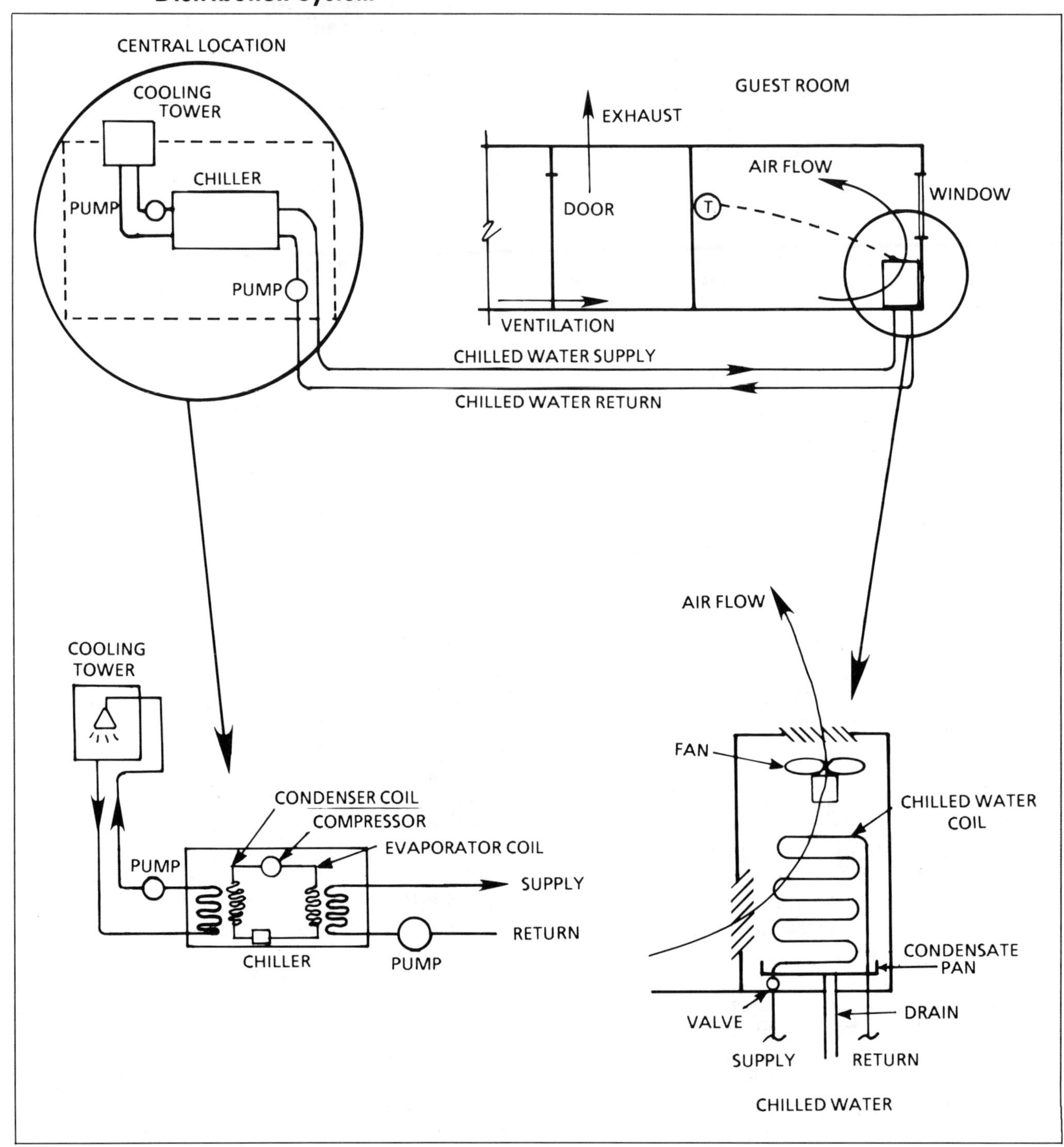

returns to the evaporator coil through the expansion valve, while the warmed condenser water is pumped to a cooling tower located outside the building. At the cooling tower, the condenser water is exposed to the outdoor air. This allows a portion of the water to evaporate, thus cooling the remaining condenser water. The evaporated condenser water is replaced with make-up water from the domestic water system. The cooled condenser water is delivered back to the condenser end of the chiller to begin the cycle again.

In this type of central system, there are three separate circulation loops: the chilled-water loop, the refrigerant loop inside the chiller, and the condenser-water loop. All three loops contribute to the transfer of heat. The chilled-water loop takes the heat from the guestroom to the evaporator end of the chiller. The refrigerant moves the heat from the lower temperature of the chilled water to the higher temperature of the condenser water. Finally, the condenser-water loop transports the heat to the outside. The first two loops are closed, while the last loop is open to the atmosphere for the purpose of evaporative cooling.

Centralized System with a Cold Air Distribution System. The components in the system configuration shown in Exhibit 8.4 are very similar to the central system with a chilled water distribution system. The fundamental difference is that the energy is extracted from the air in the central location and this cold air is distributed to the zone to cool the room. There still is a chilled-water loop, although it is shorter; the chiller still operates in the same fashion; and the condenser-water loop and the cooling tower work the same in both systems.

The air flows in this configuration most closely match those in the basic structure described earlier. The return air is taken from the room by a return-air fan. Some of it is exhausted from the building and the remainder is mixed with ventilation air. The mixed air passes over a cooling coil placed in an air duct, which is called an air handler. In the air handler, the air is cooled and dehumidified before a supply-air fan forces it back to the room.

The flows of energy in this system are identical to those in the chilled water distribution system, although one major flow takes place in a different part of the building. In the chilled water system, the heat is extracted from the room air in the room, while in this type of system, the heat is extracted from the air in a centrally located air handler. Thus, the cooling is transported to the room in the form of cold air rather than chilled water.

Common Aspects. For any of these configurations, the overall effect of the system is the removal of unwanted heat from a zone in the building and the discharge of that heat to another location. The cost of this transport of heat is for the energy to power the compressor in the refrigeration system and to run the auxiliary components such as pumps and fans.

Exhibit 8.4 Schematic of a Centralized Air Conditioning System with a Cold Air Distribution System

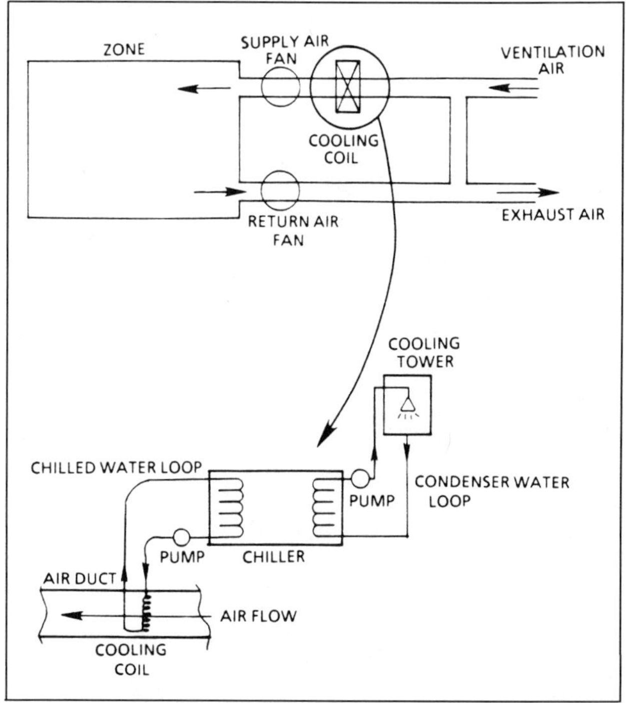

The primary controller of the system is the thermostat in the room. For a decentralized configuration, the thermostat directly controls the operation of the refrigeration system, turning it on when cooling is needed. For a centralized configuration, the control process has two steps. In a water-based system, for example, the thermostat first controls a valve which allows chilled water to flow through the cooling coils when cooling is needed in the room. The control of the central chiller, however, is not accomplished by the room thermostat. Instead, a thermostat that measures the temperature of the chilled water at the outlet of the chiller controls the operation of the chiller, thus providing the

Exhibit 8.5 Heat Transmitted Through a Roof as Affected by the Sun

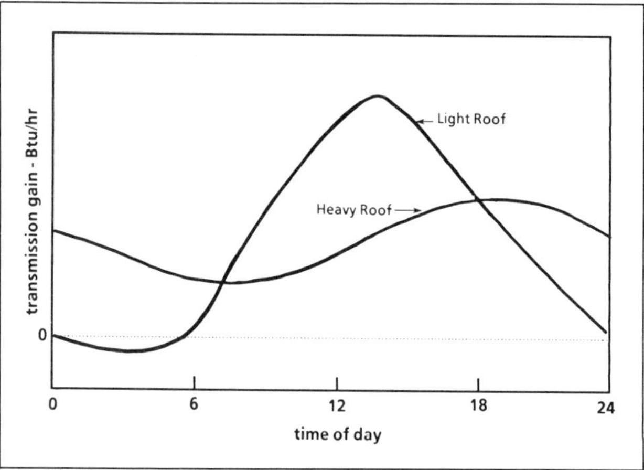

chilled water to the rooms at the proper conditions.

Cooling Loads

The heat gains for a building are classified into five categories: (1) transmission loads, (2) solar loads through windows, (3) ventilation loads, (4) infiltration loads, and (5) internal sources of heat. All are present in a property and contribute to the size and consumption of the air conditioning system. A brief description for each load follows, while a detailed presentation of the calculations used for determining each is provided later in the chapter.

For an air conditioning system, it is important to differentiate between two types of energy in the loads. Energy that is stored in an increase in the air temperature is defined as *sensible energy*, while the energy stored in water vapor evaporated in the air is defined as *latent energy*. Air conditioning systems respond differently to the two types of loads. Generally, it is more expensive in operating costs to remove latent energy than it is to remove a similar amount of sensible energy.

Transmission Loads

The definition for the transmission load is the same as for heating, except that the heat flows into rather than out of the building through the exterior surfaces. The U factor, surface area, and temperature difference still govern the amount of heat that flows through the surface.

The situation is, however, complicated by the effect of the sun that shines on the exterior surfaces. Some of the incident solar energy is absorbed by the outside surface, thus heating its outermost layer. The heat stored in this warmed outermost layer eventually travels through the wall or roof and enters the room. Consequently, more heat enters the room than can be explained by just the difference between the interior and exterior air temperatures. Therefore, the variation in this heat flow over a day is dependent on both the outdoor temperature and the solar radiation. Exhibit 8.5 shows the effect for a flat, horizontal roof. Notice that the maximum heat flow occurs some time after the peak solar load (12:00) on the exterior layer of the roof. This time delay is characteristic of the effect.

The transmission load is recorded as a sensible load on the system.

Solar Loads Through Windows

Solar energy also enters buildings through windows. The energy that enters depends on how much strikes the window and, of that, what percentage passes through the window. The percentage that passes through is usually constant, while the amount that strikes a window varies greatly.

The amount that strikes a window depends largely on the time of day and the orientation of the window. Exhibit 8.6 shows the effect for windows facing in four different directions for a day in January. Notice the strong dependence on the position of the sun relative to the window. For example, an east-facing window receives most of its energy from the sun in the morning hours because the sun is then in the eastern part of the sky.

The solar load through windows is also recorded only as a sensible load on the system.

Ventilation and Infiltration Loads

The concepts defining ventilation and infiltration loads during the heating season also apply to these loads during the cooling season, although the cooling season presents the additional problem of removing latent heat. In other words, the water vapor in the outdoor air be-

Exhibit 8.6 Typical Profile of Solar Energy Striking Windows

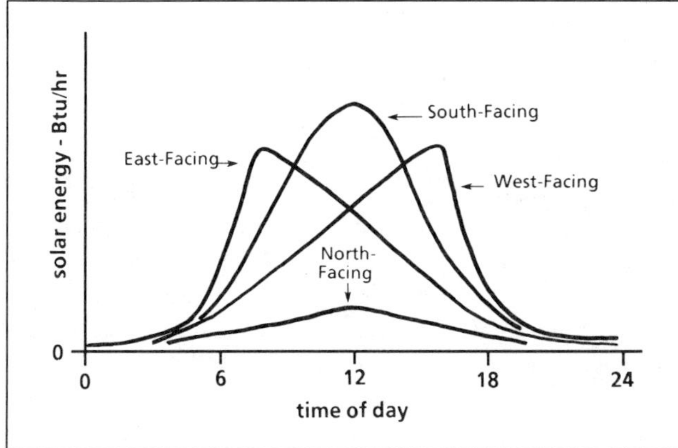

Exhibit 8.7 Typical Daily Profiles for Ventilation and Infiltration Loads for Cooling

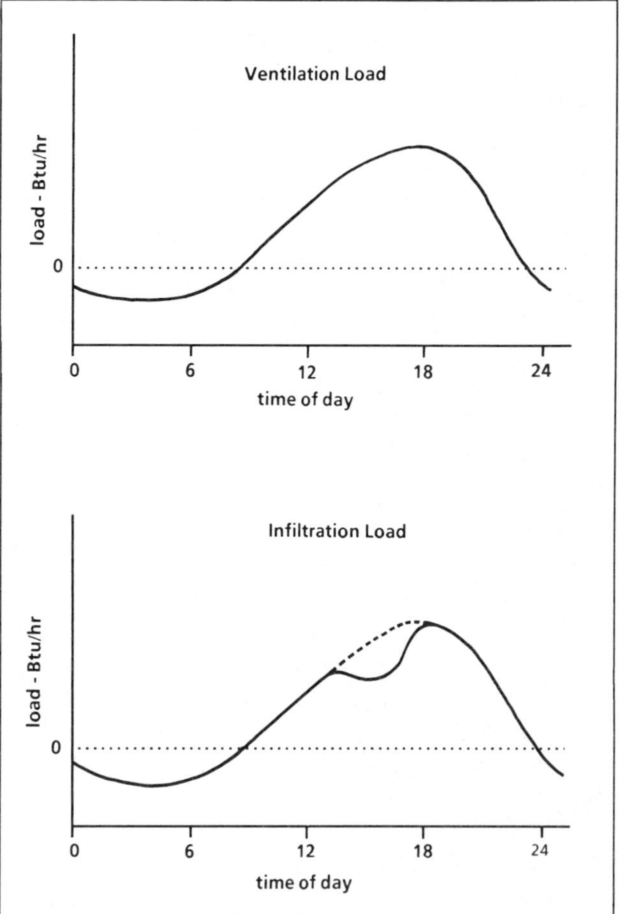

comes a load in addition to the load due to the temperature difference between the indoor and outdoor air. In hot and humid locations, this latent load often is 75% of the total load.

The magnitudes of the loads depend, as in the heating season, on the volume of the air flow and the conditions of the outdoor air. On a daily basis, the maximum ventilation load occurs when the outdoor weather is at its extreme conditions (usually late in the afternoon), while the maximum infiltration load occurs when the combined effects of the volume of air and the outdoor conditions produce the maximum load (also usually late in the afternoon). Typical profiles on a daily basis are shown in Exhibit 8.7.

A portion of the maximum of each load is recorded as a sensible load, while the remainder is recorded as a latent load. The size of these portions is very dependent on the weather conditions. In extremely humid areas, the latent load is more than the sensible load, while the opposite is true in dry areas.

Internal Sources of Heat

In the heating season, internal sources such as lights, people, and equipment are treated only as offsets to the heating losses. For cooling, however, they must be carefully analyzed as part of the loads on the system.

Their contribution to the loads depends on when they are activated (that is, when lights or equipment are on or people are in the building) and how much energy is dissipated into the room at these times. A further consideration is the type of energy—sensible or latent—that is dissipated. On a daily basis, the timing of the loads depends on the operational characteristics of the property (for example, when the people are there, when the lights are on, when the kitchen is operating), while the amount of energy and its proportion of sensible and latent contribution depend on data that is well documented later in this chapter. Possible profiles for the people and lighting contributions in two areas of a property—guestrooms and function spaces—are shown in Exhibit 8.8. Lighting and motors contribute only to the sensible load. People and equipment that gives off water vapor (for example, a coffee brewer) contribute to both types.

System Characteristics

Size

Properly sizing the air conditioning system is more complex than sizing the heating system because the timing of the individual cooling system loads is more varied. In the heating season, all of the loads are assumed to peak at the same time, so the sum of the maximums of the individual loads is a proper estimate of the size after the offsets for internal heat are considered. This is not the case in the cooling season. For example, the cooling load in an east-facing guestroom might peak at mid-morning, while the load on the west-facing room on the other side of the corridor might not peak until late in the afternoon. Add to this the scheduling of the functions in the ballroom and the problem becomes even more complex.

Within this additional complexity, the size of the air conditioning system depends, as does the heating system, on two major factors: (1) the size and type of construction of the building and (2) the weather for the location. Exhibit 8.9 shows typical system sizes for the same building in various locations and Exhibit 8.10 shows how the parts of the system might be distributed to the different areas of a property.

Exhibit 8.8 Possible Daily Profiles for People and Lighting

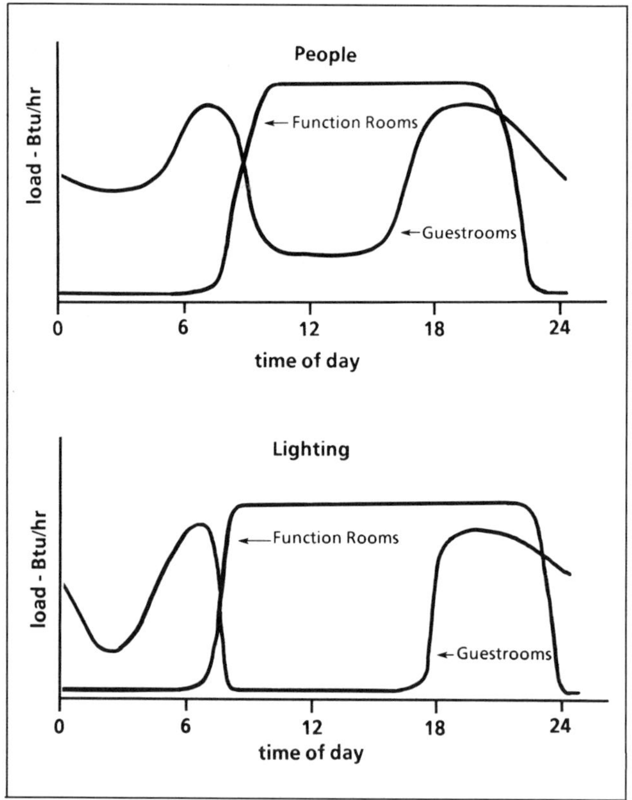

Consumption

As with heating systems, the relative importance of the air conditioning system and the amount of energy it consumes is extremely dependent on the location of the property. Exhibit 8.9 presents consumption data for the same building in different locations, while Exhibit 8.10 documents how the consumption is proportioned over the various functional areas of a different property. Exhibit 6.6 in Chapter 6 shows the consumption of the air conditioning system relative to consumption for an entire property.

Exhibit 8.9 Size and Consumption of Cooling Systems for Guestrooms

Location	Size Tons/100 ft^2	Consumption Btu/ft^2-year
Syracuse, N.Y.	.206	3,200
Minneapolis, Minn.	.219	3,400
Denver, Colo.	.203	2,700
Seattle, Wash.	.176	2,500
San Francisco, Cal.	.158	2,600
Memphis, Tenn.	.241	7,800
Los Angeles, Cal.	.204	7,700
Phoenix, Ariz.	.250	16,300
San Antonio, Tex.	.228	11,400
Miami, Fla.	.225	18,400

Source: Armand Domanic Iaia, *Computer Modeling of Building Criteria to Determine Their Efficiency in Different Climates*, Monograph, School of Hotel Administration, Cornell University, 1983.

System Design

Load Calculations

The size and operating costs of the air conditioning system are directly dependent on the size and timing of the loads. For a cooling system, the loads occur from the five basic sources discussed earlier in this chapter. The total energy gain is the sum of the individual

Exhibit 8.10 Air Conditioning Loads

Space	Peak Tons	Consumption: Ton-Hours x 1,000	Percentage of Consumption
Guest Rooms and Corridors	258	86	23.8
Ballroom	195	101	28.0
Meeting Rooms	67	39	10.8
Offices	13	12	3.3
Lounge and Restaurant	43	49	13.6
Lobby and Court	35	38	10.5
Indoor Pool	14	8	2.2
Kitchen	0	0	0
Laundry	7	6	1.7
Back of House	31	22	6.1
TOTAL	**465***	**361**	**100.0**

* Peak for the property is not the sum of the individual space peaks because the peaks in each space do not occur simultaneously.

Source: Robach Inc., Torrance, Calif., 1984.

components, where two separate totals—one for the sensible energy gain (Q_{GS}) and one for the latent energy gain (Q_{GL})—must be kept.

Transmission Loads. As discussed in Chapter 6 for heating loads, heat flows from a region of higher temperature to a region of lower temperature according to the equation $Q_T = U \times A \times TD$. The influences of the construction and size of the wall are contained in the U factor and the area, respectively. The temperature difference is determined differently, depending on whether the surface is an exterior or an interior surface.

The temperature difference across interior surfaces is

$$TD = T_{In} - T_I$$

where T_{In} is the air temperature in the nth adjacent space in °F and T_I is the air temperature inside the space. A zone may have many interior surfaces surrounding it, so each surface is calculated. In most cases, however, the heat flow is zero because there usually is no temperature difference between two adjacent rooms.

The situation for exterior walls and roofs is complicated by the effect of the sun striking their outside surfaces. This effect is accounted for by defining a *cooling load temperature difference (CLTD)* in F° that depends on the factors which control the amount of heat that travels through the surface. These factors are the composition and weight of the wall or roof, the color of the outermost layer, and the orientation of the outermost layer. Charts that summarize these effects are available. Exhibits 8.11 and 8.12 are samples of the information for roofs and walls, respectively.

A review of the values of CLTD for roof numbers 2 and 8 as shown in Exhibit 8.11 demonstrates the important effects. Although the incident sun energy on a flat roof is at the maximum at 1200 hours, the maximum flow of energy through roof number 2 into the space below the roof does not occur until three hours later as indicated by the fact that the CLTD is 52F° at 1200 hours and is 74F° at 1500 hours. This delay in the transmission of heat is caused by the thermal storage capacity of the material from which the roof is built. Notice that some heat energy is passed from the roof into the room even in the early morning hours. Comparing this profile of CLTD with the profile for roof number 8 demonstrates the delaying effect of heavier construction. The maximum flow for the heavier roof does not occur until 2000 hours and it is smaller in magnitude. This observation can be generalized for all roofs. Heavier construction both delays the timing of the peak load and reduces its magnitude in comparison to lighter construction.

The information in this chart is based on several assumptions which are stated at the bottom. Consult the source for this chart for information on adjusting these figures for situations not conforming to the stated assumptions.

A similar review of Exhibit 8.12 for walls introduces the effect of orientation. Within a

Exhibit 8.11 Typical Cooling Load Temperature Differences for Dark Roofs

Roof No.	Description of Construction	Weight lb/ft²	U-value Btu/(h-ft²-F°)	Solar Time, h 1	2	3	4	5	6	7	8	9	10	11	12	13	14	15	16	17	18	19	20	21	22	23	24
				Without Suspended Ceiling																							
1	Steel sheet with 1-in. (or 2-in.) insulation	7 (8)	0.213 (0.124)	1	-2	-3	-3	-5	-3	6	19	34	49	61	71	78	79	77	70	59	45	30	18	12	8	5	3
2	1-in. wood with 1-in. insulation	8	0.170	6	3	0	-1	-3	-3	-2	4	14	27	39	52	62	70	74	74	70	62	51	38	28	20	14	9
3	4-in. w. concrete	18	0.213	9	5	2	0	-2	-3	-3	1	9	20	32	44	55	64	70	73	71	66	57	45	34	25	18	13
4	2-in. h.w. concrete with 1-in. (or 2-in.) insulation	29	0.206 (0.122)	12	8	5	3	0	-1	-1	3	11	20	30	41	51	59	65	66	66	62	54	45	36	29	22	17
5	1-in. wood with 2-in. insulation	9	0.109	3	0	-3	-4	-5	-7	-6	-3	5	16	27	39	49	57	63	64	62	57	48	37	26	18	11	7
6	6-in. l.w. concrete	24	0.158	22	17	13	9	6	3	1	1	3	7	15	23	33	43	51	58	62	64	62	57	50	42	35	28
7	2.5-in. wood with 1-in. insulation	13	0.130	29	24	20	16	13	10	7	6	6	9	13	20	27	34	42	48	53	55	56	54	49	44	39	34
8	8-in. l.w. concrete	31	0.126	35	30	26	22	18	14	11	9	7	7	9	13	19	25	33	39	46	50	53	54	53	49	45	40
9	4-in. h.w. concrete with 1-in. (or 2-in.) insulation	52 (52)	0.200 (0.120)	25	22	18	15	12	9	8	8	10	14	20	26	33	40	46	50	53	53	52	48	43	38	34	30
10	2.5-in. wood with 2-in. insulation	13	0.093	30	26	23	19	16	13	10	9	8	9	13	17	23	29	36	41	46	49	51	50	47	43	39	35

Direct Application Without Adjustments: Values were calculated using the following conditions:

- Dark flat surface roof("dark" for solar radiation absorption)
- Indoor temperature of 78° F
- Outdoor maximum temperature of 95° F with outdoor mean temperature of 85° F and an outdoor daily range of 21 F°
- Solar radiation typical of 40 deg. North latitude on July 21
- Outside surface resistance, R_o = 0.333ft² × F × h/Btu
- Without and with suspended ceiling, but no attic fans or return air ducts in suspended ceiling spaces
- Inside surface resistance, R_i = 0.685 ft² × F × h/Btu

group of walls of similar construction, orientation plays an important role in the timing of the transmission load. With group G as an example, the transmission load is at a maximum on an east-facing wall at 1000 hours, on a south-facing wall at 1400 hours, and a west-facing wall at 1700, each time being a delay of approximately two hours from the time that the maximum solar energy is incident on the surface. Notice that the maximum value of CLTD is largest on the west-facing wall.

After the CLTD is determined from the chart, its value is substituted for TD in the transmission equation to determine the amount of heat flowing into the space behind the surface.

Exhibit 8.13 shows a sample calculation for a roof and a wall.

Solar Loads Through Windows. Energy enters a building through a window in two ways: conduction through the glass and solar radiation. The amount of energy flow for each mechanism is determined separately.

The heat that is conducted through the window is estimated in a manner similar to that for roofs and walls. A CLTD is selected from a table such as in Exhibit 8.14. This CLTD is then

Exhibit 8.12 Cooling Load Temperature Differences for Various Walls

a.) Groups of Wall Construction

Group No.	Description of Construction	Weight (lb./ft²)	*U*-Value (Btu/h × ft² × F)
4-in. Face Brick + (*Brick*)			
C	Air Space + 4-in. Face Brick	83	0.358
D	4-in. Common Brick	90	0.415
C	1-in. Insulation or Air Space + 4-in. Common Brick	90	0.174-0.301
B	2-in. Insulation + 4-in. Common Brick	88	0.111
B	8-in. Common Brick	130	0.302
A	Insulation or Air Space + 8-in. Common Brick	130	0.154-0.243
4-in. Face Brick + (*H.W. Concrete*)			
C	Air Space + 2-in. Concrete	94	0.350
B	2-in. Insulation + 4-in. Concrete	97	0.116
A	Air Space or Insulation + 8-in. or more Concrete	143-190	0.110-0.112
4-in. Face Brick + (*L.W. or H.W. Concrete Block)*			
E	4-in. Block	62	0.319
D	Air Space or Insulation + 4-in. Block	62	0.153-0.246
D	8-in. Block	70	0.274
C	Air Space or 1-in. Insulation + 6-in. or 8-in. Block	73-89	0.221-0.275
B	2-in. Insulation + 8-in. Block	89	0.096-0.107

b.) Cooling Load Temperature Difference for Group A, F, and G Walls

North Latitude Wall Facing	Solar Time 1	2	3	4	5	6	7	8	9	10	11	12	13	14	15	16	17	18	19	20	21	22	23	24
Group A Walls																								
N	14	14	14	13	13	13	12	12	11	11	10	10	10	10	10	10	11	11	12	12	13	13	14	14
NE	19	19	19	18	17	17	16	15	15	15	15	15	16	16	17	18	18	18	19	19	20	20	20	20
E	24	24	23	23	22	21	20	19	19	18	19	19	20	21	22	23	24	24	25	25	25	25	25	25
SE	24	23	23	22	21	20	20	19	18	18	18	18	18	19	20	21	22	23	23	24	24	24	24	24
S	20	20	19	19	18	18	17	16	16	15	14	14	14	14	14	15	16	17	18	19	19	20	20	20
SW	25	25	25	24	24	23	22	21	20	19	19	18	17	17	17	17	18	19	20	22	23	24	25	25
W	27	27	26	26	25	24	24	23	22	21	20	19	19	18	18	18	18	19	20	22	23	25	26	26
NW	21	21	21	20	20	19	19	18	17	16	16	15	15	14	14	14	15	15	16	17	18	19	20	21
Group F Walls																								
N	8	6	5	3	2	1	2	4	6	7	9	11	14	17	19	21	22	23	24	23	20	16	13	11
NE	9	7	5	3	2	1	5	14	23	28	30	29	28	27	27	27	27	26	24	22	19	16	13	11
E	10	7	6	4	3	2	6	17	28	38	44	45	43	39	36	34	32	30	27	24	21	17	15	12
SE	10	7	6	4	3	2	4	10	19	28	36	41	43	42	39	36	34	31	28	25	21	18	15	12
S	10	8	6	4	3	2	1	1	3	7	13	20	27	34	38	39	38	35	31	26	22	18	15	12
SW	15	11	9	6	5	3	2	2	4	5	8	11	17	26	35	44	50	53	52	45	37	28	23	18
W	17	13	10	7	5	4	3	3	4	6	8	11	14	20	28	39	49	57	60	54	43	34	27	21
NW	14	10	8	6	4	3	2	2	3	5	8	10	13	15	21	27	35	42	46	43	35	28	22	18
Group G Walls																								
N	3	2	1	0	-1	2	7	8	9	12	15	18	21	23	24	24	25	26	22	15	11	9	7	5
NE	3	2	1	0	-1	9	27	36	39	35	30	26	26	27	27	26	25	22	18	14	11	9	7	5
E	4	2	1	0	-1	11	31	47	54	55	50	40	33	31	30	29	27	24	19	15	12	10	8	6
SE	4	2	1	0	-1	5	18	32	42	49	51	48	42	36	32	30	27	24	19	15	12	10	8	6
S	4	2	1	0	-1	0	1	5	12	22	31	39	45	46	43	37	31	25	20	15	12	10	8	5
SW	5	4	3	1	0	0	2	5	8	12	16	26	38	50	59	63	61	52	37	24	17	13	10	8
W	6	5	3	2	1	1	2	5	8	11	15	19	27	41	56	67	72	67	48	29	20	15	11	8
NW	5	3	2	1	0	0	2	5	8	11	15	18	21	27	37	47	55	55	41	25	17	13	10	7

Reprinted by permission from *1985 ASHRAE Handbook—Fundamentals.*

used in the familiar transmission equation, $Q_T = U \times A \times CLTD$.

The load on the cooling system from energy that enters the window as solar energy depends on the size and type of window, its orientation, the time of day, the interior shading of the window, and the construction of the room. These factors are combined in the following equation for the cooling load from solar radiation:

$$Q_S = A \times SC \times MSHG \times CLF$$

where Q_S is the cooling load in Btu/hr; *A* is the area of the window in ft^2; *SC* is a shading coefficient whose value is between 0 and 1.00; *MSHG* is the maximum solar heat gain in Btu/hr-ft^2; and *CLF* is a cooling load factor whose value is between 0 and 1.00. The specific values for these variables are determined from charts such as shown in Exhibits 8.15, 8.16, and 8.17.

Exhibit 8.15 documents the maximum amount of solar energy that is incident on windows for various orientations for each month of the year. For example, a south-facing window receives 95 Btu/hr-ft^2 of energy in June and 254 Btu/hr-ft^2 during January.

This maximum amount of energy falling on the window is modified by the shading coefficient, which is a measure of the percentage of energy that passes through the window, to determine the maximum amount that could enter the room. Values for SC are shown in Exhibit 8.16 for various types of glass.

The maximum amount of solar energy that could enter the room must be modified by the time of day and the construction characteristics to determine the cooling load. These effects are included in the cooling load factor (CLF), which is the percentage of the maximum available energy that actually results in a load on the cooling system, as shown in Exhibit 8.17. Notice that the time at which the largest CLF occurs is always later in the day than the time at which the maximum solar energy is entering the window. This delay is caused by the absorption effect of the furnishings in the room. Also notice that heavier construction characteristics delay the timing of the peak and reduce its size.

Sample calculations for the cooling load from energy that passes through the windows for four guestrooms, each with a different orientation, are shown in Exhibit 8.18.

Exhibit 8.13 Sample Transmission Load Calculations for Cooling

A. Roof—Data:

Day: July 21
Roof construction: 4 in. h.w. concrete with 1 in. insulation; dark color
Inside temperature: 78°F
Outside temperature: range—21F°; maximum—95°F; average—85°F
Time of day: 12:00 and 18:00
Area: 12′ × 27′

What is the amount of transmission heat flow?

Calculation:

Basic equation: $Q_T = U \times A \times CLTD$
From Exhibit 8.11: U = .2; CLTD = 26F° and 53F°
At 12:00
$Q_T = .2 \times (12 \times 27) \times 26 = 1{,}684$ Btu/hr
At 18:00
$Q_T = .2 \times (12 \times 27) \times 53 = 3{,}434$ Btu/hr

B. Wall—Data:

Wall construction: 4 in. face brick, insulation, 8 in. concrete
Orientation: south
Area: 12′ × 3′
Other data is the same as in part A

What is the amount of transmission heat flow?

Calculation:

From Exhibit 8.12:
Wall type A; U = .11; CLTD = 14F° and 17F°
At 12:00
$.11 \times (12 \times 3) \times 14 = 55$ Btu/hr
At 18:00
$.11 \times (12 \times 3) \times 17 = 67$ Btu/hr

Infiltration and Ventilation Loads. In contrast to the infiltration and ventilation loads as described in Chapter 6, these loads for cooling must include the effect of the water vapor in the air. Consequently, the equations for the loads are derived from the "wet air" approach discussed in Chapter 7. In addition, the cooling load for sensible energy must be separated from the cooling load for latent energy.

The sensible and latent cooling loads from infiltration and ventilation are calculated using the following two equations, respectively:

Exhibit 8.14 Cooling Load Temperature Differences for Conduction Through Glass

Solar Time, h	0100	0200	0300	0400	0500	0600	0700	0800
CLTD, F°	1	0	−1	−2	−2	−2	−2	0
	0900	1000	1100	1200	1300	1400	1500	1600
	2	4	7	9	12	13	14	14
	1700	1800	1900	2000	2100	2200	2300	2400
	13	12	10	8	6	4	3	2

Reprinted by permission from *1985 ASHRAE Handbook—Fundamentals.*

Exhibit 8.15 Maximum Solar Heat Gain Data

Maximum Solar Heat Gain Factor, Btu/h-ft^2 for Sunlit Glass, North Latitudes

40° North Latitude

	N (shade)	NNE/ NNW	NE/ NW	ENE/ WNW	E/ W	ESE/ WSW	SE/ SW	SSE/ SSW	S	HOR
Jan.	20	20	20	74	154	205	241	252	254	133
Feb.	24	24	50	129	186	234	246	244	241	180
Mar.	29	29	93	169	218	238	236	216	206	223
Apr.	34	71	140	190	224	223	203	170	154	252
May	37	102	165	202	220	208	175	133	113	265
June	48	113	172	205	216	199	161	116	95	267
July	38	102	163	198	216	203	170	129	109	262
Aug.	35	71	135	185	216	214	196	165	149	247
Sept.	30	30	87	160	203	227	226	209	200	215
Oct.	25	25	49	123	180	225	238	236	234	177
Nov.	20	20	20	73	151	201	237	248	250	132
Dec.	18	18	18	60	135	188	232	249	253	113

Reprinted by permission from *1985 ASHRAE Handbook—Fundamentals.*

$$Q_{I(V)S} = 1.08 \times \text{cfm} \times \text{TD}$$

and

$$Q_{I(V)L} = 4840 \times \text{cfm} \times \text{WD}$$

where $Q_{I(V)S}$ is the sensible load for either infiltration or ventilation and $Q_{I(V)L}$ is the latent load for either in Btu/hr. The first equation is the familiar "dry air" equation used for heating load calculations. The second equation, which has a similar form, accounts for the water vapor in the air. *WD* is the difference in the water contents of the indoor and outdoor air measured in lb water/lb dry air. This value is shown on a vertical scale on the right-hand side of the psychrometric chart in Appendix B. For example, interior air at 78°F and 50% relative humidity (rh) contains .0104 lb water/lb dry air, while outdoor air at 95°F and 60% rh contains .0218 lb water/lb dry air. The constant 4840, which accounts for the properties of air and water and the conversion from minutes to hours, is very similar in purpose to the constant 1.08.

The values of the remaining variables, cfm and TD, are determined from the design requirements of the system. The amounts of cfm are determined from code regulations for ventilation and from calculations similar to those in Chapter

Exhibit 8.16 Shading Coefficients for Glass

A. Single Glass

Type of Glass[a]	Nominal Thickness[b]	Solar Trans.[b]	Shading Coefficient $h_o = 4.0$	Shading Coefficient $h_o = 3.0$
Clear	1/8in.	0.86	1.00	1.00
	1/4in.	0.78	0.94	0.95
	3/8in.	0.72	0.90	0.92
	1/2in.	0.67	0.87	0.88
Heat Absorbing	1/8in.	0.64	0.83	0.85
	1/4in.	0.46	0.69	0.73
	3/8in.	0.33	0.60	0.64
	1/2in.	0.24	0.53	0.58

B. Insulating Glass

Type of Glass[a]	Nominal Thickness[b]	Solar Trans.[b]	Shading Coefficient $h_o = 4.0$	Shading Coefficient $h_o = 3.0$
Clear Out, Clear In	1/8in.[c]	0.71[e]	0.88	0.88
Clear Out, Clear In	1/4in.	0.61	0.81	0.82
Heat Absorbing[d] Out, Clear In	1/4in.	0.36	0.55	0.58

[a]Refers to factory-fabricated units with 3/16, 1/4 or 1/2-in. air space or to prime windows plus storm sash.

[b]Refer to manufacturer's literature for values.

[c]Thickness of each pane of glass, not thickness of assembled unit.

[d]Refers to gray, bronze and green tinted heat-absorbing float glass.

[e]Combined transmittance for assembled unit.

Reprinted by permission from *1985 ASHRAE Handbook—Fundamentals.*

Exhibit 8.17 Cooling Load Factors for Glass Without Interior Shading

Fenestration Facing	Room Construction	Solar Time 1	2	3	4	5	6	7	8	9	10	11	12	13	14	15	16	17	18	19	20	21	22	23	24
N (Shaded)	L	0.17	0.14	0.11	0.09	0.08	0.33	0.42	0.48	0.56	0.63	0.71	0.76	0.80	0.82	0.82	0.79	0.75	0.84	0.61	0.48	0.38	0.31	0.25	0.20
	M	0.23	0.20	0.18	0.16	0.14	0.34	0.41	0.46	0.53	0.59	0.65	0.70	0.73	0.75	0.76	0.74	0.75	0.79	0.61	0.50	0.42	0.36	0.31	0.27
	H	0.25	0.23	0.21	0.20	0.19	0.38	0.45	0.49	0.55	0.60	0.65	0.69	0.72	0.72	0.72	0.70	0.70	0.75	0.57	0.46	0.39	0.34	0.31	0.28
E	L	0.04	0.03	0.03	0.02	0.02	0.19	0.37	0.51	0.57	0.57	0.50	0.42	0.37	0.32	0.29	0.25	0.22	0.19	0.15	0.12	0.10	0.08	0.06	0.05
	M	0.07	0.06	0.06	0.05	0.05	0.18	0.33	0.44	0.50	0.51	0.46	0.39	0.35	0.31	0.29	0.26	0.23	0.21	0.17	0.15	0.13	0.11	0.10	0.08
	H	0.09	0.09	0.08	0.08	0.07	0.20	0.34	0.45	0.49	0.49	0.43	0.36	0.32	0.29	0.26	0.24	0.22	0.19	0.17	0.15	0.13	0.12	0.11	0.10
S	L	0.08	0.07	0.05	0.04	0.04	0.06	0.09	0.14	0.22	0.34	0.48	0.59	0.65	0.65	0.59	0.50	0.43	0.36	0.28	0.22	0.18	0.15	0.12	0.10
	M	0.12	0.11	0.09	0.08	0.07	0.08	0.11	0.14	0.21	0.31	0.42	0.52	0.57	0.58	0.53	0.47	0.41	0.36	0.29	0.25	0.21	0.18	0.16	0.14
	H	0.13	0.12	0.12	0.11	0.10	0.11	0.14	0.17	0.24	0.33	0.43	0.51	0.56	0.55	0.50	0.43	0.37	0.32	0.26	0.22	0.20	0.18	0.16	0.15
W	L	0.12	0.10	0.08	0.06	0.05	0.06	0.07	0.08	0.10	0.11	0.12	0.14	0.20	0.32	0.45	0.57	0.64	0.61	0.44	0.34	0.27	0.22	0.18	0.14
	M	0.15	0.13	0.11	0.10	0.09	0.09	0.09	0.10	0.11	0.12	0.13	0.14	0.19	0.29	0.40	0.50	0.56	0.55	0.41	0.33	0.27	0.23	0.20	0.17
	H	0.14	0.13	0.12	0.11	0.10	0.11	0.12	0.13	0.14	0.14	0.15	0.16	0.21	0.30	0.40	0.49	0.54	0.52	0.38	0.30	0.24	0.21	0.18	0.16
HOR	L	0.11	0.09	0.07	0.06	0.05	0.07	0.14	0.24	0.36	0.48	0.58	0.66	0.72	0.74	0.73	0.67	0.59	0.47	0.37	0.29	0.24	0.19	0.16	0.13
	M	0.16	0.14	0.12	0.11	0.09	0.11	0.16	0.24	0.33	0.43	0.52	0.59	0.64	0.67	0.66	0.62	0.56	0.47	0.38	0.32	0.28	0.24	0.21	0.18
	H	0.17	0.16	0.15	0.14	0.13	0.15	0.20	0.28	0.36	0.45	0.52	0.59	0.62	0.64	0.62	0.58	0.51	0.42	0.35	0.29	0.26	0.23	0.21	0.19

L = Light construction: frame exterior wall, 2-in. concrete floor slab, approximately 30 lb. of material/ft^2 of floor area.
M = Medium construction: 4-in. concrete exterior wall, 4-in. concrete floor slab, aproximately 70 lb. of building material/ft^2 of floor area.
H = Heavy construction: 6-in. concrete exterior wall, 6-in. concrete floor slab, approximately 130 lb. of building material/ft^2 of floor area.

Reprinted by permission from *1985 ASHRAE Handbook—Fundamentals.*

Exhibit 8.18 Heat Entering Windows per Square Foot of Window

Data:

	Orientation of glass N	E	S	W
Time: 16:00				
CLTD	14	14	14	14
U factor	1.0	1.0	1.0	1.0
SC	.94	.94	.94	.94
Month: June				
MSHG	48	216	95	216
Medium construction				
CLF	.74	.26	.47	.50
Area (ft^2)	1.0	1.0	1.0	1.0

What is the heat entering a square foot of window?

Calculation:

	N	E	S	W
$Q_T = U \times A \times CLTD$	14.0	14.0	14.0	14.0
$Q_S = A \times SC \times MSHG \times CLF$	33.4	52.8	42.0	101.5
Total Btu/hr-ft^2	47.4	66.8	56.0	115.5

6 for infiltration. The temperature difference is the same as that used for the transmission calculation.

Exhibit 8.19 Sample Calculations for Infiltration and Ventilation Loads for Cooling

Data:

Exterior conditions: temperature—90°F; 60% rh; water content—.0182 lb/lb of air
Interior conditions: temperature—78°F; 50% rh; water content—.0102 lb/lb of air
cfm ventilation: 75
cfm infiltration: 30

What are the sensible and latent loads for ventilation and infiltration?

Calculation:

	Infiltration	**Ventilation**
Sensible load—Btu/hr (1.08 × cfm × TD)	389	972
Latent load—Btu/hr (4,840 × cfm × WD)	1,162	2,904
Total Load—Btu/hr	1,551	3,876

Exhibit 8.19 shows sample calculations for an infiltration and a ventilation load.

Internal Loads. Loads on the cooling system are produced by people and equipment inside the

Exhibit 8.20 Rates of Heat Gain from Occupants of Conditioned Spaces

Degree of Activity	Typical Application	Total Heat Btu/h	Sensible Heat Btu/h	Latent Heat Btu/h
Seated at rest	Theater, movie	350	210	140
Seated, very light work writing	Offices, hotels, apts.	420	230	190
Seated, eating	Restaurant	580	255	325
Seated, light work, typing	Offices, hotels, apts.	510	255	255
Standing, light work or walking slowly	Retail Store, bank	640	315	325
Light bench work	Factory	780	345	435
Walking, 3 mph. light machine work	Factory	1040	345	695
Moderate dancing	Dance hall	1280	405	875
Heavy work, heavy machine work, lifting	Factory	1600	565	1035
Heavy work, athletics	Gymnasium	1800	635	1165

Reprinted by permission from *1985 ASHRAE Handbook—Fundamentals.*

building. The actual effect of these sources of energy on the system is a combination of the amount of energy produced by the source and the profile of time over which the produced energy becomes a cooling load. For simplicity of discussion in this section, all produced energy is assumed to be an instantaneous load on the system. Therefore, no time delay effects are presented.[1]

People produce heat and dissipate it to the surrounding air in the forms of sensible and latent energy. Exhibit 8.20 documents this amount of energy for numerous common activities.

Equipment such as lights and display cooking appliances contribute heat to the cooling loads. For lights, the contribution is estimated at the rated wattage plus any auxiliary ballast, converted into Btu/hr by the conversion factor of 3.413 Btu/hr for each watt. Exhibit 8.21 shows a sample of the data for commercial cooking appliances. Notice the effect of installing the equipment under a hood.

System Size

Total Loads. Unlike the situation for heating loads (where the maximums of the components of the total load are assumed to occur at approximately the same time of day), the maximums of the components of the total cooling load do not occur at the same time of day or the same time of year. For example, the ventilation load is usually at its maximum in the afternoon of the warmest month, the maximum people load occurs at maximum occupancy, and the largest solar load happens at various times of the day and year depending on the orientation of the window. Consequently, the calculation to determine the maximum cooling load is more complicated than just summing the largest loads of the components. Usually, the calculation for each component and the total cooling load is performed for various times of the day and for various days of the year in order to determine which time results in the largest total.

Experience and knowledge of the contributing loads help to pinpoint the likely times for the largest total load. If the zone is an interior function room without any exterior walls or roof, the largest total might occur late in the afternoon during the hottest month. If the zone is a south-facing guestroom in a warm climatic zone, the largest load might occur during the afternoon in the month of January because the solar load is a maximum at that time.

Exhibit 8.21 Recommended Rate of Heat Gain for Commercial Cooking Appliances Located in an Air Conditioned Area

Appliance	Capacity	Overall Dim., Inches Width x Depth x Height	Miscellaneous Data	Manufacturer's Input Rating Btuh	Probable Max. Hourly Input Btuh	Recommended Rate of Heat Gain, Btu/h — Without Hood: Sensible	Without Hood: Latent	Without Hood: Total	With Hood: All Sensible
			Gas-Burning, Counter Type						
Broiler-griddle		31 x 20 x 18		36,000	18,000	11,700	6,300	18,000	3,600
Coffee brewer per burner			With warm position	5,500	2,500	1,750	750	2,500	500
Water heater burner			With storage tank	11,000	5,000	3,850	1,650	5,500	1,100
Coffee urn	3 gal	12-inch dia.		10,000	5,000	3,500	1,500	5,000	1,000
	5 gal	14-inch dia.		15,000	7,500	5,250	2,250	7,500	1,500
	8 gal twin	25-inch wide		20,000	10,000	7,000	3,000	10,000	2,000
Deep fat fryer	15 lb fat	14 x 21 x 15		30,000	15,000	7,500	7,500	15,000	3,000
Dry food warmer per sq ft of top				1,400	700	560	140	700	140
Griddle, frying per sq ft of top				15,000	7,500	4,900	2,600	7,500	1,500
Short order stove, per burner			Open grates	10,000	5,000	3,200	1,800	5,000	1,000
Steam table, per sq ft of top				2,500	1,250	750	500	1,250	250
Toaster, continuous	360 slices/hr	19 x 16 x 30	2 slices wide	12,000	6,000	3,600	2,400	6,000	1,200
	720 slices/hr	24 x 16 x 30	4 slices wide	20,000	10,000	6,000	4,000	10,000	2,000

Reprinted by permission from *1985 ASHRAE Handbook—Fundamentals.*

Exhibit 8.22 Form for Summarizing Cooling Loads

Time of day:
Time of year:

Category	Sensible	Latent
Transmission		
Solar		
Infiltration		
Ventilation		
Internal		
TOTAL LOADS Btu/hr		

The chart in Exhibit 8.22 helps to organize the results when the calculations are performed.

Timing of Components of the Total Load. Exhibit 8.23 demonstrates for three types of surfaces (glass, a typical wall, and a typical roof) the tremendous variation in loads that occurs over a day. In the top graph, the amount of energy entering the room through the glass is shown in Btu/hr-ft^2 for four different window orientations. In the bottom graph, similar data for walls of four orientations and a flat, horizontal roof is provided. These two graphs can be used to calculate the total load from transmission and solar contributions for a guestroom of any size that is constructed from the building materials assumed for the generation of the graphs. Exhibit 8.24 shows an example of this calculation.

Exhibit 8.25 shows the results of such calculations for four guestrooms at various times of the day. The cooling load in the east-facing guestroom peaks at 0800 hours, in the south-facing room at 1300 hours, in the west-facing room at 1700 hours, and in the north-facing room at 1800 hours.

The effect of this variation in the size and timing of the peak loads for guestrooms of different orientations on the selection of equipment is important. If decentralized cooling units were purchased for each separate room, the size of the systems would be approximately 14,500, 8,800, 18,000, and 7,900 Btu/hr, respectively. This requires purchasing and stocking units of

Exhibit 8.23 Cooling Loads for Various Building Surfaces

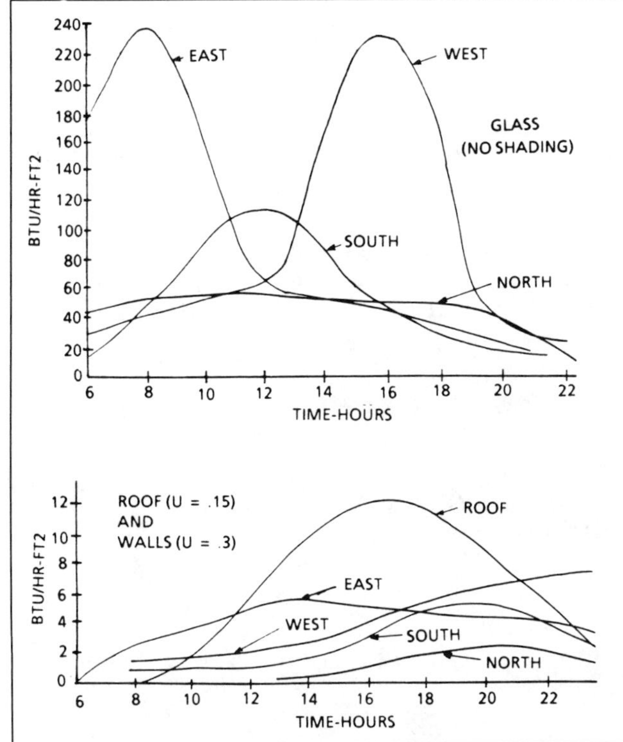

Exhibit 8.24 Transmission and Solar Loads for a Guestroom (based on Exhibit 8.23)

Data:

Window: 60 ft^2
Exterior wall: 40 ft^2
Roof: 340 ft^2
Orientation: south
Time: 12:00

Determine the transmission and solar loads for the guestroom.

Calculation:

Energy transmitted (from Exhibit 8.23):
Window: 115 Btu/hr-ft^2
Wall: 1.2 Btu/hr-ft^2
Roof: 5.4 Btu/hr-ft^2

$$\text{Total energy} = (115 \times 60) + (1.2 \times 40) + (5.4 \times 340) = 8{,}784 \text{ Btu/hr}$$

Exhibit 8.25 Cooling Loads for Guestrooms with Different Orientations

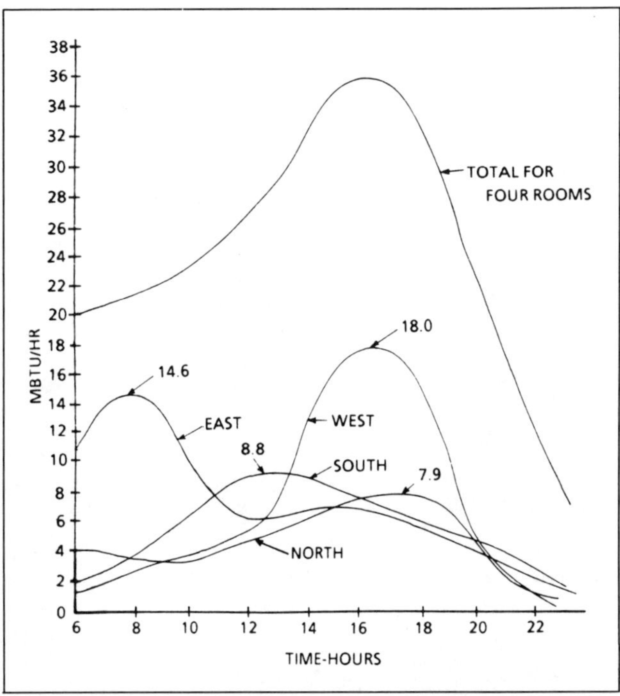

various sizes for the different rooms. Usually it is impractical to specify many different sizes, but often two or three sizes are used to accommodate the difference in the loads for east- and west-facing rooms or for rooms with and without roofs.

If, however, the four rooms were connected to a centralized system, their contribution to the size of the system would be approximately 36,000 Btu/hr. Notice that this is substantially smaller than the sum (49,200 Btu/hr) of the capacities of the four decentralized units. This effect, which highlights one of advantages of a centralized system, happens because the peaks of the loads do not occur at the same time. The advantage, however, is partially offset by the extra requirements for auxiliary equipment such as piping for the chilled-water lines and circulation pumps.

System Consumption

Coefficient of Performance. As with refrigeration systems for food service applications as described in Chapter 7, a coefficient of performance for the cooling unit can be determined. The definition of the coefficient, which is the cooling output of the unit divided by the re-

Exhibit 8.26 Approximate Power Requirements for Cooling Systems

System	Compressor kw/ton	Auxiliaries kw/ton
Window units	1.46	0.32
Through-wall units	1.64	0.30
Dwelling unit, air-cooled	1.49	0.14
Central, group or bldg. cooling plants		
(3 to 25 tons) Air-cooled	1.20	0.20
(25 to 100 tons) Air-cooled	1.18	0.21
(25 to 100 tons) Water-cooled	0.94	0.17
(Over 100 tons) Water-cooled	0.79	0.20

Reprinted by permission from *1985 ASHRAE Handbook—Fundamentals.*

quired energy input to the unit, is the same as for a food service refrigeration system. The coefficient may sometimes, however, be expressed in units because the performance of cooling equipment is stated in two forms: (1) Btu/hr output per watt of input and (2) Btu/hr of output per Btu/hr of input, without any units. The COPs of food service refrigeration equipment are stated in the unitless form, while the COPs of cooling units are stated in both forms depending on the size and installation type of the unit. The values for decentralized units are given with units (that is, Btu/watt-hour or wh), while the values for large centralized units are stated in unitless form. The two ways of expressing the efficiency of the unit are equivalent. A multiplication by 3.413 Btu/wh converts from the unitless form to the form with units. In common practice, the form with units is known as the *EER* (*energy efficiency ratio*) and the unitless form is called the COP. The relationship between the two is

$$\text{EER} = \text{COP} \times 3.413$$

The range of values of EER for decentralized cooling equipment is from 5 to approximately 12. Cooling units that have values below 6 are considered very energy inefficient, while units with values over 9 are energy efficient.

For large cooling units, the efficiency is sometimes stated in kw/ton, the amount of electricity that is necessary to power the unit compared to the output cooling capacity. This ratio is inversely proportional to the COP according to the expression

$$\text{kw/ton} = 3.52/\text{COP}$$

Exhibit 8.26 contains typical values of kw/ton for various sizes of cooling units. The power input for each system is divided into two parts: the power for the compressor and the power for the auxiliary equipment. Care must be used when comparing the stated values for different types of systems to the manufacturer's information because, for example, the information on the efficiency of a large chiller does not include the power to run the auxiliaries. The EERs, however, for decentralized units are for the entire unit and therefore include the power for the auxiliaries.

There are two trends obvious in the data. First, the larger systems require less power per ton of output to run than do the smaller units. Second, the water-cooled units require less power per output unit than do the air-cooled units. This second fact is a logical extension of the discussion in Chapter 7 on the effect of condenser coil temperature on the operating efficiency of a compressive refrigeration system.

Energy Requirements. The prediction of a cooling system's energy consumption relies on the same three types of methods used for heating systems: single-measure, simplified multiple-measure, and detailed simulation. The task, however, is much more difficult for cooling systems because the timing of the loads is more varied and the sources of the loads are more diverse. Therefore, the single-measure methods are used only for coarse estimates in the early planning stages of a building. Simplified multiple-measure methods might be used in the beginning stages of design for the systems, but only detailed simulation provides results that are accurate enough for decisions on design tradeoffs.

The easiest single-measure method employs the concept of equivalent full load hours of operation. This concept relies on an estimate for the number of hours the system would have to run at full capacity to accomplish the same amount of cooling that is needed over the entire average cooling season. This number of hours is known as the equivalent hours of operation at rated load. Exhibit 8.27 is a sample of the data for several locations in the country.

Exhibit 8.27 Equivalent Full Load Hours of Operation

Albuquerque, NM	800-2200	Indianapolis, IN	600-1600
Atlantic City, NJ	500-800	Little Rock, AR	1400-2400
Birmingham, AL	1200-2200	Minneapolis, MN	400-800
Boston, MA	400-1200	New Orleans, LA	1400-2800
Burlington, VT	200-600	New York, NY	500-1000
Charlotte, NC	700-1100	Newark, NJ	400-900
Chicago, IL	500-1000	Oklahoma City, OK	1100-2200
Cleveland,OH	400-800	Pittsburgh, PA	900-1200
Cincinnati, OH	1000-1500	Rapid City, SD	800-1000
Columbia, SC	1200-1400	St. Joseph, MO	1000-1600
Corpus Christi, TX	2000-2500	St. Petersburg, FL	1500-2700
Dallas, TX	1200-1600	San Diego, CA	800-1700
Denver, CO	400-800	Savannah, GA	1200-1400
Des Moines, IA	600-1000	Seattle, WA	400-1200
Detroit, MI	700-1000	Syracuse, NY	200-1000
Duluth , MN	300-500	Trenton, NJ	800-1000
El Paso, TX	1000-1400	Tulsa, OK	1500-2200
Honolulu, HI	1500-3500	Washington, DC	700-1200

Reprinted by permission from *1985 ASHRAE Handbook—Fundamentals.*

Exhibit 8.28 Sample Operating Cost Estimate for a Cooling System

Data:

Size of system: 12,000 Btu/hr
EER: 9.0 Btu/hr-watt
Location: St. Petersburg, Florida
EFLH: 1,500 hr/year (from Exhibit 8.27)
Cost of electricity: $.10/kwh

Estimate the annual energy cost for operation.

Calculation:

Basic equation:

$$\text{COST} = \text{SIZE} \times \text{COST}_{\text{KWH}} \times \text{EFLH}/(\text{EER} \times 1{,}000)$$
$$\text{COST} = 12{,}000 \times \$.10 \times 1{,}500/(9.0 \times 1{,}000) = \$200/\text{year}$$

Using this data, the operating cost of a system for the season is estimated as follows:

$$\text{COST} = \text{SIZE} \times \text{COST}_{\text{KWH}} \times \text{EFLH}/(\text{EER} \times 1000)$$

where *COST* is for the cooling season; *SIZE* is the rated capacity of the cooling unit in Btu/hr; $COST_{KWH}$ is the price of electricity per kwh; *EFLH* is the equivalent full load hours of operation from Exhibit 8.27; and *EER* is the energy efficiency for the unit in Btu/wh. Exhibit 8.28 shows a sample calculation. This method is most appropriate for situations in which most of the loads on the system are caused by the weather. If the load is predominantly from people or has a large component from the sun, then this method does not provide reasonable results. Generally, this method works for predicting the consumption requirements of systems that cool guestroom blocks but does not work for the public and function areas of lodging properties.

Applications

8.1 Energy Conservation Opportunities

The opportunities for energy conservation in cooling systems fall into three categories: (1) reductions in cooling loads, (2) increases in the performance of the distribution systems, and (3) increases in the efficiency of the primary energy conversion equipment.[2] Although we separate the categories to organize the opportunities, the effects of the opportunities are interrelated. For example, a reduction in a cooling load allows a reduction in the capacity of the distribution system, which further saves energy, and permits the selection of a smaller capacity primary energy conversion unit, which further saves in costs of installation and operation.

For cooling systems powered by electricity, the savings in operations that result from savings in energy consumption have two benefits. The obvious benefit is the lower consumption. The less obvious savings is the reduction in the electrical demand (in kw) and the lower demand charge. This second effect happens because the cooling system usually is operating when the peak demand period occurs. Therefore, a reduction in the electrical demand from the cooling system reduces the billing demand for the property. This effect is further magnified if the rate structure includes a demand ratchet clause, because a savings in the demand charge for the month with the largest demand also provides the potential for savings in the billing demand in the other months of the year. For example, a savings of 1 kw of demand in the month of August at the billing rate of $5/kw could save $48 for the year when the ratchet clause is based on an 80% rate of demand carry-over.

8.2 Reductions in Cooling Loads

The references cited in Note 2 of this chapter contain numerous suggestions for conserving energy by reducing the cooling loads. The effect of every suggestion can be determined through the equations that determine the cooling load for the building. Some suggestions that are important to hospitality properties are as follows: (1) control of the interior air temperature, (2) reduction of solar effects, (3) improving exterior wall construction, (4) reducing ventilation loads, and (5) reducing internal heat loads from lighting.

The temperature and humidity differences between indoor and outdoor air control the size of the cooling load from transmission, infiltration, and ventilation. Therefore, maintaining the highest possible temperature and humidity that still are within the comfort zone saves a substantial percentage of the energy required to respond to these loads. The current suggestions for interior air conditions are 78°F and 50% rh. In a location similar to Washington, D.C., keeping the thermostat set at 75°F, a temperature that is only 3F° below the suggested value, may cause an increase of 60% in the energy consumption related to the cooling loads that are caused by a temperature difference.

The amount of solar energy that enters the building can be reduced in three ways: (1) increase the exterior shading of the windows by adding overhangs on the outside of the building or by setting the window back into the wall, both of which are accomplished during the design stages for a new property; (2) increase the interior shading of the windows by selecting a tinted glass during the design stages, by adding a solar film to existing windows, or by installing and using decorative drapes; and (3) reduce the ratio of glass to wall in the exterior surface of the building during the design stages.

The U factor, thermal mass, and color of the exterior surface are the controlling parameters for the amount of cooling load that occurs because of the surface. Improving these characteristics has important effects on both the electrical consumption and demand of the cooling system.

Control of the ventilation loads is accomplished by either controlling the amount of ventilation air or by reducing the energy content of the incoming air before it passes over the cooling coils. The former can be implemented by controlling the exhaust fans on the exhaust ducts for

Exhibit 8.29 Schematic of Economizer Cycle Dampers

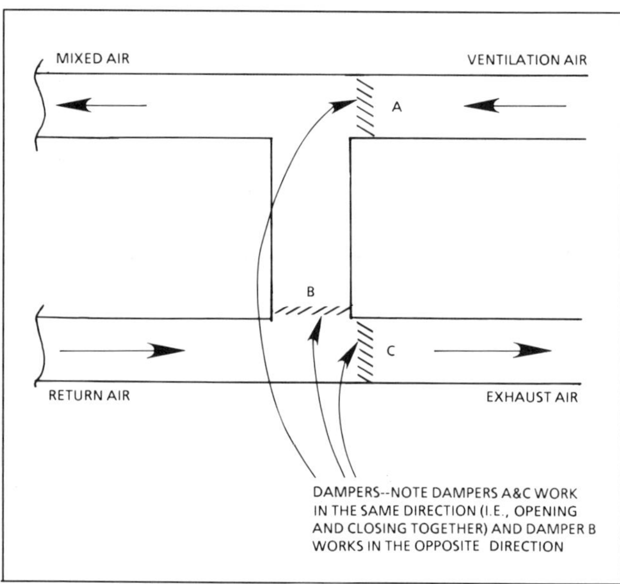

the bathrooms in the guestrooms so that little or no air is exhausted from an unoccupied guestroom and by shutting off the ventilation to function rooms that are not in use. The latter requires the installation of sensors and equipment to operate an economizer cycle in the air ducts. Exhibit 8.29 shows a schematic of the system. Dampers are inserted in the ventilation, exhaust, and cross-over section of the return air ducts so that the percentage of ventilation versus cross-over return air may be controlled.

There are two types of systems available which measure the energy content of the incoming air differently. In the simpler system, which measures temperature, when the outdoor temperature is above the desired room air temperature, then the percentage of ventilation air should be the minimum allowed by the codes. When the outdoor air temperature, however, is below the desired room temperature, then the ventilation air should be 100% and all of the return air should be exhausted. In this way, "free" cooling of the building is accomplished by cool outdoor air. The more complex system, which measures enthalpy (the total energy from temperature *and* humidity in the air), uses the same control logic, but compares enthalpy instead of temperature.

The magnitude of the reduction that can be

received from either system is highly dependent on the location in that the system only provides such a benefit when the conditions of the air are within a certain band. If the conditions are too hot and humid, then the system will not open the ducts; if the conditions are too cold, then the heating system will operate instead. Properties in regions of temperate climate are likely to benefit the most from using such systems.

The effect of lighting on the cooling system can be reduced by replacing low efficiency light bulbs with their high efficiency equivalent, using lumens/watt as the measure of efficiency. Both incandescent and fluorescent bulbs should be replaced in this manner. In addition, fluorescent bulbs should replace incandescent bulbs wherever possible because of the former's substantially higher efficiency.

The overall effect of reducing cooling loads is always to improve the energy consumption characteristics of the building and to reduce the amount of the electric bill during the cooling season. The reduction, however, may not be as large as expected. First, the reduction is not on a Btu-for-Btu basis. For example, reducing the amount of solar energy that enters a guestroom by 72,000 Btu/day does not save 21.1 kwh (the electrical equivalent) per day because the cooling system transfers energy at a COP greater than 1.0. Instead, for a system with a COP of 3.0 (the equivalent of 1.17 kw/ton), the savings in electricity would be 7.04 kw/day. Second, the percent reduction that is obtained by a conservation measure only applies to the portion of the total load that is caused by the effect. For example, if the transmission load contributes only 20% of the total load, then a 30% reduction in the transmission load would save only 6% of the total load. This latter insight is important to remember when discussing with vendors the desirability of purchasing equipment which they claim should save 30%.

Exhibit 8.30 Improvement in Chiller COP as a Function of Chilled Water Discharge Temperature

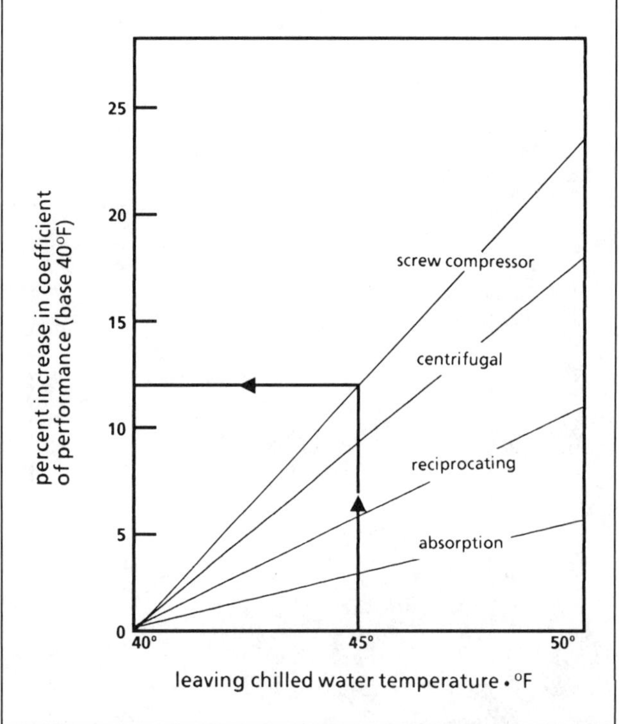

Reprinted by permission of Dubin-Bloome Associates, East Norwalk, Conn.

8.3 Increases in the Performance of the Distribution System

The performance of the distribution system can be improved in several ways: (1) reduce the flow of the cooling medium (cold air or chilled water), (2) reduce the resistance to flow, (3) reduce the losses of the cooling effect in the system, and (4) maintain the efficiency of the drive equipment. In the first situation, the designer often overdesigns the system, causing a flow rate of the cooling medium that is unnecessarily high. This is particularly unfortunate because the energy to pump either water or air is proportional to the cube of the volume of flow. Therefore, a 10% reduction in the flow rate saves 27% in the energy to pump the fluid. In the second situation, components in the system such as air filters, air diffusers, and water coils contribute resistance to the flow. Careful maintenance and cleaning ensures that these components are as resistance free as possible. Third, some of the cooling effect is lost through the pipes or duct work as heat is transmitted from the warm surroundings into the cold air or chilled water. Proper insulation of these components minimizes the losses. Fourth, the electric motors, drive pulleys, pumps, and their bearings should be maintained properly. A substantial portion of the output energy of a motor can be wasted in bad bearings, pulleys, or belts.

Exhibit 8.31 Improvement in Chiller COP as a Function of Condensing Temperature

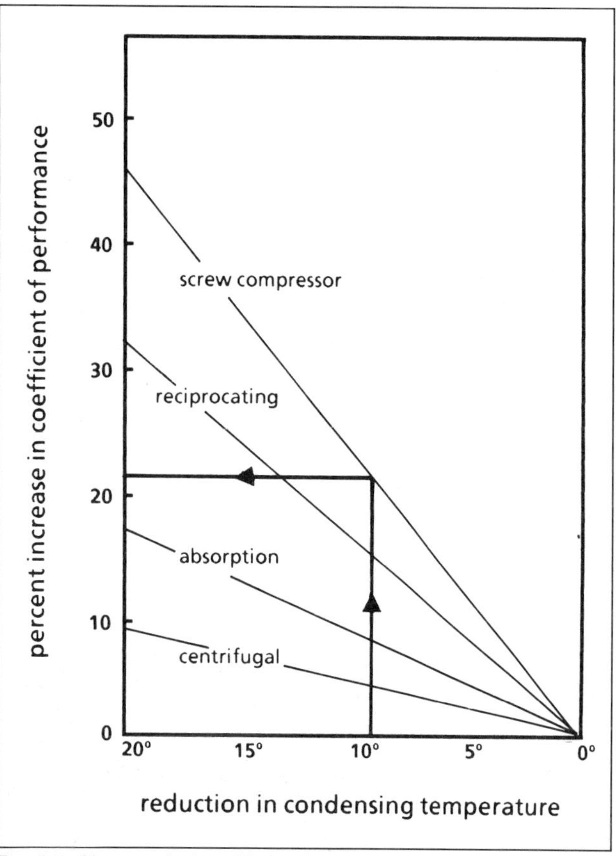

Reprinted by permission of Dubin-Bloome Associates, East Norwalk, Conn.

Exhibit 8.32 The Effect of Fouling on Chiller COP

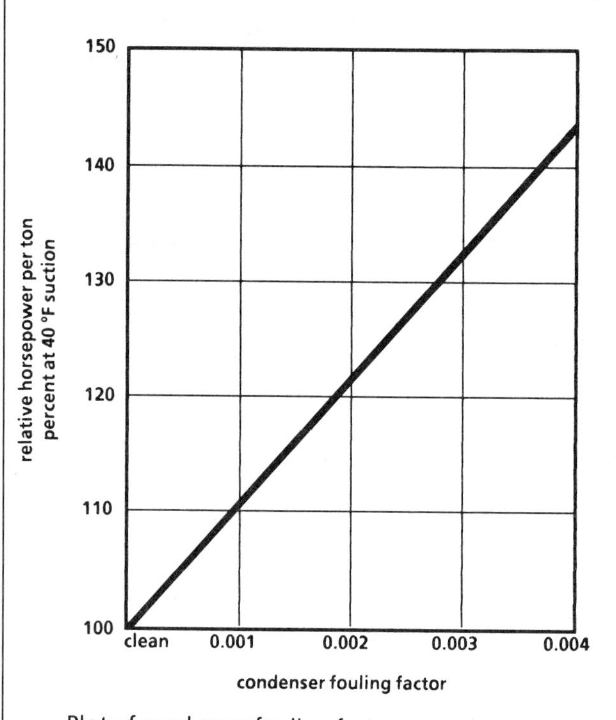

Plot of condenser fouling factor versus hp per ton shows the effect of tube scaling.

The Effects of poor Maintenance on the Efficiency of a Reciprocating Compressor, Nominal 15-Ton Capacity

Conditions	(1) *°F*	(2) *°F*	(3) *Tons*	(4) *%*	(5) *HP*	(6) *HP/T*	(7) *%*
Normal	45	105	17	-	15.9	0.93	-
Dirty Condenser	45	115	15.6	8.2	17.5	1.12	20
Dirty Evaporator	35	105	13.8	18.9	15.3	1.10	18
Dirty Condenser and Evaporator	35	115	12.7	25.4	16.4	1.29	39

(1) Suction Temp., °F
(2) Condensing Temp., °F
(3) Tons of refrigerant
(4) Reduction in capacity %
(5) Brake horsepower
(6) Brake horsepower per Ton
(7) Percent increase in compressor bh per/ton

Courtesy of Attaviano Technical Services, Inc., Melville, New York.

8.4 Increases in the Efficiency of the Primary Energy Conversion Equipment

The maximum efficiency of a cooling unit such as a chiller can be managed by proper attention to the temperatures of the evaporator and the condenser and the fouling factor of the coils in the unit. The temperature of the evaporator is determined by the set point for the discharge temperature of the chilled water. The discharge temperature is dependent on the magnitude of the loads on the terminal equipment. Thus, when the total load is at less than its maximum, the discharge temperature can be increased without any loss in performance, thereby improving the COP of the chiller. See Exhibit 8.30 for a graph that indicates the potential savings for this approach. Second, a similar effect on the COP occurs when the discharge temperature of the condenser water can be lowered. This reduction in temperature can be implemented during times when the wet-bulb temperature (see Appendix B) of the outdoor air is low. During these times, the cooling tower is able to cool the condenser water to a lower temperature, thus lowering the condenser temperature in the chiller. This lower temperature improves the COP according to the graph shown in Exhibit 8.31. Finally, as the purpose of the chiller is to transfer heat from the evaporator to the condenser, any fouling (that is, deposits on or encrustation) of the heat transfer surfaces markedly affects the efficiency of the transfer. Exhibit 8.32 shows the magnitude of the effect for a water-cooled chiller.

Any improvement in the COP of the chiller affects all of the consumption caused by the cooling loads. For example, a 10% increase in the seasonal effective COP reduces the consumption of electricity by 10%. Therefore, maintaining the highest possible COP for the system is a very important part of an energy conservation program.

Notes

1. If more accurate results are necessary, consult *1985 ASHRAE Handbook—Fundamentals* (Atlanta, Ga.: The American Society of Heating, Refrigerating, and Air-conditioning Engineers, 1985), Chapter 26.
2. Some of the information in these Applications is drawn from the following references: Victor B. Attaviano, *Energy Management* (Melville, N.Y.: Attaviano Technical Services, 1982); Fred S. Dubin et al., *How to Save Energy and Cut Costs in Existing Industrial and Commercial Buildings* (Park Ridge, N.J.: Noyes Data Corporation, 1976), Sections 6 and 7; *Energy Conservation Manual, Volume I* and *Energy Maintenance Manual, Volume II* (New York: Hospitality, Lodging, & Travel Research Foundation, Inc., American Hotel & Motel Association, 1977); Robert E. Aulbach, *Energy Management* (East Lansing, Mich.: Educational Institute of the American Hotel & Motel Association, 1984); and Frank D. Borsenik, *The Management of Maintenance and Engineering Systems in Hospitality Industries* (New York: John Wiley & Sons, Inc., 1979).

9

Integrated Heating, Ventilating, and Air Conditioning Systems

Today's lodging guests expect all-season conditioning of the air and individual control of the systems in guestrooms, function rooms, and restaurants. They want either heating or cooling to be available upon their command. Meeting these guest expectations requires a property to integrate the operation of its heating and cooling systems. Whether this integration involves operating separate systems or a single integrated system, the concepts behind the need to integrate are the same.

Basic Configurations

During periods of very cold temperatures, every zone requires heating, while during periods of warm temperatures, all of the zones require cooling. However, during the times of intermediate temperatures, some spaces need heating while others need cooling.

In theory, the integrated system for providing the heating and cooling is designed to deliver either effect at any time. In practice, however, only a decentralized system is operated this way. A centralized system is rarely operated to produce the opposite effect during either strong heating or strong cooling periods because of the high overhead cost for operating the central unit and distribution system at very little or no load. Centralized systems do, however, deliver both effects during the periods when it is likely that both heating and cooling would be needed by different rooms in the property.

Decentralized Systems

All of the important elements of decentralized heating and air conditioning systems as described in Chapters 6 and 8 are included in one integrated package which is installed inside or very near the zone that the decentralized system conditions. Exhibit 9.1 is a schematic of a typical installation in a guestroom. The return air from the room is filtered before it is mixed with the outdoor air. The mixed air passes over heating and cooling elements before a fan supplies the air back to the room.

Typical Installations. The heating and cooling components and the selection of the utility are very similar from property to property. For all installations, the cooling is provided by a self-contained refrigeration system powered by electricity. For those installations that are inside the building shell or outside the shell but near operable windows, the heating is provided by either an electric resistance element or a heat pump that uses the same refrigeration system used for the cooling. In either case, electricity is the utility because of code restrictions on other fuels in these systems. For installations on a roof, as shown in Exhibit 9.2, the heating is

Exhibit 9.1 Typical Decentralized HVAC System Installed in a Guestroom

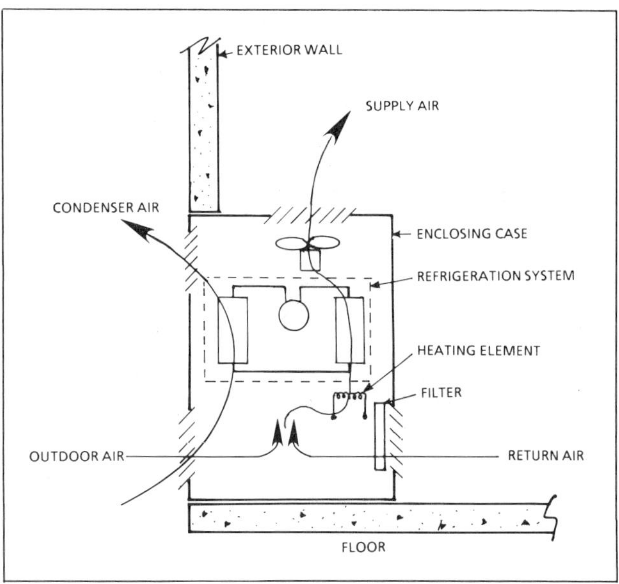

Exhibit 9.2 Typical Decentralized HVAC System Installed on a Roof

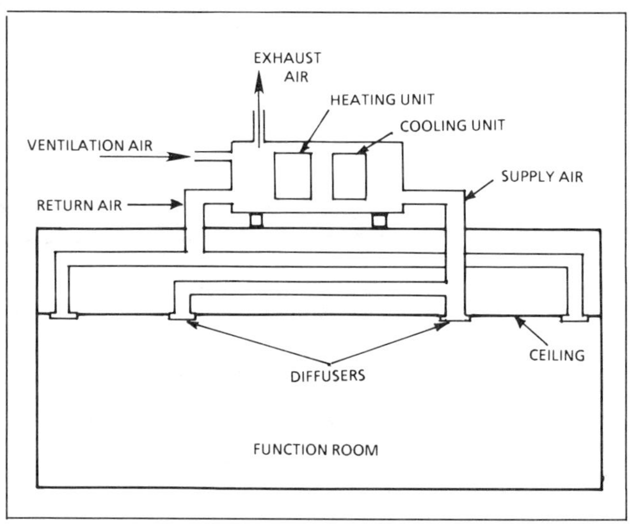

sometimes provided by natural gas instead of electrical resistance or electrical heat pumps.

Occupant Control Over the System. The selection of whether the unit is delivering heating or cooling is totally under the control of the guest or the employee. Each zone has a separate thermostat that measures the zone's air temperature and a controller that interprets the signal from the thermostat thereby signaling the heating or cooling elements for action when desired. The controls are usually mounted for easy access inside the units that are installed in guestrooms and on the wall with a wire connection to the units installed on the roof. The occupant turns the unit on by selecting the desired mode of operation—heating or cooling—and the unit responds to the difference between the actual air temperature and the set point of the thermostat.

The thermostat and the controller have several characteristics that are important for their effective operation in a hotel/motel environment. In many installations, the occupant has access to the set point of the thermostat so that the system can effectively respond to different individuals' definitions of a comfortable temperature. Some units, however, have preset set points that can only be changed by opening the enclosing cover of the unit. The former permits more occupant control, but often causes more energy consumption when the occupant changes the set point to extreme values. All units have a heating/cooling thermostat so that the action of the controller can be reversed—an air temperature below the set point signals heating while an air temperature above the set point signals cooling—for all-season operation. All units have a small dead band (that is, a temperature difference over which no action occurs) to prevent the constant cycling back and forth between the heating and cooling modes. Finally, some installations allow the remote setting of the set point in order to conserve energy when the room is not occupied. This control may be exercised through the use of a motion detector in the room or by the front desk clerk. In these circumstances, the set point is changed to a set-back value that is either lower in the heating season or higher in the cooling season, thereby reducing the transmission load on the system. When this option is used, the system should have the capacity to quickly condition the air temperature when the set-back action is deactivated so that, when the guest arrives in the room, the air temperature is not uncomfortable.

System Characteristics. Decentralized systems have numerous advantages for many types of lodging properties. The most important of these advantages are:

- Initial cost of the entire system is low.
- Maintenance of the system is easy. No trained operators are required. Replacement units can be kept on hand so the entire unit can be replaced when a problem arises.
- Less space is needed for installation because there are no requirements for a central mechanical room or a distribution system.
- Failure of a unit only affects one zone rather than a major portion of the building.
- Heating or cooling can be provided at all times independent of the operation of the other HVAC systems in the building.
- The systems are designed and built with matched components by one manufacturer, which results in higher quality control.

This type of system does, however, have its drawbacks as well:

- The life expectancy is short, usually less than 10 years.
- The level of guest satisfaction may be low because of the sound levels generated by the system and the lack of good humidity control.
- The options for placement of the unit within the zone are very limited, since the unit must be located on the outside wall.
- In general, the cost of operation due to energy consumption is usually higher than for central systems. The cost of operation is high when the heating is provided by electricity because of its usually high cost. The efficiency for the cooling components (EER) of the units is lower than for central systems (though this effect is often offset by the lack of operating costs for the auxiliary pumps or fans in the distribution system). Sophisticated control schemes such as an economizer cycle are not available.

Centralized Systems

A centralized system produces heating or cooling in a central location and transports that effect to the separate zones through the distribution system. All of the important components of the centralized heating and cooling systems as described in Chapters 6 and 8 are included in one integrated system. The pieces of equipment that produce the heating and cooling are located together in a central mechanical room and the distribution system connects the equipment with the zones for both heating and cooling.

Typical Installations. The two basic types of all-season systems are defined by the distribution medium that they use. Exhibits 9.3 and 9.4 are schematics for a water-based and an air-based system, respectively. In the central equipment room shown in Exhibit 9.3, a boiler produces hot water while a chiller produces chilled water (see Chapter 10 for a description of this equipment). The choice of the fuel for the boiler is usually made based on the relative cost of the available alternatives, with fossil fuels typically being the least expensive. The chiller using the compressive refrigeration cycle is usually operated with electricity, but some chillers operate using an absorption cycle (see Chapter 10) powered by steam or hot water. In either case, the excess heat is usually removed from the chiller by a condenser-water loop connected to a cooling tower.

The hot or chilled water is available for distribution and use by each zone in the building. The water is distributed to and from the zone through pipes—one pipe for the supply and one pipe for the return. At the zone, the water flows through a coil located in a terminal unit which transfers the effect to the air flowing over the coil. The conditioned air either heats or cools the room.

The air-based system (Exhibit 9.4) uses the same central equipment as the water-based system to produce the primary effects. A boiler provides either hot water or steam, and a chiller provides chilled water. These heating and cooling effects, however, are transferred into hot or cold air in a central air-handling unit rather than being distributed directly to the zones. The conditioned air is then distributed to each of the

Exhibit 9.3 Schematic of a Water-Based Centralized System

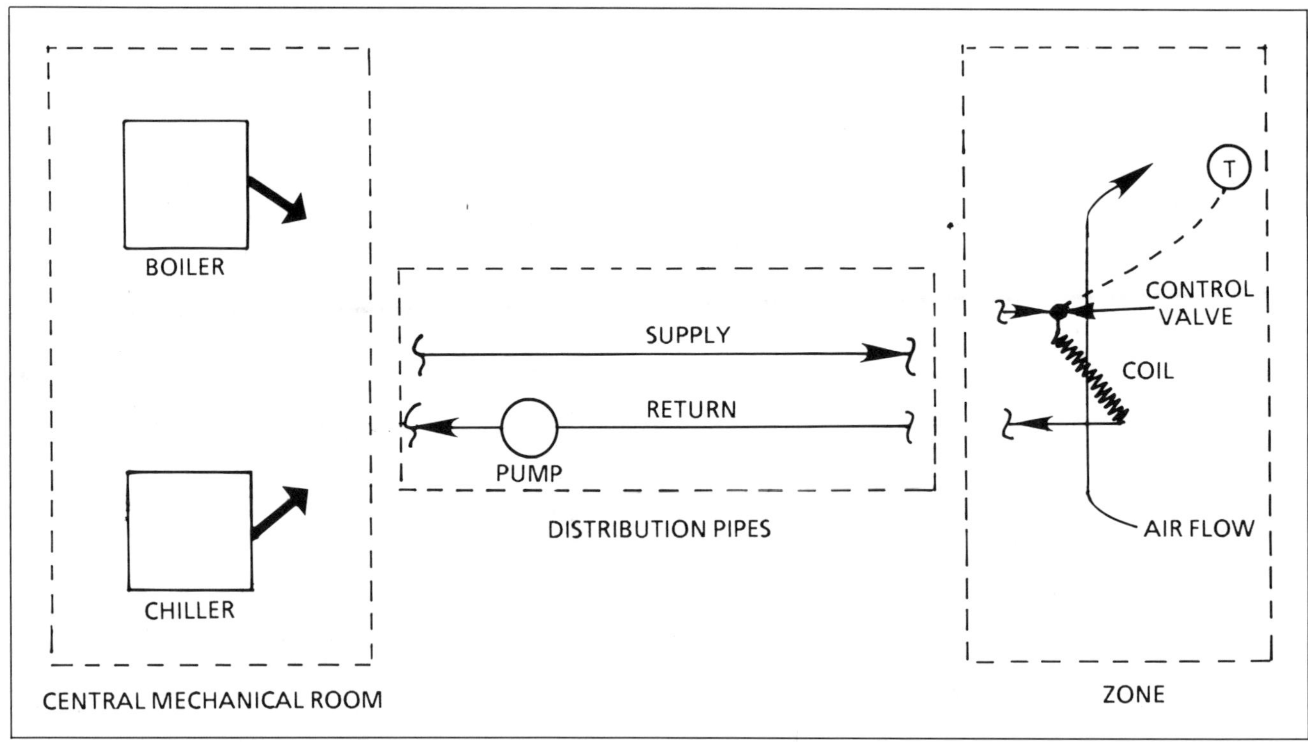

Exhibit 9.4 Schematic of an Air-Based Centralized System

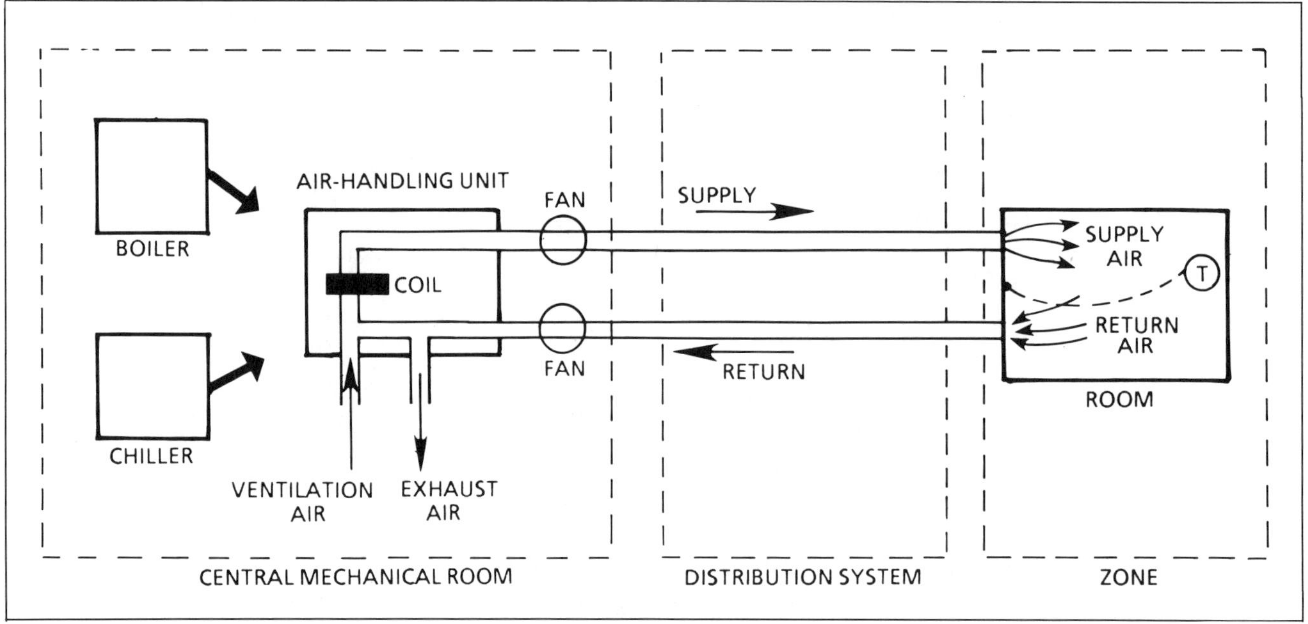

zones through a supply and return duct. At the zone, the air is inserted into and removed from the room through supply and return air grates.

Occupant Control Over the System. The occupant of an individual zone only has control over whether the effect that is delivered by the distribution system enters the room. In a water-based system, the thermostat operates a valve in the supply pipe that either allows or prevents the flow of water through the coil. In an air-based system, the thermostat regulates either the temperature or the volume of the conditioned air that enters the room.

The operation of the central equipment is accomplished by the engineering staff. The staff decides whether to run the chiller or the boiler and at what temperatures to provide the air or water for the distribution system. The continuous control of the output of the equipment is provided by thermostats built into the central equipment. The boiler or chiller and all of the auxiliary pumps or fans must run even though only a few of the zones in the entire building are requesting heating or cooling.

System Characteristics. Centralized systems have several advantages for many types of lodging properties. The most important of these advantages are:

- In general, the cost of operation due to energy consumption is lower than for decentralized systems. More flexibility in the choice of utilities is allowed. More sophisticated control systems and equipment can be implemented. The central plants have higher operating efficiencies than the decentralized units (though this advantage is partially offset by the need to operate the auxiliary equipment, particularly during low load conditions).
- The level of occupant satisfaction is high because of the low sound levels of the terminal equipment and the improved humidity control, especially with an air-based system.
- There is more flexibility in the location of the terminal equipment within the zones.
- Consolidation of equipment in a central location facilitates ease of maintenance and operation by engineering staff.
- The life expectancy of the equipment is long.

There are, however, several disadvantages to these types of systems which are not associated with decentralized systems.

- Initial cost for the entire system is high. A water-based system is less costly than an air-based system.
- Trained staff is required for the system's operation.
- More space is required in the building because of the central mechanical room and the distribution system. This requirement is strongest for an air-based system because of the large air-handling units and the size of the duct work.
- Failure of an important component in the central plant may disable the entire system.
- For heating and cooling to be provided at all times, large-capacity equipment must be operated even at very low load conditions. This is especially a problem during intermediate seasons when one portion of the building is requesting cooling while the other is asking for heating.
- The systems are assembled on the job site using components from many different manufacturers.

Air-Based Central Systems

The differences among the various types of air-based systems occur in the configurations of the air-handling unit and duct system. All of the systems require hot water or steam from a boiler to provide the heating effect and chilled water from a chiller to provide the cooling effect. In the following discussion, the existence of these central plants is assumed.

Constant Volume Single-Zone System

The air-handling unit for the basic air-based system serving one zone has for its components a supply and a return duct to and from the zone backed up by an air-handling unit which includes heating and cooling coils. Exhibit 9.5 shows a schematic of this type of system. Return air is drawn from the zone by the return-air fan.

Exhibit 9.5 Schematic of a Constant Volume Single-Zone HVAC System

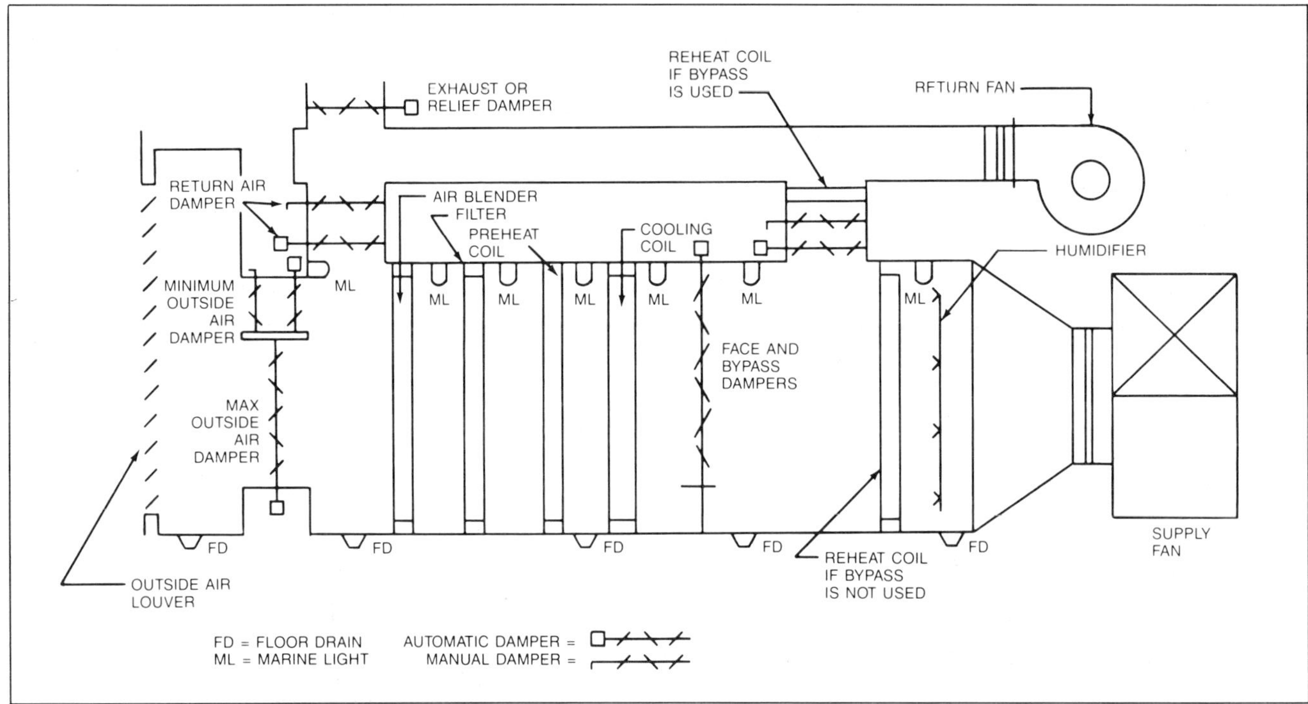

Reprinted by permission from *1987 ASHRAE Handbook—HVAC Systems and Applications.*

A portion of it is exhausted from the building and the remainder passes through the return-air dampers to be mixed with the outdoor air which enters the building through the outdoor-air dampers. The mixed air passes through a filter and over a preheat coil that is used to warm extremely cold mixed air during times when the outdoor temperature is very low. This air then passes through a humidifying section, if humidity control is important, and over a cooling coil. Finally, the air passes through face dampers that control the amount of air that passes through the coils versus the amount that is bypassed. Before the air is supplied to the zone by the supply-air fan, it must pass over the reheat coil for conditioning to the correct final temperature.

The size of each component is determined by the design calculations at maximum heating and cooling loads. The cooling coil must be capable of extracting the sensible and latent cooling loads, while the heating coils (preheat and reheat) must have the capacity to deliver the design total heat loss. The amounts of air flow are determined as follows: the amount of supply air is calculated based on the sensible cooling or heating load; the amount of outdoor air is determined by code regulations; the amounts of return air and exhaust air are similar to the amounts of supply air and outdoor air, respectively.

The system responds to variations in the loads under the control of the thermostat in the zone. The volume of air flow through the system remains constant, while its temperature is varied in response to the varying loads. During the heating season, the thermostat controls a valve on the reheat coil that modulates the amount of hot water or steam that flows through the coil, thus varying the temperature of the air as it enters the room. During the cooling season, the thermostat controls either the amount of heat that is used to reheat the overcooled air when humidity control is important or the amount of air that is allowed to bypass the cooling coil. Increasing the amount of reheat energy or the amount of bypass air increases the temperature of the air just before it enters the room.

Constant Volume Multi-Zone System

This type of system is an extension of the single-zone system in that the same basic components are used and the same control scheme of varying the temperature of the air as it enters the zone is implemented. The significant differ-

Exhibit 9.6 Schematic of a Constant Volume Multi-Zone HVAC System

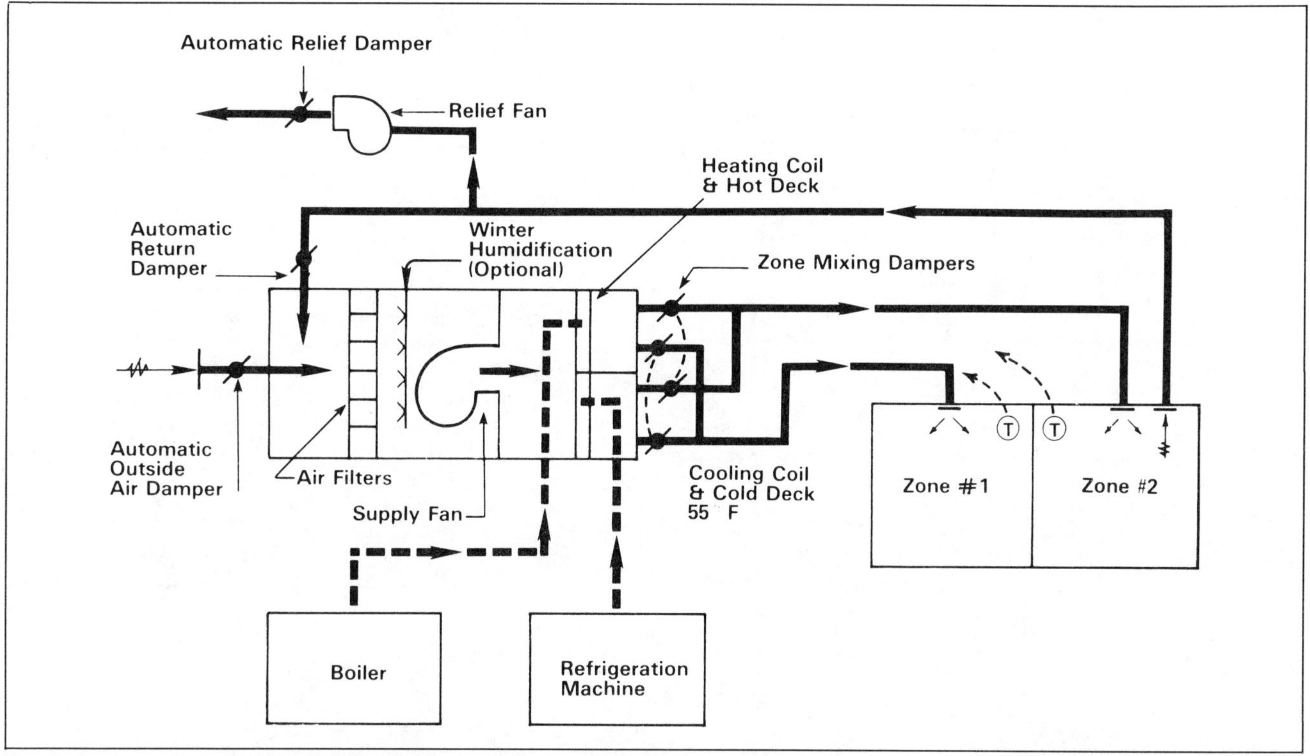

Permission to reprint granted by Building Owners and Managers Institute International, 1987.

ence is that the system must have the capability to respond to varying loads in several zones at one time.

As shown in Exhibit 9.6, hot and cold air is provided at all times in the hot and cold decks of the air handler, respectively. The temperature of the air in the supply duct to each zone is varied by altering the proportion of air that is extracted from the hot and cold decks under the control of the zone thermostat. The total amount of air that flows to each zone remains constant, while the temperature of the air in each zone's supply duct is different.

This system allows the all-season conditioning of the air in several zones using one central air-handling unit.

Constant Volume Dual Duct System

This system is a refinement of the multi-zone system in that it provides all-season conditioning to several zones. The mixing of the hot and cold air is accomplished by a mixing box near the zone, rather than near the hot and cold decks as in the previous system. Exhibit 9.7 shows a schematic of the arrangement of the distribution system. Two ducts (one for the cold air and the other for the hot air) run from the air-handling unit to each zone. At the zone, a mixing box proportions the amount of air that enters the room from each duct, thereby controlling the temperature of the supply air to the zone. This mixing box is under the control of the thermostat for the zone.

This type of system has the capability to provide better quality conditioning to more zones than the multi-zone arrangement. In the multi-zone configuration, the number of zones is limited to the number of single separate ducts (called duct runs) that can emanate from one air-handler. In the dual duct set up, the number of zones is limited only by the space above the ceiling that is allotted to the two duct runs.

Variable Air Volume System

A different control scheme to respond to the varying loads is applied in variable air volume (*vav*) systems. Instead of having a constant volume of air flow provided at varying temperatures, the temperature of the air is the same, but

Exhibit 9.7 Schematic of a Constant Volume Dual Duct HVAC System

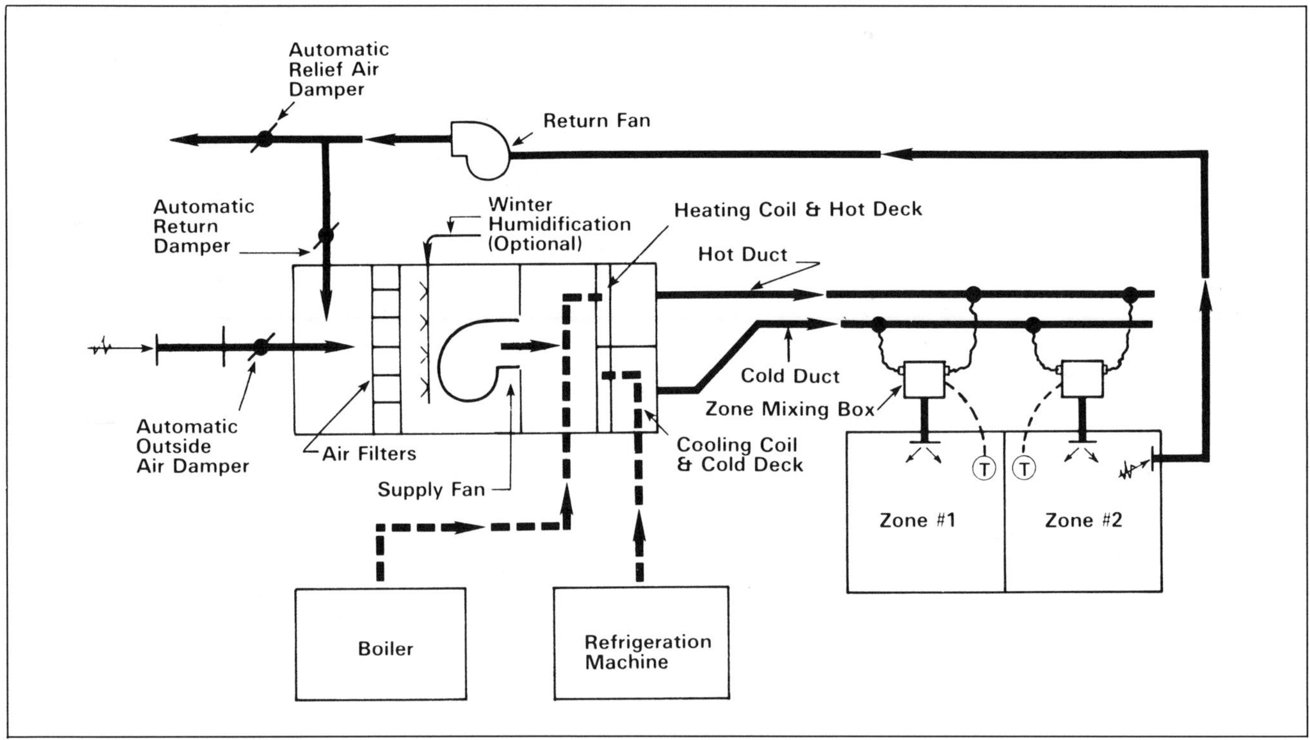

Permission to reprint granted by Building Owners and Managers Institute International, 1987.

the volume of the air is reduced to respond to lower loads. In a single-zone vav system, the room thermostat controls the volume of the air provided by the supply air fan using a variable volume fan. A thermostat measuring the temperature of the supply air determines the amount of heating or cooling that occurs in the coils. In a dual duct vav system, the hot and cold decks provide conditioned air as in the constant volume dual duct arrangement, but the volume of air flow into each zone is controlled by the zone thermostat.

The primary advantage of the vav system for a configuration that must condition several zones simultaneously is the savings in energy consumption. In the dual duct system, the air supplied to each room is either overcooled or overheated and then tempered by the other air stream. This practice is a waste of energy in that heating is used to cancel cooling and vice-versa. This does not occur in a vav application.

Water-Based Central Systems

The differences in the four types of systems depend on the number of pipes used to distribute water to and return it from each separate zone and on whether a fan causes forced air circulation over the coils.

One-Pipe System

A one-pipe system has limited application in that it provides only heating to the zone. It is, however, a very low cost way of providing that heating.

Exhibit 9.8 is a schematic of the system. A boiler provides the hot water to the single-pipe distribution network. The water is forced through the pipe by a supply pump. At each terminal or baseboard unit, a portion of the water flowing in the supply line is diverted through the coil inside the unit. This hot water heats the coil and the surrounding air by natural convection. When the system is used for just one zone, its thermostat controls the circulation pump. When the system heats more than one zone, the circulation pump runs continuously and the zone's thermostat activates a valve in the branch line to each baseboard unit.

The primary advantage of this system is its low cost of installation and operation. A minimal amount of piping is needed and no electricity is necessary to operate a circulation fan. These advantages are offset by the lack of capability to provide all-season conditioning and the lower heating capability of the last few terminal units in the circuit because of the lower hot water temperature.

Two-Pipe System

When a two-pipe system is installed with fan-coil units as the terminal units, it is capable of providing either heating or cooling to all of the zones in the building. As shown in Exhibit 9.9, the water is supplied to each fan-coil unit by a supply line and is brought back to the central location by a return line. A circulation pump is necessary to deliver the water through the lines. The fan-coil unit has a fan included in it that forces the circulation of air over the coil.

The load demands of the building determine the temperature of the water in the distribution system. During the heating season, hot water is circulated, while during the summer season, chilled water is provided. As the system cannot provide both heating and cooling simultaneously, a change-over procedure must occur for the system to switch from one to the other. Special controls must be installed to prevent chilled water from entering the boiler or hot water from entering the chiller.

The thermostat in each zone controls a valve located in the branch line to each fan-coil unit, thereby allowing the flow of water when conditioning is desired. The thermostat must be a reversible type, so that the valve can be opened during the heating and cooling season.

The system is very satisfactory when the entire building requires either heating or cooling, but it does not provide the all-season conditioning during the intermediate seasons that most guests expect.

Three-Pipe System

The three-pipe system (shown in Exhibit 9.10) does allow all-season conditioning on demand by an occupant in any zone if both the boiler and the chiller are operated at all times. Hot water and chilled water are supplied to each room by separate supply lines and any water that flows through the fan-coil unit is returned to the central equipment room by a common return line. The flow of water into the unit's coil

Exhibit 9.8 Schematic of a One-Pipe Water-Based HVAC System

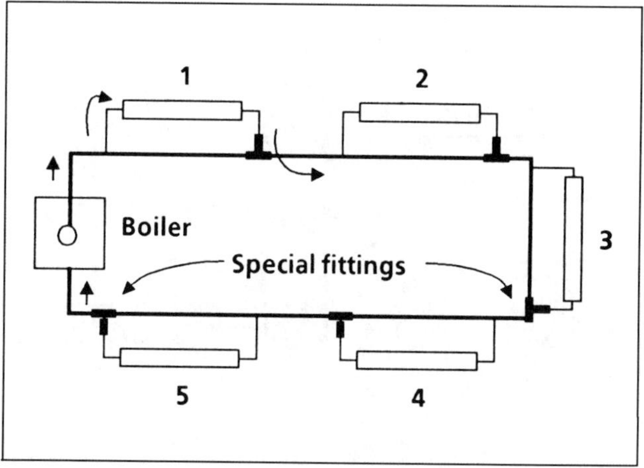

is controlled by a three-way mixing valve activated by the zone's thermostat.

Although this system provides the necessary industry standard for thermal comfort, the operating costs for the system are extremely high during the intermediate seasons. When some rooms require heating and the others ask for cooling, the used hot and chilled water is mixed together in a common return line. When this return water arrives back at the boiler and the chiller, it must be heated and chilled to the correct distribution temperatures for each separate circuit. Because some of the heating and cooling effects were wasted in the mixing process, the amount of energy required by the boiler and the chiller is much more than the energy required by the zones. Therefore, although many hotels that were built in the late 1960s and early 1970s have three-pipe systems installed in them, they are usually operated as two-pipe systems because of the prohibitive cost of operating three-pipe systems.

Four-Pipe System

The four-pipe system supplies both hot and chilled water to each zone and collects the return water through two return lines, one for the hot and the other for the chilled water. As shown in Exhibit 9.11, this arrangement allows all-season conditioning and eliminates the waste of energy associated with a three-pipe system. The fan-coil

Exhibit 9.9 Schematic of a Two-Pipe Water-Based HVAC System

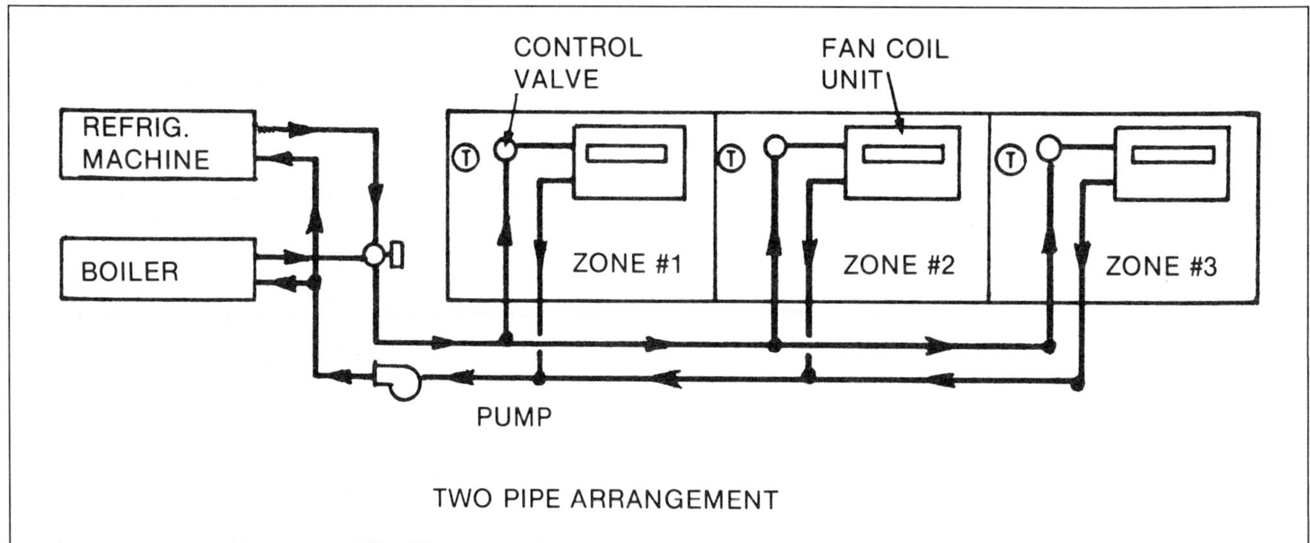

Permission to reprint granted by Building Owners and Managers Institute International, 1987.

Exhibit 9.10 Schematic of a Three-Pipe Water-Based HVAC System

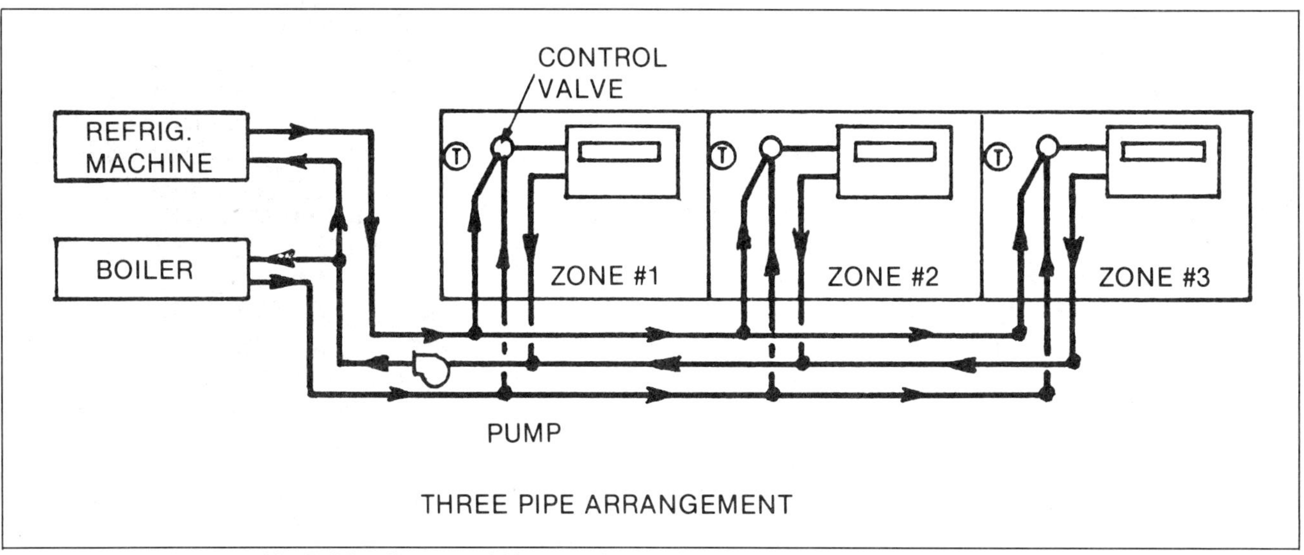

Permission to reprint granted by Building Owners and Managers Institute International, 1987.

unit usually has two separate coils, one for hot water and the other for chilled water. When the zone requires conditioning, the thermostat opens the appropriate valve, allowing the water to flow through the unit.

This system provides cost effective heating and cooling effects in climates that have both strong heating and cooling requirements. Occupant satisfaction with the system is very high because of the quality of the conditioning and the low noise levels.

Steam-Based Central Systems

Steam systems are not installed in new buildings as much as they once were, but they still have application for some situations in new construction and, of course, some of the old systems still exist.

Central steam systems are used to heat buildings, to provide steam for kitchen and laundry applications, and to power turbines that drive refrigeration systems. For these applica-

Exhibit 9.11 Schematic of a Four-Pipe Water-Based HVAC System

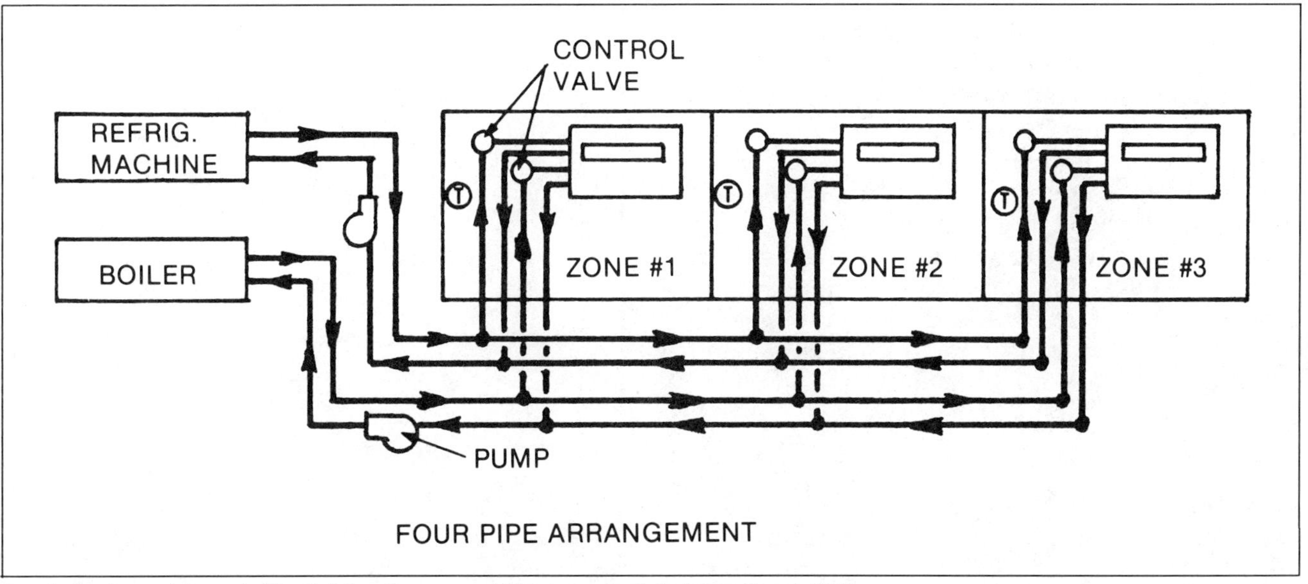

Permission to reprint granted by Building Owners and Managers Institute International, 1987.

tions, the steam is provided by either a one-pipe or a two-pipe system. The following discussion assumes the existence of a steam boiler with the necessary piping and controls (which are discussed in Chapter 10).

One-Pipe System

The one-pipe system is less expensive to install as only one run of steam piping is required and no steam traps are used. It has very limited application to space heating in the industry because its performance characteristics are not acceptable for guestrooms and are only marginally acceptable for back-of-the-house spaces.

Exhibit 9.12 diagrams the important aspects of an installation. Steam from the boiler and the condensate (the hot water after the steam has condensed and given up its latent heat) both flow in the same pipe. No steam traps are used, but an air vent for each terminal unit vents the air in the system, thus allowing the steam to enter the heater. Temperature control over the space is provided by temperature sensitive valves that control the flow of steam into the heater.

Two-Pipe System

Exhibit 9.13 shows a two-pipe system. Each terminal unit has a steam supply line and a condensate return line that runs through a steam trap. The purpose of the steam trap is to prevent the loss of the steam before it has given up its latent energy and has condensed into water. The trap allows only the passage of condensate and air that is in the steam lines. Temperature control of the zone is maintained by a thermostatically controlled valve in the supply line to each terminal unit.

This system does provide adequate comfort conditioning during the heating season.

Exhibit 9.12 Schematic of a One-Pipe Steam-Based System

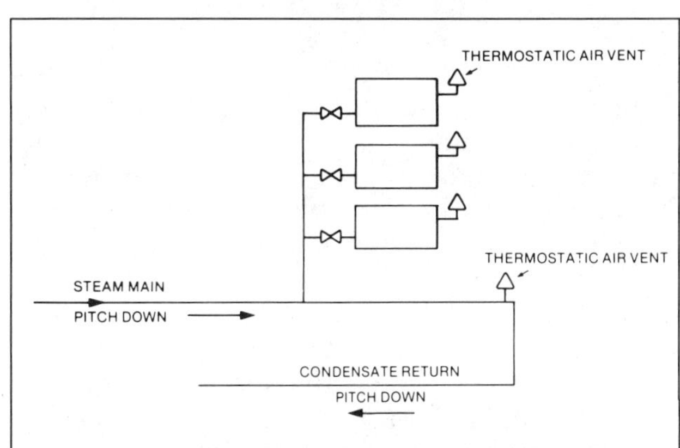

Reprinted by permission from *1987 ASHRAE Handbook—HVAC Systems and Applications.*

Combination Systems

Hybrid systems—systems that combine decentralized and centralized elements—are installed in numerous properties in order to take advantage of the best characteristics of both types of systems. One of the advantages of the decentralized system is its low initial cost. An advantage of the centralized system is the high energy efficiency of its central boiler or chiller. Two hybrid systems that combine these advantages are (1) a two-pipe hydronic system with electrical resistance heaters in each zone and (2) individual water-source heat pumps connected by a common water loop.

Two-Pipe Hydronic System with Electrical Resistance Heaters. This type of system comes in two versions. The first version is found in locations that have substantial cooling requirements most of the year and small, but necessary, heating requirements for short periods of time during the remainder of the year. In this case, the two-pipe system always delivers chilled water for cooling and the electrical resistance heater in the zone provides the heating as required.

The second version is installed in locations that have swing seasons (times of the year when both heating and cooling are required in different parts of the building, especially from the daytime to the nighttime) of substantial duration as well as strong heating and cooling seasons. In this application, the two-pipe system is operated as a cooling system during the cooling and swing seasons with small electrical resistance elements (that is, trimmer heaters) providing the heating when necessary. The two-pipe system is then changed over to a heating system during the periods of strong heating requirements. This technique is especially cost effective in locations that have electrical rates that are lower during the night.

Water-Source Heat Pumps with Common Water Loop. This system relies on decentralized heat pumps in each zone connected together by a central water loop. Exhibit 9.14 shows a schematic of a typical installation. The electric heat pump in each zone operates independently, providing the heating or cooling as required by the zone. The source for the absorbed heat and the sink (that is, where the heat is dumped) for the dissipated heat is the central water loop.

Exhibit 9.13 Schematic of a Two-Pipe Steam-Based System

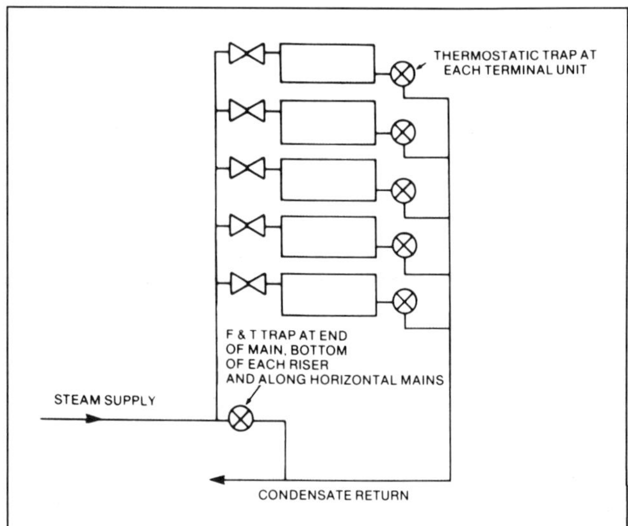

Reprinted by permission from *1984 ASHRAE Handbook—Systems.*

Exhibit 9.14 Water-Source Heat Pumps with Connecting Water Loop

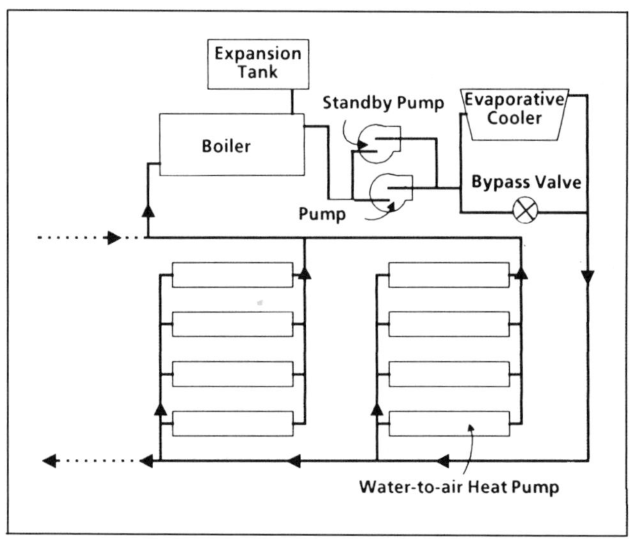

In a central location, heat must be added to or extracted from the water loop to maintain its temperature between 60 and 90°F. A boiler is used to add heat and a cooling tower is used to extract heat. A change-over procedure is required to switch the system from heating to cooling.

This system has several advantages. First,

the central plant provides only the net amount of heating or cooling for the building, thus conserving energy when part of the building requires heating and the other part requires cooling. Second, the cooling can be provided by a cooling tower rather than a chiller, since the operating temperature of the water loop is only 60 to 90°F rather than the 40 to 45°F for a chilled water loop. Thus, the operating cost of the central cooling system is substantially lower. Of course, this effect is partially offset by the operating costs of the heat pumps in the individual zones. Third, the water loop does not require insulation because of its temperate operating conditions. Fourth, the size of the central boiler is smaller than in the normal situation because the heat pumps are providing some of the heating energy.

Exhibit 9.15 Heat Recovery Using a Double-Bundle Condenser

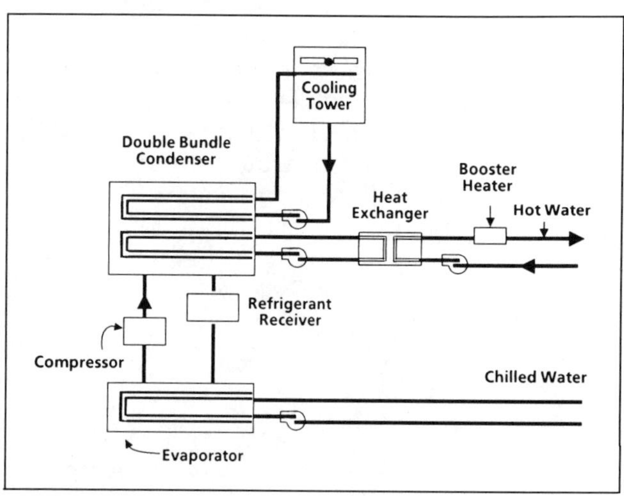

Applications

As the chapters on heating and air conditioning include descriptions of conservation opportunities focused on the separate systems, the discussion in this section emphasizes conservation measures for the integrated systems.[1] Some of the conservation measures are inherent in the selection of the system. For example, the variable air volume (vav) system operates with reduced quantities of supply air, thus eliminating the necessity of expensive reheating of the air to maintain the desired comfort levels. The other important opportunities rely on the efficient operation of the central equipment or the reclamation of heat from the central equipment.

9.1 Reset Control on Supply Air Temperature

In an air-based system, the desired temperature of the supply air provided to the zone is set by the controller for the system. The energy consumption of the central plant can be improved if this temperature is continually reset depending on the air temperature in the zone. For example, during the cooling season, if the air temperature in the zone is slowly increasing, then the supply air temperature is too high and it must be lowered to maintain the comfort of the occupants of the zone. If, however, the air temperature in the zone is slowly decreasing, then the central system is overcooling the air and energy could be saved by resetting the desired supply air temperature to a higher value.

9.2 Heat Exchange Between Chilled Water and Condenser Water

Normally, heat is transferred from the chilled water to the condenser water by the operation of the chiller which consumes electricity. This is necessary because the chilled water is normally maintained at 40 to 45°F and the condenser water can be cooled down only to the wet-bulb temperature (see Appendix B) of the outdoor air, which is usually warmer than the chilled water temperature. When the outdoor air temperature is cold enough, however, the chilled water system can be operated at a higher temperature (55 to 60°F) because the cooling loads are substantially reduced and the condenser water can be cooled to a temperature below the chilled water temperature. In this situation, the operation of the refrigeration system in the chiller is not necessary, and "free" cooling of the chilled water by the colder condenser water is obtained. This technique is implemented by a special design feature in the chiller that allows heat exchange between the chilled water and the condenser water when the compressor is not operating.

9.3 Heat Recovery from the Chiller

Heat is normally rejected from the condenser coil of the chiller into the condenser water for eventual dissipation from the building by the cooling tower. This heat, however, can be reclaimed and used to preheat the domestic hot water for the building. Exhibit 9.15 shows a schematic of the system. The cold water from the domestic system is pumped through a separate bundle of coils in the condenser of the chiller (hence the name "double-bundle condenser"). Some of the heat rejected in the condenser is absorbed by the domestic water, thus preheating it before it enters the water heater. This saves money and energy because the amount of energy needed to heat the water is substantially reduced due to the preheating effect.

Notes

1. Fred S. Dubin et al., *How to Save Energy and Cut Costs in Existing Industrial and Commercial Buildings* (Park Ridge, N.J.: Noyes Data Corporation, 1976), Sections 5 and 7.

10

Heating, Ventilating, and Air Conditioning Equipment

In Chapters 6–9, the complete systems for refrigeration and HVAC were described as assemblies of separate components with emphasis on the operation of the overall system. In this chapter, the focus is on the characteristics of the individual pieces of equipment.

Heating Equipment

As stated in Chapter 6, the most common sources for heat are electricity, fossil fuels (natural gas, fuel oil, and LPG), and steam. The selection of the source for the heating system determines the primary heating equipment.

Electrical Resistance

Electricity may be used to produce heat almost anywhere within a property. It is used for space heating in most decentralized equipment and as duct heaters in centralized systems with air distribution. In water-based heating systems, the boiler can be electrically heated. There are electric water heaters for domestic hot water. The heaters for wash tanks in dishwashers and the booster heaters for the final rinse are often electrically powered. Electric boilers are used in the kitchen to produce steam for other cooking equipment such as steam kettles and convection steamers. Finally, electricity is used to heat cooking equipment such as ranges and broilers.

In all of these applications, electricity is turned into heat by having an electric current flow through a material with resistance. In the applications that directly heat a substance other than water (for example, the burner on a range), the current flows through a metal heating element. In applications that heat water by having the heating element immersed in the water, the current flows through either a metal heating coil or through the water between two electrodes. In either case, the flow of current through the resistance of the conducting material causes heat to be generated (according to the principles of electricity described in Appendix A). This generated heat is then transferred to the element's surroundings, thus causing the water to heat or the steak to broil.

There are several advantages to using electricity as a source of heat. In general, equipment that uses electricity rather than a fossil fuel is less expensive to construct. Further, there are no products of combustion from the conversion process, so that no chimney or other type of venting is necessary and the installation is not influenced by regulations for the control of emissions. Finally, the equipment is usually easier to maintain due to less complex controls and no accumulation of dirt from the combustion process.

These advantages, however, are often offset by one very important disadvantage. The cost of electricity for the effective heat content is usually much higher than that for fossil fuels. The substantially higher operating costs often overwhelm the savings in construction and maintenance costs.

Fossil Fuel Boilers and Heaters

The energy in fossil fuels is converted into heat by the combustion of the fuel in two different categories of equipment: boilers and heaters. The heat is transferred into either water or steam in a boiler and into air in a heater. Because the distribution medium used by the equipment must match the need for heat in the property, the choice of which type of equipment to install is strongly dependent on the application.

Boilers are commonly used in the following situations. They provide space heating in centralized systems with either water-based or steam-based distribution; water for the domestic hot water system; and steam for special applications such as laundry and kitchen equipment. They are sized in either *boiler horsepower* (*BHP*) or Btu/hr of output, with one BHP equivalent to 33,475 Btu/hr.

Heaters are used for space heating in systems with air-based distribution. This category of equipment is often used as rooftop units on single-story buildings used for public and function space. Heaters are sized in MBtu/hr of output (one MBtu is 1,000 Btu).

In some properties, the need for a boiler or heater is satisfied by purchasing steam from a utility company. Either the steam is used throughout the building in a steam distribution system or the heat in the steam is transferred to water or air for distribution through a heat exchanger. Properties that buy steam are usually located in large metropolitan areas.

Boilers and heaters are primarily classified by six major factors: (1) fuel type, (2) method for introducing combustion air, (3) distribution medium, (4) operating pressure and temperature, (5) configuration of heating surfaces, and (6) construction material. The following discussion highlights the important differences in the equipment within each classification.

Many boilers and heaters use a fossil fuel, though electric boilers are also available. If the fuel is a gas under pressure (for example, natural gas), then it flows unaided into the burner where it is combusted. If the fuel is fuel oil, then it is pumped through an orifice in order to atomize it before it is burned. The heavier fuel oils (such as #6) may require preheating to make the oil flow easier.

The efficient combustion of a fossil fuel requires that the correct amount of air be available during the burning process and that combustion by-products be removed from the combustion chamber. The flow of air (called *draft*) is either natural or forced. In a natural-draft system, air flows from outside the building through an intake grate into the boiler room, through the burner into the combustion chamber, and out of the building through a chimney because of the density difference in the air caused by the combustion of the fuel. In a forced-draft system, the air flows along the same path but its movement is assisted by a fan at either the inlet to the burner or the outlet from the combustion chamber. Forced-draft equipment usually requires a smaller chimney, thus lowering the installation cost. Its more complete mixing of the fuel and its control of the combustion air during operations improves the efficiency of the system.

A heater, by definition, distributes the produced heat by air, while a boiler does this by either water or steam. The choice of medium depends on the application. If steam is needed for an important special application within the property, then a boiler is selected for steam. The steam is then used to produce hot water wherever it is required. Recently, however, many installations have used a water boiler for space heating and domestic hot water, while producing the steam necessary for the kitchen with very small steam boilers located in the kitchen. Heaters are used for space heating of public and function areas in unitary or rooftop units.

Boilers are designed to operate at different temperatures and pressures based on the application. Most water boilers in use in lodging properties operate at low temperatures (that is, below 250°F). The other types of systems available are medium (250–350°F) and high (greater than 350°F) temperature. Steam boilers are classified as low pressure (15 psi or less) and high pressure (greater than 15 psi). The higher temperature and pressure systems allow more heat transport for a given distribution system, but for application to lodging properties, this advantage is not enough to overcome the extra cost of construction for stronger components.

Boilers are further classified by whether the combustion occurs inside tubes surrounded by water (a fire tube type) or outside of the tubes filled by water (a water tube type).

Finally, the material out of which the boiler is fabricated helps to classify the equipment. Either steel or cast iron is the primary material used. Due to limitations in the fabrication process, cast iron is limited to smaller boilers. Very large boilers are made from steel.

Fossil fuel boilers and heaters have one major advantage over electric resistance heating and it is so overpowering that it deserves special attention. In most locations, the cost of fossil fuel is so much lower than the cost of electricity for the equivalent amount of heat that fossil fuels are the fuel of choice if there is a substantial heating requirement.

The comparative disadvantages of fossil fuel boilers and heaters are numerous. The equipment costs more to buy initially, takes up more space in the building, requires more time and money for repair and maintenance, and requires more highly skilled employees.

Hot Water and Steam Distribution Systems

The various configurations for the water-based systems (that is, two-pipe, three-pipe, and four-pipe) and steam-based systems (one-pipe and two-pipe) have been documented in the previous chapter. For typical lodging properties, the water system has practical advantages over the steam system.

The distribution piping for a steam-based system is more complex than for a water-based system. The pipes themselves must be larger. Either the condensate must be pumped back to the central location or the piping must be sloped down toward the boiler so gravity can bring it back. Extra components such as steam traps are required throughout the system. Larger floor heights are required in the building to allow installation of the sloping condensate lines. However, the flow of steam through the system occurs without the assistance of pumps as required in hot water systems. Steam systems are installed in very few new lodging buildings.

Heat Pumps

A heat pump, another name for a compressive refrigeration system installed in a special way, can be used for water and space heating. Although it may seem contradictory to use a refrigeration system to provide heating, recall that the system rejects heat to its surroundings from the condenser coil. If this heat can be rejected into a tank of water or a building space that requires heating, then the system can provide heating.

Exhibit 10.1 Schematics for an Air-to-Air Heat Pump

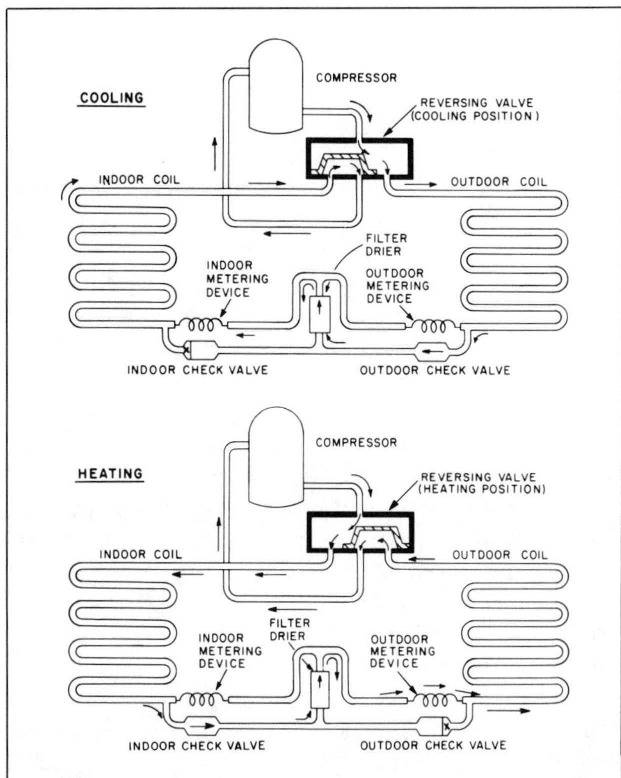

Reprinted by permission from *1983 ASHRAE Handbook—Equipment.*

An easy application of this concept is found in guestrooms with decentralized air conditioning units. A different, yet similar, unit could work as an air conditioner in the cooling season and a heat pump in the heating season. In fact, the air conditioner contains the four major components (evaporator coil, compressor, condenser coil, and expansion valve) of a compressive refrigeration system. Exhibit 10.1 shows the interconnections of the components for the cooling and heating modes. In theory, all that is required to turn these components into a heat pump is a switching valve that makes the refrigerant flow around the system in the opposite direction. When this occurs, the roles of the two coils are reversed. The evaporator coil is now outside the building and the condenser coil is inside the guestroom. Heat is absorbed by the evaporator from the outside air and rejected from the condenser coil into the room. Electricity powers the compressor.

In practice, the system needs an extra expansion valve (labeled in the exhibit as a metering device) and two check valves (valves that allow flow in only one direction) to function properly. When the system is in the cooling mode, the refrigerant flows from the exit of the outdoor coil (that is, the condenser) through the outdoor check valve, bypassing the outdoor metering device. The fluid then flows through the filter drier, the indoor metering device, and into the entrance to the indoor coil (that is, the evaporator). In the heating mode, the flow is in the opposite direction, with the fluid bypassing the indoor metering device and flowing through the outdoor one.

The system's primary advantage is a lower heating cost using electricity. Instead of producing heat at only 3,413 Btu/kwh as it does in resistance heating, the electricity powering the system transports heat from the outside air into the room at a much higher effective ratio. Heating ratios of 5,000 to 10,000 Btu/kwh are common for heat pumps. For a ratio of 10,000 Btu/kwh, the cost is reduced to approximately one third of the resistance heating cost.

A measure of the effectiveness of a heat pump has been defined in a manner similar to the COP for a refrigeration system. The efficiency of the system, called the *seasonal performance factor* (*SPF*), is the ratio of the amount of electricity necessary to heat the room with resistance heating to the amount needed to heat the room with a heat pump, measured for the entire heating season. Typical values range from 1.5 to 3.0. An SPF of 3.0 is equivalent to a heat ratio of approximately 10,000 Btu/kwh.

Heat pumps should not be used in all regions of the country. When the weather is cold, the system does not work as efficiently as it might appear. First, the heat pump is usually sized to produce the correct amount of heat when the outside temperature is in the range of 30–35°F. When it is colder than this outside, supplementary electric resistance elements must be used to provide some of the heating. Furthermore, the efficiency of the refrigeration system is reduced as the evaporator temperature is lowered. Exhibit 10.2 shows these effects. These two effects lower the SPF for systems installed in very cold climates.

Exhibit 10.2 Heat Output and COP for a Guestroom Heat Pump

Outdoor Temperature °F	Output Btu/hr	COP
62	9,800	3.1
57	9,300	3.0
52	8,600	2.8
47	7,900	2.6
42	7,500	2.5
37	6,600	2.3
32	6,100	2.2

Controls

The operation of boilers and heaters requires several different control devices. Their purposes fall into two different categories: proper operation and safety.

Proper operation requires three basic types of controls. First, temperature and pressure sensors determine when the equipment needs more heat and turn the burner on and off appropriately. Second, the amount of combustion air can be controlled in both forced-draft and natural-draft systems to improve the efficiency of operation. In a forced-draft system, the amount of air that is supplied by the fan can be controlled depending on the rate of flow of the fuel. Third, in systems with multiple boilers, controls can sense when the load is large enough to start another boiler.

Safety considerations for boilers require even more types of controls. Four of the five types automatically shut down the burner if a problem is sensed. The first automatic control senses abnormally high temperatures and pressures. This control has a manual reset requirement so that the boiler cannot be restarted without operator assistance. A second control senses whether there is enough water, while a third senses high or low pressure in the fuel line. The fourth control senses whether the flame is burning when the fuel is flowing. This controller also has a manual reset feature. The fifth type of safety control is a manual relief valve that prevents a boiler from rupturing when all else fails.

Repair and Maintenance Considerations

Because the operation of the heating equipment has an important impact on the energy consumption of the property and on guest satisfaction, special attention should be paid to this equipment. This attention should be shown both in the design and operational stages of the property.

During design, two important issues should be investigated. First, there should be enough space around the equipment to allow proper inspection and service by a mechanic. There must be some way to bring this large equipment into the building during construction and some space to remove the tubes from the boiler for replacement later in its life. Second, redundancy should be built into the system. Instead of using one large boiler to handle the entire building load, two boilers can be used, each capable of providing (for example) 65% of the total load. This provides a backup position if one boiler fails, allows one boiler to be taken out of service periodically for maintenance, and improves the operating efficiencies of the boilers at partial loads.

During operation, the boiler or furnace must be kept clean in order to maintain the highest possible operating efficiencies. The proper flow of air should be maintained at all times. Periodic calibration of the burner should be performed by measuring the products of combustion in the chimney. The chimney or flue should be inspected in order to avoid plugs or leaks that could cause carbon monoxide poisoning. Both sides of the burning surface (that is, the fire side and the water side) should be cleaned periodically. Soot should be removed from the fire side and scale from the water side by blowing down the boiler. Of course, treatment of the water entering the boiler and the heating system should be monitored.

Air Conditioning Equipment

The equipment that supplies cooling to the HVAC system is divided into two categories according to the degree of assembly of the individual components. If a refrigeration system (usually in sizes of from 3/4 to 115 tons, with a "ton" of cooling equivalent to 12,000 Btu/hr) comes installed inside a cabinet with additional fans and controls, then the entire assembly is considered either a *unitary* or a *packaged* system. If the refrigeration system is purchased separately (usually in sizes greater than 50 tons), then the equipment is labeled a *chiller*. The following sections describe the characteristics for these two types of equipment.

Unitary and Packaged Systems

Unitary and packaged systems are manufactured to a high degree of assembly, with the entire refrigeration system complemented by the necessary controls, fans, cabinet, and accessory components such as air filters and grills. The capability to provide heating in the same unit is also available. Unitary systems are built to provide air conditioning for more than one room, while the packaged units (packaged terminal air conditioners—PTACs) are intended for only a single room. Therefore, PTACs are most commonly applied in decentralized systems as the air conditioning unit in guestrooms. Unitary systems are installed in larger applications as the source components when air is used as the distribution medium. They are often used as rooftop units for public and function areas and provide the conditioned air that is supplied into the corridors of guestroom blocks. Exhibits 10.3 and 10.4 show examples of a unitary and a PTAC system, respectively.

Both kinds of systems have several positive characteristics that are evident in both the design and operational stages of a property. In the design stage, these systems simplify the designer's task by offering standardized designs in various configurations. They are certified by recognized testing laboratories such as Underwriters Laboratory (UL) and are rated by the Air-conditioning and Refrigeration Institute (ARI). They are easier to install on the construction site because they have standardized installation procedures and require a minimal amount of field wiring. In the operational stage, the equipment usually is more reliable and has better performance balance among its components because it was designed, manufactured, and tested as a unit. The ability to service the unit is enhanced by the ready availability of replacement parts and service manuals. Questions may be directed to and assistance obtained from a single manufacturer.

There are several special considerations that apply to PTACs. First, the wall box becomes an integral part of the exterior wall of the building. Therefore, it must have adequate weatherproofing to prevent water, wind, and insects from entering the building. Second, the equipment must be extremely corrosion resistant, since it is

Exhibit 10.3 Sketches of a Unitary Air Conditioning System

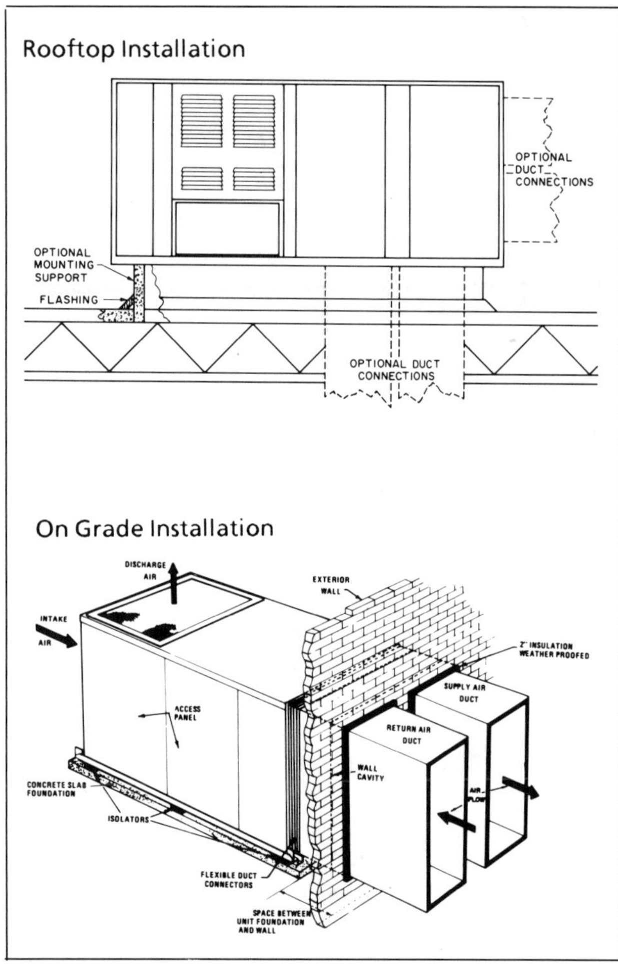

Reprinted by permission from *1983 ASHRAE Handbook—Equipment*.

Exhibit 10.4 Sketch of a PTAC Air Conditioning System

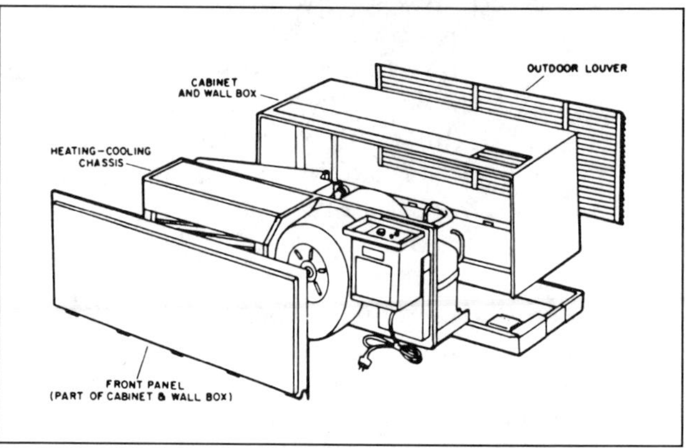

Reprinted by permission from *1983 ASHRAE Handbook—Equipment*.

exposed to the external elements. Its service life can be dramatically reduced due to exposure to corrosive elements, especially salt. Third, condensate disposal must be designed into the equipment, usually by rejection into the air blown over the condenser, so that the condensate does not drip down the side of the building. Fourth, the refrigeration system should be mounted on a removable chassis so that maintenance personnel can repair the system by removing the entire chassis and replacing it with another working unit.

Chillers

Chillers are large refrigeration systems which are used to produce chilled water, typically at temperatures of 42–45°F. They are installed as the source component for cooling in centralized water-based HVAC systems, with the chilled water distributed throughout the property to provide the cooling. Their most common application is in properties where the guest expects a low level of noise from the air conditioning unit in the room. For this situation, the most common choice is a fan-coil unit supplied with chilled water because the PTAC units described in the previous section are generally too noisy.

The operation of a chiller is based on one of two refrigeration cycles: the compression cycle or the absorption cycle. Compression chillers use exactly the same principles of operation as the refrigeration system described in Chapter 7 for food service applications, although the size and capacity of the components are substantially different. Absorption chillers, however, operate on an entirely different principle. Instead of requiring mechanical power from a motor to operate the cycle as does a compression system, the absorption cycle uses heat from steam, hot water, or the combustion of a fuel to energize the system. (We will turn to a more detailed discussion of absorption chillers shortly.)

As with all refrigeration equipment, the heat absorbed in the evaporator coil (in this case, from the chilled water) must be dissipated from the system to the external environment (in this case, the outdoor air). This dissipation is accomplished in three ways depending on the type of the condenser coil. The energy is rejected directly into the outdoor air by either an air-cooled or an evaporative-cooled condenser or it is rejected into water (which dissipates the heat to the outdoor air through a cooling tower) by a water-cooled condenser. Exhibit 10.5 shows a schematic for each type of condenser.

Chillers are also classified by the type of compressor that drives the system. As with food service refrigeration equipment, there are three types of compressors: reciprocating, rotary, and centrifugal. Most chillers in lodging properties have either rotary or centrifugal compressors, primarily because of the low vibration levels associated with balanced rotary motion.

In addition, a centrifugal chiller is often chosen because of its ability to operate easily at less than full load. Although the capacity of the chiller is selected to meet the peak demand for cooling in the property as described in Chapter 8, it operates most of the time at partial loads. Therefore, the ability of the chiller to efficiently operate under these conditions is very important to the cost-effective operation of the building. One of the primary advantages of a centrifugal compressor is its ability to operate over a range of loads from 10 to 100% of its design capacity. Either (1) inlet vanes control the flow of the refrigerant with some loss in efficiency while the compressor continues to turn at a steady speed or (2) a frequency inverter is used to control the frequency of the electricity for the motor and thus the speed of the compressor. The latter is more difficult to accomplish, but it makes for more efficient operations.

Absorption Cycle Chillers. Refrigeration cycles work on the principle of boiling and condensing the working fluid at two different temperatures. In a compression cycle, the compressor accomplishes this by changing the pressure of the fluid so that it can boil and condense at different temperatures. In an absorption cycle, water is the operating fluid and the evaporation is caused by the affinity that lithium bromide has for the water. Exhibit 10.6 shows a schematic of this cycle.

The refrigerant water is evaporated in an evaporator (1) (thus cooling the chilled water) and absorbed by a highly concentrated solution of lithium bromide located in an absorber (2). As the solution becomes diluted by the absorbed water, it is transferred to a generator (3) where moisture is driven off by the application of heat. The water vapor is condensed in a condenser (4) by condenser water and is returned to the evaporator to repeat the cycle. Likewise, the concentrated lithium bromide solution is returned to the absorber. A heat exchanger (5) transfers heat from the concentrated solution to the diluted solution in order to improve efficiency.

There are many similarities between this cycle and the compression cycle, and there are two major differences. As similarities, both systems have an evaporator and a condenser. They produce chilled water. In both, heat must be

Exhibit 10.5 Schematics for Three Types of Condensers for Chillers

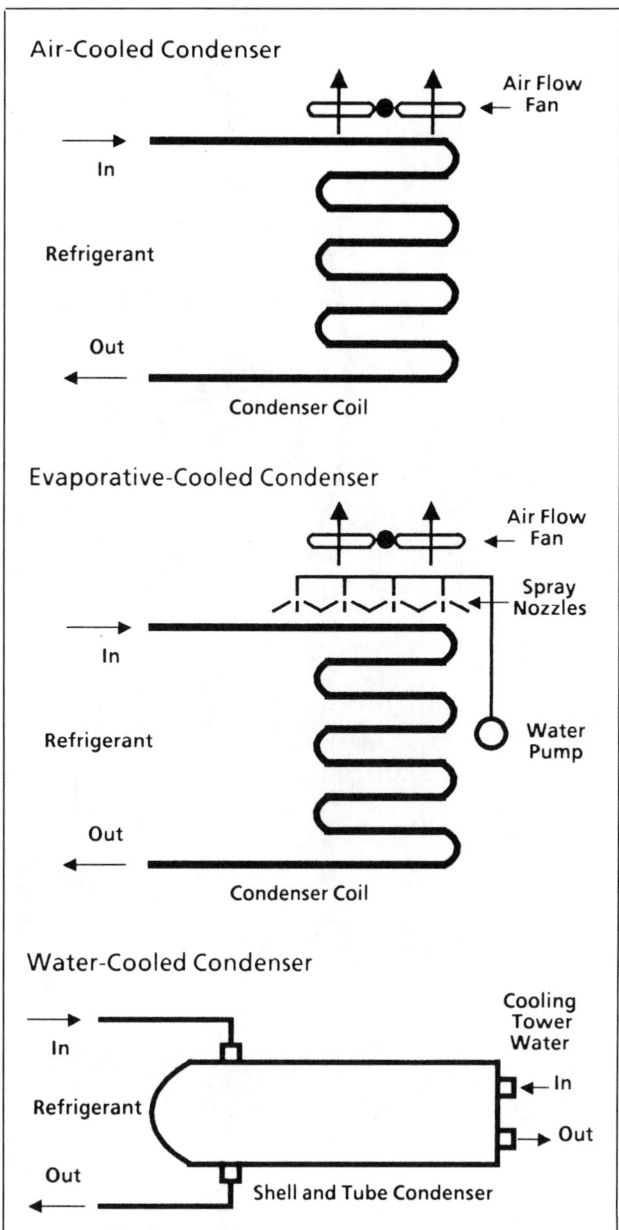

Exhibit 10.6 Schematic of an Absorption Refrigeration Cycle

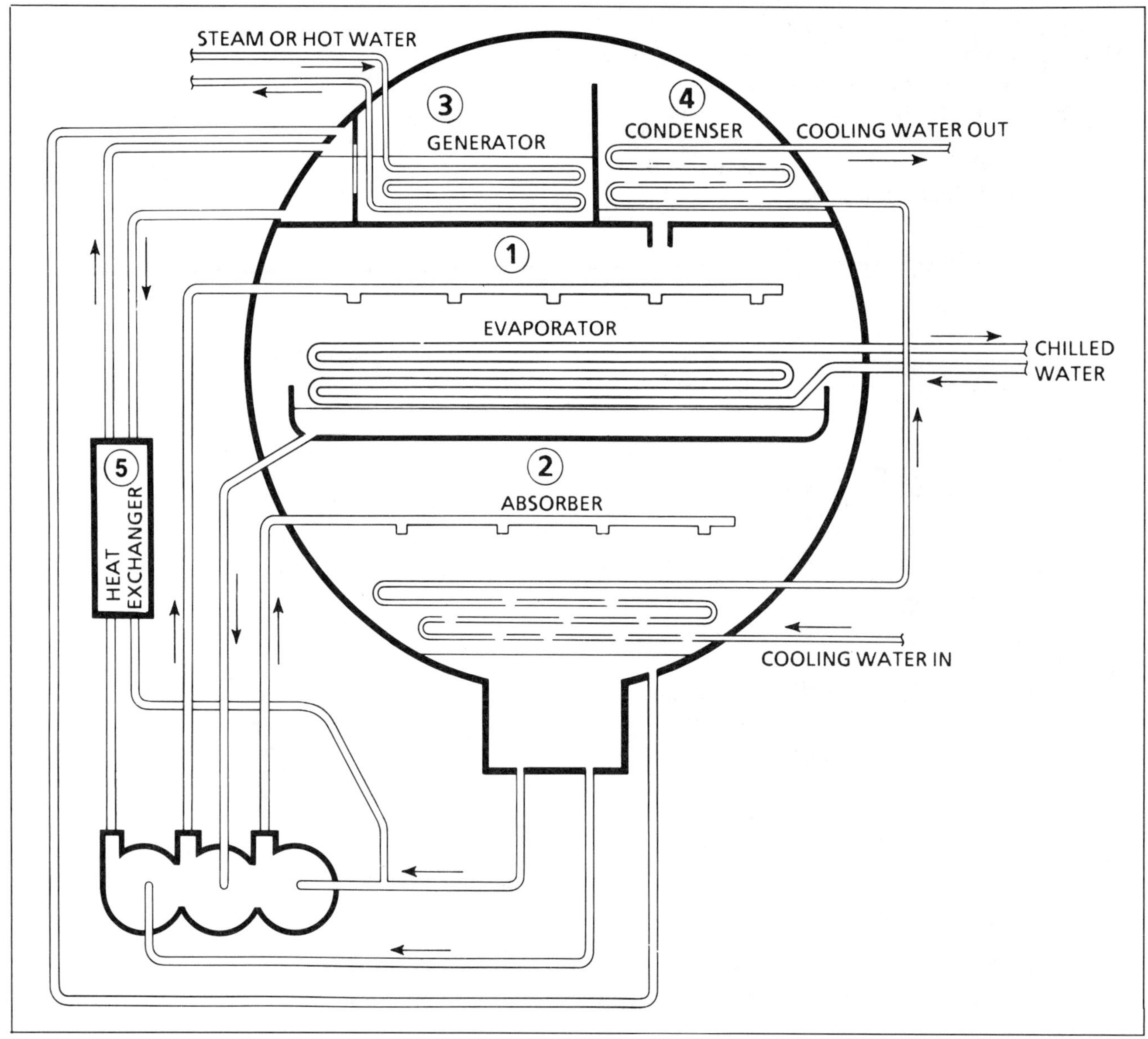

Permission to reprint granted by Building Owners and Managers Institute International, 1987.

dissipated from the condenser, although the condenser must be water-cooled for an absorption cycle. The cycles differ, however, in the type of power needed to drive them and in their efficiency of operation. The compression cycle requires mechanical power to operate a motor, while the absorption cycle requires only heat. The COPs for absorption-cycle chillers are between .5 and 1.0, while the COPs for compression-cycle chillers range from 2.5 to 6.0.

Absorption chillers are available in two types: indirect- and direct-fired. Indirect-fired chillers use steam (5 to 150 psi) or hot water (150–400°F) as the source of heat. Direct-fired chillers use a combustible fuel, such as natural gas, to energize the cycle. Direct-fired units are more efficient.

Even with the drastically lower operating efficiency, the application of an absorption chiller can be cost-effective when there is available heat energy at a cost substantially lower than the equivalent cost of electricity. For example, if natural gas that is available at an equivalent cost of $8/MMBtu is applied to a direct-fired absorption chiller with a COP of 1.0, then the cost of energy would be approximately the same as for a compression chiller with a COP of 3.6 run by electricity purchased at $.10/kwh.

Controls

The proper and reliable operation of air conditioning units requires several types of control devices which satisfy two different needs: (1) safe and reliable operation of the refrigeration system and (2) proper operation to maintain comfort conditions and to maintain the highest efficiency. The controls necessary for the first purpose are essentially the same as required for refrigeration systems for food service applications as discussed in Chapter 7. The controls for the second purpose are discussed in the following text.

The room thermostat operates in two ways, depending on the type of system it is controlling. In a decentralized system with PTAC equipment, the thermostat directly orders the on/off cycling of the refrigeration system, thus controlling the temperature of the room air. In a centralized system with a unitary unit or a chiller, the thermostat controls the valves or dampers that allow the distribution medium (air for a unitary unit and water for a chiller) to condition the room air to the proper temperature.

The room thermostat, however, does not control the central unit. That is accomplished by an additional thermostat that senses the output of the central unit (the supply air temperature for a unitary unit and the supply chilled water for a chiller). The refrigeration system is either cycled on and off or modulated in response to this thermostat, thus matching the output of the central unit with the cooling load in the building.

Controls can contribute to maintaining the highest possible operating efficiencies for the central units, especially for chillers. Normally, the temperature of the chilled water is maintained in the range of 42–45°F, especially when the system is operating under a heavy cooling load. When the loads are lower, however, the efficiency of the system can be improved if the chilled water temperature is increased slightly. This increase would have no detectable effect on the occupants in the building because the cooling load is not heavy at this time. It is accomplished by resetting the desired temperature of the supply chilled water according to the size of the load on the system.

Proper control of the condenser water temperature can also contribute to the efficient operation of the chiller. Normally, the temperature is in the range of 85–95°F for compression chillers and 85–105°F for absorption chillers. When the outdoor temperature is cooler and the humidity level is low, the temperature of the condenser water can be lower than the normal values, thus increasing the efficiency of the chiller.

Repair and Maintenance Considerations

As with heating equipment, the operation of the air conditioning equipment has an important impact on the success of the operation of the property. Therefore, special attention should be given to this equipment, both in the design stage and the operational stage.

During the design stage of the property, two factors should be considered: access and proximity for service and redundancy of the equipment. The ability to service the equipment is especially important for central units. There should be adequate circulation space around the equipment for inspection and repair. There must be room to remove the cooling tubes, to replace a circulation pump, or to repair other major components of the system. If the equipment is located in a central mechanical room, then it is easy for the mechanics to access it. Unitary units on roofs, however, are notorious for being overlooked for routine maintenance such as cleaning the filters because they are out of sight. The components of the PTAC units should be easy to remove from the room so that repair can be accomplished by replacing the broken unit and sending it out for repair.

As for redundancy of the equipment, there should be more than one pump for each of the chilled-water and condenser-water loops. Multiple chillers should be installed to prevent total loss of cooling if one chiller should fail or require repair.

During the operational stage of a property, the normal preventive maintenance suggested by the manufacturer should be attended to. Furthermore, for chillers, additional attention should be given to water treatment for both the chilled water and the condenser water. The

Exhibit 10.7 Diagram of a Forced-Draft Cooling Tower

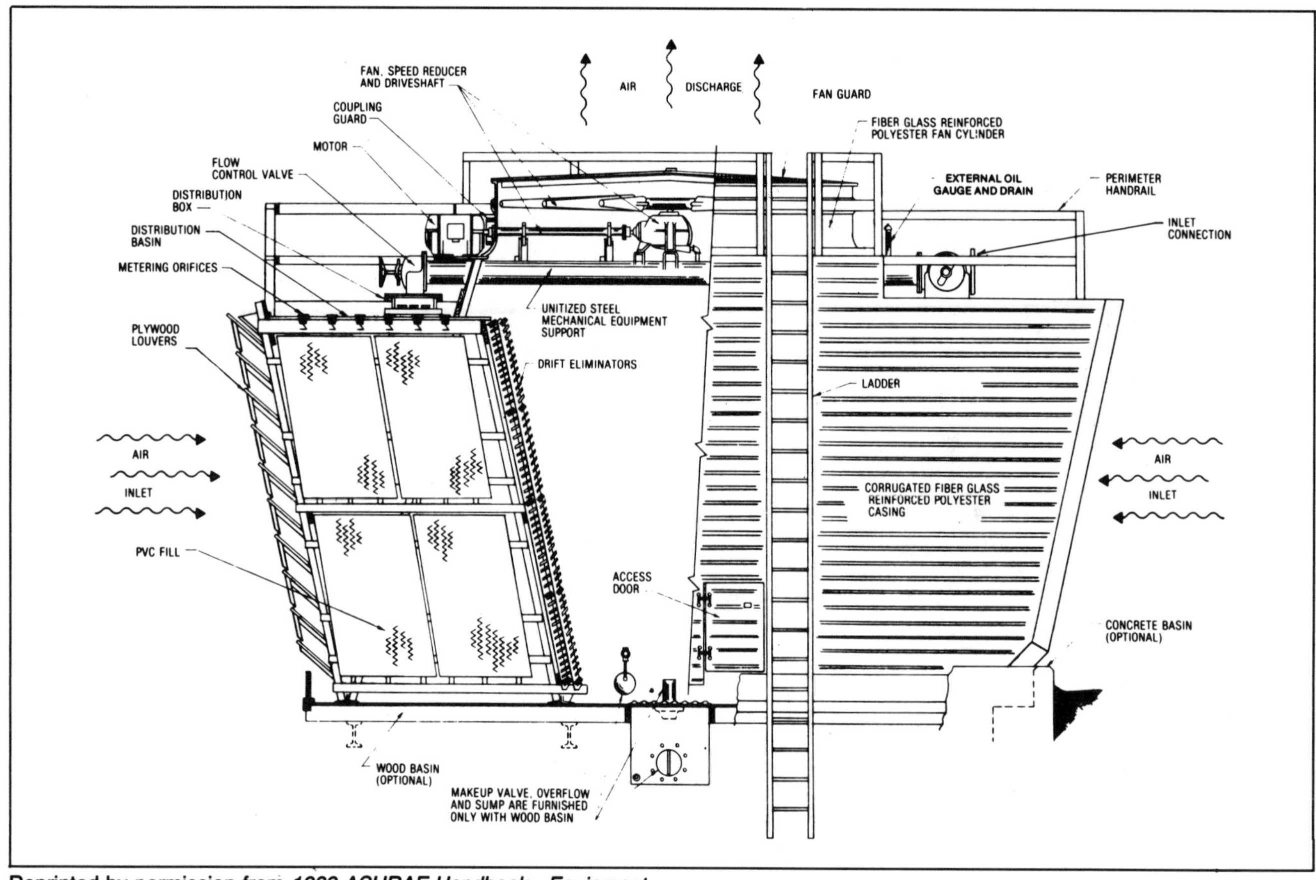

Reprinted by permission from *1983 ASHRAE Handbook—Equipment.*

chilled-water loop is a closed circuit, so treatment is only required when water is added to the system. The condenser-water loop, however, is open to the atmosphere in the cooling tower. This water should be constantly monitored and the proper water quality should be chemically maintained because cooling towers have been identified as the source for several serious diseases.

Supporting Equipment for Air Conditioning

Cooling Towers

The condenser water from the chiller must dissipate the heat that is absorbed from the chiller to the outdoor air. This is accomplished through the evaporation of some of the condenser water itself, with the necessary heat of vaporization being supplied by the dissipated heat. This process occurs in a cooling tower located outside of the building, usually on the roof or on the ground near the building.

Exhibit 10.7 shows a diagram of an induced draft tower. The condenser water from the building is sprayed over the top of the unit. The water cascades down through the core of the tower, exposing itself to the air. Some of the water evaporates into the air, thus cooling the remaining water. Most of the water reaches the bottom storage pan and is recirculated to the chiller inside the building. Outdoor air is drawn through the tower by a fan to enhance the evaporation process.

Water in addition to the condenser water must be supplied to the tower for its proper operation. Some of the condenser water is lost intentionally through evaporation and some is lost unintentionally as water droplets (*drift*) carried away by the air flow. A small portion of the water (*bleedoff*) must also be removed to prevent the buildup of impurities in the system. These losses must be replaced by makeup water piped directly to the tower.

Circulation Pumps

Circulation pumps are installed in chilled-water, hot-water, and condenser-water loops for the purpose of moving the water through the system. Almost all of these are centrifugal pumps which use impellers to push the water. The impeller converts the mechanical energy of the rotating motor, usually powered by electricity, into pressure in the water. This pressure must be sufficient to overcome the friction loss in the piping system due to components such as valves and to raise the water to the highest level in the building.

The pumps, designed for continuous operation, operate as long as there is a load on the heating or cooling system. In some installations, the pumps deliver a constant flow at all times, even when there is little water flowing through the fan-coil units in the guestrooms during a light heating or cooling load. For this to happen without overloading the pumps, the water that is not flowing through the fan-coil unit must bypass the coil so the volume of flow through the system remains constant. In other installations, the flow of the water through the loop is throttled to meet the demand of the fan-coil units. This is accomplished by using one of the following techniques: turning multiple pumps off or on, switching between speeds on two-speed motors, or using variable speed drives.

Fans

Fans are installed throughout the HVAC system for the purpose of moving air. The blade or impeller of the fan converts the power from the electric motor into pressure and flow in the air. The pressure must overcome the friction losses in the system. The flow delivers the volume of air required by the specific application.

The fans installed in lodging properties fall into one of two classifications: axial or centrifugal. The axial fan takes air in and exhausts it in a stream parallel to the axis of rotation of the fan blade—for example, a common room fan. In contrast, a centrifugal fan exhausts the air perpendicular to the axis of rotation. Axial fans produce high volumes of air flow with little ability to overcome resistance to the flow. Therefore, they are commonly used to draw air through exhaust ducts from bathrooms, to blow air over the condenser coil in a PTAC unit, or to blow air over the evaporator coil in a walk-in refrigerator. Centrifugal fans produce air flows with more pressure, so they are used in most applications that require blowing air through ducts or blowing air over coils where the air flow pattern is important. They are usually installed as the supply and return air fans in air-based centralized systems and as the supply fans in PTAC units.

Control of the fan speed is very important to the cost-effective operation of an air-based centralized HVAC system. The horsepower necessary for driving the fan is proportional to the cube of the flow rate. Therefore, doubling the flow rate of a given fan requires eight times as much power. Conversely, halving the flow rate reduces the power requirement to one-eighth of the original amount. This relationship presents several opportunities for more efficient operation. Variable speed drives should be used in vav systems, and flow rates should be checked in constant volume systems to determine that no unnecessary air is being circulated.

Filters

One of the important functions of an air conditioning system is to provide a clean atmosphere inside the building. Outdoor air brings with it pollen, insects, soot, dust, and other foreign substances. Dust, dirt, and lint are also generated inside the building. Filters are installed in the duct work of the air conditioning system in order to remove these contaminants.

There are three common types of filters: viscous impingement, dry, and electrostatic. Filters of the first type are flat panel filters made of coarse fibers with a high porosity. Oil is applied to coat the filter medium so that particles stick to the filter when they impinge on it. They have low resistance to air flow, a good efficiency with lint (but not with atmospheric dust), and a low cost. They come in two styles: disposable and permanent.

Dry filters use mats or blankets of media such as cellulose, glass fiber, wool felt, or other synthetic materials. The medium is usually supported in V-shaped pleats in order to increase the surface area of the filter. Particles larger than

Exhibit 10.8 Data on a Decentralized HVAC System for a Property in Cincinnati, Ohio

Room tower
- 247 rooms or suites
- 106,956 ft^2 of floor area
- 253 PTAC units with heat pump
  - Cooling: 8,150 Btu/hr each
  - Heating:
    - Heat pump: 7,900 Btu/hr each
    - Resistance heater: 17,800 Btu/hr each
  - Supply air: 300 cfm
  - Ventilation air: 60 cfm
- 3 rooftop units for hallways and laundry
  - Cooling: 279 MBtu/hr total
  - Heating (electric): 750 MBtu/hr total
  - Supply air: 9,000 cfm

Commercial and other areas
- 45,680 ft^2 of floor area
- 28 rooftop units
  - Cooling: 2,844 MBtu
  - Heating (electric): 5,990 MBtu/hr total
  - Supply air: 93,830 cfm

Totals
- 152,636 ft^2 of floor area
- Cooling: 5,185 MBtu/hr
- Heating: 13,242 MBtu/hr
- Supply air: 178,730 cfm

the size of the openings between the fibers are held by the filter medium. Filters of this type are usually more efficient than the viscous impingement filters and they hold more dust before cleaning is required. When dirty, the filter medium is discarded and replaced by clean material.

Electrostatic filters use the electrostatic precipitation principle to collect particulate matter. Electric charges are used to attract the particle to the filter medium. The filter medium or the collector plates are coated with an adhesive to keep the dust attached to the surface. These filters are often used in conjunction with dry filters located downstream which catch any dirt that falls off the electrostatic filter. These filters are the most effective and have a high initial cost.

Exhibit 10.9 Data on a Water-Based Centralized HVAC System for a Property in Orlando, Florida

Guestrooms
- 814 rooms
- 473,000 ft^2 of floor area
- Fan-coil units:
  - 7.5 MBtu/hr average cooling capacity
  - 1,000 watts electric heating capacity
- 58,000 cfm of makeup air supplied to corridors

Commercial and other areas
- 119,000 ft^2 of floor area
- 766 tons of cooling capacity
- 8,300 MBtu/hr of heating capacity

Central equipment
- 3 chillers at 40% of total load: 440 tons each
- 3 chilled water pumps: 60 HP motor each
- 3 condenser water pumps: 30 HP motor each
- 1 standby pump: 60 HP motor
- 1 three-cell cooling tower: 20 HP motor/cell
- 2 hot water boilers at 66% of total load: 125 BHP each
- 2 hot water pumps

Totals
- 592,000 ft^2 of floor area
- Cooling capacity: 1,320 tons
- Heating capacity:
  - 250 BHP boiler
  - 2,770 MBtu/hr electric resistance

Repair and Maintenance Considerations

Although the importance of supporting equipment may seem small, its continuous operation is essential to the performance of the HVAC system. Therefore, the preventive maintenance on this equipment should not be neglected.

This includes seeing that the motors and fans are in good working order, that the filters are cleaned or changed, that the duct work is in good shape with a clean inside and a

Exhibit 10.10 Data on a Water-Based Centralized HVAC System for a Property in New York, New York

Guestrooms
- 765 rooms
- 389,000 ft^2 of floor area
- Fan-coil units:
  - 8.3 MBtu/hr average cooling capacity
  - 5.0 MBtu/hr average heating capacity
  - 1,000 watts electric heating for intermediate seasons
- Makeup air directly into units

Commercial and other areas
- 87,000 ft^2 of floor area
- 634 tons of cooling capacity
- 8,500 MBtu/hr of heating capacity

Central equipment
- 3 chillers at 40% of total load: 500 tons each
- 3 chilled water pumps: 75 HP motor each
- 3 condenser water pumps: 100 HP motor each
- 1 standby pump: 100 HP motor
- 1 three-cell cooling tower
- No boiler--steam is purchased
- 2 steam-to-water heat exchangers
- 2 hot water pumps

Totals
- 476,000 ft^2 of floor area
- Cooling capacity: 1,500 tons
- Heating capacity: 12,325 MBtu/hr

well-insulated outside, that the drive belts for the fans are not slipping, and that the bearings for all fans, motors, and pumps are oiled.

Applications

This section contains three examples of HVAC systems as they are installed in lodging properties. Exhibits 10.8 to 10.10 summarize the data for a 247-room property located in Cincinnati, Ohio, an 814-room property in Orlando, Florida, and a 765-room property in New York, New York, respectively. The types of systems installed in the three properties are different. The system installed in the Cincinnati property is decentralized with PTAC units containing heat pumps used in the guestrooms and rooftop units for the commercial space. The Orlando property has two-pipe fan-coil or air-handling units throughout the facility and has chilled water provided to these units year-round. When heating is needed, small supplemental electric resistance heaters are used in the guestrooms and a boiler supplies hot water to the air-handling units. The system in the New York location has fan-coils and air-handling units supplied by a two-pipe system that is changed over as the seasons require. Hot water is supplied to the fan-coil units during the winter and chilled water is supplied during the spring, summer, and fall. During the spring and fall, supplemental electric resistance heaters provide heating when necessary. Steam is purchased so there are no boilers.

11
Lighting Systems

Lighting systems affect several aspects of physical plant management. The character and direction of light influences building colors and textures. Its optical characteristics affect the appearance of surface finishes and ceilings. The nature and level of illumination affect the efficiency of task performance. The lighting systems chosen influence HVAC system design and operation (because of the heat given off), building design (because of the dimensions of the lighting fixtures), electrical design, and the economics of investment (because the lamps and their controls are part of the initial investment).

Light Levels

Measurement Methods

In order to have some objective means of determining relative light levels, some standard light level units and measurement methods have been developed. The *lumen* is the most commonly used unit of light and is equal to 0.0015 watt. Light which is incident on a surface is known as *illumination*. Illumination is typically measured in *footcandles*, a term which denotes a light intensity of one lumen per square foot.

Lighting levels are most commonly measured with portable light meters which indicate the available light in footcandles. These devices are accurate to plus or minus 5% if kept calibrated. Portable light meters will often have multiple scales allowing them to measure light levels over a fairly wide range.

Recommended Light Levels

The level of illumination required in a given space is generally a function of the activities or tasks being performed within the space. The Illuminating Engineers Society (IES) has developed a method to calculate design levels for lighting which incorporates a number of task, space, and occupant parameters. An application of this method is shown in Exhibit 11.1, which lists selected footcandle levels for spaces commonly encountered in lodging properties and restaurants. While providing an idea of the likely design value for lighting of these spaces, the values shown are not standards as such.

As a result of concerns about energy consumption by lighting equipment, the federal government and various state governments have developed their own recommended levels of illumination. These may directly specify light levels or may specify the watts per square foot which the lighting system can consume. As might be expected, these specifications sometimes result in light levels which are somewhat lower than the IES levels. Care should be taken in reducing illumination levels below IES recommendations, since employee productivity and comfort may be at stake. The increased use of task lighting and video display terminals has resulted in additional concerns in the specification of lighting levels. These and other concerns must be included in the overall process of lighting system design, maintenance, and modification.

Light Sources

Light sources include *natural light, incandescent lamps*, and *electric discharge lamps*. Light sources can be categorized by many measures, including their efficiency (measured in lumens per watt) and their color rendering index. The latter is a number from 0 to 100 which states how closely the lamp approaches the color rendering capability of natural light, which has an index of 100. Another characteristic is lamp life, which is defined as the time it takes half of the lamps in a given sample to fail.

Natural Lighting

Natural light, or daylighting, is by far the most common and least expensive lighting source and is the basis for the determination of the overall color rendering characteristics of artificial lighting. The use of natural light is currently of great interest to designers of commercial buildings, especially offices and schools where lighting energy is a significant fraction of total energy use. Since clear-sky outdoor illumination levels can approach 1,000 footcandles for over 85% of the working day in some locations, the contribution of natural lighting to overall building lighting needs is potentially significant.

However, natural lighting will probably not make a significant contribution to lodging or restaurant lighting needs due to these operations' design and usage. These facilities have much of their interior office and meeting space remote from natural lighting sources. Also, unlike many other commercial buildings, a significant portion of the building operating time occurs during the evening hours when natural lighting is not available.

Incandescent Sources

Incandescent sources are quite common, especially in residences, guestrooms, and restaurants. An incandescent lamp consists of a filament inside a sealed glass bulb. Current passing through the filament heats it to incandescence, producing light. The bulb is usually etched or coated to diffuse the light produced by the filament. The electrical connection for the lamp is through the base.

Incandescent sources are characterized by relatively short lifetimes (2,000 hours or less), relatively poor efficiencies (15 to 20 lumens per watt), and good color rendition. They are capable of instant restarting, are low in cost, are readily dimmed, and have a high power factor. Their poor efficiency results in their contributing a large amount of heat to the building and in relatively high operating costs. Their short lifetime results in potentially high replacement labor costs.

The higher the wattage of an incandescent lamp, the more efficiently the lamp operates. Long-life lamps (which produce 10–20% less light per watt of power consumed) are generally

Exhibit 11.1 Lodging Applications Derived from IES Design Specifications

Space	Recommended Minimum Footcandles
HOTELS AND MOTELS	
Bathrooms	
General	10
Mirrors	30
Bedrooms	
Reading	30
Subdued environment	15
Lobby	
General	10
Reading and working	30
Power plant	
Boiler room	10
Equipment room	20
Storerooms	10
Offices	
Accounting	150
Regular office work	
Good copy	70
Fair copy	100
Corridors, elevators & stairways	20
RESTAURANTS	
Dining areas	
Cashier	50
Intimate type	
Light environment	10
Subdued environment	3
Leisure type	
Light environment	30
Quick service type	
Bright surroundings	100
Normal surroundings	50
Food displays	
Twice the general level but not under	50
Kitchen	
Inspection, checking and pricing	70
Other areas	30

less efficient than standard lamps. Any incandescent lamp will have its efficiency increased (and its life decreased) by operation at higher than its rated voltage.

Besides the conventional incandescent bulb, other types of incandescent bulbs are used for special applications. Rough service or vibration lamps are built to withstand rough handling and vibration. Extended service lamps have longer lifetimes and should be used where replacement is difficult.

Reflector lamps are incandescent lamps which contain a reflector coating to give the lamps a more directed light output. These lamps are known as spot or flood lamps. They may be installed over food counters with filters to limit the amount of heat in the light beam.

Electric Discharge Lamps

Electric discharge lamps generate light by passing an electric arc through a space filled with a specially formulated mixture of gases. This category of lamps includes fluorescent, mercury vapor, metal halide, and high- and low-pressure sodium.

Each of the electric discharge lamps requires an additional piece of equipment, a *ballast*, as part of the lighting system. The ballast, which controls the starting and operation of electric discharge lamps, acts as a small transformer in the lighting circuit. Ten to fifteen percent of the energy used by an electric discharge lighting system is consumed in the ballast and given off as heat. Ballasts are rated by their operating temperature, type of overheating protection (those that are thermally protected, self-resetting, and generally specified for commercial uses are denoted as type "P" ballasts), power factor, and noise level (rated A through F with A the quietest). Some recent trends in ballast design have included the development of electronic ballasts which consume up to 25% less energy than standard ballasts.

Fluorescent Lamps. Fluorescent lamps are the most commonly encountered form of electric discharge lamp. They are characterized by a long lifetime (7,000 to 20,000 hours) and an efficiency (40 to 80 lumens per watt) which is significantly higher than that of incandescent lamps. The color rendition of some fluorescent lamps is much poorer than that of incandescent lamps.

The label on a fluorescent lamp defines several of the lamp's characteristics. A lamp which is labeled F15T12WW is a fluorescent (F) lamp, 15 watts, of tubular (T) shape with a 12/8 inch diameter and a warm white (WW) color.

Fluorescent lamp lifetime decreases as the average number of burning hours per start decreases. This has contributed to the perception on the part of some people that it is cheaper to leave a fluorescent lamp on continuously than to switch it on and off as needed. However, in areas with high-cost electrical energy, this may not be true. When a room or area is left vacant, the lights should be turned off. The additional lamp replacement costs associated with the reduced lamp lifetime should easily be repaid by the resulting energy savings.

When selecting the ballast for fluorescent lamps, the type of lamp and the operating temperature of the ballast are important considerations. Locations which are hotter or colder than the ballast rating could potentially result in problems. Hot locations will decrease ballast life, resulting in premature ballast failure. Specification of a ballast suitable for higher temperature operation will result in longer ballast operation and fewer maintenance problems. When fluorescent lamps are installed in cold locations, ballasts which are capable of starting and operating the lamps under these cold conditions should be specified. Providing a dimming capability for fluorescent lamps requires an electronic ballast and the selection of dimming equipment suitable for the size and type of lighting system.

Other Electric Discharge Lamps. Besides the fluorescent lamp, there are other types of lamps which operate on the same principle and require a ballast for operation. These lamps include mercury vapor, metal halide, and high- and low-pressure sodium. These lamps are sometimes listed in a general category of high-intensity discharge (HID) lamps. Each lamp type may have applications within the hospitality industry.

While the incandescent and fluorescent lamps light almost immediately upon being energized, the *strike time* (the time required for the lamp to reach full output from a cold start) for HID lamps can be several minutes. In addition, the time required for a hot lamp to restrike is usually longer than the strike time. These longer strike and restrike times can be problematic in certain applications and should be considered when selecting lamp sources for such needs as emergency lighting.

Mercury vapor lamps have long been used for outdoor lighting of streets and parking lots. They have an efficiency of 15 to 60 lumens per watt and a lifetime of 12,000 to 24,000 hours. Strike times for mercury vapor lamps are 3 to 6 minutes and restrike times 3 to 8 minutes. White mercury lamps have somewhat better color rendition than clear lamps.

Metal halide (MH) lamps are basically mercury vapor lamps modified by the addition of metallic halides to improve the overall spectral emissions and to increase efficiency (80 to 100 lumens per watt). Lamp life is 7,500 to 15,000 hours, less than that for mercury vapor. Lumen maintenance is also significantly reduced later in the lamp life. Metal halide lamps have relatively short strike times, 2 to 3 minutes, but can have restrike times of up to 10 minutes.

High-pressure sodium (HPS) lamps are highly efficient light sources (85 to 140 lumens per watt) which have long life (16,000 to 24,000 hours) and a high lumen maintenance over their lifetimes. Strike times are 3 to 4 minutes, with a relatively short restrike time of about one minute. High-pressure sodium lamps are used in parking garages and parking lots and for lighting of building exteriors and entry areas. Indoor use of HPS lamps is possible if color-corrected lamps are selected or the HPS lamps are mixed with other sources which result in an appropriate spectral distribution.

Low-pressure sodium (LPS) lamps are the most efficient light sources, with efficiencies in excess of 150 lumens per watt possible. They have lifetimes of over 18,000 hours and a high lumen maintenance. Their color rendering characteristics are generally poor, since they produce a very yellow light. They are primarily used for parking lot lighting and security lighting such as after hours lighting in restaurants.

Lighting System Design

Lighting system design is an important element of the overall design of any hospitality facility. Interior and exterior lighting are crucial design components that:

- Help attract customers and make them comfortable.
- Improve employee productivity.
- Communicate a concept (your intended position in the market).
- Establish an atmosphere.

In addition, lighting can substantially affect safety and energy costs, both directly and indirectly.

Fixtures

Fixtures (also known as *luminaires*) serve several functions in lighting systems. The fixture may contribute significantly to the interior design of the space. Some fixtures are highly visible elements of the overall design, while others are virtually invisible, serving only the function of holding the lamp and directing its light output. Fixtures present a maintenance requirement both in the sense of basic cleaning needs and in the stocking of appropriate replacement items (such as decorative globes or safety covers). For lamps requiring ballasts, the fixture may also serve as the mounting location for the ballast. Finally, the type of fixture will dictate the overall efficiency of the lighting system.

Safety and maintenance concerns should be considered during fixture selection and installation. Compliance with local code requirements is very important. Plastic fixtures should only be used if the plastic materials are slow burning or self-extinguishing and have low smoke density ratings and low heat distortion temperatures. Long-term durability of fixtures when exposed to ultraviolet light should be investigated to ensure that yellowing or embrittlement will not result. Installation of fixtures should always be done in the manner recommended by the manufacturer. Fixtures should be installed in the correct orientation, provided with adequate ventilation and clearance to avoid heat build-up, and used with lamps with the proper (rated) wattage.

The efficiency of a lighting fixture is a parameter of concern in the selection process. While it is possible to determine the efficiency of the fixture itself, in general, the individual specifying the lighting fixture is more concerned about the fixture efficiency in the application being evaluated. The efficiency factor which combines the fixture efficiency (light delivered from the fixture divided by light produced by the lamp) with the room characteristics and the light distribution in the room is called the *coefficient of utilization* (*CU*). Highly efficient fixtures will have CU values of above .9, while inefficient ones will be in the range of .2 to .4.

Spectral Considerations

Since the color of the light emitted by various types of lamps differs, the impact of the type of lamp on the appearance of surfaces, finishes, and furnishings can be very significant. Exhibit 11.2 provides a brief overview of various lamp types and their color rendition.

Emergency Lighting Considerations

The requirements for emergency lighting will be specified in the local building code. These must be complied with. This discussion will draw on the requirements found in the Life Safety Code[1] and the National Electrical Code (*NEC*).[2] Local building codes will usually follow these two standards.

The *NEC* states that

> emergency illumination shall include all required means of egress lighting, illuminated exit signs, and all other lights specified as necessary to provide required illumination. Emergency lighting systems shall be so designed and installed that the failure of any individual lighting element, such as the burning out of a light bulb, cannot leave in total darkness any space which requires emergency illumination.[3]

Emergency lighting can be provided as (1) a system independent of the general lighting supply which is automatically transferred to another power source upon failure of the general lighting system or (2) two or more separate and complete systems with independent power supplies, each system providing sufficient current for emergency lighting purposes. In the event of a power failure, a delay of no more than ten seconds is permitted in the operation of the emergency lighting system. The emergency lighting system must be capable of providing a minimum of one footcandle for 1.5 hours.

A Special Consideration

Light sources in locations where the breakage of a bulb could pose a particular hazard (such as kitchens and pool areas) are required to use either a fixture with an acrylic diffuser to retain glass and lamp phosphor materials or (for fluorescent lamps) a tube safety shield around the lamp. This is usually a provision of the health code.

Lighting System Maintenance

The requirements for lighting system maintenance depend on the light source, its location, and the purpose served by the lighting. Maintenance can be as simple as replacing an incandescent bulb in a guestroom closet and as difficult as replacing the lamp and ballast on a pole-mounted fixture in the middle of a parking lot using a bucket truck.

The Effect of Lamp Properties

Since a major element of lighting system maintenance is the replacement of burned-out lamps, the type of lamps used at a property and their lifetime can have a significant impact on the overall needs for lamp replacement. A typical fluorescent lamp lifetime curve (see Exhibit 11.3) illustrates that, after the lamps have burned for approximately 60% of the lamp life, the rate of lamp failures begins to accelerate. Since the lamp life defines the time at which 50% of the lamps will have failed, significant activities to replace the lamps will have already begun well before the rated life is reached.

The use of incandescent lamps creates a potentially much greater need for lamp replacements due to the short lifetime of the incandescent lamp when compared with other options. For example, if we assume an incandescent lamp life of 1,000 hours (some may have a life of only 750 hours) and a fluorescent life of 12,000 hours, the incandescent lamp could require as many as eight replacements per year if burned continuously. The fluorescent would be replaced about once every 1.5 years under such circumstances. While the use of incandescent lamps in guestrooms may be warranted given their color rendering characteristics, their use in back-of-the-house spaces where such characteristics are unimportant and daily operating hours are long is certainly not warranted.

A further consideration when replacing fluorescent lamps is maintaining the desired color rendition. Replacing a lamp with a lamp which has a markedly different color rendition (cool white with warm white, for instance) results in a

Exhibit 11.2 A Guide for Lamp Selection Based on General Color Rendering Properties

Type of Lamp	Efficacy lm/w	Lamp Appearance Effect on Neutral Surfaces	Effect on "Atmosphere"	Colors Strengthened	Colors Grayed	Effect on Complexions	Remarks
FLUORESCENT LAMPS							
Cool white CW	High	White	Neutral to moderately cool	Orange, yellow, blue	Red	Pale pink	Blends with natural daylight--good color acceptance
Deluxe cool white CWX	Medium	White	Neutral to moderately cool	All nearly equal	None appreciably	Most natural	Best overall color rendition; simulates natural daylight
Warm white WW	High	Yellowish white	Warm	Orange, yellow	Red, green, blue	Sallow	Blends with incandescent light--poor color acceptance
Deluxe warm white WWX	Medium	Yellowish white	Warm	Red, orange, yellow, green	Blue	Ruddy	Good color rendition; simulates incandescent light
Daylight	Medium-high	Bluish white	Very cool	Green, blue	Red, orange	Grayed	Usually replaceable with CW
White	High	Pale yellowish white	Moderately warm	Orange, yellow	Red, green, blue	Pale	Usually replaceable with CW or WW
Soft white/natural	Medium	Purplish white	Warm pinkish	Red, orange	Green, blue	Ruddy pink	Tinted source usually replaceable with CWX or WWX
INCANDESCENT LAMPS							
Incandescent filament	Low	Yellowish white	Warm	Red, orange, yellow	Blue	Ruddiest	Good color rendering
HIGH-INTENSITY DISCHARGE LAMPS							
Clear mercury	Medium	Greenish blue-white	Very cool, greenish	Yellow, blue, green	Red, orange	Greenish	Very poor color rendering
White mercury	Medium	Greenish white	Moderately cool, greenish	Yellow, green, blue	Red, orange	Very pale	Moderate color rendering
Deluxe white mercury	Medium	Purplish white	Warm, purplish	Red, blue, yellow	Green	Ruddy	Color acceptance similar to CW fluorescent
Metal halide	High	Greenish white	Moderately cool, greenish	Yellow, green, blue	Red	Grayed	Color acceptance similar to CW fluorescent
High Pressure Sodium	High	Yellowish	Warm, yellowish	Yellow, green, orange	Red, blue	Yellowish	Color acceptance approaches that of WW fluorescent

Courtesy of General Electric Company.

mottled lighting effect on the interior design which can be quite disastrous.

If a property's lighting system maintenance program is designed to keep the lighting system operating in a manner which matches as closely as possible the initial condition of the system, then the lumen depreciation of the lamps is also of interest. Exhibit 11.4 illustrates typical lumen depreciation as a function of burning hours. Unless the lighting system is greatly over-designed, it may be necessary to replace lamps before they fail due to a reduction in their light output. This is sometimes the case with mercury vapor lamps whose light output drops off very dramatically as the burning hours approach the lamp lifetime.

Other characteristics of lamps which affect maintenance needs are the average burning time (see Exhibit 11.5) and the voltage of the electrical supply to the lamp. Incandescent or fluorescent lamps which are cycled often will have greatly reduced lifetimes, resulting in a greater maintenance cost, for both lamps and labor. Lamps which are supplied at a voltage different from the rated voltage (even by only a few percent) will have a reduced life if the voltage is above the rated value and an increased life if the voltage is below the rated value.

The Effect of Housekeeping Practices

The term housekeeping practices refers to the overall cleanliness of the property. The cleanliness level maintained by the property will affect the light output from lamps and luminaires, thereby affecting the ability of the lighting system to deliver its designed light levels.

Periodic cleaning of lamps and lighting fixtures will enable the lighting system to deliver a greater fraction of its light output than it does when the light is absorbed by dirt on bulbs and fixtures. The regular replacement of filters in air-handling units helps remove dust and dirt from the building air.

The Effect of Replacement Policies

Most discussions of lighting system replacement policies include a discussion of group relamping versus replacement upon burnout. Group relamping advocates suggest that wholesale replacement of all of the lamps in the lighting system (or a portion of the system) after some prescribed number of operating hours is

Exhibit 11.3 Typical Life Expectancy or Mortality Curve for Fluorescent Lamps

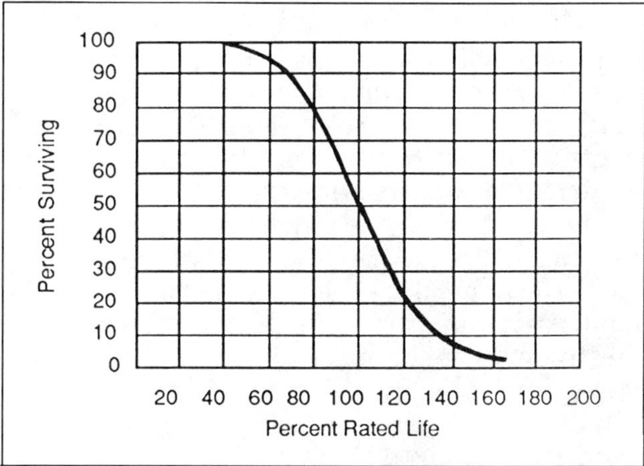

Exhibit 11.4 Approximate Lumen Maintenance of Various Cool White Fluorescent Lamps

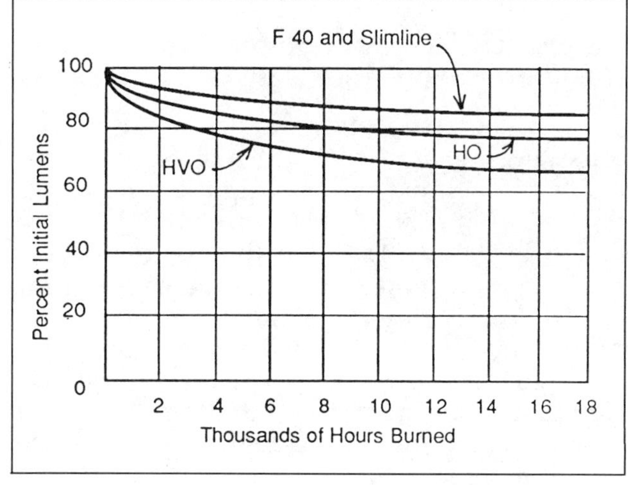

reached will result in significantly reduced costs for lamp replacement. Cost reductions are possible primarily through a labor cost reduction, although it may be possible to reduce lamp costs as well by bulk purchase of lamps.

Within hospitality facilities, however, the appearance of the facility and the guest's perceptions are so important that group relamping may not be appropriate. The bulbs which burn out shortly before the group relamping may adversely affect the guest's perceptions and the property appearance. Also, there is no easy way to judge the number of operating hours of guestroom lighting, making the timing of group relamping decisions somewhat of a problem. Group relamping is best implemented in back-of-the-house areas and in public spaces where such an activity is most likely to have a payback. It is very appropriate to any relamping task which requires significant labor simply to gain access to the lighting system—for example, convention areas and parking lots.

Depending on the length of time required to replace a lamp and the labor cost of the individual performing the replacement, lamp replacement costs can vary considerably. If lamps in guestrooms can be inspected and replaced by housekeeping staff as part of their normal rounds (and no problems arise from leaving a spare bulb in the guestroom for guest use in emergencies), the cost of lamp replacement will be low. However, if replacement is done by a member of the engineering staff dispatched via radio, the cost to replace a bulb can approach or exceed $5.00.

The Overall Effect of Lighting System Maintenance on Light Output

The combined effects of lamp properties, housekeeping practices, and replacement policies on the lighting system output can be significant. One lamp supplier has produced the curve shown in Exhibit 11.6. On this figure is illustrated the reduction in light output over time for a fluorescent lighting system as a result of the maintenance items discussed above. If the lighting system is allowed to experience such significant reductions in light output, the building will either be overlit in initial design (to compensate for the assumed maintenance methods) or the building will be underlit for large parts of its operating life. Neither situation seems to be compatible with the desire to control costs in the initial design while also providing an adequate work environment.

Energy Conservation Opportunities

For lighting systems, the two primary energy conservation opportunities are the use of more efficient lighting sources and the control of operating hours. Secondary benefits may be

Exhibit 11.5 Typical Mortality Curves as a Function of Burning Cycles for 40-Watt Rapid Start Lamps with a Rated Life of 20,000+ Hours

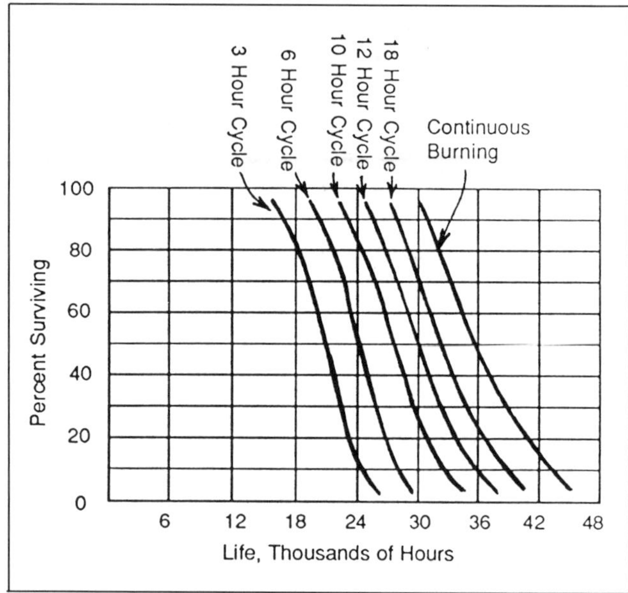

possible in the reduction of lighting in overlit spaces, but this must be approached with caution since lighting reductions may affect safety, productivity, or guests' perceptions of the property.

One of the primary concerns in the use of more efficient lighting (more lumens per watt) should be the substitution of fluorescent lamps for incandescent in as many locations as possible. Screw-in fluorescent lamps are available which can be substituted for incandescent lamps in downlights, table lamps, and ceiling-mounted lighting fixtures of various designs. The result will be a reduction of up to 75% in the electricity consumed by the lamp. In addition, there will be substantial labor savings due to the longer life of the fluorescent lamps. Attention to exterior lighting and the replacement of inefficient light sources with more efficient ones is also very appropriate (and usually results in a short payback period), since the operating hours of exterior lighting are very long. See Exhibit 11.7 for a selected list of lamps that can be used to replace standard lamps. Application 11.1 discusses retrofit lighting modifications made by one lodging chain to improve the efficiency of its lighting systems.

Exhibit 11.6 The Effect of Lighting System Maintenance on Light Output

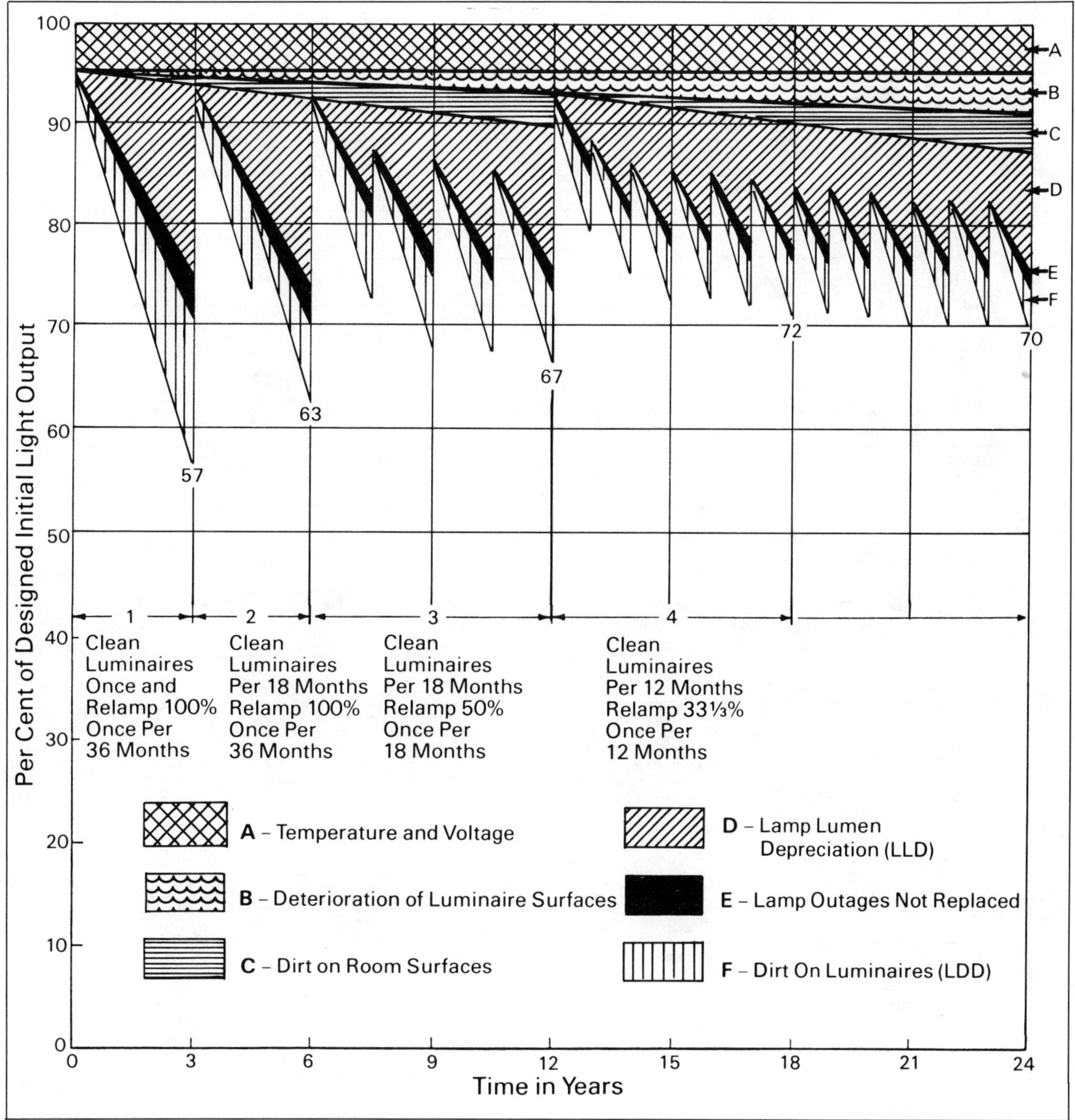

Source: *The Light Side of Energy Management* (Danvers, Mass.: GTE Products Corp., Sylvania Lighting Center, undated).

The control of lighting systems results in fewer operating hours for the systems, lower energy usage, and lower costs. Reduced burning hours also increase the time between lamp replacements. The easiest method of control is just to use the already available switch to turn off lights which are not needed. This is an activity which can be engaged in by all employees, requires no additional training, investment, or labor hours, and has immediate real benefits. Since motivating employees and management to take this responsibility has sometimes proven to

Exhibit 11.7 Interchangeability of Several Selected Lamps

Standard Lamp	Replacement Lamp	Wattage Savings[1]	Comparative Light Output of Replacement Lamp[2]	Value of Energy Savings Over Life of Replacement Lamp at $0.07/Wh	Other Benefits
60W Incandescent	Self-Ballasted Fluorescent	42	+	$22.05	X
75W Incandescent	Self-Ballasted Fluorescent	57	+	$29.93	
100W Incandescent	Self-Ballasted Fluorescent	56	=	$29.40	X
75W PAR-38 Spot or Flood Incandescent	65W PAR-38 Spot or Flood Incandescent	10	=	$1.40	
150W R-40 Flood Incandescent Downlight	75W ER-30 Incandescent Downlight	75	=	$10.50	
	120W ER-40 Incandescent Downlight	30	+ +	$4.20	X
150W PAR-38 Spot or Flood Incandescent	90W PAR-38 Spot or Flood Incandescent	60	=	$8.40	
300W R-40 Flood Incandescent Downlight	120W ER-40 Incandescent Downlight	180	-	$25.00	
500W Incandescent	450W Self-Ballasted Mercury Vapor	50	-	$56.00	
1,000W Incandescent	750W Self-Ballasted Mercury Vapor	250	--	$280.00	
F-40 Fluorescent	F-40 Reduced-Wattage, High-Efficiency Fluorescent	7	=	$9.80	
	F-40 Reduced Wattage, High-Efficiency Color-Improved Fluorescent	7	-	$9.80	
	F-40 High-Brightness Fluorescent	0	+	$0.00	X
F-96 Fluorescent	F-96 Reduced-Wattage, High-Efficiency Fluorescent	16.5	-	$20.80	
F-96 HO Fluorescent	F-96 HO Reduced-Wattage, High Efficiency Fluorescent	16.5	-	$20.80	
F-96 1,500 MA Fluorescent	F-96 1,500 MA Reduced-Wattage, High-Efficiency Fluorescent	30	-	$23.83	
175W Mercury Vapor	150W Retrofit High Pressure Sodium	40	+ +	$33.60	X
	175W Retrofit Metal Halide	0	+ +	$0.00	X
250W Mercury Vapor	215W Retrofit High-Pressure Sodium	65	+ +	$54.60	X
400W Mercury Vapor	325W Retrofit Metal Halide	70	+ +	$98.00	X
	400W Retrofit Metal Halide	0	+ +	$0.00	X
	360W Retrofit High-Pressure Sodium	60	+ +	$67.20	X
1,000W Mercury Vapor	880W Retrofit High-Pressure Sodium	160	+ +	$59.50	X
1,000W Mercury Vapor	950W Retrofit Metal Halide	50	+ +	$42.00	X

All numbers shown are approximations, and certain cases assumptions are made about the types of fixtures and other conditions involved. Consult manufacturers for acccurate data relative to direct replacements possible for a given installation as well as any ballast, operating temperatures or other restrictions which may apply.

Notes:

1. Wattage savings include ballast losses, where applicable. Actual ballast losses to be experienced depend on the specific type of ballast involved and operating conditions which affect its performance. In those cases where wattage savings exceed the difference in lamp wattage (if any), operation of the replacement lamp also has the effect of reducing ballast losses.
2. Symbols used indicate the following: + + (substantially more) + (more) = (about the same) - (less) -- (substantially less). Consult manufacturers for accurate information relative to conditions unique to the lamps and installations involved.

Source: Alan Meyers, "Hotel Lighting: Some Illuminating Facts," *Lodging Hospitality*, Dec. 1983, p. 52.

be difficult, many operations have chosen to implement mechanical methods to accomplish this same effect.

One area which certainly lends itself to mechanical control is exterior lighting, including parking lots. Photocell control for exterior lighting is highly recommended and, in comparison to either manual or time clock control, should result in substantial energy savings with a minimal initial investment. (Time clock control for this lighting must frequently be reset in order to operate the lighting only when needed.) In locations within the property which benefit from natural lighting, management may wish to install photocell control as well. In these instances, the photocell control acts to maintain a preset light level in the area and either dims or turns off lamps as the amount of natural light increases. As long as the lamps are not serving an aesthetic effect, this can be quite effective in reducing energy costs.

To control the operation of lights in meeting rooms, storerooms, mechanical spaces, and other areas where lights do not need to operate continuously, the use of ultrasonic sensors or twist timers may be appropriate. Ultrasonic sensors turn on the lights when they sense movement in the room. Following a preset period of inactivity in the room, the lights are switched off. Twist timers are manually activated by the person wanting to use the space and automatically turn off after a period of time. The length of time they operate is dictated by the type of timer and the degree to which it is turned.

Application

11.1 Case Study of Lighting Retrofit

In 1982 and 1983, the management of the Hilton Florida Center launched a major program to improve the efficiency of their lighting system and reduce their lighting costs.[4] They contracted for replacement of over 1,000 incandescent fixtures with fluorescent lamps at a cost of $17,500. They also installed reflectors in other fixtures which allowed the lamp wattage to be reduced significantly. Projected savings for these activities was over $2,000 per month at electric rates near $.07 per kwh.

Among the changes made to the lighting system were:

- Replacement of 20-watt incandescent bulbs in the exit lights with 4- or 6-watt fluorescent lamps, resulting in energy savings of $1,500 per year for an initial cost of $570. Additional benefits of this change included a doubling of the lamp life, reducing maintenance costs.
- In the bathrooms, 75-watt incandescent lamps were replaced with 9-watt fluorescents. Two 60-watt lamps were replaced with one 19-watt fluorescent. Costs were $6,700 and savings were $8,700 per year.
- In the lobby, 75-watt flood lamps were replaced with 25-watt incandescent bulbs and reflectors. In the lounge, 150-watt pink flood lamps were replaced with 60-watt lamps with reflectors. This combination of lower wattage bulbs and reflectors was used at a number of other locations within the hotel.
- Around the pool and patio, 150-watt lamps were replaced with two 13-watt fluorescent lamps with an 8-month payback.
- Further savings resulted from reducing light output from several 4-foot fluorescent fixtures which were overlighting doors, hallways, and stairs. Light levels were cut and wattage reduced by installation of a lighting control system with savings of $4,100 per year and an initial cost of $3,200.

Notes

1. NFPA 101, *Life Safety Code* (Quincy, Mass.: National Fire Protection Association, 1985).
2. NFPA 70, *National Electrical Code* (Quincy, Mass.: National Fire Protection Association, 1986).
3. Reprinted with permission from NFPA 70-87, *National Electrical Code®*, Copyright ©1986, National Fire Protection Association, Quincy, Mass., 02269. This reprinted material is not the complete and official position of the NFPA on the referenced subject, which is represented only by the standard in its entirety.
4. Warrock, Anna M., "Hotel Cedes 7 Months' Savings for Total Lighting Retrofit," *Energy User News*, 11 July 1983.

12
Fire Protection and Smoke Control Systems

Fires in the Hospitality Industry

Fire safety has long been a major concern of lodging managers, who recognize the need to devote attention and resources to this issue. Exhibit 12.1 summarizes statistics on hotel/motel fires for 1979–1985. The dollar figures reported are for property damage only. Since the cost of lost business may exceed that of property damage and since settlements of personal injury claims in some major lodging industry fires have been in the hundreds of millions of dollars, the actual dollar cost of fires is much higher than these figures indicate. And of course these figures say nothing of the cost in terms of human life and suffering. Although hotel and motel fires were responsible for less than 2% of all civilian fire deaths and less than 2.5% of all civilian fire injuries in 1985, the magnitude of certain hotel fires during the 1980s (for example, the MGM Grand in Las Vegas) has led to great public interest in lodging industry fire safety. In many instances, this interest has resulted in fire safety codes and laws which directly affect lodging properties.

Locations, Causes, and the Development of Fires

The National Fire Protection Association (NFPA) states that, since 1971, fire departments across the country have reported that hotel fires start most often in bedrooms, living rooms, storage areas, laundry rooms, and means of egress.

> The heat of ignition is most often supplied by cigarettes, matches, electrical equipment, and, in some cases, is applied by human hands. . . . Incendiarism as a cause of fatal hotel fires increases as the number of fatalities increases. For instance, in hotel fires where there are one or two fatalities, incendiary or suspicious fires account for only 11.03% of the total incidents. In fires with three or more fatalities, 32.35% of the total are incendiary or suspicious. And in fires with five or more fatalities, 50% of the fires are incendiary or suspicious.[1]

Data from one international lodging chain for fires which resulted in no deaths or serious injuries indicates that human error accounted for 72% of the reported fires over a 20-month period. Equipment failure accounted for 15%, electrical problems for 9%, and arson for 4%. Property losses were by far the largest for kitchen fires, with an average loss of almost $10,000 per incident.[2]

Given the possibility of arson, it should be apparent that hotels will never be free from the risk of fire. However, certain property design features, adequate warning and suppression equipment, sensitivity to individuals who may pose a risk to the property and its guests and employees, and the proper reaction of employees when faced with fire situations can reduce the risk of fires.

A fire will generally move through four stages. The *incipient* stage is characterized by invisible products of combustion, with no visible

Exhibit 12.1 Hotel/Motel Fires: 1979–1985

YEAR	CIVILIAN FIRE DEATHS	CIVILIAN FIRE INJURIES	NUMBER OF FIRES	PROPERTY LOSSES (MILLIONS)
1979	140	1,225	11,500	$100
1980	165	1,075	11,500	$154
1981	90	850	11,500	$ 99
1982	75	450	10,500	$ 84
1983	80	450	9,000	$ 64
1984	120	300	9,000	$ 50
1985	85	375	7,500	$ 56

Source: Compiled from *Fire Journal*, September issues of 1980–86.

smoke, flame, or appreciable heat present. At the *smoldering* stage, combustion products are visible as smoke, but flame and appreciable heat are still not present. The *flame* stage exhibits fire and smoke, but not appreciable heat. In the *heat* stage, the fire is characterized by uncontrolled heat and rapidly expanding air, with varying amounts of smoke depending on the material burning. The heat stage usually quickly follows the flame stage, while the incipient and smoldering stages may exist for many minutes or even hours.

Further definitions of terms used in fire protection can be found in Exhibit 12.2. The exhibit's definition of fire loading refers to heats of combustion, which are listed for some commonly used substances in Exhibit 12.3.

Business Implications of Fire Safety

The need for fire safety in lodging properties and the problems in the industry which have highlighted this need have had significant business impacts. Properties which have experienced a major fire are often closed for long periods in order to repair the damage. Besides the cost of this repair, there is the lost business associated with the closure of the facility, the payroll costs incurred for key personnel who are retained during this period, and the cost of training new staff when the facility is reopened. The local government's response to a major fire has often been to tighten the local fire code, resulting in the expenditure of millions of dollars for upgrading of systems at all properties in the area, even those which were unaffected by the fire. Almost invariably, when the property which has had a major fire reopens, it has installed a state-of-the-art fire protection system.

A secondary impact on the property's business arises from the actions of meeting planners and some corporations. Because of the responsibility and risk associated with being the individual(s) scheduling a meeting place, it is now a much more common practice for meeting planners to include a property's fire safety system in their evaluation criteria when assessing the property's suitability as a site for a meeting or convention. Due in part to a hotel fire in which a number of a corporation's executives attending a meeting perished, businesses have also begun to investigate the fire safety of properties at which their employees are staying. An increased emphasis on fire safety is not merely a code requirement or a decision based on the personal values of the property owner—it is also good business.

Industry Responses to Fire Protection and Smoke Control

The American Hotel & Motel Association (AH&MA) has surveyed industry technological responses to fire protection in terms of major types of technology. Exhibit 12.4 is a summary of surveys conducted in 1980 and 1983 (the most recent published surveys). Obviously, there were dramatic increases in the use of certain types of fire protection technology from 1980 to 1983.

The 1983 survey also addressed activity in two new areas, smoke control and fireproof/fire-retardant interior furnishings. Smoke control was added because the major threat to life in many fires is smoke. Fireproof/fire-retardant furnishings were of interest for the same reason, and because many fires begin in guestrooms, especially those which can be attributed to cigarettes.

The following sections of this chapter discuss several technological responses to fire protection.

Detection Systems

Detection systems are installed to warn that fire or smoke is present. Some detectors may also initiate suppression or containment actions. The type of detection system installed will depend on the location and nature of the hazards.[3]

Exhibit 12.2 Terms and Definitions

Several terms which are helpful in understanding the jargon of fire protection are defined below:

Flash point: The lowest temperature at which sufficient vapor will be given off to form an ignitable or flammable mixture with air near the surface of the material or within the container.

Ignition temperature: The minimum temperature to which a material must be heated in order to initiate or cause self- sustained combustion independent of the heating element.

Fire point: A temperature slightly above the flash point at which continuous combustion takes place.

Lower explosive or ***flammability limit (LEL):*** Minimum concentration of vapors in air or oxygen below which the propagation of flame will not occur even in the presence of an ignition source (may be expressed as a percentage or as parts per million).

Upper explosive or ***flame limit (UEL):*** A representation of the point at which there is a maximum content of vapor or gas in air, above which propagation of flame will not occur (may be expressed as a percentage or as parts per million).

Class I ("flammable") liquids: Liquids which have a flash point below 100°F. Class IA liquids have flash points below 73°F and boiling points below 100°F. Class IB liquids have flash points below 73°F and boiling points at or above 100°F. Class IC liquids are liquids with flash points between 73°F and 100°F.

Class II ("combustible") liquids: Liquids which have a flash point at or above 100°F and below 140°F.

Class III liquids: Broken down into IIIA (flash points between 140°F and 200°F) and class IIIB (flash points 200°F and above).

Fire loading: A measurement of the combustibles within an area. Where only class A materials are involved, fire-loading measurements consist of obtaining the total weight of these materials and dividing by the area to obtain an average in pounds per square foot (psf). More accurately, this should be done by calculating the caloric content of the combustibles present. Most class A materials have heats of combustion from 7,000 to 9,000 Btu/lb, while flammable liquids have approximately twice that amount. The heat values of some common substances are given in Exhibit 12.3. A structure with a low fire loading is one which does not exceed 100,000 Btu/ft^2.

Fire resistance rating: The length of time (typically in hours) which a structure or structural members can resist a fire, usually before each can no longer support loads.

Flame spread: A relative classification of the degree of promulgation of flame down a sample of material. The bases of the numeric values (which start at zero) are for the material compared with asbestos board (having a flame spread of 0) and red oak (rated 100).

Fuel contributed and smoke developed ratings: Calculated on the same basis as flame spread and with the same materials for comparison.

Interior finish classifications: Class A interior finishes have a flame spread of 0-25; class B, 26-75; class C, 76-200; class D, 201-500; and class E, over 500. The Life Safety Code stipulates the required class of interior finish for certain areas of facilities and allows higher classifications or flame spreads where sprinkler protection is provided.

Intumescence: A characteristic of fire-retardant coatings which causes them to react when exposed to flame by transforming into a thick insulating mat. Such coatings are used to reduce flame spread.

Smoke Detectors

Smoke detectors respond to minute particles generated by fire. *Ionization detectors* consist of one or two chambers containing a small source of radioactivity. Alpha or beta rays emitted from the radioactive source ionize the air between two electrically charged plates in the sensing chamber and cause a current to flow. Particles entering the chamber change the impedance, cause a voltage shift, and trigger an alarm. Ionization detectors respond most rapidly to the smaller particles created by fast-flaming fire.

Photoelectric detectors operate by responding to the reflection (scattering) or absorbtion (obscuration) of light by smoke particles. The more common type uses the light-scattering principle. A light source, usually a light-emitting diode (LED), is mounted on one side of the device, and a light receiver, usually a photo diode, is mounted on the other side so that the receiver is not directly exposed to the LED. Smoke particles entering the detector reflect light onto the receiver, changing its conductivity and causing the device to activate or sound. In obscuration detectors, the light receiver is directly exposed to the LED. Smoke particles entering the detector absorb some of the light, changing the receiver's conductivity and causing it to activate. Photoelectric detectors respond to the larger particles of smoldering fires.

Heat Detectors

Heat detectors are the least expensive type of detector and are used to protect large areas where life safety and early warning are not the major concern. They have the lowest unwanted alarm rate[4] and are the slowest to respond. There are three major types of heat detectors: fixed temperature, rate-of-rise, and rate compensation.

Fixed temperature devices activate when a preset temperature is reached, although the ambient temperature may be significantly higher due to thermal lag. Rate-of-rise detectors depend on the sharp increase in air temperature that is expected to occur in the area above a fire. These devices activate when the rate of temperature change exceeds a preset amount (usually 15F°/minute), but compensate for the normal ambient temperature changes that occur. Rate compensation detectors are similar to rate-of-rise detectors, but compensate for thermal lag in their design. They are less susceptible to unwanted alarms and more suitable to hazardous atmospheres and dirty environments than other heat detectors.

Exhibit 12.3 Heat Values of Some Commonly Used Substances

Substance	Heat of Combustion (Btu/lb)
Kraft paper	7,500
Corrugated cartons	7,700
Hardwood	8,700
Softwood	9,100
Polyvinyl chloride	8,030
Polyethylene	19,950
Polystyrene	18,700
Gasoline (various grades)	19,800-20,520
Acetone	13,228
Kerosene	19,800
Methyl alcohol	9,600
Methyl ethyl ketone	14,537
Toluol	18,252

Flame Detectors

Flame detectors optically recognize the radiation produced by fire. Flame detection systems generally are the most expensive and have a fast response time. They are found in high hazard areas. These detectors may use infrared or ultraviolet radiation detection. It is unlikely that flame detectors will be found in lodging applications, with the exception of their use on some boiler systems as safety controls.

Alarms, Controls, and Communication Systems

A fire alarm in a building can take several basic forms.[5] One form is a general building alarm in which alarms are activated for the entire building. Another form is a local alarm in which only areas near the suspected fire location are notified. Finally, the alarm may appear only at the building annunciator or control panel. An alarm may or may not automatically signal the local fire department.

Exhibit 12.4 Life Safety Technology in Use or on Order: 1983 vs 1980

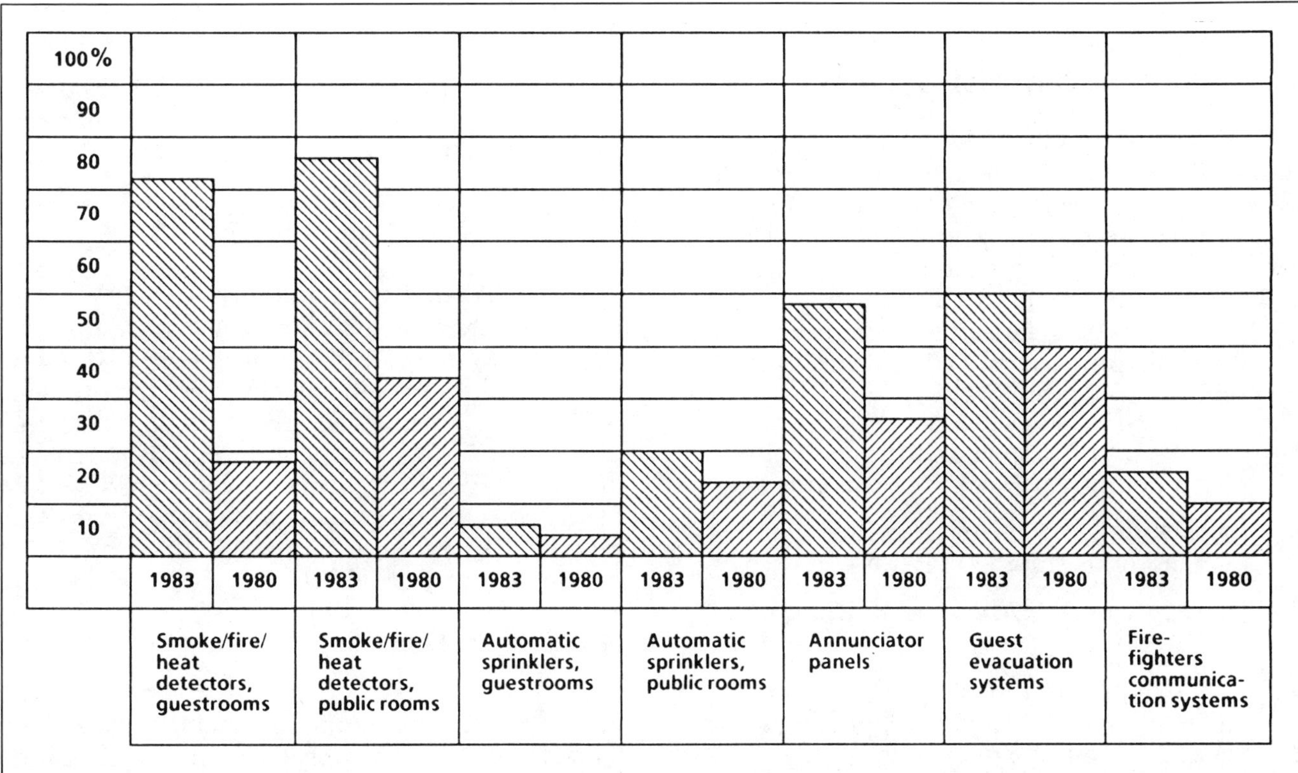

Source: *Lodging*, March 1983, p. 45.

A building (or a portion of a building) may be put into an alarm state by any of the following:

- Activation of a manual pull station
- Activation of a smoke or heat detector connected to the central building control panel
- The sensing of flow in a sprinkler standpipe
- Activation of the building alarm from the central building control panel

While the standard building alarm is still a horn or similar device, there is increased use of voice communication systems which have a recorded message and the capability for direct one-way communication to provide instructions. In addition to an audible alarm, the use of a visual alarm, such as a flashing light, is also becoming more common.

In high-rise properties, the evacuation of an entire facility under a fire alarm is difficult, potentially dangerous, and sometimes unwarranted. For these reasons, one procedure which is sometimes followed is to initiate alarm and evacuation instructions only for the floor where the fire is believed to exist and for the floor above (or the two floors above) and the floor below.

During a building alarm, the following are somewhat common control actions taken to minimize the potential hazards associated with a fire. Some are unique to high-rise buildings.

- Exhaust the fire floor and pressurize the floors above and below.
- Close fire doors and smoke doors.
- Bring elevators to the lobby and remove from service except for use by the fire department or property fire brigade.
- Notify the fire department, even if automatic notification is supposed to occur.
- Staff the fire command center.

- Station staff in fire stairwells to aid guests exiting the building.

Extinguishing Systems

All methods of fire extinguishing rely on the removal of one of the elements necessary for a fire to exist. These elements are (1) a combustible material, (2) an oxidizing agent, (3) a temperature sufficient to raise the temperature of the fuel to its ignition temperature and to sustain combustion, and (4) a means of sustaining the combustion chain or reaction. Extinguishing systems function in one of four ways:[6]

1. By lowering the temperature below the ignition point, which requires a cooling agent.
2. By excluding oxygen or air, which requires a blanketing or smothering effect.
3. By removing fuel, such as shutting off the gas supply.
4. By breaking or inhibiting the combustion chain or reaction using extinguishing agents such as Halon or dry chemicals.

Portable Extinguishers

Portable extinguishers are useful for attacking a fire in its early stages or in locations where other means of fire suppression are not available or practical. There are various types of extinguishers, denoted by the letters A, B, C, and D (which correspond to the various classes of fires). Class A extinguishers are used on wood and paper fires and basically use water, although multipurpose dry chemicals are also suitable. Class B extinguishers are useful on flammable (class I) and combustible (class II) liquids and function by either removing oxygen or inhibiting the combustion chain. Examples of class B extinguishers are those using carbon dioxide, foam, or dry chemicals. Class C extinguishers are used on energized electrical equipment where a non-conducting extinguishing material such as carbon dioxide is needed. Class D extinguishers (for use on a variety of combustible metals) are not encountered in the lodging industry.

For portable extinguishers to function effectively as part of a fire protection program:[7]

- They must be properly located.
- They must be in proper working order.
- The proper types of extinguishers must be present for the hazards encountered.
- The fire must be discovered while still small enough for the extinguisher to be effective.
- Persons who know how to use the extinguishers must be available.

The "ABC" or general purpose extinguisher is a dry chemical extinguisher which may be used on any class A, B, or C fire. For this reason, it is sometimes installed to eliminate the problem of choosing which extinguisher to purchase and use. However, the monoammonium phosphate in this type of extinguisher, when used on hot metal, forms deposits which may be difficult to remove. Therefore, use of an ABC extinguisher in kitchen areas should be avoided.

Sprinkler Systems

As with smoke detectors in guestrooms and hallways, requirements for the installation of sprinkler systems are proliferating. A basic understanding of sprinkler systems will serve the hotelier of the future well, since it is likely that these systems will be a standard feature in new construction in many locations.[8]

Sprinkler systems are installed with several purposes in mind. One purpose is to extinguish the fire. Another purpose is to delay the development of the fire to allow for occupants to exit and for the fire department to arrive. Sprinkler systems may be *wet*, meaning they are filled with water, or *dry*, meaning they are normally filled with compressed air or nitrogen. Most sprinkler heads use a fusible link (made of an alloy with a low melting point) which melts under fire conditions and causes the head to open. In a dry system, the compressed gas escapes, causing a loss of pressure that opens a water valve which supplies water to the system. In a wet system, the water is immediately available at the head. Should a fusible link sprinkler head open, water will continue to flow from it until it is replaced or the water is shut off. At least one vendor offers a head which will reseal itself when the temperature in the space drops to a preset level.

Application 12.1 discusses some suggested management concerns when installing fire protection systems.

Dry Chemical and Carbon Dioxide Systems

Dry chemical systems are installed in kitchen areas to provide protection for kitchen equipment and staff.[9] These systems typically use a sodium bicarbonate-based dry chemical and carbon dioxide which combine to form a foam which smothers the fire and inhibits reignition by preventing combustible vapors from escaping. The systems are activated by a fusible link located in the duct hood or above the cooking surface. The link will melt at between 280°F and 360°F (depending on the operating temperature of the ventilation system).

Carbon dioxide extinguishing equipment may be used in areas where special hazards exist.[10] These include areas with flammable liquids and electrical and electronic equipment. Since carbon dioxide extinguishes primarily by reducing the oxygen supply, it is not particularly effective in combating class A fires, where cooling or wetting action is required. In addition, the limited amounts of extinguishing material present in the system are quickly exhausted and require more special handling for replenishment. Since carbon dioxide leaves no residue, it is a clean extinguishing agent. If used in a flooding type of design, it can prove hazardous to human life, since it reduces the oxygen supply. The most likely location for a carbon dioxide system in a hospitality setting would be in the underfloor area of a data processing center.

Systems Based on Other Agents

Systems using Halon have been installed in certain high-risk settings where damage to sophisticated electronic equipment is a concern. In the lodging property, this could be data processing or reservations equipment. Also, Halon may be particularly desirable for total flooding protection of areas containing very valuable records or material, such as data processing tape.

Smoke Control

Smoke and toxic fumes are a major concern in the management of the risks associated with fires. Inhaling the smoke and fumes produced from the interior finishes and furnishings located in most commercial buildings may be fatal. Smoke control has emerged as a significant component of building fire protection.

Exhibit 12.5 Stairwell Pressurization by Multiple Injection with a Ground Level Fan

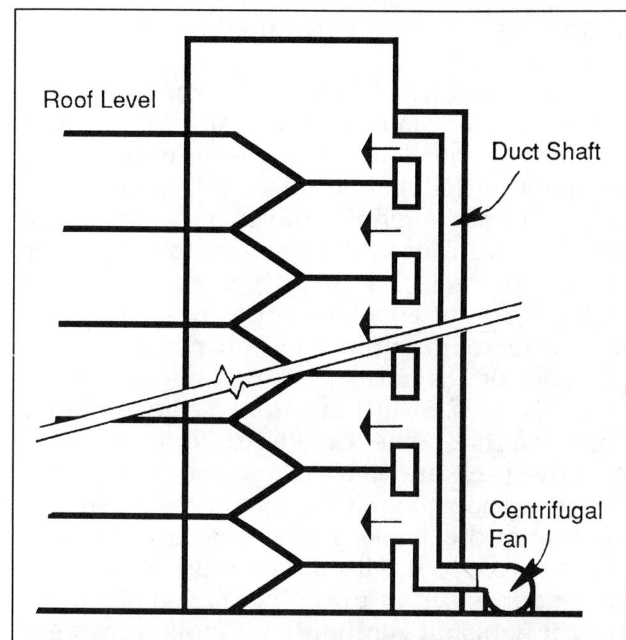

Reprinted by permission from *ASHRAE Journal*, April 1983.

Methods of Smoke Control

There are two basic principles of smoke control:

1. Airflow by itself can control smoke movement if the average air velocity is sufficient.
2. Air pressure differences across barriers can act to control smoke movement.

Smoke containment is accomplished by fixed building partitions (walls, floors) and by movable components specifically designed or installed for this purpose (such as smoke dampers in HVAC systems).

However, physical barriers are only a partial solution to smoke control. Smoke control commonly incorporates two aspects, especially in high-rise buildings. *Pressurized stairwells* are used to provide a smoke-free means of egress. *Zoned smoke control*, using pressurization and exhaust, is used to limit the migration of smoke from locations in which it is produced.

Exhibit 12.5 illustrates stairwell pressurization. The stairwell, as a means of egress, is physically separated from the building by means of fire walls and doors. When the air pressure in the stairwell is greater than that of the floors of the building, the migration of smoke into the stairwell is inhibited and the means of egress protected. In addition, a relatively smoke-free location is maintained for fire-fighting personnel.

Concerns which have been expressed about the design of stairwell pressurization systems include the need to avoid the introduction of smoke into the stairwells by the pressurization fans. Another potential problem is overpressure, which could cause difficulties in opening doors to the stairwells. At the other extreme, there may be loss of adequate pressurization during fires due to multiple door openings and the presence of fire hoses blocking doors open.

Exhibit 12.6 illustrates zoned smoke control, with the fire zone exhausted (operated at a negative pressure) and the non-fire zones immediately adjacent to the fire zone pressurized. The venting of the smoke zones to achieve negative pressure coupled with the pressurization of adjacent zones serves to confine the smoke to the zone in which it is produced. Smoke zone venting also achieves some reduction in smoke concentration in the vented zone and prevents significant overpressurization of the zone due to thermal expansion of gases caused by the fire. Smoke control zones are often floors of a building, although the floors themselves can be subdivided into zones as well.[11]

Exhibit 12.6 Smoke Control Zone Arrangements

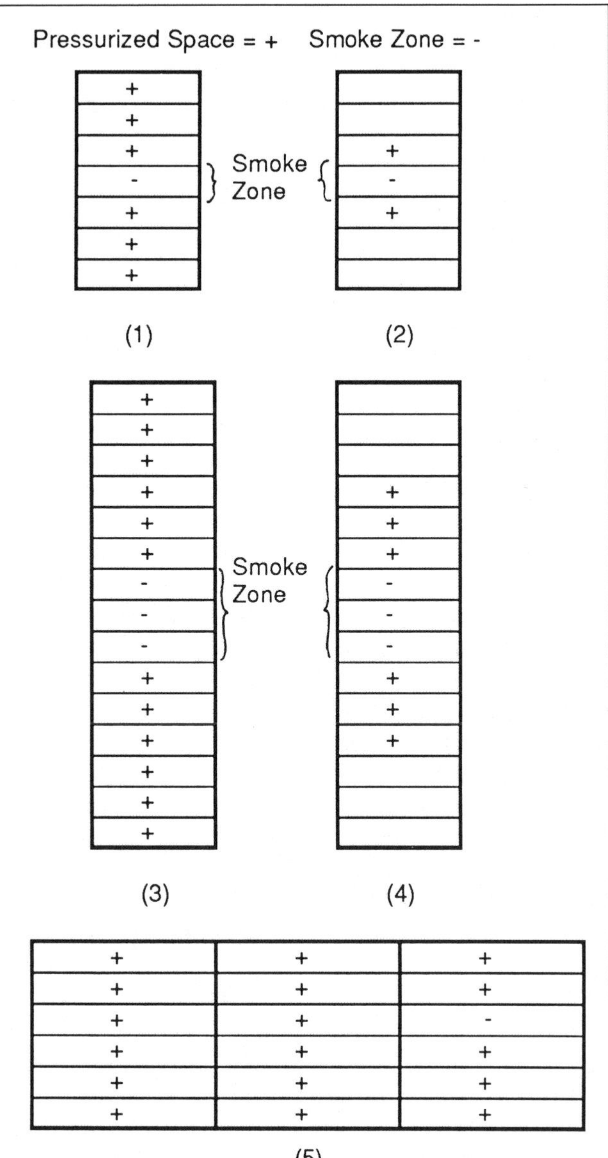

Each floor can be a smoke control zone as in (1) and (2) or a smoke zone can consist of more than one floor, as in (3) and (4). All of the non-smoke zones in a building may be pressurized as in (1) and (3), or only non-smoke zones adjacent to the smoke zone may be pressurized, as in (2) and (4). A smoke zone can also be limited to a part of a floor, as in (5).

Reprinted by permission from *ASHRAE Journal*, April 1983.

Code Regulations

Code regulations affecting fire protection and smoke control systems typically include design and structural elements (such as the fire rating of walls and doors, the flame and smoke generation allowable from wall and floor coverings, exiting requirements, and the establishment of necessary compartmentation) and provisions for building alarm systems, fire suppression equipment, smoke containment and exhaust, emergency plans, and periodic fire drills.

Exhibit 12.7 illustrates the OSHA (Occupational Safety and Health Act) requirements for fire protection systems. These are federally mandated requirements which must be complied with in addition to any local regulations.

The following discussion is based on the Life Safety Code, which serves as the basis for the fire protection codes in many locations. Not all locations will have code provisions which are

Exhibit 12.7 OSHA Requirements for Fire Protection Systems

EQUIPMENT OR SYSTEM	MANDATED OR OPTIONAL	ADVISORY OR TRAINING REQUIREMENTS	INSPECTION SCHEDULE	MAINTENANCE REQUIREMENTS	SPECIAL INSTRUCTIONS	RECORD-KEEPING REQUIREMENTS
Fire extinguisher.	Mandated.	Training to be provided in use of extinguishers at hire and retraining for all employees annually.	Visually inspected monthly.	Annual maintenance check. Dry chemical: stored pressure dry chemical emptied and provided applicable maintenance on 6-year schedule.	Hydrostatic testing of cannister every 5 years; 12 years for dry chemical. Extinguishers for wood, paper & cloth within 75 feet. Flammable liquid and electrical extinguishers within 50 feet.	Enter annual maintenance record in log. Retain for one year after last entry or life of unit, whichever is less. Date of inspection & maintenance entered on extinguisher tag.
Standpipe.	Optional, but mandated by many municipalities.	May supplant extinguishers for flammable materials (paper, wood, cloth); but local code requirements may pre-empt this OSHA option.	Employer must designate trained persons to inspect at least annually.	Lined hoses after 1/1/81. Shut-off type nozzles after 7/1/81. Maintain water supply at adequate level.	Water supply must provide 100 gallons per minute for at least 30 minutes. Valves in main piping open and operative at all times, except during repair.	Not required, but a maintenance log entry is recommended.
Automatic Sprinkler Systems.	Not mandated, but apply where sprinklers are installed.	Local waterflow alarm will provide an audible alarm on premises when water flows through the system at a rate equal to the flow from a single sprinkler. Persons trained in shut-off locations.	Main-drain flow test annually. Inspector's valve opened at least every 2 years.	Risers, lines, sprinkler heads and valves on regular maintenance schedule.	Proper acceptance tests: 1. Flushing of underground connections 2. Hydrostatic testing of system piping 3. Air tests in dry-pipe systems 4. Dry-pipe valve operation air tests 5. Test of drainage facilities. Water supply must be able to deliver design waterflow for at least 30 minutes.	Record of acceptance tests must be maintained.
Fixed extinguishing systems, usually in kitchen hoods or computer rooms.	Not mandated, but required in most local jurisdictions or by insurance companies.	If the flooding agent is a potential health hazard, as with a chemical gas in a computer room, a pre-discharge alarm-and-delay for evacuation must be incorporated in the system. Appropriate warning signs must be posted where chemical concentrations may occur. The employer shall train employees designated to inspect, maintain, operate or repair these systems, with annual retraining.	Annual system check. Weight and pressure check, as required semi-annually.	Sample dry chemical supplied at least annually to prevent caking or lumping.	At least one manual station must be provided for discharge activation. Devices must be identified as to hazard against which they provide protection. Employees must be trained in operation of such devices and use of personal protective equipment in event of total flooding of an area by a chemical suppressant.	Inspection and maintenance dates must be recorded on the container, on a tag attached to the container, or in a central location. A record of the last semi-annual check shall be maintained until the next check or for the life of the container, whichever is less.
Fire Detection.	Not mandated; but required in many jurisdictions.	All servicing, maintenance and testing of fire detection systems, including cleaning and necessary sensitivity adjustments, must be performed by a trained person. A warning for emergency action and safe escape of employees must be incorporated with a fire detection system.	On a continuing basis to meet maintenance requirements as noted in next column.	Must be tested and adjusted as often as needed to maintain proper reliability and operating condition. Fire detectors must be cleaned of dirt, dust, or other particulate to maintain a fully operational system.	All systems installed after 1/1/81 must be supervised systems. Response time for systems actuating fire extinguishment of suppression systems must be adequate for controlling or extinguishing a fire. Alarms or devices activated by detectors shall not be delayed beyond 30 seconds, unless such delay is necessary for employee safety.	Not specified, but it is suggested a log of system servicing be maintained.
Employee Alarm Systems.	Mandated.	Must provide sufficient warning for safe evacuation of employees from fire-involved areas. All employees shall be trained in nature of alarm system, how activated; and each employee's individual and appropriate response.	Test of reliability and adequacy of non-supervised employee alarm systems shall be made every two months. All supervised employee alarm systems, annually.	Back-up and power replacement supplies shall be maintained as needed.	All systems after 1/1/81 which are capable of being supervised will be supervised. Manually operated actuation devices for the employee alarms must be unobstructed, conspicuous and readily accessible.	Maintenance log recommended.

Exhibit 12.8 Summary of Selected Major Building Fire Safety System Requirements for Lodging Properties

	ATL	BOS	CHIC	DAL	HOUS	LA	NY	SF	TAM	W DC
Number of Properties	71	28	270	140*	350	227	463	500	250	111
Number of High Rise Properties (HR)	37	22	90*	35	50	30	190*	50	27	85**
Requirement:										
Fire Alarm System	Yes	Yes	Yes	Yes	Yes	Yes	Yes	Yes	Yes	Yes
Full Detection System +	No	Yes	No	No	No	No	No	No	No	No
Auto Alarm to FD/CS	Yes (HR)	Yes	Yes (HR)	Yes (HR)	No	Yes (HR)	Yes (HR)	Yes	Yes	No
Full Sprinkler Prot.	Yes (HR)	Yes (HR)	No	No	Yes (HR)	Yes (HR)	Yes	Yes (HR)	Yes (HR)	No
Water Flow Alarm to FD	Yes (HR)	Yes	Yes (HR)	No	Yes	No	Yes	Yes	Yes	No
Elev. Auto Return	Yes	No	No	Yes (HR)	Yes	Yes	Yes	Yes	Yes	Yes
HVAC Auto Controls	Yes	Yes	Yes (HR)	Yes	Yes (HR)	Yes (HR)	Yes	Yes	Yes	No + +
Public Address System	Yes (HR)	Yes (HR)	Yes (HR)	Yes	Yes (HR)	Yes	Yes	Yes (HR)	Yes	No
Self Closing Door	Yes	Yes	Yes	No	Yes	Yes	Yes	Yes	Yes	No
Guest Information	Yes	Yes	Yes	Yes	Yes	Yes	Yes	Yes	Yes	Yes
Fire Brigade	Yes	Yes	No	Yes (HR)	Yes	No	No	No	Yes	No
Carpet and Floor Finish	Yes	Yes	No	No	No	No	Yes	No	Yes	No
Curtain/Drapery	Yes	Yes	Yes	Yes	Yes	Yes	Yes	Yes	Yes	Yes
Upholstered Furniture	No	Yes	No	No	No	No	No	No	Yes + + +	No
Mattresses	No	Yes	No	No	No	No	No	No	No	No

* Estimated
** All buildings in Washington D.C. are limited in height to 13 stories, or less.
\+ Every room covered by auto detection or sprinklers
\+ + HVAC controls for buildings with atriums
\+ + + Only coverings regulated

Source: "Fire Codes and Laws for Hotels in Ten U.S. Cities" (a 1985 survey conducted by the Boston Fire Department).

as stringent and others will have more stringent provisions. Exhibit 12.8 is a summary of fire system requirements for lodging properties in major United States cities. There are obviously significant variations in the code provisions from city to city. The local codes specify the *minimum* requirements in the locality. Properties sometimes choose to exceed these minimum standards.

Assembly Occupancies

The Life Safety Code defines *assembly occupancies* as "all buildings or portions of buildings used for gathering together 50 or more persons for such purposes as deliberation, worship, entertainment, amusement, or awaiting transportation." Within the hospitality industry, the following assembly occupancies may be present: restaurants, drinking establishments, assembly halls, exhibition halls, dance halls, club rooms, theaters, and skating rinks.

Chapters 8 and 9 of the Code concern new and existing places of assembly. These chapters outline provisions for occupant loads, means of egress, interior finish, extinguishment and suppression systems, and alarm and communication systems. The alarm and communication system requirements in assembly occupancies are interrelated. No automatically sounding alarm is required (in order to avoid panicking a large group of people). Instead, the alarm is to sound in a constantly manned location. A public address system with an emergency power source is required, which can be used to communicate with the people in attendance.

Residential Occupancies

The Life Safety Code defines *residential occupancies* as "those occupancies in which sleeping accommodations are provided for normal residential purposes, [including] all buildings designed to provide sleeping accommodations." Hotels and motels are specifically considered under this classification. The Code limits the types of interior finishes which are allowed and requires:

- the enclosure of stairways, elevator shafts, and other vertical openings.
- a building alarm system which can notify occupants of the building or section thereof that is endangered by a fire.
- immediate notification of the fire department in the event of fire.

Voice communication systems in buildings over seven stories tall and emergency power to one elevator for use by the fire department in case of fire for buildings over six stories tall are required for new lodging occupancies.

Interior Finishes

The provisions of the Life Safety Code for interior finishes vary somewhat, depending on the location within the property. Finish materials are rated A–E based on their flame spread. Class A materials are required in vertical exits, while class A or B materials are required in locations of exit access and lobbies and other corridors. Individual guestrooms may have A, B or C finishes. Assembly occupancies may have class A or B finishes in general assembly areas and, in facilities with capacities of from 50 to 300 persons, may have class C materials.

Management Responsibilities

Emergency Procedures

Emergency procedures at lodging establishments are a combination of OSHA requirements, local code stipulations, corporate policies, and facility-based variations. The resulting variations in emergency procedures are quite great. In this section, we address those provisions which are found in OSHA and the Life Safety Code only. Property-specific requirements and corporate edicts, although potentially important, are too varied to be treated here.

OSHA requirements define some of the needs for emergency procedures at a property. One area specifically addressed by OSHA concerns means of egress. The Means of Egress Standard discusses employee emergency plans and fire prevention plans. The plans must:

- be written.
- indicate emergency escape procedures and route assignments.
- provide procedures for employees who remain to operate critical hotel or motel operations before evacuating.
- provide a procedure to account for all employees after an emergency evacuation has been completed.
- establish rescue and medical duties for employees or local services.
- give the preferred means of reporting fires and other emergencies.
- provide the names or regular job titles of persons or departments who can be contacted for further information or explanation of duties under the plan.

The law further requires training and annual retraining of employees to effectively implement the emergency evacuation program.

The Life Safety Code states that all employees must be instructed and drilled monthly in their emergency duties. When a fire is discovered, employees should notify the front office, the public fire department, and the private fire brigade. Guests and others who are or could be endangered should be warned and assisted to safety. Rooms should be searched to ensure that all occupants have escaped. Elevators should be competently manned. Extinguishing equipment should be used to extinguish or control the fire and the public fire department (which assumes full command upon arrival) should be met upon arrival and directed to the location of the fire.

The Life Safety Code also stipulates the treatment of certain equipment. Fire pumps and ventilating equipment should be ready for instant operation. If refrigerating equipment is clearly in danger, it should be turned off and its refrigerant should be blown to a sewer or into the atmosphere to prevent an explosion. Generators and motors should be protected from water damage by tarpaulins. While generators should keep operating to provide power to lighting and elevators, unneeded motors should be turned off. Endangered boilers should be extinguished or have their fire and lower steam pressure dumped by blowing to a sewer or the atmosphere to prevent possible explosions.

The Code also calls for emergency instructions for guests to be posted in every guestroom and establishes standards for furnishings and decorations.[12]

Applications

12.1 Preventing Pitfalls in Fire Protection Systems

While the design of a fire protection system may initially be adequate, changes in various factors can compromise the design.[13] For example, the local water supply pressure can change as the system is expanded or as additional pumping capacity or new loads are added to the system. The resulting supply pressure may be too low to adequately supply water to the building fire protection system or so high that it overpressures the system when the fire pump operates. Also, changes in the use of space can result in inadequate protection. A change in the position of storage racks can compromise the effectiveness of a sprinkler system.

Installation of fire pumps requires careful consideration and design. The potential for developing high pressures in the lines when pumps are operating must be considered and designed for. Failure to do so can lead to damaged valves and piping and injuries to fire fighters when the systems are operated. Failure to isolate the electrical supply for the fire pump from areas where a fire is likely to occur may result in a loss of power to the pump when a fire occurs. Installation of adequate indicator, alarm, and supervisory signals can help to diagnose problems and avoid operation of fire pumps at inappropriate times.

Piping installation is another possible source of problems. Cleanliness during pipe installation, adequate flushing of new piping, removal of blocks on check valves, testing of alarms, detectors, and supervisory devices, and pressure tests of systems are all important and sometimes neglected elements of proper system installation.

Ongoing maintenance is required to ensure the continued reliability of systems. Inspections for leaks, closed valves, damaged or blocked alarms, and frozen water storage tanks, draining of condensate from dry pipe systems and air compressors, testing of fire pumps, and a general awareness of potential system problems will contribute to a reliable system. NFPA 13A, *Inspection, Testing, and Maintenance of Sprinkler Systems*, provides some guidance in the care of fire protection systems. Careful attention to manufacturers' maintenance recommendations is also warranted.

12.2 Restaurant Fire Prevention and Hood Design

Since kitchen fires are potentially costly in terms of property damage and their effect on restaurant or convention food service revenue, they deserve special concern. NFPA 96, *Removal of Smoke and Grease-Laden Vapors from Commercial Cooking Equipment*, provides guidelines for not only ventilation, but also fire protection systems for kitchens.

The proper operation of grease removal devices is a key element in an overall restaurant fire protection system. If filters are used, they must be cleaned and drained of grease as needed. If extractor systems are installed, they must be washed down as needed with the appropriate detergent.

The extinguishing system includes automatic shutoffs for cooking fuel, detectors at various locations, piping and spray nozzles for the extinguishing materials, a remote manual pull located in the path of egress (for times when the system has failed to activate automatically), and an extinguishing material.

Kitchen fires pose unique problems because of the peculiar chemical nature of fats and oils used in the cooking process.[14] The ignition temperature of fat is 620°F, the fire point approximately 500°F, and the flash point 450°F. When burning within a duct in the kitchen, the flame temperature can reach more than 2,000°F. Because of these high temperatures, the use of refractory exhaust ducts is discussed in NFPA 96. Carbon steel or stainless steel exhaust ducts are not capable of withstanding these high temperatures, nor are the solder alloys used to assemble these materials.

Gladstone suggests that the exhaust fans be thermostatically controlled. This avoids the premature shutdown of the fans, which would result in a temperature increase of the filters and the possibility of fire as oil is dehydrogenated and has its flash point lowered. He further suggests that a lack of attention to maintenance results in lowered air flow—for example, when grease and dirt build up on the filter and pose additional air resistance or when the fan belt slips. Lowered air flow causes the duct temperature to rise and the amount of air moved to decrease, and contributes to an increase in the overall fire hazard. Besides these operational considerations, the designer of a hood system should remember that it is a *system*. Many components must interact with one another. Proper use of fan rating criteria, the effect on fan performance of a lack of discharge ducting, and the effect of temperature on air density are some of the points which are often neglected and which, if considered, will contribute to fire *prevention*.

Notes

1. Jon C. Jones, "A Brief Look at the Hotel Fire Record," *Hotel Fires—Behind the Headlines* (Quincy, Mass.: National Fire Protection Association, undated). This book contains case studies of several lodging industry fires and is an excellent reference for those interested in further information concerning specific fires.
2. William Webster and Valentine A. Lehr, "Statistical Analysis of Hotel Fires," *Heating/Piping/Air Conditioning*, Oct. 1985, pp. 94–101.
3. This discussion of detection systems has generally been abstracted from Jeanine Katzel, "An Overview of Automatic Fire Detectors: Smoke, Heat, and Flame," *Plant Engineering*, Sept. 27, 1984, pp. 36–42.
4. An *unwanted* alarm results from the correct functioning of the alarm at an inappropriate time—for example, a smoke alarm responding to thick cigar smoke. A *false* alarm results from malfunctioning equipment or the deliberate action of a person.
5. There exist several variations on these basic forms. For further information, see NFPA 71, *Installation, Maintenance, and Use of Central Station Signaling Systems* (Quincy, Mass.: National Fire Protection Association, 1985); NFPA 72A, *Installation, Maintenance, and Use of Local Protective Signaling Systems* (Quincy, Mass.: National Fire Protection Association, 1985); NFPA 72B, *Installation, Maintenance, and Use of Auxiliary Protective Signaling Systems* (Quincy, Mass.: National Fire Protection Association, 1986); NFPA 72C, *Installation, Maintenance, and Use of Remote Station Protective Signaling Systems* (Quincy, Mass.: National Fire Protection Association, 1986); and NFPA 72D, *Installation, Maintenance, and Use of Proprietary Protective Signaling Systems* (Quincy, Mass.: National Fire Protection Association, 1986).
6. Robert G. Planer, *Fire Loss Control: A Management Guide* (New York: Marcel Dekker, 1979).
7. See NFPA 10, *Portable Fire Extinguishers* (Quincy, Mass.: National Fire Protection Association, 1984) for details regarding the first three items on this list.
8. The installation of sprinkler systems is covered in NFPA 13, *Installation of Sprinkler Systems* (Quincy, Mass.: National Fire Protection Association, 1987). Other NFPA Standards should be consulted for items such as fire pumps, standpipes and hoses, fire hydrants, and other such items.
9. NFPA 17, *Dry Chemical Extinguishing Systems* (Quincy, Mass.: National Fire Protection Association, 1985), specifies requirements for such systems. Equipment installed to provide protection in kitchen areas should comply with NFPA 96, *Removal of Smoke and Grease-Laden Vapors from Commercial Cooking Equipment* (Quincy, Mass.: National Fire Protection Association, 1984). For a brief discussion of the issue of fire *prevention* in kitchen areas with an emphasis on design of exhaust fans and hoods, refer to Application 12.2.
10. NFPA 12, *Carbon Dioxide Extinguishing Systems* (Quincy, Mass.: National Fire Protection Association, 1985), provides a guide for the application and installation of these systems.
11. For further details on the design of smoke control systems, see *Design of Smoke Control Systems for Buildings* (Atlanta, Ga.: American Society of Heating, Refrigerating, and Air-conditioning Engineers, 1983).
12. This summary of Life Safety Code material is not the complete and official position of the NFPA, which is represented only by the standard in its entirety.
13. This discussion is derived from Walter A. Damon, "Preventing Pitfalls in Fire Protection Systems," *Heating/Piping/Air Conditioning*, April 1985, pp. 61–71, which presents the material in greater detail.
14. The remainder of this chapter is derived from John Gladstone, "Beyond NFPA 96: Practical Design for Restaurant Fire Prevention," *Heating/Piping/Air Conditioning*, Jan. 1985, pp. 97–105, which presents the material in greater detail.

13
Energy Management

History and Rationale

Corporate concern over energy management can generally be traced to the energy problems beginning in the early 1970s. These problems resulted in limited availability and rapid price increases of many energy forms. While facilities designers, developers, and managers should have been considering energy costs as part of their design and operating concerns before this period, many paid little attention until the rapidly escalating prices and supply problems forced the issue.

The energy problems of the 1970s and early 1980s resulted in a great deal of action by various governmental bodies attempting to control the amount of energy being consumed. Some of these actions included setting efficiency standards for appliances and restricting the amount of energy which could be used in buildings, usually by limiting the energy use per square foot of building. Because of shortages of some fuels, some utility companies also placed limits on the amount of energy which could be used by buildings. In order to stimulate user-produced power, incentives were developed by federal and state governments to encourage the development of small-scale power production, including cogeneration. All of these actions provided incentives for energy conservation.

Lodging Industry Interest and Response

Within the lodging industry, the American Hotel & Motel Association (AH&MA) initiated its Energy Technical Center in the late 1970s to provide information to the industry on energy conservation and management. The services of the Center included the compilation of data on energy usage in lodging facilities and a series of articles in *Lodging* magazine dealing with energy management. Exhibit 13.1 is a table summarizing lodging building energy use from 1977 through 1985 from the 1985 report of the Technical Services Center (the new title which encompasses the Energy Technical Center and other similar functions of the AH&MA). While the industry was apparently able to achieve some reductions in energy use in the late 1970s and early 1980s, the results reported for 1985 indicate this success may have been either short-lived or questionable. A look at the performance of various subgroups of the industry from 1982 through 1985, as illustrated in Exhibit 13.2, shows only one subgroup (the under-150-room classification) as having achieved any significant year-to-year reduction in energy use, and that reduction (from 1983 to 1984) may have been a statistical aberration, since consumption rebounded in 1985.

At the corporate level, most major lodging chains hired corporate energy managers who implemented sometimes extensive programs of energy monitoring at properties, began auditing electric utility bills for errors, provided information about potential energy conservation devices, and generally attempted to develop a corporate energy management program. This has proven to be fairly successful for some of the large chains, which can document reductions in energy usage at their facilities. Unfortunately, the priority given to energy management has diminished as a result of the improved availability of energy and the lack of price increases over the past few years.

Exhibit 13.1 Energy Consumption in Lodging Facilities

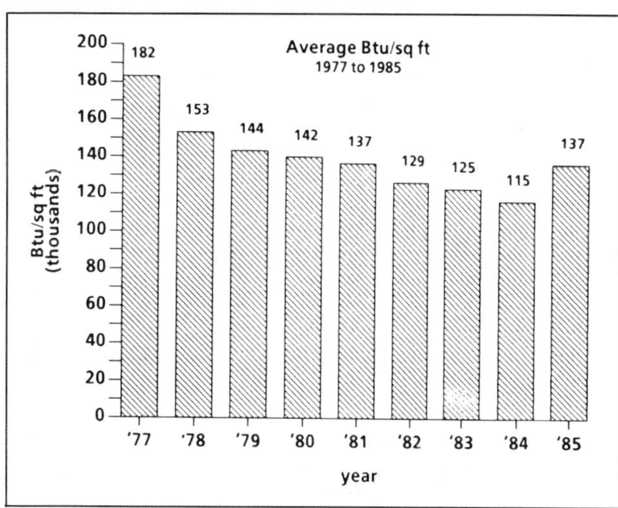

Average Btu/sq ft
1977 to 1985
Btu/sq ft (thousands)
182
153
144
142
137
129
125
115
137
'77
'78
'79
'80
'81
'82
'83
'84
'85
year

Source: *1985 Survey of Energy and Water Use in Hotels and Motels*, Technical Services Center of the Hospitality, Lodging, & Travel Research Foundation, Inc.

Methods of Approach and Program Management

While many energy programs concern themselves with the overall quantity of energy used at the property, as measured in units of Btu/ft^2, the programs really should be understood primarily as cost control programs. Energy is required at a property for many functions and its use for these purposes is a vital part of good business. No one involved in an energy management program would advocate cutting off the hot water to guestrooms to save energy. The approach of the energy management program should be to attempt to reduce energy costs to the lowest possible level consistent with the overall needs and expectations of the guests, the employees, and the building itself.

Most energy management programs begin with an audit of the building and its systems and equipment. The audit addresses such topics as

Exhibit 13.2 Energy Consumption in Lodging Facilities by Size

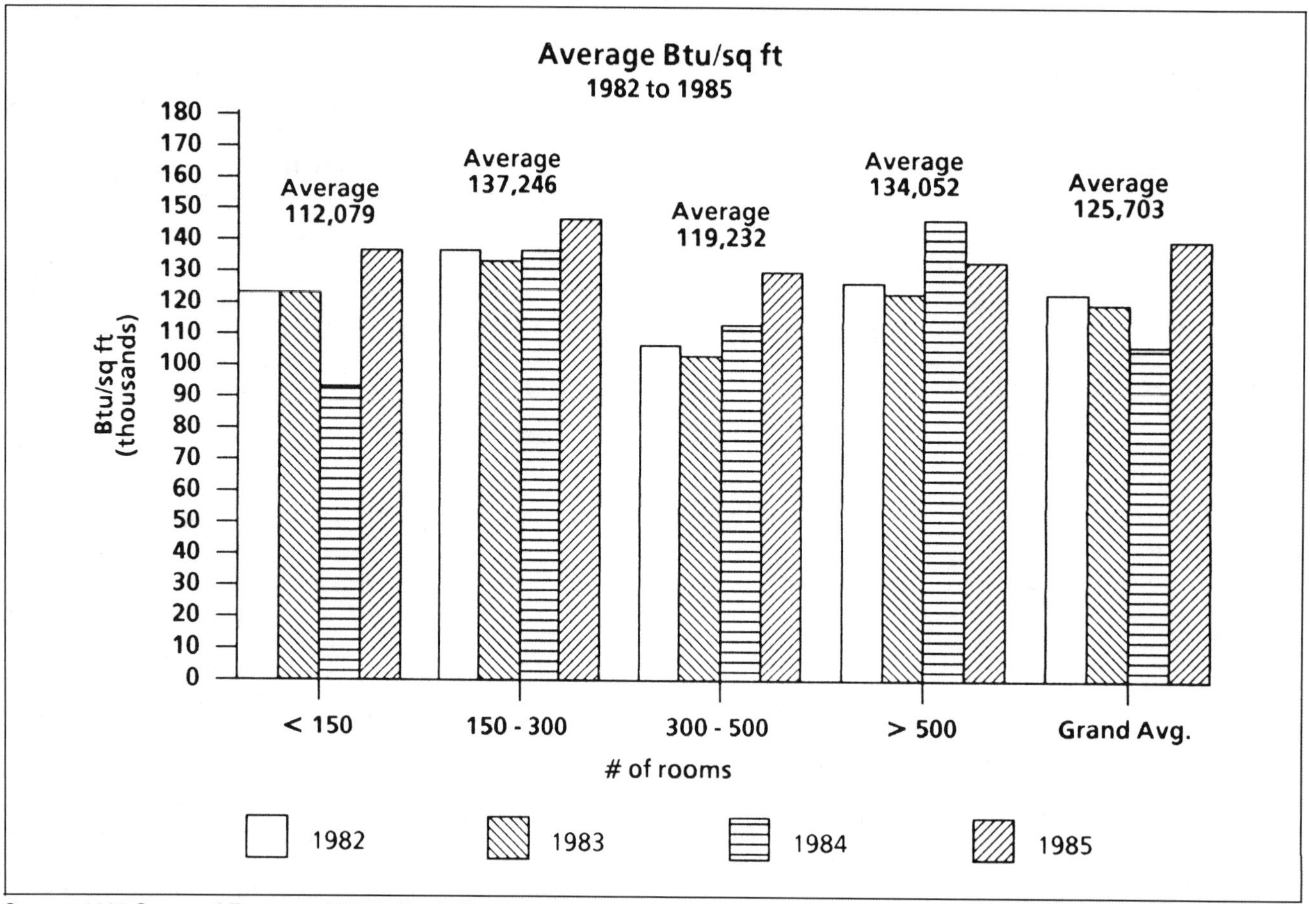

Average Btu/sq ft
1982 to 1985
Btu/sq ft (thousands)
Average 112,079
Average 137,246
Average 119,232
Average 134,052
Average 125,703
< 150
150 - 300
300 - 500
> 500
Grand Avg.
# of rooms
1982
1983
1984
1985

Source: *1985 Survey of Energy and Water Use in Hotels and Motels*, Technical Services Center of the Hospitality, Lodging, & Travel Research Foundation, Inc.

Exhibit 13.3 Monthly Energy Consumption Data for a 388-Room Hotel in Louisville, Kentucky

MONTH	KWH	THERMS
January	496,000	45,736
February	436,160	36,256
March	436,800	22,764
April	518,400	14,312
May	609,920	12,064
June	544,320	8,211
July	677,440	9,200
August	621,760	8,195
September	579,200	8,194
October	503,360	9,137
November	466,880	8,517
December	396,800	34,069

Exhibit 13.4 Graph of Electrical and Natural Gas Consumption for a 388-Room Hotel

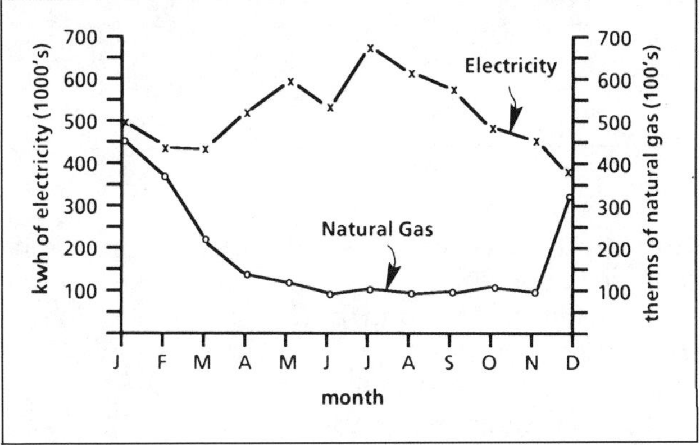

what is physically present, the efficiency and method of control of the equipment and systems, the operating hours, and the potential for modifications or changes. The audit also usually involves some analysis of utility bills to determine the amount of energy being consumed and its cost. From the audit, it is possible to develop a list of possible energy management actions and then convert the actions into estimates of energy savings and hence cost savings. Estimates of the capital cost are then used to evaluate the investment's rate of return or other relevant financial criteria. With this information, the engineering manager is in a position to approach the general manager or others with a proposed action plan for making changes in the facility to reduce its energy costs.

Exhibit 13.5 Graph of Btu Equivalents of Electrical and Natural Gas Consumption for a 388-Room Hotel

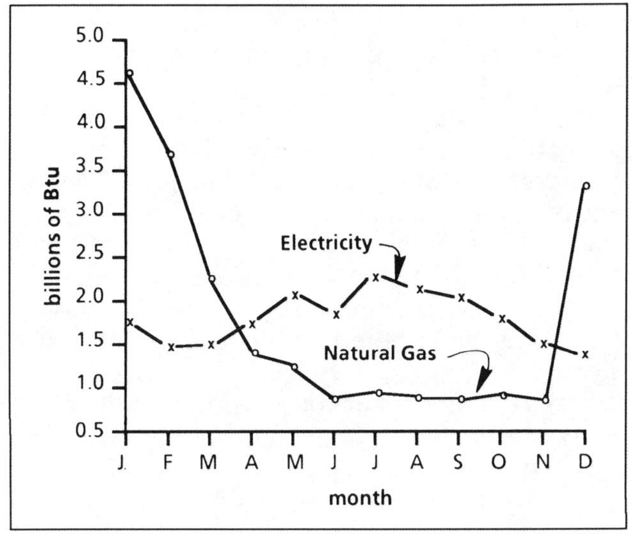

When accumulating audit information from utility bills, it is often helpful to graph the monthly energy consumption data for the property. This graph can be presented in either the actual units of consumption (for example, kwh for the electrical energy) or in common units for each fuel used, in which instance Btu would be used. Exhibits 13.3, 13.4, and 13.5 contain energy consumption data for a 388-room hotel located in Louisville, Kentucky. Exhibit 13.3 is data derived directly from the utility bills for the property showing the actual energy consumption of the facility in kwh (electricity) and therms (natural gas). Exhibit 13.4 is a graph of this consumption. Exhibit 13.5 is another graph of the energy consumption where the kwh and therms have been converted to Btu.

Exhibits 13.4 and 13.5 can be used to gain some understanding of the usage of energy at the property. With a knowledge of the systems at the facility (and with some care if occupancy shows significant monthly or seasonal variations), it is possible to broadly estimate energy consumption at the facility for certain purposes. Exhibit 13.6 illustrates a method of deriving some estimates of energy usage for space heating and cooling and other applications. These estimates can prove helpful when performing preliminary evaluations of the opportunities for energy cost control.

Since every facility is different, it is not possible to create rules which define the amount of energy which *should* be used by a facility and the purposes for which this energy should be used. In the absence of such rules or standards, individualized computer modeling of building energy usage can prove to be a helpful tool in evaluating building efficiency and the opportunity for energy conservation. Exhibit 13.7 is a summary of the results of computer modeling of energy usage for a 355-room property. While the property used to develop and test the modeling is actually located in the state of Washington, the computer model allows the property to be "moved" about the country and its energy usage estimated at various locations. As with estimates performed by analyzing utility bills, computer modeling will provide information concerning consumption for various purposes within the property. In addition, computer modeling has the potential to analyze the effect on energy consumption of changes in building design or equipment, an analysis which is somewhat difficult to perform when dealing only with data from utility bills.

The property maintenance program is one of the major allies in the property energy cost control program. Well-maintained equipment will operate more efficiently, thereby reducing energy costs. If the building exterior is well-maintained, there will be fewer air leaks, resulting in less conditioned air escaping to the outside. Repairing leaking pipes and valves conserves water and the energy used to heat this water. In addition, if the equipment installed as part of the energy management program is not maintained, a large part of its benefit may not be realized.

The AH&MA has monitored the introduction of energy control technology by periodically conducting surveys of U. S. hotels and motels. Exhibit 13.8 contains the results of one of these surveys indicating the types of technologies and the percentages of the sample using the technology, having it on order, having it under consideration, or having no interest in it. Some technologies, such as water flow restrictors, automatic time clocks, and automatic lighting controls, have achieved great industry penetration. Others, such as guestroom turndown, room occupancy sensors, and heat recapture technology, were under consideration by a large fraction of those sampled.

Exhibit 13.6 Derived Estimates of Energy Consumption

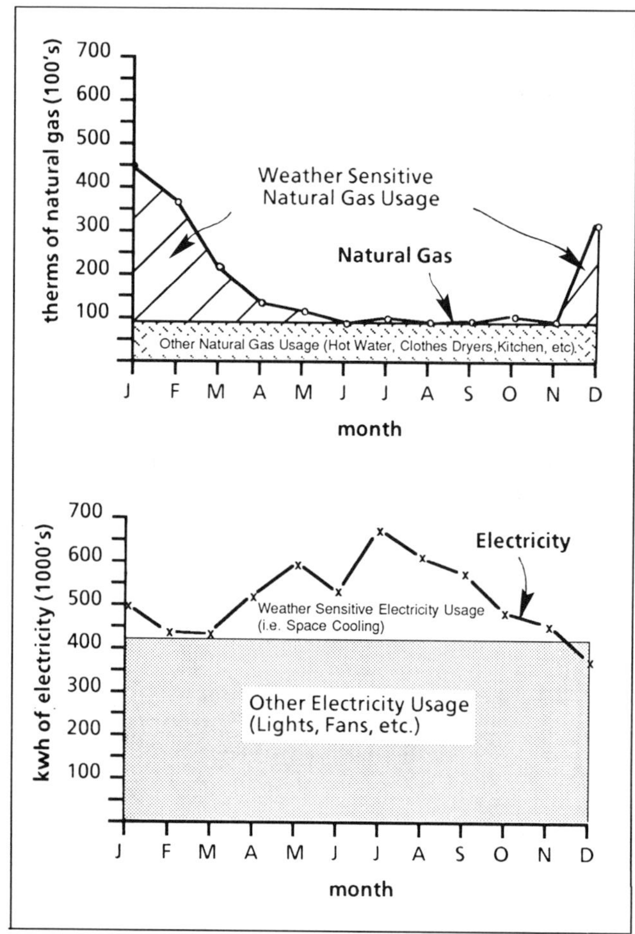

Further discussion of the energy management problems of the hospitality industry and some of the managerial issues in energy management can be found in Aulbach.[1] The remainder of this chapter will briefly discuss (1) energy management within a framework of basic techniques for reducing energy usage/cost, (2) computerized energy management systems, and (3) some considerations when evaluating the economics of capital investments in energy management.

Exhibit 13.7 Results of Computer Modeling of Energy Consumption of a 355-Room Hotel in Various U.S. Cities

	Energy Usage (percent of total) by Location				
SYSTEM	HOUSTON	SEATTLE	WASHINGTON	MILWAUKEE	LOS ANGELES
Heating	14	26	24	31	9
Cooling	18	5	11	7	14
Fan	9	7	8	6	9
HVAC Auxiliaries	2	1	2	1	2
Hot Water	22	25	24	25	28
Lighting	11	11	10	9	12
Vertical Transportation	6	6	6	5	7
Misc. Equipment	18	19	15	16	19
THOUSANDS OF BTU / FT^2--YR					
Electricity	83	65	76	70	75
Fossil Fuels	46	69	69	90	45
TOTAL	129	134	145	160	120

Source: U.S. Department of Energy, National Technical Information Service, *Recommendations for Energy Conservation Standards and Guidelines for New Commercial Buildings, Volume III: Description of the Testing Process*, PNL 4870-7, Report # DOE/NBB-0051/6 (Washington: Government Printing Office, 1983), pp. 2G 1–11.

Exhibit 13.8 Energy Control Technology Survey

	PERCENTAGE OF PROPERTIES SAMPLED*			
TYPE OF TECHNOLOGY	Using	On Order	Considering	No Interest
Water Flow Restrictors	66	1	23	11
Automatic Time Clocks	66	1	7	26
Load Cyclers/Programmable Controllers	27	1	14	58
Peak Demand Controllers	22	1	20	57
Central Building Automation	8	1	20	71
Automatic Lighting Controls	42	1	16	41
Guestroom Turndown At Check-out	10	2	25	63
Room Occupancy Sensor Control of HVAC	6	1	27	66
Combustion Control Refinements	4	<1	18	78
Chiller Load Optimization	7	<1	18	75
Heat Recapture Technology	11	1	27	61
Cogeneration	<1	<1	14	85
Solar	6	0	8	86

<1--Less than 1%
*Based on a survey of 2,500 properties with a total of 480,023 rooms

Source: *The State of Technology in the Lodging Industry*, The American Hotel & Motel Association, 1983.

Energy Management and Building Systems

While there are thousands of specific methods for reducing the energy consumption or cost of energy-using equipment in lodging facilities, there are five basic techniques by which the methods accomplish these reductions. These five basic techniques are:

- Reduction in the load.
- Improvement in the efficiency of the equipment or system.
- Reduction in the operating time.
- Recovery of waste energy.
- Use of a cheaper energy source.

Load reductions are accomplished when the factors which create the load are somehow reduced. For a building heating or cooling load, this may be a reduction in the amount of outside air brought into the building. For an electrical system, this may mean rescheduling the use of equipment to reduce the peak electrical demand, something which may not directly affect the amount of energy used, but will reduce the peak demand charge of the facility.

Improvements in the efficiency of the equipment or system result in reductions in energy usage either by increasing the amount of output from a piece of equipment or system while holding the input constant or by reducing the input to the system while holding the output constant. For water heating systems, cleaning the heat transfer surfaces in the water heater (a form of maintenance) improves efficiency by reducing the amount of heat input required for a given amount of hot water output.

Reductions in equipment operating time are often the most cost-effective options since they can be accomplished quite simply. Turning off the lights in unoccupied meeting rooms is an example. The only cost of this particular example is the amount of time it takes someone to go to the light switch and turn it off.

Recovery of waste energy makes use of energy which is being discarded by the facility. The use of refrigeration heat recovery devices and the installation of exhaust air heat exchange devices are examples of waste energy recovery. Waste energy recovery can be attractive in hospitality settings since it requires little to no input or cooperation from managers and staff in other departments and has little to no effect on the guest.

The use of a cheaper energy source does not directly result in a reduction in energy usage, but does reduce the cost of energy to the facility and, as such, fulfills the primary function of an energy management program. One method of accomplishing this is the installation of a dual fuel boiler at the property with natural gas and oil as the fuels. Many gas utilities will provide a reduced natural gas rate for what is known as interruptible service, meaning that the property must be able to shift to a fuel source other than natural gas for a short period during the winter months. In addition, when there is strong price competition between gas and oil, the property engineer can switch back and forth depending on which fuel is the cheapest.

All five of these techniques can apply to most of the major systems in lodging establishments. It is up to the building engineer to assess the application of these techniques and incorporate those which are appropriate in the property energy program. Sections of this book dealing with specific building systems have briefly addressed energy management opportunities for these systems as part of the system discussion.[2]

The balance of this chapter will be devoted to the topics of computerized energy management systems and cogeneration, which have been identified as areas of significant growth in energy control technology in lodging establishments. The complexity of these systems, their relatively high initial cost, and the special considerations which need to be evaluated when considering them warrant special managerial attention.

Computerized Energy Management Systems

Types of Systems

The following may be classified as computerized energy management systems:

- Automatic time clocks
- Load cyclers/programmable controllers
- Peak demand controllers

- Central building automation
- Automatic lighting controls
- Guestroom turndown at checkout
- Room occupancy sensor control of HVAC
- Combustion control refinements

Automatic time clocks have been used in non-computerized form for many years. The devices, which turn equipment on and off, reduce the operating hours of certain equipment. Examples include building lighting circuits, ventilation fans, and the circulation pump on domestic hot water systems.

Load cyclers/programmable controllers attempt to reduce the amount of energy consumed by systems by cycling the systems on and off during the normal operating period. An example would be a system which cycles building ventilation fans. The effectiveness of these devices has been questioned, since they may compromise building comfort, may increase equipment maintenance costs, and may not be a particularly cost-effective approach to energy management.

Peak demand controllers address only the demand portion of the electric utility bill and are therefore of interest only to properties which have demand billing and where the demand bill is a high percentage of the total utility bill. If peak demand control is to be effective, loads must be controllable—that is, it must be possible to turn them off for periods of time. This may be difficult at a lodging property with high occupancy. One of the most commonly controlled items is electric water heating. Fans and chillers are often controlled as well.

Central building automation is possibly the ultimate step in computerized energy management. With this type of system, numerous sensors installed throughout the building convey information to a central computer which makes decisions on the control of the building and its equipment. Since it represents a potentially large investment, central building automation is probably only appropriate for large facilities with both a need for this level of control and the staff to manage the maintenance (or maintenance contract).

Automatic lighting controls can take several forms, from the simple photocell operation of parking lot and exterior lights to rather involved interior lighting systems which attempt to maximize the use of daylight. With regard to the AH&MA survey cited earlier, we believe that the majority of the lodging establishments which say they use this type of control are referring to photocell control of exterior lighting.

Combustion control technology refers to a broad category of devices which attempt to maximize the combustion of fuel. While some of these devices are not computerized (for example, those devices which preheat combustion air using exhaust gases), the computerized devices monitor the overall combustion process and modify inputs to this process in order to properly control and maximize its efficiency.

Because of the unique nature of guestroom turndown and room occupancy systems, they are discussed in some detail in the following section of this chapter.

Guestroom Control Technology

Guestroom turndown at check-out and room occupancy sensor control of the HVAC system represent two types of computer-based energy management which are either unique to the lodging industry or have special concerns when applied to this industry. Both devices are primarily directed at the energy used by the guestroom HVAC units, although some may also control lights and appliances in the guestroom. Other types of guestroom energy controls include door chain, deadbolt, or door key activated switches which control energy availability in the guestroom. These devices were forerunners of today's room occupancy sensing methods.

Guestroom turndown at check-out uses equipment installed at the front desk to shift a room which is not rented to an unoccupied mode. This mode is characterized by an interior air temperature which minimizes energy use (cold in winter and warm in summer). Turndown equipment may cycle the ventilation fans in the room or in some other way maintain a minimal level of air movement and fresh air introduction to the room. This cycling or duty cycling feature may operate even when the room is rented. These devices are linked to the guestroom by direct wiring, powerline carrier (a method of transmitting control signals over the building wiring system), or the life safety and security transmission system (for example, the wiring for smoke or heat alarms wired to a central panel). Whatever the actual savings possible with such systems, they are generally limited to the periods of time when a room is not rented, a period which the average hotelier hopes is kept to an absolute minimum!

Room occupancy sensors sense whether people are present and control the HVAC system accordingly. Early versions of these devices (deadbolt, door chain, and door button devices) required a physical action of the guest to allow the guestroom HVAC (and sometimes lighting) system to operate and were prone to various problems. Room occupancy sensors today use either infrared or ultrasonic sensors to detect the presence of the guest. For those room occupancy sensors which also have a connection to the front desk, control of the room when it is not rented and even the sensing of an entry into an unrented room are possible.[3]

Concerns and Cautions

Since guestroom control technology is attempting to reduce energy usage in the guestroom, one major concern is the guest's perception of what is happening in the guestroom. When a guest pays $50 to $150 for a room, sets the room thermostat to what he or she perceives to be a comfortable level, and leaves for a drink or a meal, that guest expects the room to be at the selected temperature when he or she returns. If the room is not, the guest is likely to complain. The manager must assess whether the potential for such problems is high or significant with the device being contemplated.

One key concern regarding room occupancy devices is determining the percentage of savings possible with these devices and, as a related item, determining the total amount of energy used in the guestroom. Results of one study of these devices during a summer period in a motel in southern Texas indicated that savings ranged from 15% to 29%. With installed costs of several hundred dollars very likely at smaller properties, the savings may not warrant the investment.

Systems which use duty cycling may create additional maintenance needs due to the strain placed on equipment by the duty cycling itself. In addition, if duty cycling occurs while the guest is in the room, the on/off action of the HVAC unit may annoy the guest.

Finally, although there are other points to be made both for and against guestroom controllers, most managers could use the housekeeping staff to accomplish much of what the guestroom controllers accomplish—for example, controlling thermostat set points and shutting down or adjusting the thermostat in unrented rooms. Using the housekeeping staff to perform these functions eliminates the investment in the system.

Cogeneration

Cogeneration is the simultaneous production of work output and a usable thermal output from a single source. In its most common form, the work output drives a generator and produces electricity while the usable thermal output provides heat for either potable water heating or space heating. Cogeneration is an attempt to reduce energy costs by making a significant capital investment in equipment which will produce heat and, usually, electricity at an overall price which is less than that currently paid.

The lodging industry has long used cogeneration. In the earlier part of this century, urban hotels with coal- or oil-fired boilers commonly produced steam which was passed through a turbine/generator set before proceeding to the thermal loads in the building. The turbine/generator set produced electricity. It was often possible to generate more electricity than was needed by the hotel. As a result, hotels sometimes sold excess electricity to the local electric utility.

Methods and Applications

The cogeneration systems of the late twentieth century come in various forms, depending on the building, its systems, and the local electrical rates. The work output from cogeneration systems can be used in:

- Steam-driven turbines powering pumps which circulate either hot water, chilled water, or cooling tower (condenser) water. The steam leaving the turbine is used for whatever needs the property has for steam.
- Natural gas- or oil-fired turbines or engines. These turbines or engines usually

power electrical generators, although coupling them to power a refrigeration compressor or a pump is also possible.

The thermal output from the cogenerator can be used for providing space and/or water heating, depending on the facility needs at the time, and providing thermal energy to power an absorption chiller, which produces chilled water for building cooling.

When electrical power production is considered, the cooperation of the local electric utility is very helpful to the smooth introduction of the cogenerator. Today, most properties using cogeneration use it to supplement the local electric utility, on which they rely for some or even most of their electrical needs. The utility provides a frequency for the cogenerator to match and must be available when the cogenerator is out for service. Although rare in the United States, it is possible to operate a cogenerator as a stand-alone unit capable of operating with or without the local electric utility. In this mode, the cogenerator may also serve as the emergency power source for the building.

Lodging properties are viewed as a good application for cogeneration because they usually have a relatively good mix of thermal and electrical needs, in contrast to (for example) an office building, where the thermal needs are almost non-existent. The mix of electrical and thermal needs at lodging properties has resulted in an average unit size of 70 kw per 100 guestrooms at those properties which have installed cogenerators. Because of some mismatch in the timing of the thermal and electrical needs of lodging facilities, it is common for cogeneration installations to include additional storage for hot water (or chilled water if absorption cooling is used).

Feasibility Assessment and Economics

With the installed cost of cogeneration systems ranging from $1,000 to $2,000 per kw, the potential requirements of the local utility for interconnection, and the additional space and maintenance needs created by the system, the decision to install a cogenerator calls for careful analysis.[4]

Exhibit 13.9 illustrates the potential return which a cogeneration investment can provide for a property. In general, electric rates in excess of $.08 per kwh are needed to provide a favorable after-tax internal rate of return. Areas with rates approaching or exceeding $.10 per kwh are the most attractive investment locations. The analy-

Exhibit 13.9 Potential Return on a Cogeneration Investment for Different Electric Rates

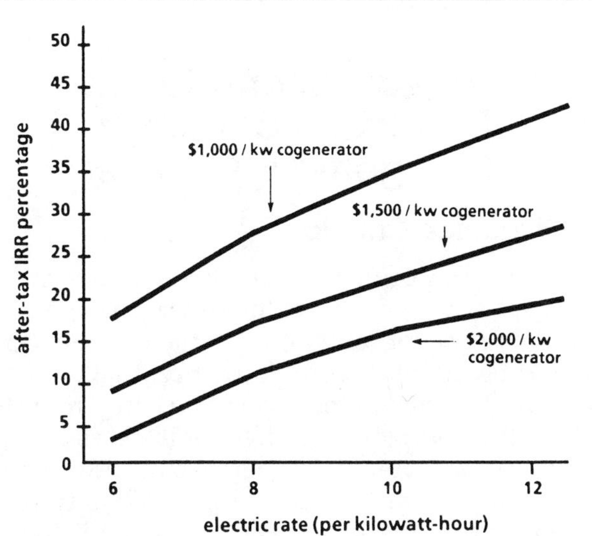

The internal rate of return (IRR) of a cogeneration project is affected by the wide variety of factors listed below. The major factors to be considered, however, are the cost of electricity compared to that of natural gas or fuel oil, and the cost per kilowatt (kw) of installing the equipment. This graph shows The IRR resulting from cogeneration projects with three different cost levels and four different electric rates. The width of the graph line represents different natural-gas rates, but these changes had little effect on IRR compared to the cost of electricity or of installation. Other assumptions are as follows:

Thermal usage	1,000,000 Btu /yr
Electric usage	1.0E + 09 / yr
Unit size	100 kw
Price of gas	$6.00 / million Btu
Operation and maintenance cost	.015
Insurance rate	.005
Property-tax rate	.05574
Generation efficiency	.27
Boiler efficiency	.75
Time in operation	.9
Waste-heat recovery rate	.85
Income-tax rate	.46
Interest rate	.13
Investment tax credit	.1
Natural-gas escalation rate	.06
Electricity escalation rate	.06
Maintenance-cost escalation rate	.06
Property-tax and insurance escalation rate	.06
Actual internal rate of return	.2481

Source: David M. Stipanuk and Thomas G. Denlea, "Cogeneration: A Way to Cut Hotel Energy Costs," *The Cornell Hotel and Restaurant Administration Quarterly*, Nov. 1986, p. 59.

sis performed for Exhibit 13.9 is based on the assumptions at the bottom of the Exhibit. An analysis for a different individual project could result in very different conclusions.

General Criteria for the Evaluation of Energy Management Activities

Performance Criteria

Since the primary purpose of energy management activities is to reduce energy usage and cost, one major criterion in their evaluation should be their actual performance, that is, how well they achieve their purpose. In order to assess the energy usage effect, it is necessary to estimate the amount of energy currently being used and the projected savings. Without submetering information, it is often difficult to secure valid estimates of existing usage, which in turn makes the performance evaluation process difficult.

One problem facing the lodging manager when assessing the potential benefit of energy management is the tendency in the lodging industry to focus on the guestroom. Industry statistics are tabulated per guestroom, a practice which can be misleading about where energy is actually required in lodging facilities. Aulbach reports energy consumption data for a medium-sized southeastern hotel (about 200,000 ft^2) where guestrooms and corridors account for only 19% of total property energy use. He further cites a large East Coast hotel (about 1,200,000 ft^2) where the guestrooms and corridors used 46% of the total energy at the property.[5] With variations such as these in the fraction of total energy being used in the guestroom, it is obvious that savings need to be estimated carefully.

When possible, it is highly desirable to install equipment on a test basis and to concurrently install equipment capable of monitoring the performance of the equipment being tested. This needs to be made a part of the contract for the installation of an energy management system. In addition, some properties require the seller to provide performance insurance which will guarantee a level of savings to the property. It is amazing how many energy management devices have been installed with no documented method established to measure the savings and no assurances that there have been actual savings.

Maintenance Criteria

Every piece of equipment installed at a property needs maintenance. This simple fact is sometimes totally disregarded when the initial purchase decision is made. For energy management systems, the results have been particularly disastrous. In some instances, the failure to maintain the equipment has, over time, effectively removed the equipment from service either directly or by greatly decreasing its effectiveness. In other instances, the company providing the equipment has gone out of business, service has been unavailable, and the property has been left with a device which cannot be maintained and which may even need to be removed at further expense.

The AH&MA solicited information from its members concerning the overall results from and maintenance service received on the energy technology they had purchased. Exhibit 13.10 contains the results of the survey of maintenance service. Automatic lighting controls, guestroom turndown, and room occupancy sensors had relatively high levels of fair responses and heat recapture technology and solar had high levels of poor responses.[6]

Financial Criteria

Financial analysis of energy cost control should consider all of the relevant costs associated with the project. In the process of converting energy savings to dollar savings, care should be taken to use the correct rate or price for energy, since the savings may occur at a rate or price which is different from the average price. Electric utility rates are an example of this. If sales tax is charged on the energy, these savings should be considered as well. Some energy actions may result in reductions elsewhere which should be considered as well. For example, a reduction in chiller operation due to a reduction in cooling load will also reduce the need to operate the cooling tower.

Maintenance costs should be incorporated into the analysis. These costs should be derived

Exhibit 13.10 Survey Respondents' Evaluation of Technology in Use

EVALUATION OF TECHNOLOGY NOW IN USE

TYPE	RESULTS (%)				MAINTENANCE SERVICE (%)			
	EXCEL	GOOD	FAIR	POOR	EXCEL	GOOD	FAIR	POOR
Water Flow Restrictors	43.6	51.4	4.2	.8	37.9	55.6	3.5	3.0
Automatic Time Clocks	38.6	49.2	10.1	2.1	40.0	47.4	8.3	4.3
Load Cyclers/Programmable Controllers	47.1	51.1	.6	1.2	55.2	40.3	2.8	1.7
Peak Demand Controllers	44.7	48.6	4.2	2.5	42.7	48.6	7.6	1.1
Central Building Automation	56.2	41.4	1.8	.6	67.8	30.0	1.0	1.2
Automatic Lighting Controls	42.6	48.3	4.4	4.7	24.6	57.8	15.4	2.2
Guestroom Turndown At Checkout	39.6	42.8	16.3	1.3	35.4	51.6	9.4	3.6
Room Occupancy Sensor Control of HVAC	32.8	36.7	26.4	4.1	40.0	50.0	10.0	.0
Combustion Control Refinements	31.3	51.8	12.7	4.2	30.7	62.8	1.7	4.8
Chiller Load Optimization	40.3	47.8	11.1	.8	26.8	71.3	1.9	.0
Heat Recapture Technology	35.1	51.8	11.5	1.6	18.6	57.4	1.6	22.4
Cogeneration	61.9	34.4	.0	3.7	26.3	70.0	1.4	2.3
Solar	17.4	52.8	22.4	7.4	22.0	64.8	.0	13.2

Source: *The State of Technology in the Lodging Industry*, The American Hotel & Motel Association, 1983.

from the property's own data or recommendations from the equipment supplier, or should be based on a maintenance contract. Some equipment, such as load shedding devices or duty cycling equipment, can result in the need for additional maintenance on other building mechanical equipment, and these factors should ideally be considered in the analysis.

During the early 1980s, it was common to use rather large projected escalation rates for energy prices. As a result, payback periods were calculated to be very short. However, many rates never rose to the projected levels and the paybacks for some projects have yet to be realized. Clearly, great care should be taken in choosing the escalation rates for the analysis. In addition, sensitivity analysis (that is, determining how sensitive your projections are to slight but reasonable variations from your assumed data) is probably helpful. Local utilities and municipal or state energy offices may prove helpful in estimating future prices of energy sources in a particular locale.

Innovative financing techniques have been available for energy conservation investments which reduce the need to provide upfront money for the investment. One of these techniques, known as *shared savings*, involves the installation of equipment at no cost to the property. Instead, the resulting savings are split by the property and equipment installer. Obviously, such an approach requires some preestablished method of measuring the energy savings and determining the cost of these savings.

Other sources of financing are available as well. Some electric utilities will cooperate in the financing of energy efficiency improvements through rebate programs for the purchase of energy-efficient appliances and lighting. These provide an excellent way to reduce the cost of energy management activities. These same utilities will sometimes assist the property with a free or low-cost energy audit to help identify energy conservation opportunities.

Incorporation of the concerns and suggestions listed in this chapter will help the manager to fully and correctly evaluate the total costs and benefits of energy management. This analysis will allow energy management to achieve its true goal of cost control without interfering with a lodging property's efforts to meet its guests' and employees' expectations.

Notes

1. Robert E. Aulbach, *Energy Management* (East Lansing, Mich.: Educational Institute of the American Hotel & Motel Association, 1984).
2. See also Aulbach and *Practical Management of Hotel and Motel Energy Costs* (New York: The American Hotel & Motel Association, undated) for suggested specific energy management actions for building systems in lodging establishments.
3. Further technical description of these and other types of guestroom controllers can be found in H. P. Becker, "How Much Sense Do Room Occupancy Sensor Controls Make?" *ASHRAE Transactions 1986*, v. 92, part 1, 1986.
4. For a discussion of some of the concerns in the cogeneration installation decision, financing methods, and methods of estimating the overall project feasibility, see David M. Stipanuk and Thomas G. Denlea, "Cogeneration: A Way to Cut Hotel Energy Costs," *The Cornell Hotel and Restaurant Administration Quarterly*, Nov. 1986, pp. 51–61.
5. Aulbach, p. 49.
6. There are other sources of information for the maintenance response aspect, among which is *Energy User News*, which periodically publishes survey results of the service responsiveness of various companies providing energy management equipment.

Appendix A
Engineering Principles

This Appendix discusses some of the key principles of physics and chemistry and their application to commonly encountered situations in the design and operation of buildings. Many of these principles are presented in courses which hospitality students may take in food chemistry or physical sciences courses at colleges and universities. While this text has been written with an attempt to avoid a highly scientific or calculational approach to the material, the reader should know that a substantial background in mathematics and the physical sciences is used in the design of building systems. An understanding of the basic principles governing engineering systems will provide a worthwhile dimension to the reader's understanding of the technical aspects of building operations.

Basic Principles

Mass, Force, Power, and Energy

Mass, force, power, and energy are key engineering concepts. Mass refers to the quantity of matter. In the English system of measurement, the unit of mass is the pound (lb). The pound is also the unit used for force in the English system, a rather unfortunate circumstance. An object with a mass of one pound will exert a force of one pound when subjected to the gravity of the earth (at certain standard conditions). In the metric system, the unit of mass is the gram (gm), a rather small unit defined as the quantity of water occupying one cubic centimeter of space. Since this unit is rather small, we often use the kilogram (kg) when speaking of mass in the metric system. One kilogram is equal to 2.205 pounds (mass).

Force is the product of mass and acceleration (or change of velocity). For example, weight, the action of the acceleration of gravity on a mass, is a force. The units of force in the English system are lb (mass)-ft/second-second or, as we have mentioned, the pound (force). In the metric system, the unit of force is the newton which is defined to be one kg-meter/sec-sec. One pound (force) is equal to 4.448 newton.

Power is defined as the rate of doing work or the work per unit time. Work can be thought of as a force acting through a distance. If a force of 1 lb acts through a distance of 1 ft, we say that 1 ft-lb of work has been performed, a basic unit of work in the English system. A power term commonly used is the horsepower, which is defined as 550 ft-lb/sec. In the metric system, the unit of work is the newton-meter (n-m) and the common unit of power the kilowatt, a term equal to 102 n-m/sec. One horsepower is equal to 0.746 kilowatt.

Energy is the capability of doing work. This capability can be present by virtue of either the condition or the position of a body. An additional form of energy is that which is due to energy chemically stored in an object such as a fuel. Energy by virtue of position means an object will do work if it is released. An example would be an object tied to a rope and suspended in the air from a pulley and connected to another weight. If the object is released, work could be performed. This type of energy is also known as potential energy. Energy by virtue of condition has as its most common form energy contained by virtue of motion or kinetic energy. In the English system, the units of energy are the British thermal unit (Btu) and the ft-lb (force). In the metric system, the units of energy are the joule and the kilowatt-hour. Since the joule is a very small unit of energy, the kilowatt-hour is more commonly used when dealing with building systems. The Btu is equal to 778 ft-lb (force) and the kilowatt-hour is equal to 3,413 Btu.

Laws of Conservation

Laws of conservation define relationships in engineering systems. Just as a proper accounting system is able to track the flow of all money entering and leaving a business, the laws of conservation account for all mass and energy in engineering systems.

The law of conservation of mass states that the mass of a body remains unchanged by any ordinary physical or chemical change to which it may be subject. Simply speaking, this law means when we start with a pound (mass) of something and process it, we are left with a pound at the end. For many normal processes, we extend this to entire systems. For example, the water which enters a building water system at the water meter should be accountable in terms of water which is used for various purposes in the building.

The law of conservation of energy states that energy can be neither created nor destroyed, but only converted from one form to another.

Application of the two laws of conservation to building systems and equipment will often provide the answers to problems relating to their operation and provide clues which will assist in optimizing their performance.

General Engineering Data and Metric Conversions

General engineering data concerning such things as the various properties of water and air and the meaning of certain terms is frequently needed by or useful to those performing the engineering function at a lodging property. Exhibit A.1 contains a variety of potentially important data. For properties adhering primarily or solely to the metric system, Exhibit A.2 presents a number of approximate metric conversion factors.

Exhibit A.1 Engineering Data

Water
- volume
  - 1 gallon = 8.33 lb = 0.134 cu. ft.
  - 1 cu. ft. = 7.48 gal. = 62.3 lb
- pressure
  - 1 lb/sq. ft. = 2.31 ft. of water
  - 1 foot column of water = 0.4331 lb/sq. in.
- specific heat
  - liquid = 1.0 Btu/lb-F°
  - ice at 32°F = .487 Btu/lb-F°
  - steam at 212°F; 14.7 psia = .482 Btu/lb-F°
- latent heat of fusion = 144 Btu/lb
- latent heat of vaporization = 970 Btu/lb (at 212°F; 14.7 psia)

Air (at 75°F; 14.7 psia)
- volume
  - 1 cu. ft. = .075 lb
  - 1 lb = 13.5 cu. ft.
- specific heat = .24 Btu/lb -F°

Power
- ton of refrigeration = 12,000 Btu/hr
- horsepower = .746 kw
- horsepower = 550 ft.-lb/sec
- boiler horsepower = 33,475 Btu/hr
- watt = 3.413 Btu/hr
- kw = 1,000 watts
- lumen = .0015 watt

Energy
- kwh = 3,413 Btu
- therm = 100,000 Btu
- MBtu = 1,000 Btu
- MMBtu = 1,000,000 Btu

Volume
- ccf = 100 cu. ft.
- mcf = 1,000 cu. ft.

Water, Air, and Steam Flow

Water, air, and steam are all fluids which are commonly used in building engineering systems. Water is a non-compressible fluid under the conditions in which we normally encounter it, while air and steam are both compressible. The term compressible means that when the material is subjected to changes in pressure, its volume changes. Each of these fluids obeys basic laws of energy and mass conservation as it is used in the building. Because of the uses made of these fluids, there are some other parameters of interest which become important to the property designer and the operating engineer. These parameters include pressure, friction, and the means of providing energy to the fluid steam (pumping, compressing, or by means of fans).

Exhibit A.2 Approximate Metric Conversion Factors

Symbol	When You Know Number of	Multiply by	To Find Number of	Symbol
		Length		
in	inches	2.54	centimeters	cm
ft	feet	.305	meters	m
yd	yards	0.9	meters	m
mi	miles	1.61	kilometers	km
		Area		
sq in	square inches	6.5	square centimeters	sq cm
sq ft	square feet	0.093	square meters	sq m
sq yd	square yards	0.836	square meters	sq m
sq mi	square miles	2.6	square kilometers	sq km
	acres	0.4	hectares	ha
		Weight (mass)		
oz	ounces	28	grams	g
lb	pounds	0.45	kilograms	kg
	short tons (2,000 pounds)	0.91	metric tons	Mg
		Volume		
tsp	teaspoons	5	milliliters	mL
Tbsp	tablespoons	15	milliliters	mL
cu in	cubic inches	16	milliliters	mL
fl oz	fluid ounces	30	milliliters	mL
c	cups	0.24	liters	L
pt	pints	0.47	liters	L
qt	quarts	0.95	liters	L
gal	gallons	3.78	liters	L
cu ft	cubic feet	.028	cubic meters	cu m
cu yd	cubic yards	0.76	cubic meters	cu m
		Pressure		
inHg	inches of mercury	3.4	kilopascals	kPa
psi	pounds per square inch	6.89	kilopascals	kPa
		Temperature (exact)		
Btu	British thermal unit	.252	kilocalories	kcal
°F	degrees Fahrenheit	5/9 (after subtracting 32)	degrees Celsius	°C
		Other		
	Btu/sq ft	2.71	kilocalories/square meter	kcal/sq m
mpg	miles per gallon	.43	kilometers/liter	km/L
	Btu/lb	.556	kilocalories/kilogram	kcal/kg
cfh	cubic feet/hour	.028	cubic meters/hour	cmh
cfm	cubic feet/minute	.028	cubic meters/minute	cmm

Adapted from U.S. Department of Commerce, *Metric Style Guide for the News Media* (Washington, D.C.: National Bureau of Standards, 1976).

Pressure

The pressure of a fluid is measured in force per unit area, with the most commonly encountered units being pounds per square inch or psi. The force which creates pressure can be developed as the result of a large mass of fluid, the storage of energy in the fluid, or fluid flow. The pressure readings which are talked about on the evening news weather report are due to the force of the mass of the column of air which extends to the end of the earth's atmosphere. The pressure which occurs inside a pressure cooker is caused by the transfer of energy into the water inside causing it to change to steam. The ability of an airplane to achieve lift is due to a difference between the forces on the top and the bottom of the wings generated by different rates of air flow over each wing surface.

The pressure caused by the atmosphere of the earth is continuously present. Rather than have this pressure show up on our measuring devices, we have calibrated most of them not to include the atmospheric pressure. If this were not true, a bathroom scale which was 1 ft square (144 square inches) would show a weight of 2,117 lbs (14.7 psi due to the atmosphere times 144 square inches). Pressure measurements which use the atmospheric pressure as a datum (zero value) are called gauge pressures and would commonly be represented by the units psig. Measurements which include the atmospheric pressure are noted by the units psia. If the units are given as psi, the assumption is generally made that gauge pressure is being used.

In water systems, we are concerned about the pressure produced by and required for tall columns of water in the piping systems in high-rise buildings. A column of water one foot high with a density of 62.3 pounds per cubic foot exerts a pressure of .433 psi. Therefore, a building which is 20 stories tall with an average floor-to-ceiling height of 12 feet has a pressure at the base of a water pipe of 104 psi due to the weight of the water. If we are to move water in this pipe to the top of the building, we must inject the water into the base of the pipe at 104 psi or greater, a pressure which is higher than that usually available from the local water utility.

In air systems, we are rarely concerned about the pressure created by tall columns of air since even for a 100-story building the resulting air pressure would be less than 1 psi. Building air-handling systems are concerned with friction and pumping (fan) requirements to move air about the building. Compressed air may be used in the building for operation of the building control system, but this is a specialized application.

Steam systems create pressure by confining water within a boiler and steam piping and by heating the water until it evaporates. The eventual steam/water temperature depends on how high the pressure is allowed to go (assuming heat is continually added). Exhibit A.3 illustrates the relationship between the pressure of steam and the temperature. This relationship is true only for what is known as saturated steam—steam that has just left the surface of a pool of boiling water.

Exhibit A.3 Pressure and Temperature for Saturated Steam

Gauge Pressure (psi)	Temperature (°F)
0	212
5	227
10	240
20	260
50	298
75	320
100	337
125	353

Friction

Friction represents the resistance of an object to the flow or movement of another object along its surface. The presence of friction in fluid flow results in a drop in the pressure of the fluid. Charts are available for flow systems (both pipes and ducts) which correlate the pressure drop (in psi per unit of length) with the flow rate of the fluid and the diameter of the pipe or duct. Valves and other devices installed in these systems will also create pressure losses. There are tables which list the losses in pressure associated with these devices as well.

The amount of friction in a flow system is dependent upon the characteristics of the pipe or duct, the material flowing through the pipe or duct, and the velocity of flow. Of particular concern is the velocity of flow, since the amount of friction is proportional to the square of the velocity. The Darcy-Weisbach equation illustrates these factors for liquid flow in a circular pipe where

$$\text{Loss of pressure due to friction} = \frac{f \times L \times V^2}{d \times 2g}$$

where *f* is a dimensionless friction factor derived from test data for the pipe; *L* is the length of the pipe; *d* is the pipe diameter; *V* is the velocity; and *g* is the acceleration of gravity. This equation allows us to determine the amount of energy which must be input to the fluid in order to overcome friction.

Pumping

In order to overcome friction, energy is added to a fluid. This energy addition is accomplished by pumps for water systems, fans for air-handling systems, and a combination of pumps and the addition of heat for steam systems. In each instance, the pressure of the fluid is increased in order to compensate for the losses in pressure which will occur because of friction.

For water systems, the pumps will also compensate for differences in water pressure required because of the height of water in the building piping.

Exhibit A.4 illustrates the relationships between various parameters which define pump or fan performance. Capacity refers to the quantity of fluid moving through the pipe, usually expressed in gallons per minute (pumps) or cubic feet per minute (fans). Pressure refers to the discharge pressure from the pump or fan. For a pump, this term is often referred to as head in units of feet of water. For a fan, the units are psi or inches of water. Efficiency refers to the percentage of the input energy to the pump or fan which is transferred to the fluid and power is the rate of input of energy to the pump or fan. System pressure losses represents the pressure drop which is expected for the system on which the pump or fan is operating at the flow rate given on the horizontal axis.

Exhibit A.4 illustrates several important factors in pump/fan selection and operation. Since a pump/fan is normally chosen for some peak level of flow (the load), a knowledge of the pressure needed to supply this load is important. For water systems, the head is a combination of the amount of lift we must give the fluid above the pump position, the friction in the pipe from the pump to the load, and the desired pressure at the load itself. Air systems will generally have systems curves which incorporate the friction in the duct work and the desired delivery pressure at the load. An increase in the overall pressure of the system which must be matched by the pump/fan will reduce the quantity of fluid delivered by the pump. In addition, there is a certain range at which the pump/fan operates with a high efficiency. When selecting equipment for a given application, consideration of its operating efficiency in the application is important. Applications with highly varying flow requirements may warrant the use of variable speed equipment capable of operating close to its maximum efficiency over a range of applications or the installation of multiple pieces of equipment with a staging capability.

Exhibit A.4 Relationships Between Capacity and Maximum Values of Head, Efficiency, Power, and Pressure Losses for Flow Systems

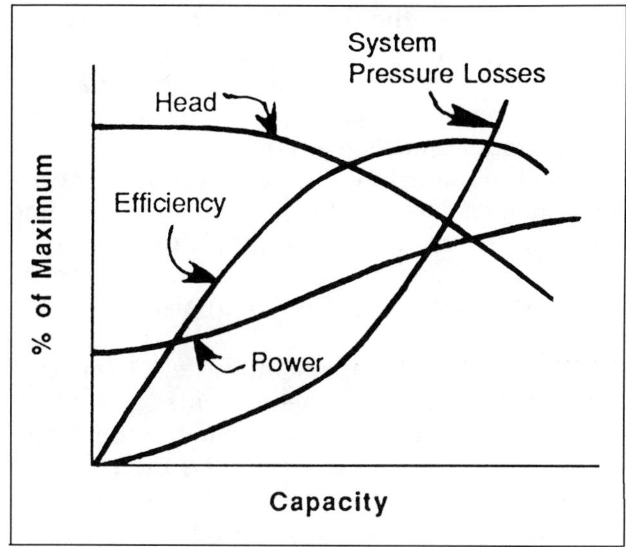

Electricity

Electricity is a form of energy consisting of a quantity of electrons (measured in amperes or amps) flowing between two points of different electrical potential (measured in volts). One ampere represents 6.251×10^{18} electrons per second passing through a cross section of the conductor. The voltage between two points represents a net difference between the number of negative charges (electrons) at the two points. A point or object with more negative charges than another point or object is said to have a negative voltage. Note that voltage is a relative measurement. A voltage measurement is either made relative to ground—usually the earth at a given location—or relative to some other point, such as the voltage between two terminals of a battery.

In electrical systems, the flow of electricity does not proceed unhindered. The characteristic which measures the difficulty that electricity has in flowing through a material is called resistance. The lower the resistance of a material, the better a conductor of electricity the material is. Good conductors such as copper and aluminum are used to make building wiring. Poor conductors, such as glass, porcelain, rubber, and some plastics, are used to make insulating materials which protect us from electricity. The equipment being powered (called the load) also has resistance.

As an aid to understanding electrical systems, analogies are sometimes made between electrical and water systems. The flow of water is similar to the flow of electricity; the pressure in a water system is similar to the voltage in an electrical system; and the resistance of a wire to the flow of electricity is similar to the friction which occurs when water flows through a pipe. The analogies can further extend to pieces of equipment found in the systems as well—for example, the similarity between a pump and a battery and between a valve and a switch.

Current, Resistance, and Power—DC Systems

The discussion of the mathematical relationships which govern electricity will begin with the form of electricity known as direct current or DC. This is the type of electricity produced by a battery. It is characterized by current flow in a single direction, with the normal convention of electrical terminology showing flow from the positive (+) cell of the battery to the negative (−) cell. This rather strange convention concerning electrical flow is due to a misunderstanding of the nature of electricity which occurred hundreds of years ago. While the actual flow of electricity (electrons) is from negative to positive, the convention is to show flow from positive to negative.

When discussing DC systems and the mathematical relationships which govern these systems, the current is usually designated in equations by I, the voltage by V, and the resistance by R. Units of current flow are amps, units of voltage are volts, and units of resistance are ohms. These three terms are linked by the relationship known as Ohm's law, which states that the current in a DC circuit is directly proportional to the voltage and inversely proportional to the resistance. In equation form, Ohm's law is

$$I = V/R$$

Since our normal use of electricity is as a source of power and energy, the relationships which allow us to calculate the amount of power and energy available from an electrical source are of interest. Electrical power is measured in watts (W), where watts are the product of current (I) and voltage (V). When we couple this with the relationship for Ohm's law, we can define electrical power by the following formulas:

$$W = VI = I^2R = V^2/R$$

These formulas reveal some interesting characteristics of electrical power. If we increase the voltage (V) supplied to a constant load, denoted in the equation by the R value, the power required will increase by the square of the voltage. Therefore, if the voltage is increased by a factor of two, the power will be increased by a factor of four. A similar increase occurs if the current is doubled.

The item which we control in electrical systems is the voltage. The resistance is a physical characteristic of the load and the current results from Ohm's law given the voltage and resistance. If we think of the R value in the power equation as representing the resistance of the wires carrying the electricity, we can see why higher voltages are used to deliver higher power requirements. If we wish to provide 100 watts of power using a 20 volt source, we will need 5 amps of current. If this current flows through a wire with a resistance of 2 ohms, the resulting power loss in the line will be 50 watts. In order to deliver 100 watts, we will have to provide 150 watts due to the losses in the line. On the other hand, if we provide electricity at 40 volts, the required current will be 2.5 amps and the power loss in the line only 12.5 watts, only one-fourth of that calculated previously. Providing electrical energy at higher voltages greatly reduces line losses. It also reduces the need for large wires to carry high levels of current flow.

Energy measurements in electrical systems are made by simply multiplying the power by the length of time that level of power is used. If 1,000 watts of power are used for one hour, the amount of energy consumed is 1,000 watt hours or one kilowatt-hour.

Current, Impedance, and Power—AC Systems

While the relationships and physics associated with DC power systems are relatively straightforward, the realm of AC systems is more complex and less easily grasped. Since the vast majority of our uses of electricity are in the form of AC power, an understanding of this common form of electricity is particularly helpful. Fortunately, several of the characteristics of DC electricity are also true of AC.

While the flow of electricity in a DC system is always in one direction, the direction of flow in an AC system oscillates following a generally symmetrical pattern known as a sinusoidal (or sine) wave. Exhibit A.5 illustrates several waves of AC current. When the curve begins to repeat itself, we say one cycle of AC current has passed. The distance along the horizontal axis which is associated with the curve beginning to repeat itself is called a cycle. The standard North American power system operates at 60 cycles per second, also known as 60 hertz. Therefore, the time required for one cycle is 1/60th of a second. The number of cycles per second is also known as the frequency.

The voltage and the current in AC systems are sine waves with the same frequency. Because of the wave nature of AC voltage and current, it is not possible to actually assign a constant value to either of these parameters. Also, because their average value is zero, the use of an average value is useless. The value we use to measure the current and voltage is actually the peak value of each divided by 1.414 (the square root of 2). All electrical instruments commonly used to measure AC current and voltage are set up to divide the peak value of the AC sine wave by 1.414 and show this on the display of the instrument.

In AC systems, the unit of current is still the amp and the unit of voltage the volt with the symbols I and V used to denote each. The unit of resistance is somewhat more complex than

Exhibit A.5 Wave Representation of AC Current or Voltage

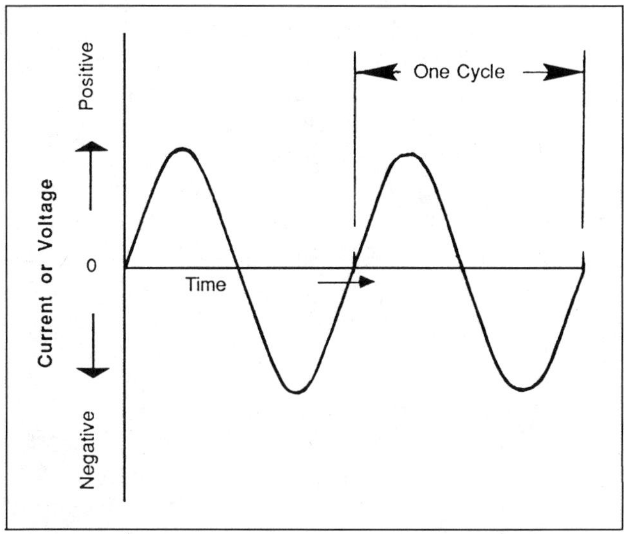

in DC circuits. It is denoted by a Z and referred to as impedance, a term which incorporates both resistance as it is thought of in DC circuits and reactance, an additional type of resistance. Reactance occurs in AC circuits because of the changing (cyclic) nature of the voltage and current flows and the tendency of the material through which the electricity is flowing to resist the change in the voltage and current flows as well as the actual current flow itself.

If an AC circuit is supplying only what is known as a resistive load, the same power relationships are used for AC as are used for DC. However, if the load being supplied has any reactive resistance, as is true of such devices as electric motors, then we must calculate power in a different manner. We will find that the voltage and the current do not occur at exactly the same time due to the reactive resistance that is present. As a result, there is a time separation between their peak values which results in less power being delivered to the load than we would calculate from the calculation ($W = V \times I$) we would perform for a DC power source. A measure of the degree of separation between the timing of the peaks of the voltage and current waves is the power factor (pf) of the load, a number with a value of 1 for purely resistive loads and less than one for loads with reactive components. For such circumstances, the equation for power is given by

$$W = V \times I \times pf$$

This equation is actually valid for both single-phase AC and DC calculations, since the power factor for DC is 1. Energy calculations are still performed by multiplying the power by the time (in hours) over which the power is used.

The world of AC power is further complicated by the presence of three-phase power systems. In three-phase systems, there are three wires, each of which functions like a single AC line. Exhibit A.6 illustrates wave forms for a three-phase power supply. Within any single cycle of the power system, a load connected to a three-phase power supply will receive three impulses of current and voltage. Such a load, such as a three-phase motor, will have a wire for each of the three phases connected to separate connections on the motor and is only capable of operating properly when provided with three-phase electricity. For applications which need a single phase, such as a wall outlet, one of the three phases is used.

With three-phase power, it should be obvious that standard power relationships will not work properly since we are dealing with three lines providing power. Power calculations in three-phase circuits are governed by the relationship

$$W = V \times I \times pf \times \sqrt{3}$$

The relationships discussed and developed between current, voltage, power, and energy for AC and DC circuits are useful for property engineers when dealing with electrical systems at lodging facilities. Exhibit A.7 presents sample calculations which use the relationships developed in this Appendix in the context of problems which might face a property engineer. The problems are simplified for the purpose of these examples.

Exhibit A.6 Wave Representations of Three-Phase AC Current or Voltage

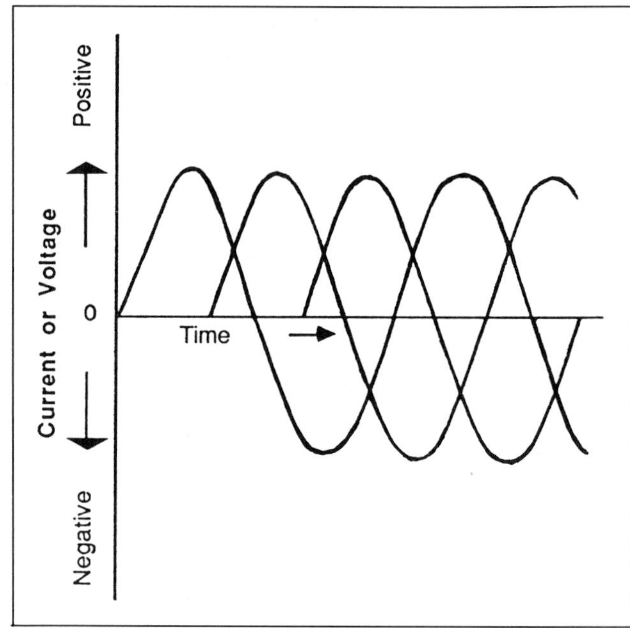

Thermodynamics

Temperature

Temperature must be defined in an indirect manner using the concept of equality of temperature. When two bodies, one hot and the other cold, are placed in contact with each other, the hot body will over time become cooler and the cold body will become warmer. Eventually, all changes in the properties of the bodies will cease and the bodies will be at thermal equilibrium (that is, they will have the same temperature). Therefore, two bodies or systems have equal temperature when no changes occur in their properties when they are brought in contact with each other.

A practical temperature scale has been developed by assigning specific, yet arbitrary, values of temperature to two easily reproducible temperatures: the freezing and boiling points of water at standard atmospheric pressure. In the English system of units, the Fahrenheit scale assigns a temperature of 32°F to the freezing point and 212°F to the boiling point.

So far, this definition of temperature only applies between the freezing and boiling point of water. But the temperature scale can be extrapolated beyond these boundaries in both directions. Therefore, the temperature in a blast freezer and a boiler can be measured as −10°F and 250°F, respectively.

Heat

Heat is a form of energy defined by temperature. When two bodies of different temperatures are brought in contact with each other,

Exhibit A.7 Sample Electrical Calculations

Problem 1: Evaluate the cost of lighting a guestwing corridor.

A corridor in the guestwing of a property is lighted by 50 lighting fixtures, each of which contains a 100-watt lamp. The lamps operate 24 hours a day, 365 days a year. The local cost of electrical energy is $.08 per kwh. What is the annual operating cost of the lamps?

The starting point for this problem is to determine the total lighting power (P) and from this to determine the energy (E) consumed by multiplying the power by the number of hours the lamps operate. The cost is then calculated by multiplying the amount of energy by the cost per unit of energy.

P = 100 watt/lamp × 50 lamps = 5,000 watts or 5 kw
E = P × time = 5 kw × 24 hrs/day × 365 days/year = 43,800 kwh/year
Cost = E × rate per kwh = 43,800 kwh/year × $.08/kwh = $3,504/year

Problem 2: Determine the current draw of a resistive load.

Determine the current draw (how many amps) of the lighting system in Problem 1. (Such a calculation may be required if additional equipment is to be connected to the lighting circuit to determine whether adequate capacity is available in the system.)

Each lamp is rated at 100 watts. Using the definition of power (P = V × I), we can calculate the current draw of each lamp. P is 100 and V is the voltage of the lamps, 120 volts being common. Solving for the current, we have

I = P/V = 100 watts per lamp/120 volts = .833 amps per lamp

The total current flow is 41.7 amps (.833 × 50).

Problem 3: Determine the efficiency of an electric motor.

An electric motor producing 5 HP (horsepower) is operated at 208 volts, single phase. The nameplate of the motor indicates the motor has a power factor of 85% and draws a full load current of 27 amps at rated horsepower. What is the motor efficiency? (A calculation of this type is necessary if a comparison is to be made between the existing motor and a new motor.)

Efficiency = Output/Input
Output = 5 HP × .746 kw/HP = 3.73 kw
Input = V × I × pf = 208 volts × 27 amps × .85 = 4.774 kw
Efficiency = 3.73 kw/4.774 kw = .78 or 78%

Problem 4: Determine the heating capacity of an electric heating element operated at other than its rated voltage.

An electric water heater installed as a booster heater for a dishwasher is rated at 4.5 kw when installed on a single phase 240 volt line. The electric service in the kitchen is 208 volts. What is the heating capability of the heater?

In this problem, the resistance of the heater is a constant value. Using a combination of a power relationship and Ohm's law, we can calculate the resistance of the heater from the following equation

$P = V^2/R$ = 240 volts × 240 volts/R = 4.5 kw

Solving for R:

R = 240 volts × 240 volts/4.5 kw = 12.80 ohm

When operated at 208 volts, the resulting power delivered by the heating element (heating capability) is

$P = V^2/R$ = 208 volts × 208 volts/12.80 ohm = 3.38 kw

they eventually reach thermal equilibrium and a common temperature. The energy that was transferred between the two bodies because of their temperature difference is defined as heat. The direction of the heat flow will always be from the body with the higher temperature to the body with the lower temperature, with the convention that the flow of heat out of a body is considered negative and the flow of heat into a body is considered positive.

The amount of heat can be measured by raising the temperature of the mass of a specific material by a specific temperature difference. The Btu (British thermal unit) is defined as the amount of heat required to raise one pound of water by one Fahrenheit degree. Materials other than water require more or less heat to increase their temperatures by one Fahrenheit degree. This amount of heat is defined as the specific heat, C_P, for that material. Air, for example, has a specific heat of .24 at typical atmospheric conditions.

States of Matter

At the environmental temperatures normally associated with buildings, all matter exists in three states: solid, liquid, or gaseous. These states can be distinguished by observation of certain characteristics of the material. A solid is rigid and maintains its shape without the help of a container. Its volume changes only slightly as the environmental conditions change. A liquid takes the shape of the lower portion of its container, but maintains a horizontal upper surface. Its volume also changes only slightly as the environmental conditions change. A gas fills the entire container without maintaining shape or volume.

The same substance can exist in any of the three different states, depending on its temperature and pressure. At standard atmospheric pressure, water exists as ice (a solid) when its temperature is below 32°F, as steam (a gas) when its temperature is above 212°F, and as a liquid when the temperature is between these two values. As the pressure changes, the temperatures that identify the boundaries between the states change. At a pressure of 15 psig, water will remain in the liquid state up to a temperature of 249.7°F. At a pressure of 50 psig, the boiling point of water increases to 297.7°F.

These specific conditions of water can be observed readily in a lodging facility. The temperature of the ice in the bin of an ice maker must be lower than 32°F, while the temperature of a drink made with shaved ice is exactly 32°F. Water boiling in a stock pot is approximately 212°F. The temperature of the cooking environment or the steam in a high-pressure steam cooker is approximately 250°F because the pressure in such a unit is 15 psig. The steam being produced from a boiler set at 50 psig must be at a temperature greater than approximately 298°F.

Many of the important thermal processes that occur in a lodging property operate on the basis of a change of state for the working substance. During these changes of state, energy is either added to or extracted from the substance. Ice is produced in an ice maker by extracting heat energy from water, thus changing its temperature and state from liquid to solid. Steam is produced in a boiler by adding heat to water, thus increasing its temperature and changing its state from liquid to gaseous. A phase change in the reverse direction is used to cook food in a steamer. Water changing from the gaseous state to the liquid state as the steam is condensed in the steamer gives off heat that is used to cook the vegetables. The Freon in a guestroom air conditioner cools the room by undergoing a change from the liquid state into the gaseous state, taking the necessary heat from the room.

The two changes of state that are common are the change between the solid and liquid states and the change between the liquid and gaseous states. The first change is usually called melting or freezing, depending on the direction of the change. The latter is commonly called boiling or evaporation when the change is from the liquid to the gaseous state and condensation when the change occurs in the opposite direction. Although uncommon in a property, the third possible change of state—from a solid to a gas—is called sublimation. When dry ice (solid CO_2) is used to create "smoke" for a display, the carbon dioxide is changing directly from the solid state to the gaseous state.

An exchange of energy is always associated with any change of state. This addition or subtraction of energy does not affect the temperature of the substance, but rather only affects the form of the substance. At standard atmospheric pressure, both ice and liquid water exist at 32°F and both liquid water and steam exist at 212°F. When water at either of these two conditions changes from one state to the other, it does not change its temperature even though energy has been added or subtracted from it. The energy connected with these changes is designated latent energy, because no temperature change occurs in the process. The energy associated with the change from a solid to a liquid is called the latent heat of fusion, while the energy involved in the change of state from liquid to gaseous is called the latent heat of vaporization. For water at standard atmospheric pressure, the values are 144 Btu/lb and 970 Btu/lb, respectively.

Heat Transfer

Heat energy is transferred between two bodies that have different temperatures by three modes: conduction, convection, and radiation. In the conduction mode, energy is transferred by the direct interaction of molecules. The vibrational energy of one molecule is passed on to its neighbors by direct contact or collision, but the molecules themselves do not move a significant distance through the substance. Conduction occurs in all three states of matter, but is usually associated with solids. The heat that is transferred from the burner of a range into the stock in a stock pot is conducted through the metal container.

Heat transfer in the convection mode is accomplished through the large-scale motion of molecules in currents. Using the example of the heating of a stock in a stock pot, the molecules of the stock that touch the inside surface of the container are heated by conduction. When they are warmed, the density of the liquid decreases and the warmed molecules begin to rise through the stock. As these molecules rise, they are cooled by the surrounding cooler stock. The cooled molecules then return to the bottom of the container. This cyclical heating and cooling of the molecules sets up convection currents in the liquid. The heating of the entire liquid is accomplished by the continuous mixing caused by these currents. Convection is only associated with liquids or gases and does not occur in solids.

Radiation heat transfer occurs when energy from a hot body is converted into electromagnetic energy and is transmitted to another body with a lower temperature. This transmission of energy occurs even through a vacuum without any intermediate medium and is essentially the same as the transmission of radio or television signals. This mode of transfer usually occurs between two solids, with the color of the surfaces of the solids greatly affecting the amount of radiation transfer. Black surfaces emit and absorb energy very readily, while white surfaces inhibit the emission and absorption of radiation energy. In a radiation broiler, the heating element is heated to an extremely high temperature, and the cooking of a steak is accomplished by the radiation of heat from the element to the surface of the steak.

In most actual situations, the heat transfer between two bodies or systems is accomplished by a combination of the three modes. In the stock pot example, the heat is convected and radiated from the gas flame in the burner to the bottom surface of the container, conducted through the metal to the stock that is touching the inside surface of the container, and convected to the remaining stock though currents. For the steak, the heat is initially transferred to the surface of the meat primarily by radiation, although some convection heating also occurs. The heat is then conducted into the center of the steak. In the heating season, heat is lost through the walls of a guestroom because of the difference between the inside air temperature and the outside air temperature. The heat is convected to the inside surface of the wall, conducted through the inside surface material, convected and radiated through any air spaces in the wall, conducted through the outside surface material, and finally convected to the outside air.

In these practical situations where more than one mode of heat transfer occur, the effects of the individual modes are combined into an overall heat transfer coefficient. The total heat transfer can be determined based on the geometric configuration, material properties, and terminal temperatures. The theory for combining modes of heat transfer is based on the concept of thermal circuits or thermal resistance, a direct analogy with electrical circuits and electrical resistance.

Combining the separate effects, however, requires an understanding of the equations and terminology for each of the three modes. For the conduction of heat through a solid, three thermal properties of the material are defined: conductivity (k), conductance (C), and thermal resistance (R). The definition of conductivity is best shown by performing an experiment with a specific material in the following way.

Exhibit A.8 Thermal Properties for Some Typical Building Materials

Building Material	k (Btu/hr-ft^2-F°-in)	C (Btu/hr-ft^2-F°)	R (hr-ft^2-F°/Btu)
Gypsum plasterboard (.5 in)	1.11	2.22	0.45
Fiberglass insulation (4 in)	0.25	0.0625	16.0
Brick, common (4 in)	5.0	1.25	0.80
Concrete block, 3 oval cores (8 in)	----	0.90	1.11
Plywood (.5 in)	0.806	1.61	0.62
Plate glass (.25 in)	2.77	11.1	0.09

Reprinted by permission from *1985 ASHRAE Handbook—Fundamentals.*

A one-inch thick slab of the material with a surface area of one square foot is subjected to a one Fahrenheit degree temperature difference between the two flat surfaces of the slab. Heat will flow through the one-inch dimension of the material because of the temperature difference. The conductivity (k) of the material is defined as the rate of heat in Btu/hr that flows in this specific configuration, and is expressed in units of Btu/hr-ft^2-F°-in. Therefore, this thermal property only applies to a one-inch thick sample of the material.

Since the materials in most practical situations have a thickness different than one inch, the property of conductivity is generalized to the property of conductance (C) for a specific thickness of the material other than one inch. Conductance is defined by the following equation, where x is the specific thickness in inches, and is expressed in units of Btu/hr-ft^2-F°:

$$C = k/x$$

When x is one inch, then $C = k$ as it should by definition. When x is greater than one inch, the conductance is less than the conductivity because a thicker sample of the material conducts less heat. Conversely, the conductance is greater than the conductivity when the thickness is less than one inch because a thinner sample of the material conducts more heat. Finally, a thermal resistance (R) for the material is defined as the reciprocal of the conductance, in units of hr-ft^2-F°/Btu:

$$R = 1/C$$

Exhibit A.9 Typical Convection Heat Transfer Coefficients

Situation	h_c (Btu/hr-ft^2-F°)
Still air; vertical surface	1.46
7.5 mph wind; vertical surface	4.00
15 mph wind; vertical surface	6.00
Still water; vertical surface	1.00

Reprinted by permission from *1985 ASHRAE Handbook—Fundamentals.*

While the conductance is a measure of the amount of heat that flows through a layer of material, the resistance is a measure of the material's ability to resist the flow of heat. Hence, the two properties are reciprocal in nature. Values of these thermal properties for some typical building materials are shown in Exhibit A.8.

For the convection heat transfer in a liquid or gas, the entire effect is expressed in a convection coefficient, h_c, in units of Btu/hr-ft^2-F°. The coefficient includes the effects of the type of convection (natural or forced), the geometry of the situation, and the type of fluid (for example, water or air). Values for some common situations are given in Exhibit A.9. A larger value for h_c indicates a higher rate of heat flow. The interpretation of this coefficient is analogous to that for the conductance of a solid. The resistance to convective heat flow is the reciprocal of the convection coefficient.

Similarly, the overall effect of radiation heat transfer is expressed by a radiation coefficient, h_r, with the same units. This coefficient also includes all of the effects due to the properties of material (for example, surface color) and geometry of the situation. Again, the analogy with the conductance of a solid holds, and the resistance to radiation heat flow is the reciprocal of the radiation coefficient.

With the heat transfer characteristics of individual layers of materials defined, they may be combined into composite assemblies that represent actual configurations that are common in hospitality properties. Refer to Exhibit A.10 for this discussion. The exterior wall of a guestroom could be built of several layers of building materials (for example, wall board, concrete block, face brick), but in this example only two layers are used. The conductivities or conductances of the solid layers are obtained from tables of design values for such materials. Two additional layers of air (inside air film and outside air film) contribute to the thermal properties of the wall. The heat transfer coefficients for these layers are obtained from tables similar to Exhibit A.9. In addition, the value of any radiation heat transfer coefficient should be obtained if it is appropriate. The resistances for each of these layers can then be calculated by taking the appropriate reciprocals.

The overall heat transfer capability of the entire wall may now be determined by combining the effects of the individual layers using the concept of thermal resistance. When the layers of the wall are in series (that is, all of the heat flows through each layer), the total resistance of the composite wall is the sum of the individual resistances for each layer. A common sense analysis of the situation supports this method for combining separate layers. As more layers are added to a wall, the amount of heat that flows through it is reduced, thus increasing the wall's resistance to heat flow. Note that it is not the conductances (the ability to transfer heat) but rather the resistances (the ability to resist heat transfer) of the individual layers that are added together to determine the overall thermal effect of the composite wall. If the conductances were added as the number of layers were increased, then the heat flow through the wall would increase, and this effect is contrary to actual experience.

The overall thermal effect of the wall could remain expressed in terms of its resistance, but most applications require the effect expressed in terms of its ability to transfer heat. Therefore, an overall coefficient, the *U factor*, expressed in units of Btu/hr-ft²-F°, is calculated by taking the reciprocal of the total resistance:

$$U = 1/R_T$$

This U factor represents the aggregate effect of all the layers, including the air films, on the ability of the wall or any other configuration (for example, the stock pot when heating water) to transfer heat from the higher temperature region on one side of the barrier to the lower temperature region on the other side.

Exhibit A.10 Thermal Effect of Combining Building Materials

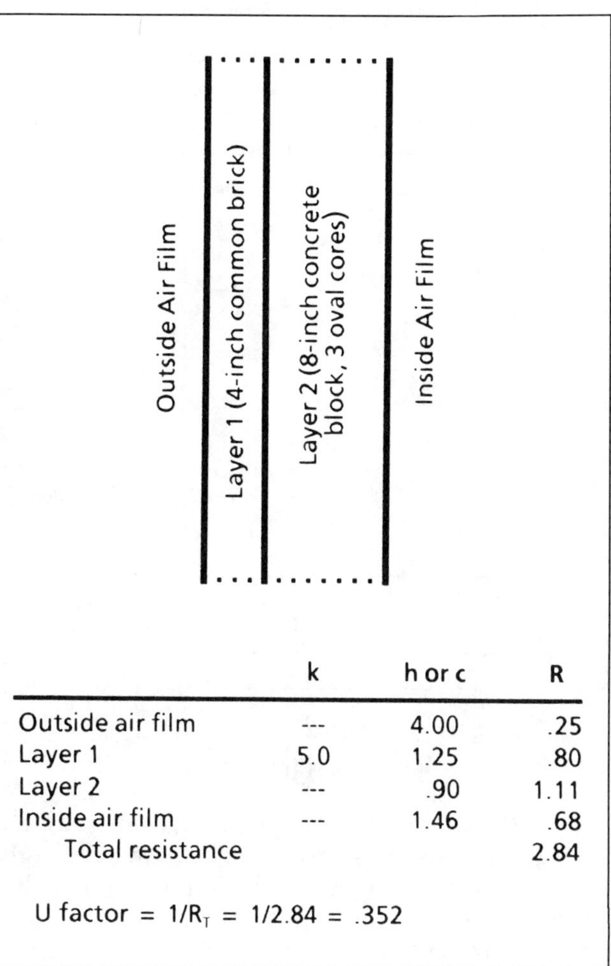

	k	h or c	R
Outside air film	---	4.00	.25
Layer 1	5.0	1.25	.80
Layer 2	---	.90	1.11
Inside air film	---	1.46	.68
Total resistance			2.84

U factor = $1/R_T$ = 1/2.84 = .352

Exhibit A.11 Spectrum of Electromagnetic Radiation

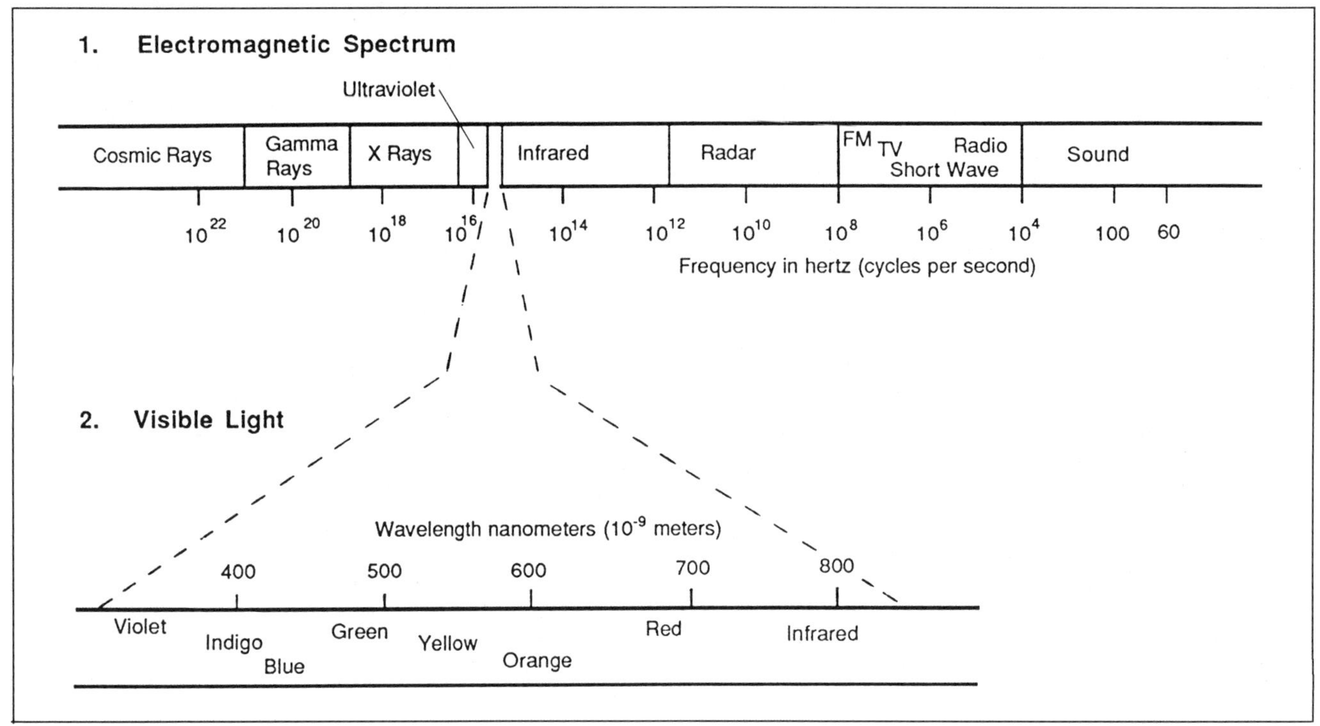

Light

Light is defined most simply as radiated energy that can be seen by the human eye. Light exhibits wave properties similar to other phenomena such as radio, microwave, and X rays, and is part of the electromagnetic spectrum as shown in Exhibit A.11. As such, light has both wave length and frequency as do all these types of radiation. These two properties are inversely related through the constant for the speed of light as follows. With frequency in cycles per second (Hz or cps), wave length in meters (m), and the speed of light as 3×10^8 m/sec, the relationship is expressed as

$$l = c/f$$

where *l* represents the wave length, *f* the frequency, and *c* the speed of light. Note that metric units have been used here because most of the literature on lighting uses them.

Color

Different wave lengths or frequencies of light are interpreted by the human eye as different colors of light. The wave lengths of visible light extend from 380 nanometers (a nanometer is 10^{-9} meters) to 760 nanometers, with the former frequency corresponding to violet light and the latter corresponding to red light. Light of wave lengths in between these two values is associated with the common colors as shown in the second section of Exhibit A.11. The acronym ROY G BIV identifies these colors as red, orange, yellow, green, blue, indigo, and violet. White light contains energy in equal amounts at all the wave lengths in this range.

Light Sources. Light that is produced by practical sources has different color characteristics because the light is emitted at various frequencies rather than just one. The frequencies that dominate in the spectrum cause the human eye to interpret the light as the colors associated with the dominant frequencies. Exhibit A.12 shows the spectral distributions of the following common light sources: noon sunlight, a typical light bulb with a tungsten filament, and a typical fluorescent lamp that has not been corrected for color rendition.

The human eye interprets daylight as having a near-white quality, but with a slight tone of yellow, while it sees the color of the light from

Exhibit A.12 Spectral Characteristics of Light Sources

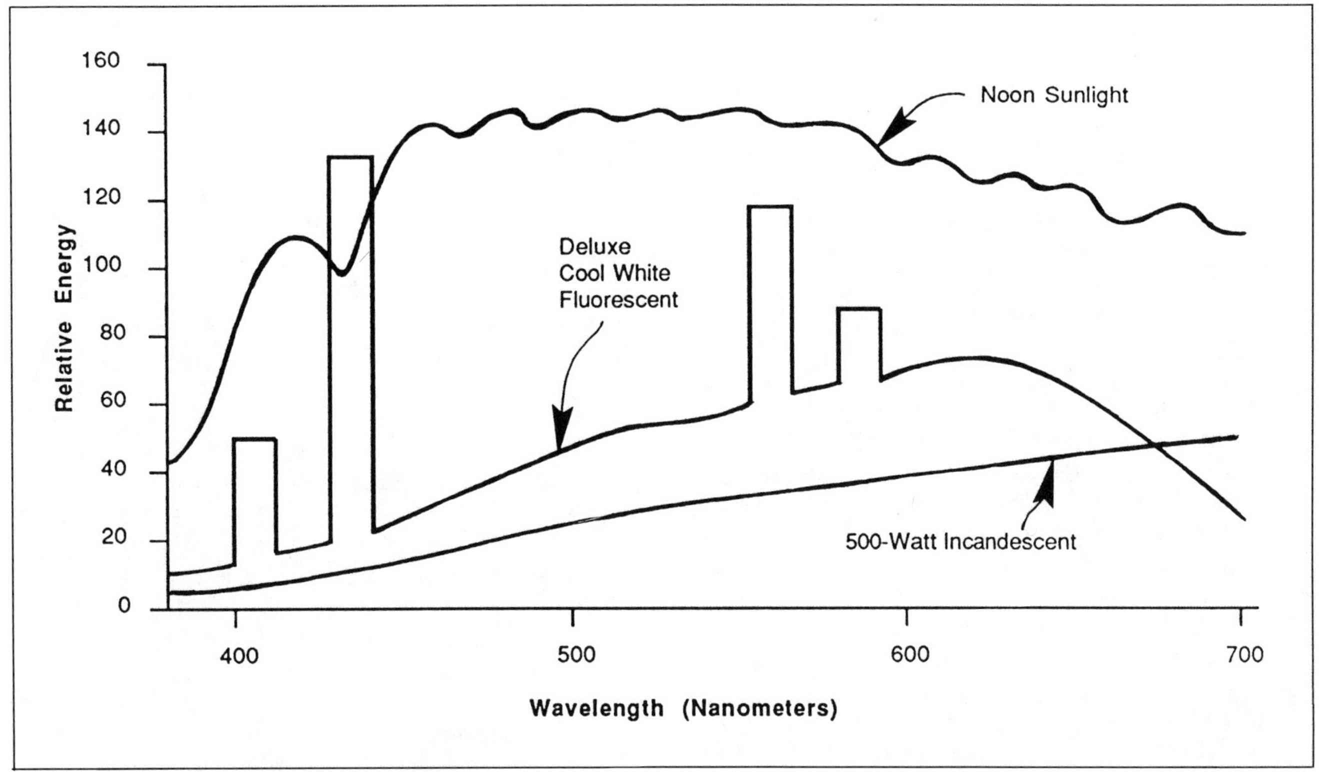

the artificial sources as substantially different from that of daylight. The light from the incandescent (tungsten filament) bulb is seen as yellow-orange and the light from the fluorescent lamp appears stronger in the blue range and very weak in the orange-red range. Therefore, the lamps that are used to light the interiors of buildings may not give the building's interiors the same color characteristics exhibited during the daylight hours.

Effect of Surfaces. When the light from a source strikes a surface, the light is absorbed, reflected, or transmitted in various proportions, depending on the material characteristics of the surface. Some of the light always is absorbed and converted into energy that increases the temperature of the surface. The remaining light is predominantly either reflected or transmitted, thus categorizing the material as either opaque or transparent, respectively.

The color of the light that is either transmitted or reflected by the surface depends on the interaction of the color of the incident light and the absorption characteristics of the surface material. Since the color of the transmitted or reflected light is interpreted by the eye as the color of the object, this interaction is extremely important in determining the color of objects as perceived by people in actual settings.

Different frequencies of light are absorbed by materials in different amounts by a process of selective absorption in which most of the light is absorbed and the remaining light is reflected or transmitted in a very narrow band of frequency. This reflected or transmitted light exhibits a distinct color or hue. For example, a red napkin absorbs almost all of the light from the visible spectrum except for those frequencies associated with the color red; yellow flowers in the atrium absorb all of the frequencies except those for yellow.

The color spectrum of the incident light is modified by the selective absorption characteristics of the surface material to determine the color of the object. When white light is incident on the surface, all colors in the spectrum are present in the incident light and the perceived color of the object is dependent on which light frequencies are absorbed by the material. For example, white light on a "red" surface appears red. When light of a specific color is incident on a surface, only light of the frequencies associated with that color is present and the perceived color of the object is dependent on which light frequencies remain after the existing light frequencies are absorbed selectively by the surface. There are two possible situations. One, when (for example) violet light strikes an object in which the material absorbs all the frequencies except those associated with the color violet, the object looks violet to the observer. Two, when the same violet light strikes an object in which the material absorbs all the frequencies except those associated with the color red, the object appears black because little or no light is reflected from the object.

Knowledge of this interaction between the color of the light source and the color absorption characteristics of an object influences many of the lighting decisions that affect the appearance of lodging facilities to their guests and employees. Foods such as beef or tomatoes that are rich in red and orange colors must be lighted by artificial sources that contain a sufficient amount of light in the red and orange frequencies or they appear dull, dark, and unappetizing to the dining room guest. Human skin must also be lighted by a source with desirable color characteristics so that it shows its natural beauty to guests as they view themselves in any of a property's mirrors.

Intensity

Power of Light Source. A standardized light source that emits radiation equally in all directions from one point is used to define the power of practical light sources. The output of the standardized light source is quantified by measuring the amount of light which strikes a spherical surface that is centered on the light source and has a radius of one foot. The unit of measurement for the total quantity of visible radiation emitted by the source is the lumen. The amount of light in a lumen is based on the light output of a wax candle, which emits approximately 12.57 lumens.

The efficacy, or the efficiency of the production of the light, of a light source is expressed by an input-output ratio. For an electrically powered light source, the efficacy is measured in lumens per watt, where lumens measure the output of the light and watts measure the electrical input. While the theoretical maximum efficiency of light production is approximately 220 lumens per watt, the efficacies of actual light sources are substantially less than this value (usually 15 to 150 lumens/watt) because a large proportion (typically 75–95%) of the input energy is converted into heat which is dissipated by the light bulb.

Inverse Square Law. The light output of a light source is measured using a spherical surface centered on the light source with a radius of one foot. The extension of this measurement of light intensity to distances other than one foot requires the development of the relationship between the amount of light (lumens) and the intensity or density of light (lumens/ft^2). A *footcandle* (*fc*) is defined as the intensity of light of one lumen per square foot.

For a standardized light source emitting 12.57 lumens, the intensity of light measured at the surface of the unit sphere is one footcandle because the output of 12.57 lumens shines equally on 12.57 ft^2 of surface area. The intensity of light on a spherical surface centered on the same light source with a radius of two feet, however, is only .25 fc because the surface area of the sphere is 50.28 ft^2, while the output of the light source is 12.57 lumens.

This reduction in the intensity of light as the distance from the light source increases is governed by the inverse square law. The relationship can be expressed mathematically by

$$\text{fc} = \text{lm}/(12.57 \times d^2)$$

where the distance (d) from the light source is measured in feet. For a light source of a given power, the intensity of the light decreases in proportion to the square of the distance from the source, hence the name "inverse square law."

Effect of Surfaces. When the light from a source shines on a surface, some of the light is absorbed and the remainder is transmitted or reflected, depending on whether the surface is primarily transparent or opaque. In either case, the intensity of the light that leaves the surface is dependent on two factors: (1) the intensity of the light striking the surface and (2) the material properties and geometry of the surface. The relationship among these variables can be expressed as

$$\text{fc} = \text{fc}_I \times \text{factor}$$

where fc_I is the intensity of the light incident on

the surface, *factor* represents the aggregate effect of the surface on the intensity of the light, and *fc* is the intensity of the light leaving the surface.

The actual factors are expressed as values in percentages ranging from 0% for a surface that absorbs all the incident light to 100% for a surface that returns all the incident light, and are described in the literature as either the reflectance or transmittance of the surface, depending on whether the surface primarily reflects or transmits the incident light.

Appendix B Psychrometrics and Human Comfort

Psychrometry

Psychrometry is the study of the thermodynamic properties of a combination of dry air and water vapor. A manager should be aware of this subject because the comfort of guests and the comfort and productivity of the employees are highly dependent on the conditions of the air inside a hospitality building. In order to maximize guest satisfaction and employee productivity with minimal cost, the conditions of the environment within the facility must be controlled properly and carefully. Knowledge of the appropriate conditions and of the best methods for control is based on the scientific properties of moist air, the mixture of dry air and water vapor.

The properties of moist air that are important to the understanding of psychrometrics are dry-bulb temperature (°F db), wet-bulb temperature (°F wb), moisture content (pounds of water vapor per pound of dry air), relative humidity (% rh), dew point (dp), specific enthalpy (h in Btu/lb of dry air), and specific volume (ft^3/lb of dry air). The definitions for each property are developed in the following sections.

Temperature

Dry-bulb and wet-bulb temperatures are best defined by a simple experiment in which two identical common thermometers are used to measure the temperature of a sample of moist air. One of the thermometers measures the dry-bulb temperature and the other the wet-bulb temperature. A wick or piece of fabric that is soaked with water is attached around the mercury reservoir of the wet-bulb thermometer, while nothing is attached to the reservoir of the dry-bulb thermometer. When the mercury reservoir of the dry-bulb thermometer is exposed to the air sample, the reading obtained from the scale is called the dry-bulb temperature—the temperature of the air as reported in weather reports. The wet-bulb temperature is read from the scale on the wet-bulb thermometer in exactly the same manner.

The two temperature readings are usually different because of the effect of the soaked wick on the reservoir of the wet-bulb thermometer. If the air sample is able to absorb some of the water in the wick, then the water in the wick evaporates into the air sample. When this evaporation occurs, the necessary heat of vaporization is extracted from the wick and the mercury reservoir, thus cooling the reservoir. Therefore, the reading from the wet-bulb thermometer is lower than the reading from the dry-bulb thermometer. This difference between the dry-bulb and wet-bulb temperatures is inversely related to the amount of water vapor that is in the air sample. If the air sample contains a substantial amount of water vapor, then the amount of water that can evaporate from the wick is reduced, reducing the cooling effect and the temperature difference between the two temperature readings. Conversely, if the air sample contains little or no water, then the amount of water that evaporates is increased, increasing the cooling effect and the temperature difference.

Thus, the two temperature readings together indicate both the actual temperature of the air and the amount of water vapor in a sample of moist air. These two temperatures are the bases for defining the other important properties of moist air.

Moisture Content

The following experiment assists in the development of the definition of moisture (or water) content. A one-pound sample of dry air at standard atmospheric pressure and a specific temperature is exposed to a source of water at the same temperature. The water is allowed to evaporate into the sample of air and heat is added to maintain the specified temperature. After some time, the air sample cannot absorb any more water from the water source. The moist air in the sample at this condition is defined as *saturated* because no more water can be evaporated into it. The amount of water that was evaporated in this process is recorded. The same experiment is run several times at various specific temperatures. The data from such an experiment is plotted in Exhibit B.1. Note that the amount of water that can be evaporated into a sample of dry air increases as the temperature of the dry air increases. Since this curve represents the maximum amount of water that can be evaporated into dry air, it is called the saturation line. On this line, the air is 100% saturated or is in a state of 100% relative humidity.

At a given dry-bulb temperature, the relative humidity of the moist air is determined by the amount of water vapor that is actually evaporated into the air compared to the maximum that could be evaporated. If the actual amount is one half of the maximum, then the relative humidity of the moist air is 50%. For each dry-bulb temperature, the necessary amount of water for 50% relative humidity can be determined by comparison with the saturation amount of water at that given temperature. These amounts of water can be plotted on a graph as shown in Exhibit B.2. This line is labeled as the 50% relative humidity line. Likewise, the lines for all other possible relative humidity levels can be plotted and labeled.

The moisture content of a sample of moist air is defined as the amount of water vapor actually held in the sample measured in pounds of water per pound of dry air. Since this parameter represents only the numerator of the ratio that determines the relative humidity of the moist air, the distinction between the moisture content and the relative humidity is very important. The moisture content measures the actual amount of water vapor in the air in an absolute sense, while the relative humidity measures this amount in a relative sense in comparison to the maximum that could be present. Notice in Exhibit B.2 that the moisture content of air at a condition of 95°F db and 50% relative humidity actually is greater than the moisture content of air at a condition of complete saturation at 70°F db, even though the relative humidity of the former is lower.

Exhibit B.1 The Saturation Line

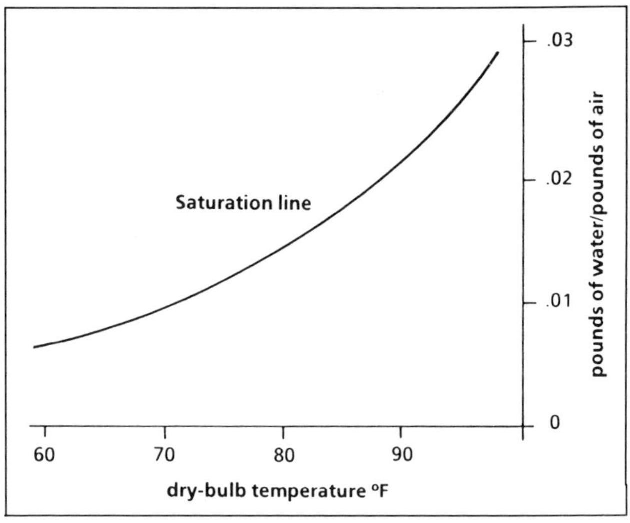

Exhibit B.2 Relative Humidity

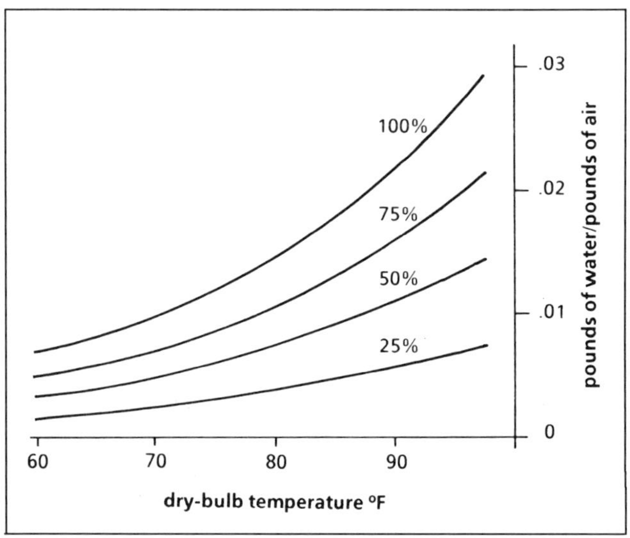

Psychrometric Chart

The graphs plotted in the previous section are the basis for the development of the psychrometric chart, a graphical presentation of the important parameters of moist air. The three parameters—dry-bulb temperature, moisture content, and relative humidity—have already been included on the chart as shown. The four remaining important parameters—wet-bulb temperature, dew point, specific enthalpy, and specific volume—can be added through their relationship to the present parameters in the following ways.

The wet-bulb temperature and the dry-bulb temperature of saturated air are the same as explained in the definition of the wet-bulb temperature. Therefore, the saturation line on the graph can be labeled with wet-bulb temperatures for every dry-bulb temperature, as shown in Exhibit B.3.

With this new temperature scale, the definition of wet-bulb temperature can be extended to all the conditions of moist air shown on the graph. When the moist air is at a condition of less than saturation, the wet-bulb temperature is always lower than the dry-bulb temperature and the reading depends on the amount of water vapor in the air. Therefore, the relative humidity and the wet-bulb temperature of a sample of air are interrelated and lines of constant wet-bulb temperature can be added to the graph to show this interconnection. These straight parallel lines slope from the upper left region to the lower right region of the graph. For example, moist air at the condition of 80°F db and 50% relative humidity has a wet-bulb temperature of approximately 67°F wb.

Another of the parameters, dew point, can be added to the graph by referring to a common occurrence in everyone's experience. When warm moist air is brought in contact with a cold surface such as a cold glass of water or a cold window pane in winter, some of the water vapor in the moist air condenses on the cold surface, forming water droplets. This occurs because the moist air is cooled below saturation by the cold surface and the water is forced to condense because the air is no longer able to hold it. This process can be traced on the graph as follows. Warm moist air at 75°F db and 50% rh is cooled as it contacts the cold surface through convection of heat from the air to the surface. As the air

Exhibit B.3 Wet-Bulb Scale

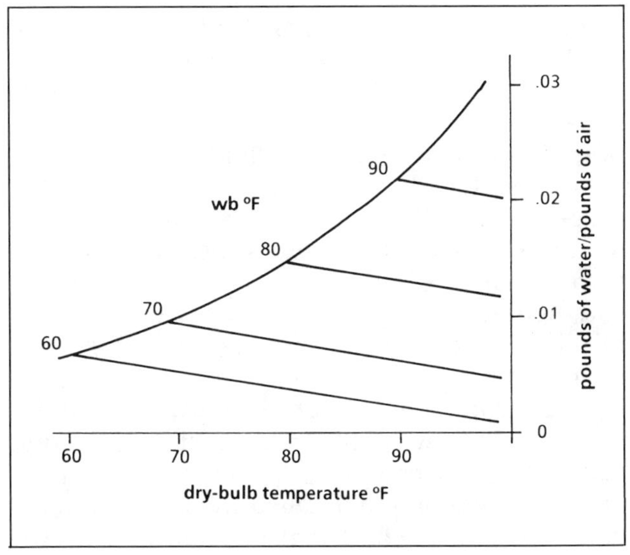

cools, the condition of the air changes initially by a lowering in the dry-bulb temperature without any reduction of the moisture content. Therefore, the initial trace of the process on the graph is a horizontal line moving to the left from the beginning condition of the air. As the air continues to cool, this horizontal line intersects the saturation line. At this point, the air holds the maximum amount of water that it can contain at this temperature. This temperature is designated as the dew point for the condition of the original air because if the air is cooled below this temperature, water droplets or dew will form.

Lines of constant dew point and a dew point scale that has exactly the same values as the wet-bulb temperature can be added to the graph as shown in Exhibit B.4. These straight parallel lines are horizontal on the graph and are each related to a moisture content. Therefore, the dew point of air at a specific condition is determined by the moisture content and not the relative humidity.

The final two parameters—specific enthalpy and specific volume—can be added by the measurement of two properties of the moist air. The total energy that is contained in the moist air, from both the dry air and the water vapor, is determined in Btu/lb of dry air and is called specific enthalpy (h). The values of specific enthalpy are based on a reference of zero specific enthalpy at 0°F. The scale for this quantity of energy is added above the saturation line and the wet-bulb temperature scale. Lines of constant specific enthalpy are essentially parallel to the lines of constant wet-bulb temperature and for common usage they are considered the same lines. Specific volume (v) is the volume of one pound of dry air at a given condition. Although the value for this parameter varies over the range of conditions normally associated with air mixtures in hospitality properties, an approximate value of 13.5 ft^3/lb is used. This value corresponds with a specific density of dry air of .075 lb/ft^3. Lines of constant specific volume are overlaid on the graph as shown in Exhibit B.5.

The completed graph as shown in Exhibit B.5 contains all of the important information about the parameters of the mixture of dry air and water vapor and is called the psychrometric chart. A similar chart that is published by the Carrier Corporation is shown in Exhibit B.6. This chart or similar charts are the basis from which all calculations regarding heating, ventilation, and air conditioning systems and determinations about human comfort are made.

Applications

Changing the conditions of moist air is accomplished through four distinct processes which are differentiated by their direction of movement on the psychrometric chart. The process that moves the condition of the air horizontally while increasing its dry-bulb temperature is designated *sensible heating*, because the air is being heated without changing its moisture content. Likewise, the process that moves the condition of the air horizontally while decreasing its temperature is called *sensible cooling*. A process that increases the moisture content without changing the air temperature is designated *humidification*, while one that decreases the moisture without changing the air temperature is called *dehumidification*.

In practice, the conditioning of the air in hospitality facilities is usually a combination of these four basic processes. In the summer, warm and moist air is both dehumidified and cooled in order to maintain the guests' and employees' comfort. In a northern location in the winter, the cold and dry outdoor air is heated and sometimes humidified to maintain desirable inside comfort conditions. In extremely dry and hot locations, the cooling of hot outside air is accomplished by allowing the air to humidify itself.

Exhibit B.4 Dew Point Scale

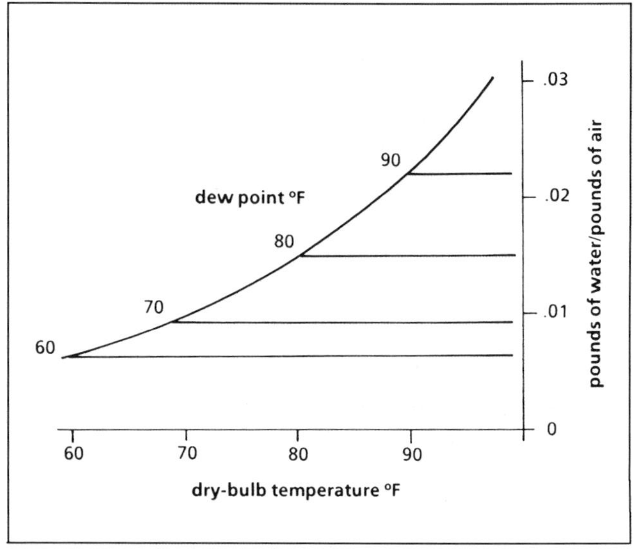

Exhibit B.5 Specific Volume Scale

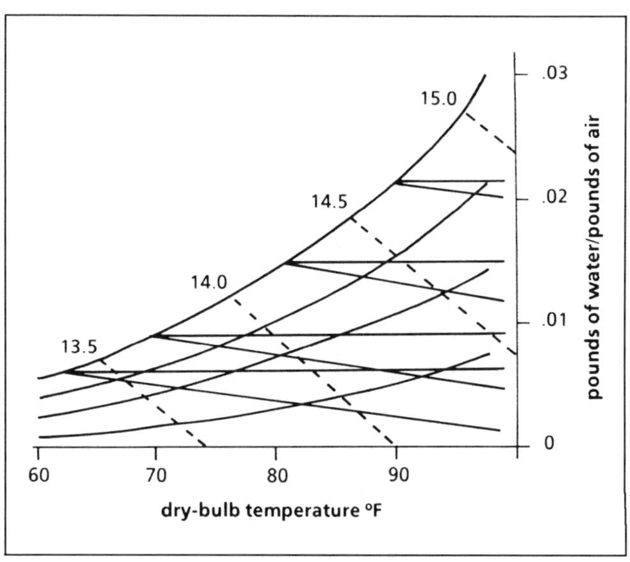

The characteristic of the dew point of moist air is demonstrated in numerous situations within hospitality facilities. The condensation of water on the inside of window panes in the winter, the condensation of water on a glass containing a cold beverage, the formation of an ice coating on cooling coils of a freezer, the formation of water droplets on the inside surfaces of a walk-in refrigerator, and the conden-

Exhibit B.6 Psychrometric Chart

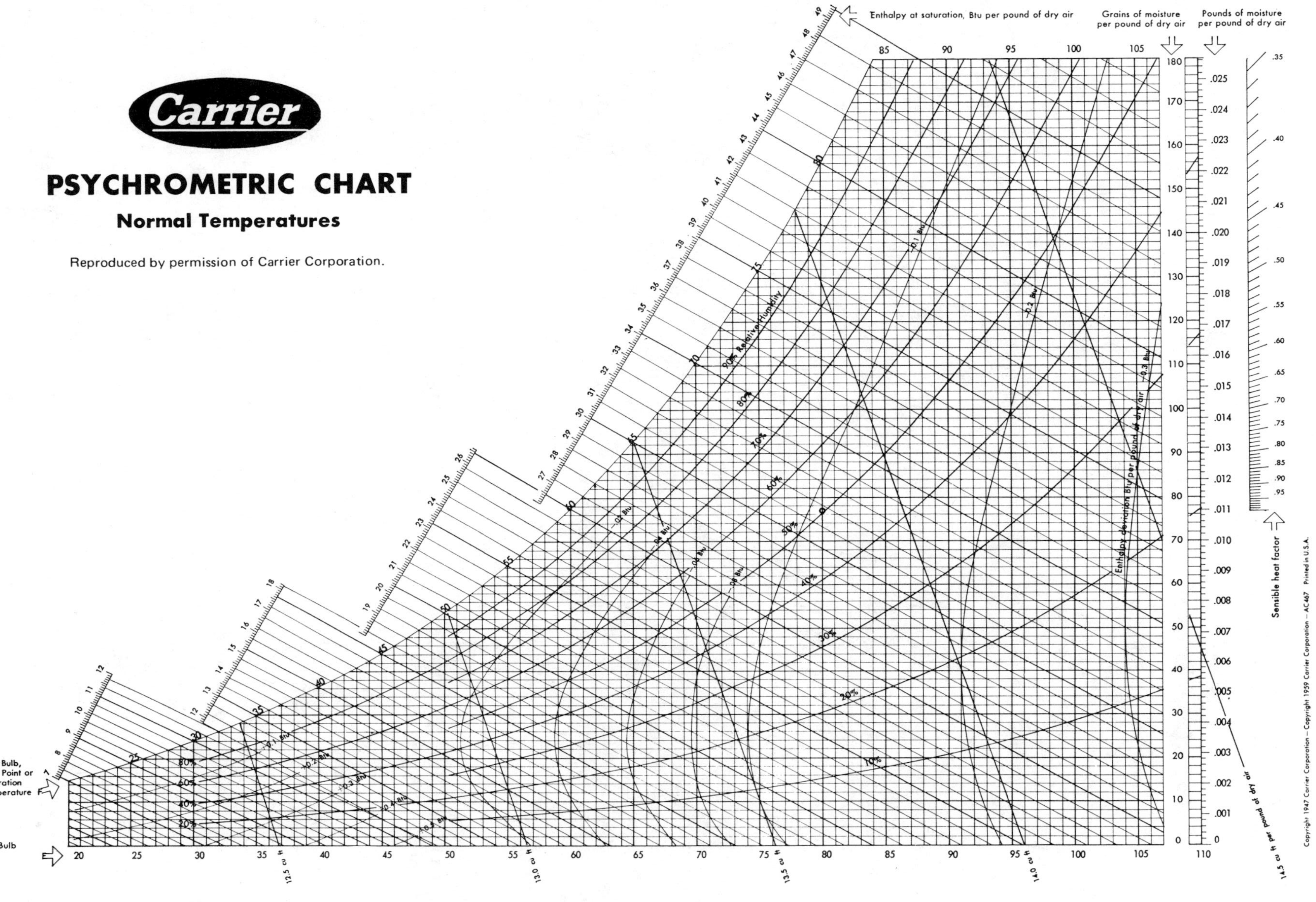

sation of water on the outside of cold water pipes are all examples of this phenomenon.

Human Comfort

A guest's opinion of a hospitality property is extremely dependent on the condition of the thermal environment. When the thermal environment makes the guest feel comfortable, then he or she completely forgets about it and enjoys the other attractions and amenities of the facility. However, when the thermal environment makes the guest feel uncomfortable, then he or she usually focuses on the negative sensations and does not notice the positive attributes of the facility. Consequently, the operator of a facility should strive to maintain environmental conditions within the range of comfort while minimizing the costs of providing them.

There are several factors that influence the environmental comfort of a guest: (1) the dry-bulb temperature of the air, (2) the humidity of the air, (3) the velocity of the air moving over the guest, (4) the temperature of the surfaces of the room, (5) the volume of fresh air that is supplied to the guest, and (6) the quality of the air. The first four factors affect the thermal comfort of the guest, while the last two factors are considered primarily as life-safety aspects of the environment.

Thermal Comfort

The thermal comfort of a guest is defined as that condition of the mind which expresses satisfaction with the thermal environment. It is the mind's interpretation—a very subjective judgment—of the body's physiological reactions to those factors that influence the energy balance for the human body. The human body automatically attempts to maintain a constant deep body temperature by keeping a balance between the energy produced by the body and the energy dissipated by the body to the surrounding environment, while the mind registers the reaction to the environment in categories such as cold, cool, slightly cool, neutral, slightly warm, warm, and hot.

For the body to remain at a constant temperature, the heat that is produced by the body's metabolic process must be transferred away from the body. This heat balance, expressed by

$$M + C + R + E = 0,$$

is dependent on the metabolic production of energy (M), the heat absorbed or dissipated through convection with the surrounding air (C), the heat transferred through radiation with the surrounding structures (R), and the heat lost through the evaporation of perspiration (E). When the air temperature is below 98.6°F, C always has a negative sign, and when the air temperature is above 98.6°F, the sign is positive. As with C, the sign of R depends on the surface temperatures of the surrounding structures compared to 98.6°F, because heat always flows from the region of higher temperature to the region of lower temperature. E always has a negative sign because the body can only lose energy through evaporation.

The body's metabolic production of heat energy is extremely dependent on the activity level of the individual. This relationship is shown in Exhibit B.7 where the amount of heat production is expressed in *met units*, a unit which is the energy produced by a seated person at rest. For an average individual, a value of 1.0 met is equivalent to an energy production of 360 Btu/hr. For hospitality employees, the metabolic heat production ranges from a low of 1.0 met for seated work up to 3.4 met for heavy housecleaning tasks; for guests, the range is from .7 met for sleeping up to 7.2 met for playing squash.

The body's thermal control systems regulate the amount of energy dissipated through convection, radiation, and evaporation in order to balance the amount of heat production so that the body has no net heat gain. Within the normal comfort region, this control is accomplished by changing the surface temperature of the body through the control of blood flow near the surface of the skin and by changing the amount of sweat secreted from the skin. The body's surface temperature affects the transfer of heat through convection and radiation because these mechanisms are dependent upon a temperature differential between the heat source and the region that absorbs the heat; the amount of sweat secretion affects the quantity of water and the corresponding heat of vaporization that is removed from the body.

Environmental factors also affect these three mechanisms. The air temperature of the room has an effect on the amount of heat that is convected from the body; a lower air temperature increases the heat flow, while a higher air temperature decreases the flow. The temperatures of the surfaces in a room (that is, ceilings, walls, and floors) influence the amount of radiation heat transfer; a higher average surface temperature allows less heat transfer, while a lower temperature requires more heat flow. The humidity of the air affects the amount of evaporative heat loss; air with a lower relative humidity permits a faster rate of evaporation than does air with a higher relative humidity.

When the body's thermal control systems respond to changes in metabolic rate or environmental factors, the body first relies on the convective and radiative mechanisms before it uses the evaporative mechanism. In the case of a seated person at rest who is producing 1.0 met or 360 Btu/hr in a room at 60°F and 45% rh, the body is dissipating almost all of the 360 Btu/hr of heat through convection and radiation. As the air temperature in the room increases, the amount of heat transferred through these two mechanisms decreases because there is a lower temperature difference between the body and its surroundings. Therefore, the body must dissipate an increasing amount of heat through evaporation in order to maintain the total dissipation rate of 360 Btu/hr. This trend continues until the room temperature is 98.6°F, at which point the entire 360 Btu/hr is being lost through evaporation. Exhibit B.8 summarizes this effect.

In the case of a similar person in a room in which the temperature is lowered, the body takes action to maintain the total heat loss at 360 Btu/hr even though the temperature difference is increased. First, it shuts down the evaporative mechanism. If that does not have enough effect, the body begins to lower its surface temperature in order to reduce the temperature difference. If that is not sufficient, the body attempts to produce more metabolic energy to offset the increased rate of heat loss by inducing involuntary muscle action or shivering.

The Comfort Zone

From this discussion, it is obvious that the thermal comfort of the guest is connected to several factors that have an interrelated effect on the guest's perception of the thermal environment. The aggregate effect of these factors has been combined into a concept called the *comfort zone*. This zone is defined as containing all the combinations of air temperature and relative humidity that satisfy at least 80% of the population with regard to their thermal comfort.

Exhibit B.7 Metabolic Rate at Different Typical Activities

Activity	Metabolic Rate in Met units
Resting	
Sleeping	0.7
Reclining	0.8
Seated, quiet	1.0
Standing, relaxed	1.2
Walking	
On the level mph	
2	2.0
3	2.6
4	3.8
Miscellaneous Occupations	
Bakery (e.g., cleaning tins, packing boxes)	1.4 to 2.0
Brewery (e.g., filling bottles, loading beer boxes onto belt)	1.2 to 2.4
Carpentry	
Machine sawing, table	1.8 to 2.2
Sawing by hand	4.0 to 4.8
Planing by hand	5.6 to 6.4
General Laboratory Work	1.4 to 1.8
Machine Work	
Light (e.g., electrical industry)	2.0 to 2.4
Heavy (e.g., steel work)	3.5 to 4.5
Shop Assistant	2.0
Teacher	1.6
Watch Repairer, Seated	1.1
Domestic Work, Women	
House cleaning	2.0 to 3.4
Cooking	1.6 to 2.0
Washing by hand and ironing	2.0 to 3.6
Shopping	1.4 to 1.8
Office Work	
Typing	1.2 to 1.4
Miscellaneous office work	1.1 to 1.3
Drafting	1.1 to 1.3
Leisure Activities	
Stream fishing	1.2 to 2.0
Calisthenics exercise	3.0 to 4.0
Dancing, social	2.4 to 4.4
Tennis, singles	3.6 to 4.6
Squash, singles	5.0 to 7.2
Golf, swinging and golf cart	1.4 to 1.8

Reprinted by permission from *1985 ASHRAE Handbook—Fundamentals.*

Exhibit B.8 Distribution of Heat Loss for a Human

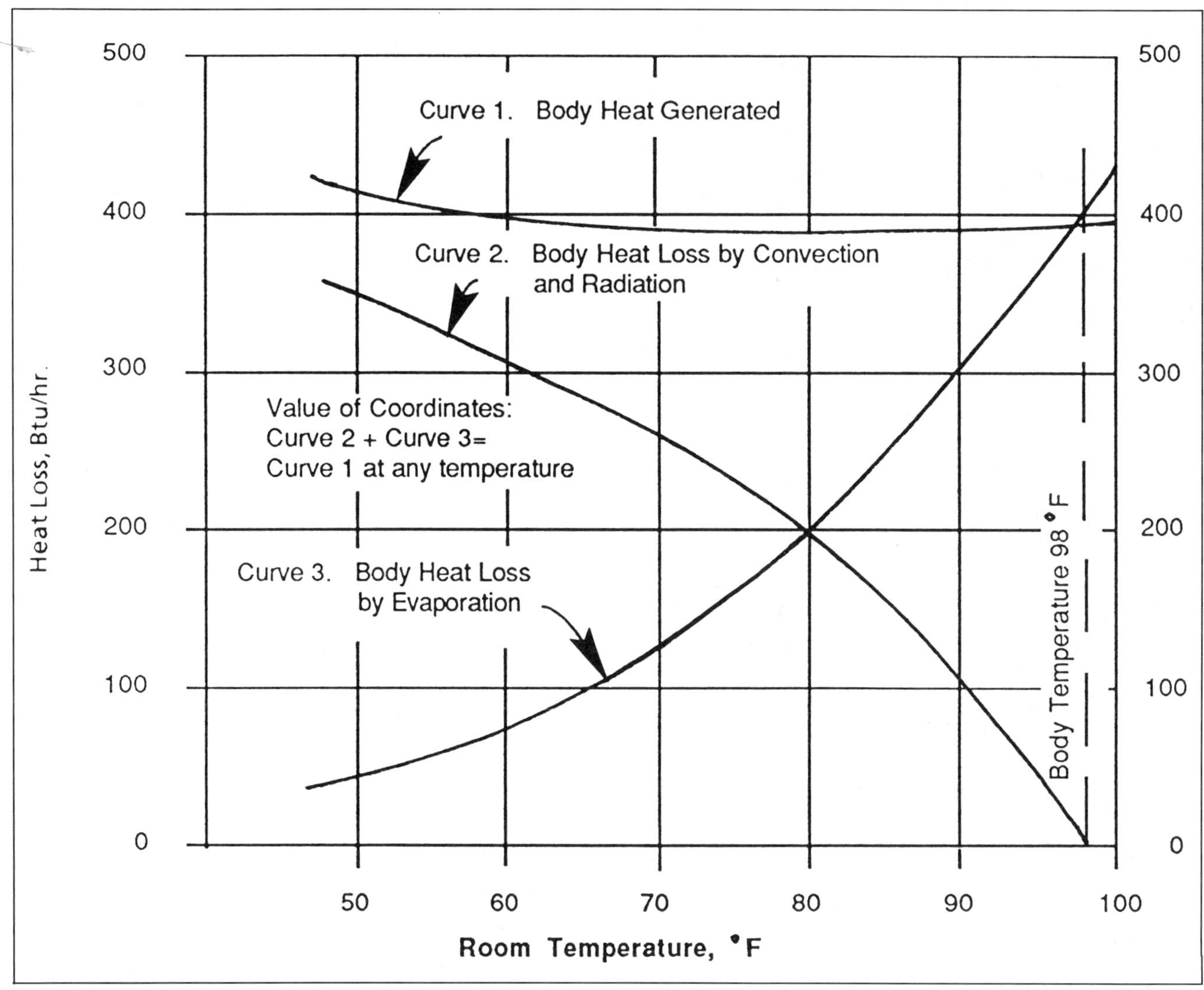

In Exhibit B.9, the comfort zones for typical winter and summer clothing are plotted separately on a portion of a psychrometric chart. The almost vertical boundaries (that is, the left and right sides) of the zones were determined by extensive testing of samples of people exposed to different air conditions. Each boundary represents those combinations of temperature and relative humidity that are perceived by the guest to be equivalent to one another and that are comfortable to exactly 80% of the tested populations. The points between the two boundaries for each zone indicate combinations of air conditions that are comfortable to more than 80% of the people.

The steep downward slope of the boundaries shows an inverse tradeoff between the temperature of the air and its relative humidity in determining the comfort of a guest. For example, air at 68.5°F and 30% rh offers the same level of comfort as air at 67.0°F and 70% rh. This tradeoff is a result of the interaction of the heat transfer mechanisms that depend on a temperature difference (convection and radiation) with the mechanism that depends on the humidity in the air (evaporation). The loss in evaporative heat transfer due to the increase in relative humidity must be offset by an increase in the convective and radiative losses accomplished by a lower air temperature.

The horizontal boundaries of the comfort zones (that is, the top and bottom) are set for considerations that partially relate to thermal comfort as well as to other practical considerations. Air that contains less moisture than is in the air at the lower boundary (a dew point temperature of 35°F) causes people to exhibit symptoms of very dry skin, dry throats, and respiratory problems. The same air also contributes to the excessive drying and deterioration of wood furniture, some building materials, and painted surfaces. Air that is wetter than the air at the upper boundary (a dew point temperature of 62°F) causes mold growth and condensation of water droplets on cool building parts such as cold water lines which are not insulated or the inside surfaces of windows in the winter. Consequently, air that is either too dry or too wet is undesirable for the successful operation of a facility.

The primary difference between the comfort zones for the winter and the summer is the amount of clothing worn by the test subjects. For the winter, the typical description of the clothing is heavy slacks, long sleeve shirt, and sweater; for the summer, the description is light slacks and a short sleeve shirt. Therefore, the apparent distinction between two different seasons is not due to intrinsic aspects of the seasons such as acclimatization, but rather to the differences in the amount of clothing that is normally worn during these seasons.

The comfort zones shown in Exhibit B.9 are based on several assumptions regarding the factors that affect the thermal comfort of guests. The activity level is light, mainly sedentary with a met value of 1.2. The average temperature of the room's surfaces (mean radiant temperature, abbreviated as MRT) is assumed to be the same as the air temperature. The velocity of air movement is less than 30 feet per minute (fpm) for the winter zone and less than 50 fpm for the summer zone.

The two comfort zones can be extended to include situations that have characteristics different from the assumptions listed above. An increase in activity level for each 0.1 met moves the winter comfort zone by approximately 1.0F° and the summer comfort zone by approximately 0.8F° toward cooler temperatures. A change in the MRT of the room surfaces for each 1.0F° moves the comfort zones approximately 0.5F°; the comfort zones move toward warmer temperatures when the MRT decreases and toward cooler temperatures when the MRT increases. Air movement in excess of the stated limit of 30 fpm for the winter comfort zone is not acceptable, while an increase in air movement is acceptable for the summer comfort zone, when the comfort zone is moved 1.0F° toward warmer temperatures for each 30 fpm increase in air movement up to a maximum air movement of 160 fpm. Air movement beyond this level causes visible movement of loose paper, hair, and other light objects.

Exhibit B.9 The Comfort Zone

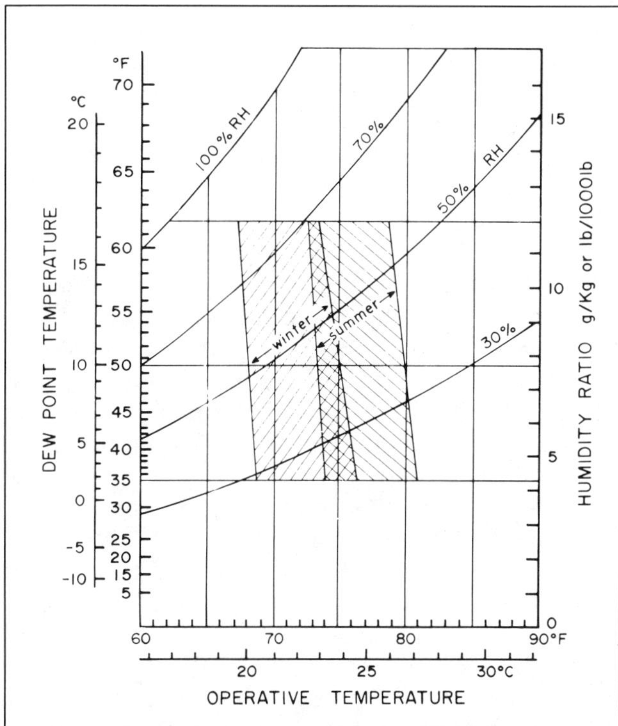

Reprinted by permission from ASHRAE Standard 55-1981.

Maintaining Acceptable Indoor Air Quality

Both the physiological and psychological needs of humans require that an adequate supply of outside air of acceptable quality be circulated through a building. For physiological reasons, the air circulation system must supply the necessary amount of oxygen for metabolism and remove the by-products of metabolism that are present in the exhaled air, as well as control the amount of carbon dioxide in the air so that minimum standards are met. The system also must control the level of various contaminants that enter the air from either outside sources (such as general industrial pollution) or inside sources of pollutants (such as formaldehyde from insulation or carbon monoxide from faulty heating systems). For psychological reasons, the body odor of occupants and the moisture contributed to the air either by humans or other sources (for example, cooking, taking showers) must be removed from the occupied space.

Except in the locations where the quality of the outdoor air is unacceptable, the ventilation system of a building could in theory maintain acceptable indoor air quality just by circulating massive amounts of outdoor air. However, this is not a viable practical solution because the circulated outdoor air must be conditioned when it is brought into the building. When the outside air is cold, the heating system must heat the air to an acceptable temperature; when the outside air is hot and humid, the air conditioning system must cool and dehumidify the air to an acceptable temperature. Both of these processes consume substantial amounts of energy. In addition, large circulation fans powered by electric motors consume energy just to circulate the air. Therefore, the designers of building ventilation systems specify the minimum ventilation rate which will provide desirable indoor air quality in order to minimize the construction and operating costs of the building.

There are two methods—the *ventilation rate procedure* and the *indoor air quality procedure*—that indicate how to achieve acceptable air quality. The first procedure is prescriptive in nature in that specified minimum ventilation rates of acceptable outside air are provided. This method assumes that this "clean" outside air should dilute and remove the contaminants from interior sources so that their levels in the interior air are acceptable. The second procedure is performance-oriented in that the maximum allowable levels of contaminants are provided for acceptable indoor air quality. No specified ventilation rates are provided, however; their actual choice is at the discretion of the designer of the ventilation system as long as the allowable levels of contaminants are not exceeded.

Ventilation Rate Procedure. The acceptable levels of pollutants for outdoor air can be obtained from several sources.[1] If the outdoor air in a specific location satisfies these levels, then the air may be used directly to ventilate a building. However, if the outdoor air contains contaminants that exceed these levels, then the air must be treated before it may be used in a building's ventilation system.

Exhibit B.10 shows the outdoor air requirements for ventilation for various types of businesses or buildings. The requirements are stated in cfm/person, cfm/ft^2 of floor area, or cfm/functional unit (for example, room in a hotel or bed in a hospital). By the application of this method, indoor air quality is considered acceptable if the required rates of acceptable outdoor air are provided for the occupied space and no unusual contaminants are present.

Higher ventilation rates are specified for the spaces in which smoking is permitted, because tobacco smoke is one of the most difficult contaminants to control at the source. When smoking is not permitted in designated spaces, the lower values of ventilation rates may be applied. In numerous applications, this reduction in ventilation rates can substantially affect the operating cost of the heating, ventilating, and air conditioning (HVAC) system. Therefore, use of no smoking areas in lodging properties should be strongly encouraged because of its desirable effect on the operating costs of the building.

Indoor Air Quality Procedure. Under this method, acceptable indoor air quality is provided by the ventilation system if the level of contaminants in the *indoor* air does not exceed the levels as specified for *outdoor* air. In addition, acceptable levels of contaminants from indoor sources must also be met.

There are, however, numerous substances for which no regulations have yet been developed (for example, mercury), substances that have not yet been identified as harmful to humans (for example, unknown environmental carcinogens), and substances for which no regulations are likely to be developed because they are such complex mixtures (tobacco smoke). In order to respond to these substances, this method allows a subjective evaluation of the indoor air quality.

The following steps should be used to ensure the validity of the subjective evaluation. A panel of at least 20 untrained observers should enter a space in the manner of a normal

Exhibit B.10 Outdoor Air Requirements for Ventilation—Commercial Facilities

	Estimated Occupancy, persons per 1000 ft.^{3} or 100 m^2 floor area. Use only when design occupancy is not known.	Outdoor Air Requirements Smoking	Non-Smoking	Comments
Food & Beverage Services		cfm/person		
Dining rooms	70	35	7	
Kitchens	20	--	10	
Cafeterias, fast food facilities	100	35	7	
Bars and cocktail lounges	100	50	10	
Hotels, Motels, Resorts, Dormitories, & Correctional Facilities		cfm/room		
Bedrooms (single, double)	5	30	15	Independent of room size
Living rooms (suites)	20	50	25	Independent of room size
Baths, toilets (attached to bedrooms)		50	50	Independent of room size: installed capacity for intermittent use.
		cfm/person		
Lobbies	30	15	5	
Conference rooms (small)	50	35	7	
Assembly rooms (large)	120	35	7	
Gambling Casinos	120	35	7	
Offices				
Office Space	7	20	5	
Meeting & waiting spaces	60	35	7	
Public spaces		cfm/ft^2 floor		
Corridors & utility rooms		0.02	0.02	
		cfm/stall or urinal		
Public restrooms	100	75	--	
		cfm/locker		
Locker & dressing rooms	50	35	15	
Sports & Amusement Facilities		cfm/person		
Ballrooms & Discos	100	35	7	
Bowling alleys (seating area)	70	35	7	
Playing floors (e.g., gymnasiums, ice arenas)	30	--	20	When internal combustion engines are operated for maintenance of playing surfaces, increased ventilation rates will be required.
Spectator areas	150	35	7	When internal combustion engines are operated for maintenance of playing surfaces, increased ventilation rates will be required.
Game rooms (e.g., cards & billiards rooms)	70	35	7	
Swimming pools		cfm/ft^2 area		
Pool & deck areas	--	--	0.5	Higher values may be required for humidity control.
		cfm/person		
Spectators area	70	35	7	

Reprinted by permission from ASHRAE Standard 62-1981.

visitor and should render a judgment of acceptability within 15 seconds. Each observer should make the evaluation independently of the other observers and without influence from a panel leader. The air can be considered acceptably free of annoying contaminants if at least 80% of the observers deem the air to be not objectionable.

Notes

1. See, for example, ASHRAE Standard 62-1981—*Ventilation for Acceptable Indoor Air Quality* (Atlanta, Ga.: American Society of Heating, Refrigerating, and Air-conditioning Engineers, 1981), and *1985 ASHRAE Handbook—Fundamentals* (Atlanta: American Society of Heating, Refrigerating, and Air-conditioning Engineers, 1985), Chapter 11.

Index

T

U

V

W

Z

The Educational Institute Board of Trustees

The Educational Institute of the American Hotel & Motel Association is fortunate to have both industry and academic leaders, as well as allied members, on its Board of Trustees. Individually and collectively, the following persons play leading roles in supporting the Institute and determining the direction of its programs.

Ronald F. Cichy, Ph.D., CHA
Director
School of Hotel, Restaurant and Institutional Management
Michigan State University
East Lansing, Michigan

Douglass C. Cogswell, CHA
General Manager
The Westin Resort
Vail, Colorado

Caroline A. Cooper, CHA
Department Chair
Hospitality/Tourism
Johnson & Wales University
Providence, Rhode Island

Edouard P.O. Dandrieux, CHA
Director & Founder
H.I.M., Hotel Institute Montreux
Montreux, Switzerland

Ronald A. Evans, CHA
President & CEO
Best Western International, Inc.
Phoenix, Arizona

Robert C. Hazard, Jr., CHA
Chairman & CEO
Choice Hotels International, Inc.
Silver Spring, Maryland

Arnold J. Hewes
Executive Vice President
Minnesota Hotel & Lodging Association
St. Paul, Minnesota

Richard M. Kelleher
President
Guest Quarters Suite Hotels
Boston, Massachusetts

Donald J. Landry, CHA
President
Manor Care Hotel Division
Silver Spring, Maryland

Bryan D. Langton, C.B.E.
Chairman
Holiday Inn Worldwide
Atlanta, Georgia

Lawrence B. Magnan, CHA
Chief Operating Officer
Spa Suites Corporation
Mercer Island, Washington

Jerry R. Manion, CHA
Executive Vice President - Operations
Motel 6
Dallas, Texas

Joseph A. McInerney, CHA
President & CEO
Travelodge International
El Cajon, California

John A. Norlander, CHA
President
Radisson Hotels Corporation
Minneapolis, Minnesota

Michael B. Peceri, CHA
Chairman of the Board
Marquis Hotels & Resorts
Fort Meyers, Florida

M.O. "Bus" Ryan, CHA
Senior Vice President
Marriott Hotels-Resorts-Suites
Atlanta, Georgia

William J. Sheehan
President & CEO
Omni Hotels
Hampton, New Hampshire

Thomas W. Staed, CHA
President
Oceans Eleven Resorts, Inc.
Daytona Beach Shores, Florida

William R. Tiefel
President
Marriott Hotels & Resorts
Washington, D.C.

The Educational Institute Fellows

Respected experts dedicated to the advancement of hospitality education

Michael J. Beckley, CHA
President
Commonwealth Hospitality,Ltd.
Toronto, Ontario
Canada

William H. Edwards, CHA
Vice Chairman and Director Emeritus
Hilton Hotels Corporation
Beverly Hills, California

John L. Sharpe, CHA
Executive Vice President
Four Seasons Hotels & Resorts
Toronto, Ontario
Canada

Stephen W. Brener, CHA
President
Stephen W. Brener Associates, Inc.
New York, New York

Creighton Holden, CHA
President, Hotels Division
Encore Marketing International
Columbia, South Carolina

Larry K. Walker, CHA
President
Cypress Hotel Management Company
Orlando, Florida

Melinda Bush, CHA
Executive Vice President, Publisher
Hotel & Travel Index
Reed Travel Group
Secaucus, New Jersey

Allen J. Ostroff
Senior Vice President
The Prudential Property Company
Newark, New Jersey

Paul E. Wise, CHA
Director
Hotel, Restaurant & Institutional Management
University of Delaware
Newark, Delaware

Robert S. DeMone, CHA
President, Chairman & CEO
Canadian Pacific Hotels & Resorts
Toronto, Ontario
Canada

Harold J. Serpe, CHA
President
Midway Hospitality Corporation
Brookfield, Wisconsin